Appetite

Appetite

Neural and Behavioural Bases

Edited by

CHARLES R. LEGG

Psychology Department,
School of Social Sciences,
The City University, London

and

DAVID BOOTH

School of Psychology,
The University of Birmingham

Oxford   New York   Tokyo
OXFORD UNIVERSITY PRESS
1994

Oxford University Press, Walton Street, Oxford OX2 6DP

Oxford   New York
Athens   Auckland   Bangkok   Bombay
Calcutta   Cape Town   Dar es Salaam   Delhi
Florence   Hong Kong   Istanbul   Karachi
Kuala Lumpur   Madras   Madrid   Melbourne
Mexico City   Nairobi   Paris   Singapore
Taipei   Tokyo   Toronto
and associated companies in
Berlin   Ibadan

Oxford is a trade mark of Oxford University Press

Published in the United States
by Oxford University Press Inc., New York

© European Brain and Behaviour Society, 1994

A catalogue record for this book is available from the British Library

Library of Congress Cataloging in Publication Data
Appetite : neural and behavioural bases / edited by Charles R. Legg and D.A. Booth. – 1st
ed.
Includes bibliographical references.
1. Appetite.   2. Desire.   3. Appetite disorders.
4. Neuropsychology.   I. Legg. Charles R., 1949–   .   II. Booth, D. A. (David Allenby),
1938–   .
QP136.A678 1994   153.8–dc20   94–11806
ISBN 0 19 8547870

Typeset by The Electronic Book Factory Ltd, Fife, Scotland

Printed in Great Britain by
Biddles Ltd,
Guildford & King's Lynn

Foreword

Terje Sagvolden, *Series Editor*

The Committee of the European Brain and Behaviour Society is constantly trying to improve the quality of its service to the members. One way of doing this is by organizing high-quality meetings. EBBS organizes both Annual General Meetings and high-quality workshops. The workshops have been our Society's benchmark and have received substantial attention. The EBBS Publication Series is a new initiative, providing collections of specially written and edited chapters on interesting elements of the workshop in question.

Welcome to this new publication series.

Preface

Forty years ago, Stellar (1954) proposed his 'two-centre' theory of motivation, according to which actions such as eating, drinking, and copulating are under the control of mutually antagonistic hypothalamic centres. Like all good review papers Stellar's article highlighted what was not known as much as what was known at the time. Although he was writing about the hypothalamus Stellar was acutely aware that, whatever role it had in motivation, it acquired that function as a result of being located in a much larger system. That system had to include a 'final common path for behaviour', inputs from exteroceptive systems, inputs from the internal environment, and inputs from the neural mechanisms underlying cognitive function; but Stellar was unable to specify these in detail. Thanks to the diligence of all those studying motivation and to advances in technique our understanding of organization of this wider neural system has since flourished. We now know, for example, something of how visual information about food is processed in the brain, and the sites at which this information could be integrated with olfactory and visceral information. We also know more about the brainstem mechanisms controlling the motor side of eating.

In addition to the things known by Stellar, we have also acquired an impressive body of information about systems not included in his model. Of these the most significant is the existence of a neural system within which chemical or electrical stimulation can mimic many of the reinforcing effects of natural rewards such as food, water, or sexual contact. The phenomenon of intracranial self-stimulation has revolutionized the way psychologists and physiologists think about motivation since it was first described by Olds and Milner (1954).

There have also been major advances in the way in which psychologists think about motivation. Stellar's model was significant for incorporating cybernetic concepts. The two hypothalamic centres he described were part of a negative feedback loop that was completed by the impact of the final common path for behaviour on the internal and external environment. The assumption behind this approach is that the link between the hypothalamic excitatory centre and the final common path for behaviour is direct, and that motivated behaviour is somehow switched on and off by the waxing and waning of the motivational state. So long as psychologists and physiologists contented themselves with studying the eating behaviour of rats presented with a single food source in a monotonous environment with no competing demands on their time or energy, this is a reasonable simplification but it does not do justice to the complexities of human motivation. Psychological research over the past 40 years has confirmed what is enshrined in our day-to-day language, that motivation involves a disposition to act rather than the activation of specific behaviour. Moreover, the disposition to act is translated into behaviour through a process of choice. Except in pathological circumstances we choose whether to eat, drink, or have sex. Having made that basic choice, we then choose how we will indulge ourselves. The indirectness of the link between what Morgan (1960) called the 'central motive state' and the motivated choices we make is encapsulated in the term 'appetite'.

This book was conceived as a celebration of what we have learned about motivation since the publication of Stellar's paper. It combines chapters that review our current knowledge of the psychological bases of appetitive behaviour with those that review recent advances in our understanding of the neural systems involved. Wherever possible, the authors were asked to focus on work on appetitive processes in humans or, where that was not available, to consider the implications of work on other species for appetitive processes in humans. We have intentionally defined 'appetite' in the loosest possible way in order to encourage debate about the nature of appetite, particularly about whether there are common mechanisms underpinning the diverse appetites we experience or whether it is more appropriate to talk about appetites.

REFERENCES

Morgan, C.T. (1960). Physiological theory of drive. In *Psychology: A study of a science* (ed. S. Koch). McGraw-Hill, New York.

Olds, J. and Milner, P. (1954) Positive reinforcement produced by electrical stimulation of septal area and other areas of rat brain. *Journal of Comparative and Physiological Psychology*, **47**, 419-27.

Stellar, E. (1954). The physiology of motivation. *Psychological Review*, **61**, 5-22.

London   C.R.L.
October 1993

Contents

Contributors

David Booth School of Psychology, University of Birmingham, Edgbaston, Birmingham B15 2TT, UK

Douglas Carroll Department of Psychology, Glasgow Polytechnic, Cowcaddens Road, Glasgow G4 0BA, UK

Steven J. Cooper School of Psychology, University of Birmingham, Edgbaston, Birmingham B15 2TT, UK

R.P.J. Freeman School of Psychology, University of Birmingham, Edgbaston, Birmingham B15 2TT, UK

E.L. Gibson School of Psychology, University of Birmingham, Edgbaston, Birmingham B15 2TT, UK

Steven Glautier National Addiction Centre, Institute of Psychiatry, De Crespigny Park, Denmark Hill, London SE8 8AF, UK

Suzanne Higgs Laboratory of Psychopharmacology, School of Psychology, University of Birmingham, Edgbaston, Birmingham B15 2TT, UK

Justine A.A. Huxley School of Psychology, University of Birmingham, Edgbaston, Birmingham B15 2TT, UK

Anita Jansen Department of Mental Sciences, Limburg State University, PO Box 616, 6200 MD, Maastricht, The Netherlands

Charles R. Legg Psychology Department, School of Social Sciences, The City University, Northampton Square, London EC1V 0HB, UK

R.J. Levin Department of Biomedical Science, University of Sheffield, Western Bank, Sheffield S10 2TN, UK

N. Mei CNRS Neurobiology Laboratory, Equipe de Neurobiologie, Intéroception 31 Chemin J. Aiguier, F13402 Marseille 9, France

Edmund T. Rolls Department of Experimental Psychology, Oxford University, South Parks Road, Oxford OX1 3UD, UK

Anne-Marie Toase School of Psychology, University of Birmingham, Edgbaston, Birmingham B15 2TT, UK

Frederick Toates Department of Biology, The Open University, Walton Hall, Milton Keynes MK7 6AA, UK

David M. Warburton Department of Psychology, University of Reading, Building 3, Earley Gate, Whiteknights, Reading RG6 2AL, UK

Roy A. Wise Center for Studies in Behavioural Neurobiology, Sir George Williams Campus, Concordia University, 1455 De Maisonneuve Boulevard West, Montreal, Quebec H3G 1M8, Canada

H. Philip Zeigler Department of Psychology, Hunter College, 695 Park Avenue, New York, NY 10021, USA

1

Appetite—a psychological concept

Charles R. Legg

INTRODUCTION

If you were to ask any group of psychologists to define a concept dear
to their hearts, you would probably end up with more definitions than
there were people in the room. It is therefore a foolhardy editor who
starts a book on a topic such as appetite by trying to define it. Instead,
this chapter has two aims. The first is to explore some of the ways
in which scientists and lay people use the term 'appetite' and to
indicate how it is being used in this book. The second is to review
how psychologists and psychobiologists have approached the topic of
motivation, to determine whether 'appetite' remains a useful scientific
concept.

THE CONCEPT OF APPETITE

Like many concepts in contemporary psychology, 'appetite' has been
adopted from common language, where it is used as part of a
commonsense model of human psychological processes (Harré and
Secord, 1972). The scientific use of the term has grown out of its
day-to-day use, and lack of precision in its meaning reflects both the
lack of clarity of common language and the way in which language
evolves through use. We can obtain a sense of that lack of clarity
and change of use by looking at dictionary definitions. *The Shorter
Oxford English Dictionary* gives eight separate meanings of 'appetite',
ranging from the very general 'bent of the mind' through to 'craving
for food'. The root of the word is the Latin word *appetitus*, which
The Collins Latin Dictionary defines as 'craving; natural desire (as
opposed to reason)'. Despite the range and the changes over time, four
significant themes emerge from the dictionary definitions: (i) appetites
are *dispositions* to act, they are not the actions themselves; (ii) appetites
imply knowledge of the object to which the actions should be directed,
prior to encountering the object; (iii) appetites can be considered to

be *causes* of people's behaviour; and (iv) appetites *conflict* with other causes of behaviour, such as the application of reason.

Two other features of the day-to-day use of 'appetite' deserve mention. The first is that the term itself is a category label and the second is that the way the word is used depends on the viewpoint of the user. On the first point, if we ask people why they do things, they rarely explain their actions in terms of 'appetite' itself but prefer to name the specific appetites involved. Thus, people say that they did things because they were hungry, thirsty, or sexually aroused. 'Appetite' is a generic term encompassing these sorts of explanations and, as such, it is a class of lay psychological constructs rather than a description of an underlying psychological process. Consequently, there is no *a priori* reason to presuppose that appetites such as hunger and thirst have anything in common other than that they label states in which individuals feel predisposed to do something. Whether they have anything more in common is an empirical matter, rather than one of definition.

The viewpoint of the user is important because we use appetitive terms in two ways; one is as a *justification* of our own behaviour and the other is as an *explanation* of somebody else's behaviour. We tend to treat them as the same thing but there is no good reason to suppose that the rules for attributing an appetite to oneself are the same as the rules for attributing appetites to other people. Outsiders have to make their attributions on the basis of behaviour alone, whereas the individual can also make use of subjective states not accessible to the outsider. The commonsense view is that appetite involves the subjective experience of desire (Bolles, 1980) and that, when we attribute an appetite to someone, we also attribute that subjective experience, but the experience of desire may occur without appetitive behaviour, and vice versa. This distinction between desire and action is reflected in the way many authors write as though appetites are something to be resisted and that yielding to appetite is a sign of moral degeneracy. The distinction between subjectively experienced appetite and appetitive behaviour is familiar to anyone who has ever tried to diet. Imagine a person observing a strict diet shopping for themselves in a 'supermarket', with every form of food available. As they wander around the shop they will encounter sights and smells, such as those emanating from the bakery, that evoke the subjective state of appetite for forbidden fruits like Danish pastries. Nevertheless, if you look at their shopping behaviour, and subsequent consumption of food, you will see that they buy and eat such things as chicken, fresh salad, and crispbread, which they then have to instruct themselves to eat. The experience of appetite can clearly occur without the behaviour of eating and the behaviour of eating can occur without the experience of appetite. As scientists we cannot gain access to the subjective states of our subject and we are, therefore, obliged to work with appetites as states that we attribute to other people and animals. Consequently, when we consider scientists' accounts of 'appetite' it is inappropriate to relate them to our individual, subjective notions of what appetite involves. On the positive side, since appetites are attributions rather than descriptions of subjective experiences, we are at liberty to make them for animals as well as people.

The commonsense view of appetites is that they are internal states or dispositions to act that can cause behaviour. Appetites are goal directed, in that part of experiencing an appetite involves being able to specify what will assuage it. They are dispositions to *act* rather than *react*, in that they lead the individual to seek out the goal object rather than merely to react to it when it appears. Appetites are not the only causes of behaviour and find themselves in conflict with other potential causes, such as the operation of reason. The term 'appetite' labels a category behavioural and subjective phenomena, and it is used in an attributional rather than in a descriptive way. Is this multifaceted concept of any value in the *scientific* study of behaviour?

PSYCHOBIOLOGICAL APPROACHES TO MOTIVATED BEHAVIOUR

Appetite, being a mentalistic concept, was effectively written out of the behaviourist psychological theories of the first half of this century. Behaviourists were largely concerned with the learning process, as they saw the acquisition of new 'conditioned' reflexes as the basis of behaviour. To the extent that behaviourists thought about issues of motivation they saw them in terms of unpleasant bodily stimuli, arising from deprivation states, that force the animal to act. According to this view there was no difference between being motivated by food deprivation and being motivated by a continuous sequence of electric shocks. This view of motivation was echoed by physiologists such as Cannon (1947), working at around the same time. According to authors such as Hull (1952), this *drive* had two roles in the acquisition of conditioned responses. The first was to underpin reinforcement which, according to Hull, involved stimulus response associations being enhanced by large decreases in drive strength immediately following particular conjunctions of stimuli and responses. The second role was as an energizer of behaviour, habit strength being multiplied by drive level to determine the behavioural 'reaction potential'. The energizing effect of drive was viewed as being completely independent of the reinforcements used to establish the associations in the first place, so all response tendencies are enhanced by all drive-inducing tissue states. Other authors, such as Guthrie (1935), took a more extreme view, arguing that associative strength changed solely as a result of contiguity between stimuli and responses and that the only function of drive was to energize behaviour. Significantly, Guthrie and his colleagues allowed for the fact that an animal in a drive state would do things that an unmotivated animal would not do, such as hungry animals apparently looking for food, but they did not pursue the issue of how these effects were mediated. Thus authors such as Hull and Guthrie wrote about the role of *drive* in learning and performance, but had no place for appetite.

The essence of this early behaviourist position is that all that is learned are associations between stimuli and responses, so that an organism faced with the same set of stimuli on a number of occasions will emit the same responses, once those responses have been established by reinforcement. The organism learns nothing about the nature of the reinforcement and it is not clear that learning provides any knowledge about the source of the drive state. Thus a hungry rat running a maze for food reward neither knows that there is food at the end of the maze nor does it know, in advance of consuming the reinforcement, that it is food, not water or sex, that it needs to reduce its drive state.

This simplistic reflex approach was shaken by a number of demonstrations that animals did not just learn to perform instrumental behaviours; they also learned about the nature of the reinforcement. One of the first demonstrations of this possibility was a simple study by Tinkelpaugh (1928), in which a monkey was trained to carry out a simple task for a tasty food reward. Once the behaviour was well established, Tinkelpaugh carried out probe trials in which lettuce leaves were substituted for the expected food. In those trials the monkey behaved as if upset and rejected the lettuce leaves. An anthropocentric observer would have said that the monkey expected the food and was upset at finding only a lettuce leaf.

Later studies offered better controlled demonstrations of expectation of reward and quantified the effects of changes in reinforcement on behaviour. For example, sudden changes in the quantity of reinforcement led to 'behavioural contrast' effects, in which animals shifted from large to small reinforcements performed worse than those trained with small reinforcements right from the start (Bower, 1961; Crespi, 1944).

In response to these challenges, behaviourists incorporated 'incentive' concepts into their models to reflect the fact that not only did animals learn about the nature of the reward but they were also sensitive to its magnitude and quality. The notion of 'incentive' relates directly to the commonsense view of appetite that it involves knowledge of what will assuage the appetite and of the actions that will lead to that outcome. Hull (1952) argued that incentive acted multiplicatively with drive and habit strength to produce behaviour. However, Hull's incentive concept was firmly embedded in a stimulus–response framework, with incentives taking the form of covert responses, called fractional anticipatory goal responses, that were components of the behaviour normally elicited by the reinforcement and that became conditioned to stimuli leading to the goal. The fractional anticipatory goal responses then acted as stimuli to which the instrumental behaviour was conditioned. Changes in the quality and quantity of reinforcement influence behaviour by modifying the fractional anticipatory goal responses.

More recent authors have abandoned attempts to cast incentive motivation in terms of covert responses, and have happily acknowledged that animals are capable of learning directly about relationships between the stimuli present in their environments without mediation by responses (Bindra, 1978; Davey, 1989; Dickinson, 1980). However, as Bindra acknowledged, the problem with such stimulus–stimulus learning models is in explaining how the knowledge is translated into action, since they otherwise leave animals lost in mazes 'buried in thought', as Guthrie (1935) put it. In other words, these models need motivational components to explain how knowledge of the reinforcements available in a situation is translated into behaviours and to predict what those behaviours will be.

The starting point for a lot of thinking on this issue is the proposal, by Morgan (1943, 1960), of the existence of 'central motive states'. Central motive states exist at two levels of explanation, the behavioural and the neurophysiological. At the behavioural level, a central motive state is a predisposition to react to particular stimuli in particular ways, and not to respond to others, that is produced by specific bodily states, such as food deprivation or increased levels of hormones. It is also a predisposition to emit behaviours related to the bodily state in the absence of external stimuli. When combined with stimulus–stimulus learning models, the concept of the central motive state also allows for complex interactions between environmental stimuli and the motivational state. For example, Bindra's (1978) model allows for incentive stimuli, such as food and sexual partners, and stimuli associated with incentive stimuli through associative conditioning, to elicit the relevant central motive state in the absence of strong internal stimuli. At the neurophysiological level, a central motive state is the result of increased neural activity in specific neural sub-systems. Since different central motive states are associated with different behaviours, each one must involve unique neural sub-systems but it is possible for them to share common system elements.

Shorn of its behaviourist language, the concept of the central motive state looks very much like our commonsense view of appetite. The state involves a *predisposition* to act and react, rather than a mechanical linkage between bodily state and action. In other words, the concept allows for behavioural flexibility, even to the point at which the central motive state is not directly translated into action. Central motive states may arise spontaneously with respect to the environment, as a result of unobserved changes in the state of the body. Conversely, they may be evoked by a range of environmental contingencies such as food deprivation, the presentation of food, or even the presentation of stimuli previously associated with the presentation of food.

Morgan's concept of the central motive state goes beyond common-sense views of appetite by postulating that appetitive processes have specific neurophysiological substrates, but Morgan did not specify the circuits involved. The first systematic attempt to integrate a behavioural theory of motivation with a neurophysiological model was Stellar (1954), with his two-centre model of hunger and satiety. Stellar's model was explicitly developed to account for eating behaviour but the intention was to offer a general model of motivated behaviour. Although some aspects of Stellar's model reflect the preoccupations of motivational theorists working 40 years ago, it is still relevant because it set the agenda for much of the current neurophysiological model of motivation. While the incorporation of separate inhibitory and excitatory centres, and the identification of these centres with the ventromedial nucleus of the hypothalamus and the lateral hypothalamus, is probably an historical accident there is still a lot of current work on the role of the hypothalamus in motivation (Grignaschi *et al.*, 1992; Kalra *et al.*, 1991; Le Magnen, 1985). At the behavioural level, Stellar's recognition of the range of factors that need to be integrated by the central nervous system remains relevant.

Stellar's model went beyond the central motive state by incorporating a feedback component that gave behavioural motivation a central role in regulating the internal environment. Whereas Cannon (1947) had maintained that homeostasis was maintained by internal regulatory processes and that behaviour was motivated by peripheral irritation, Stellar's model incorporated a behavioural loop that allowed behaviour to modify the state of the internal environment and thus modulate the signals that controlled motivated behaviour. This approach has encouraged theorists who have approached motivation from the point of view of systems theory (Toates, 1986).

Despite the attempts of early behaviourists to get rid of appetitive constructs, contemporary accounts of motivated behaviour need to talk in terms of *predispositions* to act rather than of unvarying reflex responses to the environment. Accounts of motivation also need to attribute to animals and humans the capacity to anticipate what will satisfy their needs and to select behaviour in anticipation of the outcome achieving that end. The research literature therefore compels us to discuss motivation in appetitive terms.

APPETITE AND BEHAVIOUR: THE CURRENT SITUATION

While it is useful to entertain appetitive concepts and to talk of 'appetites' in the plural, we are left with the question of whether it is helpful to talk about 'appetite' in the singular. What do we add to the debate about human and animal motivation by talking about appetite rather than 'hunger', 'thirst', or 'sex-drive'? We know too much about the nuances of motivation to believe that all motivational processes are the same, or to make sweeping classifications such as 'homeostatic' and 'non-homeostatic' drives for reasons other than editorial neatness. Nevertheless, the concept of appetite has considerable power deriving from its heuristic implications. Talking about motivational states as appetites invites us to think about them within a common conceptual framework, which suggests both the questions we can ask about them and the sorts of answers we might give. The advantage of an heuristic framework is that it directs us to do work that elaborates our understanding of motivational processes while providing us with a universal language in which to discuss results.

One element of the heuristic framework that has proved to be of enduring value is the systems approach, introduced into the study of motivation by Stellar (1954). Irrespective of the appetites concerned, the systems involved need information about: the current state of the internal environment, which means access to both blood borne signals and sensory afferents from the autonomic nervous system; incentive stimuli in the external environment and learned stimuli associated with incentive or internal stimuli; information about the nature of the associations between these two types of stimuli; and the system needs access to the motor system to control motivated behaviour. The systems need rules for integrating these classes of information and decision rules for translating the information into behaviour. These issues are addressed in many of the chapters in this book (e.g. Levin, Mei, Rolls, Toates, and Zeigler).

The appetite framework also leads us to ask questions about the possibility of common underlying processes. These processes can be specified at either the psychological or neural level. A good example of the possibility of common psychological processes derives from the issue of what makes an 'incentive' an incentive. Neither Morgan's 'central motive state' nor Stellar's extension of it explain how incentive objects acquire the property of acting as incentives. It is usually taken for granted that hungry rats will find 45 mg dried food pellets rewarding and treat them as incentive objects, but anyone who has ever had to train rats in behavioural tasks knows that the first thing the animals have to learn is that they can eat the pellets. Identifying which objects are relevant to a particular physiological state involves sophisticated learning processes that can relate the physiological consequences of the consummatory act to the object of that act. These processes are discussed by Booth *et al.* (this volume).

Under appropriate conditions, the feedback systems relating the consequences of consummatory acts to their objects leads to adaptive behaviour. Food energy intake, for example, often matches the current need for energy very closely. However, one of the reasons why appetites raise practical as well as theoretical issues is that many people develop inappropriate appetites. They either have heightened or attenuated appetites for 'natural' incentive objects such as food (Jansen, this volume) or sexual partners (Levin, this volume), or they develop appetites for biologically inappropriate incentive objects, such as drugs (Cooper, Glautier, Warburton, Wise, this volume) or gambling machines (Carroll, this volume).

At the level of potential common neural substrates, our understanding of how objects acquire incentive properties was boosted by the discovery of self-stimulation of the brain, presumed to be mediated by direct reward effects of the electrical stimulation (Olds and Milner, 1954; Rolls, 1975). Brain stimulation reward is important for two reasons. The first is that it allows us to explore the neural substrates of a reinforcement process and attempt to relate these to the neural substrates of natural motivational processes. The second is that it enables us to bypass conventional rewards and thus study a different set of processes underlying the acquisition of incentive properties. The history of the study of brain stimulation reward is beyond the scope of this chapter, but some of the conclusions of this work are important for our approach to appetite.

The first conclusion is that reinforcing brain stimulation assigns incentive properties to environmental stimuli, rather than stamping-in stereotyped movement patterns. This was apparent in the first study of the phenomenon (Olds and Milner, 1954), in which rats were observed to return to the place in which they had previously received brain stimulation, and confirmed in later studies by Olds (1956), showing that rats could learn to negotiate mazes to obtain this sort of reward and that their performance was similar to that of a food-rewarded group.

The second conclusion is that brain stimulation reward interacts with 'natural' incentive processes. For example, according to Hoebel (1968), the response rates of rats working for lateral hypothalamic stimulation depend on their level of food deprivation. Deprivation enhances responding and satiation reduces it. Other work has indicated that brain stimulation reward is more effective, in some instances, if natural rewards are simultaneously available.

The third conclusion is that brain stimulation reward is dependent on a dopaminergic pathway running from the ventral tegmental area to the nucleus accumbens septi. Destruction of this pathway disrupts reward effects from stimulation applied at many sites in the brain, and there is evidence that disruption of this pathway interferes with the reinforcing properties of food without reducing consumption, indicating that it is important for the assignment of incentive properties to environmental cues (see Wise, this volume).

The final conclusion is that activation of the brain's reward mechanisms may be the basis of the acquisition of 'unnatural' appetites, such as an appetite for drugs (Cooper, Toates, Wise, this volume). This suggestion is based in part on evidence that many addictive drugs activate the dopaminergic pathway emanating from the ventral tegmental area and in part on the similarities between behaviour towards natural incentive objects and behaviour towards drugs and the paraphernalia surrounding their ingestion. Work on drug addiction suggests that the study of addiction provides a powerful tool for analysing the processes underlying the development of appetites. It also suggests that a proper understanding of appetitive mechanisms may provide an insight into the development of addictions and thus into how to cure people of them.

CONCLUSIONS

Appetite remains a useful concept in contemporary psychology for two reasons. The first is that appetitive concepts are necessary to make sense of the experimental literature on motivation and the second is that it acts as a fruitful heuristic device in guiding investigations of the processes involved in motivated behaviour. The goal or research on appetite is to characterize individual appetites as fully as possible within a coherent conceptual framework, allowing for the plurality of forms and expressions of appetites while identifying processes, both psychological and neural, that may be common to all appetites.

REFERENCES

Bindra, D. (1978). How adaptive behaviour is produced: a perceptual–motivational alternative to response–reinforcement. *Behavioural and Brain Sciences*, **1**, 41–91.

Bolles, R.C. (1980). Historical note on the term 'appetite'. *Appetite*, **1**, 3–6.

Bower, G.H. (1961). A contrast effect in differential conditioning. *Journal Experimental Psychology*, **62**, 196–9.

Cannon, W.B. (1947). *The wisdom of the body*. Kegan Paul, London.

Crespi, L.P. (1944). Amount of reinforcement and the level of performance. *Psychological Review*, **51**, 341–57.

Davey, G.C.L. (1989). *Ecological learning theory*. Routledge, London.

Dickinson, A. (1980). *Contemporary animal learning theory*. Cambridge University Press, Cambridge.

Grignaschi, G., Mantelli, B., and Samanin, R. (1993). The hypophagic effect of restraint stress in rats can be mediated by 5-HT2 receptors in the paraventricular nucleus of the hypothalamus. *Neuroscience Letters*, **152**, 103–6.

Guthrie, E.R. (1935). *The psychology of learning*. Harper, New York.

Harre, R. and Secord, P.F. (1972). *The explanation of social behaviour*. Blackwell, Oxford.

Hoebel, B.G. (1968). Inhibition and disinhibition of self-stimulation and feeding: hypothalamic control and postingestional factors. *Journal of Comparative and Physiological Psychology*, **66**, 89–100.

Hull, C.L. (1952). *A behavior system: an introduction to behavior theory concerning the individual organism*. Yale University Press, New Haven.

Kalra, S.P., Dube, M.G., Sahu, A., Phelps, C.P., and Kalra, P.S. (1991). Neuropeptide-Y secretion increases in the paraventricular nucleus in association with increased appetite for food. *Proceedings of the National Academy of Sciences USA*, **88**, 10931–5.

Le Magnen, J. (1985). *Hunger*. Cambridge University Press, Cambridge.

Morgan, C.T. (1943). *Physiological psychology*. McGraw Hill, New York.

Morgan, C.T. (1960). Physiological theory of drive. In *Psychology: A study of a science*, (ed. S. Koch). McGraw-Hill, New York.

Olds, J. (1956). Runway and maze behaviour controlled by basomedial forebrain stimulation in the rat. *Journal of Comparative and Physiological Psychology*, **49**, 507–12.

Olds, J. and Milner, P. (1954). Positive reinforcement produced by electrical stimulation of septal area and other areas of rat brain. *Journal of Comparative and Physiological Psychology*, **47**, 419–27.

Rolls, E.T. (1975). *The brain and reward*. Pergamon Press, Oxford.

Stellar, E. (1954). The physiology of motivation. *Psychological Review*, **61**, 5–22.

Tinklepaugh, O.L. (1928). An experimental study of representative factors in monkeys. *Journal of Comparative Psychology*, **8**, 197–236.

Toates, F. (1986). *Motivational systems*. Cambridge University Press, Cambridge.

2

Neural processing related to feeding in primates

Edmund T. Rolls

INTRODUCTION

From clinical evidence it has been known since early this century that damage to the base of the brain can influence food intake and body weight. Later it was demonstrated that one critical region is the ventromedial hypothalamus, for bilateral lesions here in animals led to hyperphagia and obesity (see Grossman, 1967, 1973). Then Anand and Brobeck (1951) discovered that bilateral lesions of the lateral hypothalamus can lead to a reduction in feeding and body weight. Evidence of this type led, in the 1950s and 1960s, to the view that food intake is controlled by two interacting 'centres', a feeding centre in the lateral hypothalamus and a satiety centre in the ventromedial hypothalamus (see Grossman, 1967, 1973; Stellar, 1954).

Soon, problems with this evidence for a dual centre hypothesis of the control of food intake appeared. For example, lesions of the lateral hypothalamus which were effective in producing aphagia also damaged fibre pathways coursing nearby such as the dopaminergic nigro-striatal bundle, and damage to these pathways outside the lateral hypothalamus could produce aphagia (Marshall, Richardson, and Teitelbaum, 1974). Thus by the mid-1970s it was clear that the lesion evidence for a lateral hypothalamic feeding centre was not straightforward, for at least part of the effect of the lesions was due to damage to fibres of passage travelling through or near the lateral hypothalamus (Stricker and Zigmond, 1976). It was thus not clear by this time what role the hypothalamus played in feeding. In more recent investigations it has been possible to damage the cells in the lateral hypothalamus without damaging fibres of passage, using as neurotoxins ibotenic acid or N-methyl-D-aspartate (NMDA) (Clark *et al.*, 1991; Winn, Tarbuck, and Dunnett, 1984; Dunnett, Lane, and Winn, 1985). With these techniques, it has been shown that damage to lateral hypothalamic cells does produce a lasting decrease in food intake and body weight, and that this is not associated with

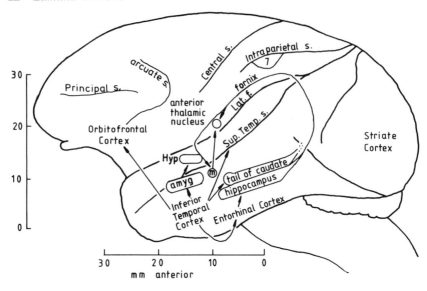

Fig. 2.1 Some of the pathways described in the text are shown on this lateral view of the brain of the macaque monkey: amyg = amygdala; central s = central sulcus; Hyp = hypothalamus / substantia innominata / basal forebrain; Lat f = lateral (or Sylvian) fissure; m = mammillary body; Sup. temp. s = superior temporal sulcus; 7 = posterior parietal cortex, area 7.

dopamine depletion due to damage to dopamine pathways, or with the akinesia and sensorimotor deficits which are produced by damage to the dopamine systems (Dunnett, Lane, and Winn, 1985; Winn, Tarbuck, and Dunnett, 1984; Clark *et al.*, 1991). The lesioned rats do not respond normally to acute glucoprivic challenges (Clark *et al.*, 1991). Thus the more recent lesion evidence does suggest that the lateral hypothalamus is involved in the control of feeding and body weight.

The evidence just described implicates the hypothalamus in the control of food intake and body weight, but does not show what important functions in feeding are being performed by the hypothalamus and by other brain areas. More direct evidence on the neural processing involved in feeding, based on recordings of the activity of single neurons in the hypothalamus and other brain regions, is described next. These other brain systems include systems that perform sensory analysis involved in the control of feeding, such as the taste and olfactory pathways; brain systems involved in learning about foods including the amygdala and orbitofrontal cortex; and brain systems involved in the initiation of feeding behaviour such as the striatum. Some of the brain regions and pathways described in the text are shown in Fig. 2.1 on a lateral view of the brain of the macaque monkey.

NEURONAL ACTIVITY IN THE LATERAL HYPOTHALAMUS DURING FEEDING

It has been found that there is a population of neurons in the lateral hypothalamus and substantia innominata of the monkey with responses which are related to feeding (see Rolls, 1981*a,b*, 1986). These neurons, which comprised 13.6 per cent in one sample of 764 hypothalamic neurons, respond to the taste and/or sight of food. The neurons respond to taste in that they respond only when certain substances, such as glucose solution but not water or saline, are in the mouth, and in that their firing rates are related to the concentration of the substance to which they respond (Rolls, Burton, and Mora, 1980). These neurons did not respond simply in relation to mouth movements, and comprised 4.3 per cent of the sample of 764 neurons. The responses of the neurons associated with the sight of food occurred as soon as the monkey saw the food, before the food was in his mouth, and occurred only to foods and not to non-food objects. These neurons comprised 11.8 per cent of the sample of 764 neurons (Rolls, Burton, and Mora, 1976, 1980). Some of these neurons (2.5 per cent of the total sample) responded to both the sight and taste of food (Rolls, Burton, and Mora, 1976, 1980). The finding that there are neurons in the lateral hypothalamus of the monkey which respond to the sight of food has been confirmed by Ono, Nishino, Sasaki, Fukuda, and Muramoto (1980).

Effect of hunger

The responses of these neurons only occur to the sight, or to the taste, of food if the monkey is hungry (Burton, Rolls, and Mora, 1976). Thus neuronal responses which occur to food in the hypothalamus depend on the motivational state of the animal. This provides evidence that these neurons have activity which is closely related to either or both autonomic responses and behavioural responses to the sight and taste of food, which only occur to food if hunger is present.

The signals which reflect the motivational state and perform this modulation include the following in the monkey. Gastric distension is one signal, as shown by the finding that after a monkey has fed to satiety, relief of gastric distension by drainage of ingested food through a gastric cannula leads to the almost immediate resumption of feeding (Gibbs, Maddison, and Rolls, 1981). (Because feeding is reinstated so rapidly, it is probably due to relief of distension rather than to the altered availability of metabolites in later parts of the gut.) Another signal is provided by the presence of food in the duodenum and later parts of the gut, as shown by the finding that if ingested food is allowed to drain from a duodenal cannula (situated near the pylorus), then normal satiety is not shown, and the monkey feeds almost continuously (Gibbs, Maddison and Rolls, 1981). Under these sham feeding conditions, food does not accumulate normally in the stomach, showing that, normally, influences of duodenal or more distal origin control gastric emptying, allowing gastric distension to build up and make its normal contribution to satiety. In this way an 'enterogastric loop' contributes to satiety. The presence of food in the duodenum also contributes to satiety, as shown by the finding that duodenal infusions of food at rates similar to those of gastric emptying reduce the rate of feeding (Gibbs, Maddison, and Rolls, 1981). Although there is no direct evidence in the monkey, it is very likely that rich information about nutrients in the gut and about gastric and gut distension reaches the nucleus of the solitary tract via the vagus, as it does in rats (Ewart, 1993; Mei, 1993, and this volume). Other signals which influence hunger and satiety presumably reflect the metabolic state of the animal, and may include such signals as glucose level in the plasma (Le Magnen, 1992). The glucose level may be sensed by cells in the hindbrain near the area postrema in the rat (Ritter, 1986). In the monkey, there is less evidence on where the crucial sites for glucose sensing that control food intake are located. It is known that there are glucose-sensitive neurons in a number of hindbrain and hypothalamic sites, as shown by micro-electro-osmotic techniques (Aou *et al.*, 1984; Oomura and Yoshimatsu, 1984).

The hypothalamus is not necessarily the first stage at which processing of food-related stimuli is modulated by hunger. Evidence on which is the first stage of processing where modulation by hunger occurs in primates is considered for the taste system below. To investigate whether hunger modulates neuronal responses in parts of the visual system through which visual information is likely to reach the hypothalamus (see below), the activity of neurons in the visual inferior temporal cortex was recorded in the same testing situations. It was found that the neuronal responses here to visual stimuli were not dependent on hunger (Rolls, Judge, and Sanghera, 1977). Nor were the responses of an initial sample of neurons in the amygdala, which connects the inferior temporal visual cortex to the hypothalamus (see below), found to depend on hunger (Rolls, 1992*b*; Sanghera, Rolls, and Roper-Hall, 1979). However, in the orbitofrontal cortex, which receives inputs from the inferior temporal visual cortex, and projects into the hypothalamus (see below and Russchen, Amaral, and Price, 1985), neurons with visual responses to food are found, and neuronal responses to food in this region are modulated by hunger (Thorpe, Rolls, and Maddison, 1983; see below). Thus for visual processing, neuronal responsiveness only at late stages of sensory processing and in the hypothalamus has been found to be modulated by hunger. The adaptive value of modulation of sensory processing only at late stages of processing, which also occurs in the taste system of primates, is discussed when food-related taste processing is described below.

Sensory-specific modulation of the responsiveness of lateral hypothalamic neurons and of appetite

During these experiments on satiety it was observed that if a lateral hypothalamic neuron had ceased to respond to a food on which the monkey had been fed to satiety, then the neuron might still respond to a different food (see example in Fig. 2.2). This occurred for neurons with responses associated with the taste (Rolls, 1981*b*; Rolls *et al.*, 1986) or sight (Rolls and Rolls, 1982; Rolls *et al.*, 1986) of food. Corresponding to this neuronal specificity of the effects of feeding to satiety, the monkey

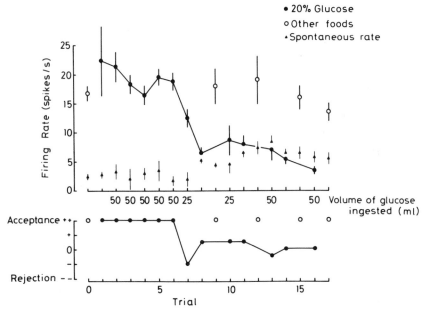

Fig. 2.2 The effect of feeding the monkey to satiety with 20 per cent glucose solution on the responses of a hypothalamic neuron to the taste of the glucose (filled circles) and to the taste of other foods (open circles). After the monkey had fed to satiety with glucose, the neuron responded much less to the taste of glucose, but still responded to the other foods. The satiety of the monkey, shown below, was measured by whether he accepted or rejected the glucose. (From Rolls *et al.*, 1986.)

rejected the food on which he had been fed to satiety, but accepted other foods on which he had not been fed.

As a result of these neurophysiological and behavioural observations showing the specificity of satiety in the monkey, experiments were performed to determine whether satiety was specific to foods eaten in man. It was found that the pleasantness of the taste of food eaten to satiety decreased more than for foods that had not been eaten (Rolls, Rolls, Rowe, and Sweeney, 1981). One implication of this finding is that if one food is eaten to satiety, appetite reduction for other foods is often incomplete, and this should mean that in man also at least some of the other foods will be eaten. This has been confirmed in an experiment in which either sausages or cheese with crackers were eaten for lunch. The liking for the food eaten decreased more than for the food not eaten and, when an unexpected second course was offered, more was eaten if a subject had not been given that food in the first course than if he had been given that food in the first course (98 per cent vs 40 per cent of the first course intake eaten in the second courses, $p < 0.01$, Rolls, Rolls, Rowe, and Sweeney, 1981). A further implication of these findings is that if a variety of foods is available, the total amount consumed will be more than when only one food is offered repeatedly. This prediction has been confirmed in a study in which humans ate more when offered a variety of sandwich fillings than one filling or a variety of types of yoghurt which differed in taste, texture, and colour (Rolls, Rowe, Rolls, Kingston, Megson, and Gunary, 1981). It has also been confirmed in a study in which humans were offered a relatively normal meal of four courses, and it was found that the change of food at each course significantly enhanced intake (Rolls, van Duijenvoorde, and Rolls, 1984). Because sensory factors such as similarity of colour, shape, flavour, and texture are usually more important than metabolic equivalence in terms of protein, carbohydrate, and fat content in influencing how foods interact in this type of satiety, it has been termed 'sensory-specific satiety' (B.J.Rolls, 1990; Rolls and Rolls, 1977, 1982; Rolls, Rolls, Rowe, and Sweeney, 1981; Rolls, Rowe, and Rolls, 1982; Rolls, Rowe, Rolls, Kingston, Megson, and Gunary, 1981). It should be noted that this effect is distinct from alliesthesia, in that alliesthesia is a change in the pleasantness of sensory inputs produced by internal signals (such as glucose in the gut) (see Cabanac, 1971; Cabanac and Duclaux, 1970; Cabanac and Fantino, 1977), whereas sensory-specific satiety is a change in the pleasantness of sensory inputs which is accounted for at least partly by the external sensory stimulation received (such as the taste of a particular food), in that, as shown above, it is at least partly specific to the external sensory stimulation received.

The parallel between these studies of feeding in humans and of the neurophysiology of hypothalamic neurons in the monkey has been extended by observations that in humans, sensory-specific satiety occurs for the sight as well as for the taste of food (Rolls, Rowe, and Rolls, 1982). Further, to complement the finding that in the hypothalamus neurons are found which respond differently to food and to water (Rolls and colleagues, unpublished observations), and that satiety with water can decrease the responsiveness of hypothalamic neurons which respond to water, it has been shown that in man motivation-specific satiety can also be detected. For example, satiety with water decreases the pleasantness of the sight and taste of water but not of food (Rolls, Rolls, and Rowe, 1983).

The enhanced eating when a variety of foods is available, as a result of the operation of sensory-specific satiety, may have been advantageous in evolution in ensuring that different foods with important different nutrients were consumed, but in man today, when a wide variety of foods is readily available, it may be a factor which can lead to overeating and obesity. In a test of this in the rat, it has been found that variety itself can lead to obesity (Rolls, van Duijenvoorde, and Rowe, 1983; see, further, B.J.Rolls and Hetherington, 1989).

Advances in understanding the neurophysiological mechanisms of sensory-specific satiety are being made in analyses of information processing in the taste system, as described below.

In addition to the sensory-specific satiety described above which operates primarily within (see above) and in the post-meal period (Rolls, van Duijenvoorde, and Rolls, 1984), there is now evidence for a long-term form of sensory-specific satiety (Rolls and de Waal, 1985). This was shown in a study in an Ethiopian refugee camp, in which it was found that refugees who had been in the camp for six months found the taste of their three regular foods less pleasant than that of three comparable foods which they had not been eating. The effect was a long-term form of sensory-specific satiety in that it was not found in refugees who had been in the camp and eaten the regular foods for two days (Rolls and de Waal, 1985). It is suggested that it is important to recognize the operation of long-term sensory-specific satiety in conditions such as these, for it may enhance malnutrition if the regular foods become less acceptable and so are rejected, exchanged for other less nutritionally effective foods or goods, or inadequately prepared. It may be advantageous under these circumstances to attempt to minimize the operation of long-term sensory-specific satiety by providing some variety, perhaps even with spices (Rolls and de Waal, 1985).

Effects of learning

The responses of these hypothalamic neurons in the primate become associated with the sight of food as a result of learning. This is shown by experiments in which the neurons come to respond to the sight of a previously neutral stimulus, such as a syringe, from which the monkey is fed orally; in which the neurons cease to respond to a stimulus if it is no longer associated with food (in extinction or passive avoidance); and in which the responses of these neurons remain associated with whichever visual stimulus is associated with food reward in a visual discrimination and its reversals (Mora, Rolls, and Burton, 1976; Wilson and Rolls, 1990). This type of learning is important for it allows organisms to respond appropriately to environmental stimuli which previous experience has shown are foods. The brain mechanisms for this type of learning are discussed below.

The responses of these neurons suggest that they are involved in responses to food. Further evidence for this is that the responses of these neurons occur with relatively short latencies of 150–200 ms, and thus precede and predict the responses of the hungry monkey to food (Rolls, Sanghera, and Roper-Hall, 1979).

Evidence that the responses of these neurons are related to the reward value of food

Given that these hypothalamic neurons respond to food when it is rewarding, that is, when the animal will work to obtain food, it is a possibility that their responses are related to the reward value which food has for the hungry animal. Evidence consistent with this comes from studies with electrical stimulation of the brain. It has been found that electrical stimulation of some brain regions is rewarding in that animals, including man, will work to obtain electrical stimulation of some sites in the brain (see Olds, 1977; Rolls, 1975, 1976, 1979). At some sites, including the lateral hypothalamus, the electrical stimulation appears to produce reward which is equivalent to food for the hungry animal, in that the animal will work hard to obtain the stimulation if he is hungry, but will work much less for it if he has been satiated (see Hoebel, 1969; Olds, 1977). There is even evidence that the reward at some sites can mimic food for a hungry animal and at other sites water for a thirsty animal, in that rats chose electrical stimulation at one hypothalamic site when hungry and at a different site when thirsty (Gallistel and Beagley, 1971). It was therefore very interesting when it was discovered that some of the neurons normally activated by food when the monkey was hungry were also activated by brain-stimulation reward (Rolls, 1975, 1976; Rolls, Burton, and Mora, 1980). Thus there was convergence of the effects of natural food reward, and brain-stimulation reward at some brain sites (e.g. the orbitofrontal cortex and amygdala), on to single hypothalamic neurons. Further, it was shown that self-stimulation occurred through the recording electrode if it was near a region where hypothalamic neurons had been recorded which responded to food, and that this self-stimulation was attenuated by feeding the monkey to satiety (Rolls, Burton, and Mora, 1980).

The finding that these neurons were activated by brain-stimulation reward is consistent with the hypothesis that their activity is related to reward produced by food, and not to some other effect of food. Indeed, this evidence from the convergence of brain-stimulation reward and food reward on to these hypothalamic neurons, and from the self-stimulation found through the recording electrode, suggests that animals work to obtain activation of these neurons by food, and that this is what makes food rewarding. At the same time this accounts for self-stimulation of some brain sites, which is understood as the animal seeking to activate the neurons which he normally seeks to activate by food when he is hungry. This and other evidence (see Rolls, 1975, 1982) indicates that feeding normally occurs in order to obtain the sensory input produced by food which is rewarding if the animal is hungry.

Sites in the hypothalamus and basal forebrain of neurons which respond to food

These neurons are found as a relatively small proportion of cells in a region which includes the lateral hypothalamus and substantia innominata and extends from the lateral hypothalamus posteriorly through the anterior hypothalamus and lateral preoptic area to a region ventral to and anterior to the anterior commissure (see Fig. 2.3 reproduced from Fig. 7 of Rolls *et al.*, 1979).

Useful further information about the particular populations of neurons in these regions with feeding-related activity, and about the functions of these neurons in feeding could be provided by evidence on their output connections. It is known that some hypothalamic neurons project to brainstem autonomic regions such as the dorsal motor nucleus of the vagus (Saper *et al.*, 1976, 1979). If some of the hypothalamic neurons with feeding-related activity projected in this way, it would be very likely that their functions would include the generation of autonomic responses to the sight of food. Some hypothalamic neurons project to the substantia nigra (Nauta and Domesick, 1978), and some neurons in the lateral hypothalamus and basal magnocellular forebrain nuclei of Meynert project directly to the cerebral cortex (Divac, 1975; Heimer and Alheid, 1990; Kievit and Kuypers, 1975). If some of these were feeding-related neurons, then by such routes they could influence whether feeding is initiated. To determine to which regions hypothalamic neurons with feeding-related activity project, electrical stimulation is being applied to these different regions to determine from which regions hypothalamic neurons with feeding-related activity can be antidromically activated. It has so far been found in such experiments by E.T. Rolls, E. Murzi, and C. Griffiths that some of these feeding-related neurons in the lateral hypothalamus and substantia innominata project directly to the cerebral cortex, to such areas as the prefrontal cortex in the sulcus principalis and the supplementary motor cortex. This provides evidence that at least some of these neurons with feeding-related activity project this information to the cerebral cortex, where it could be used in such processes as the initiation of feeding behaviour. It also indicates that at least some of these feeding-related neurons are in the basal magnocellular forebrain nuclei of Meynert, which is quite consistent with the reconstructions of the recording sites (Fig. 2.3).

In addition to a role in food reward and thus in the control of

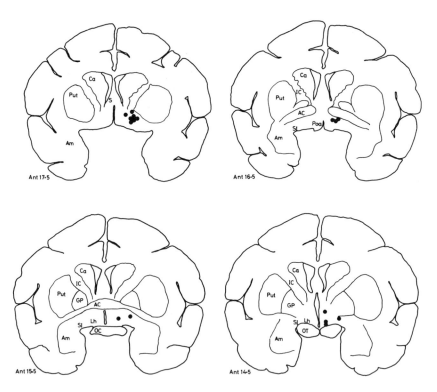

Fig. 2.3 Sites in the lateral hypothalamus and basal forebrain of the macaque at which neurons were recorded that responded to the sight of food. Abbreviations: AC, anterior commissure; Am, amygdala; Ca, caudate nucleus; GP, globus pallidus; IC, internal capsule; Lh, lateral hypothalamus; OC, optic chiasm; OT, optic tract; Poa, preoptic area; Put, putamen; S, septal region; SI, substantia innominata. (From Rolls *et al.*, 1979.)

feeding, it seems quite likely that at least some of the hypothalamic feeding-related neurons influence brainstem autonomic motor neurons. Consistent with this, it is known that there are projections from the lateral hypothalamus to the brainstem autonomic motor nuclei, and that lesions of the lateral hypothalamus disrupt conditioned autonomic responses (LeDoux, Iwata, Cichetti, and Reis, 1988).

Functions of the hypothalamus in feeding

The functions of the hypothalamus in feeding are thus related, at least in part, to the inputs which it receives from the forebrain, in that it contains neurons which respond to the sight of food, and which are influenced by learning. (Such pattern-specific visual responses, and their modification by learning, require forebrain areas such as the inferior temporal visual cortex and the amygdala, as described below.) This conclusion is consistent with the anatomy of the hypothalamus and substantia innominata, which receive projections from limbic structures such as the amygdala which in turn receive projections from the association cortex (Herzog and van Hoesen, 1976; Nauta, 1961). The conclusion is also consistent with the evidence that decerebrate rats retain simple controls of feeding, but do not show normal learning about foods (Grill and Norgren, 1978). These rats accept sweet solutions placed in their mouths when hungry and reject them when satiated, so that some control of responses to gustatory stimuli which depends on hunger can occur caudal to the level of the hypothalamus. However, these rats are unable to feed themselves, and do not learn to avoid poisoned solutions. The importance of visual inputs and learning to feeding, in relation to which some hypothalamic neurons respond, is that animals, and especially primates, may eat many foods every day, and must be able to select foods from other visual stimuli, as well as produce appropriate preparative responses to them such as salivation and the release of insulin. They must also be able to initiate appropriate actions in the environment to obtain food. Before any activation of motor neurons, such as those that innervate the masticatory muscles, involved in feeding, it it normally necessary to select which reinforcer in the environment should be the object of action, and then to select an appropriate (arbitrary) action to obtain the selected reinforcer. This indicates that direct connections from food reward systems or feeding control systems in the brain directly to motor neurons are likely to be involved only at the lowest level in the sense of Hughlings Jackson (Swash, 1989) of the control of behaviour. Instead, food reward systems may be expected to project to an action control system, and therefore connections from the lateral hypothalamus, amygdala, and orbitofrontal cortex to systems such as the basal ganglia are likely to be more

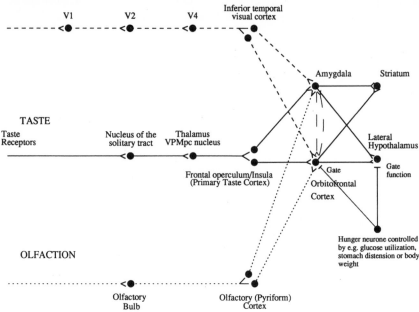

Fig. 2.4 Schematic diagram showing some of the gustatory, olfactory, and visual pathways involved in processing sensory stimuli involved in the control of food intake.

important as routes for the initiation of normal feeding (see section on the striatum below).

ACTIVITY IN THE GUSTATORY PATHWAYS DURING FEEDING

Given that there are neurons in the hypothalamus that can respond to the taste (and/or sight) of foods but not of non-foods, and that modulation of this sensory input by motivation is seen when recordings are made from these hypothalamic neurons, it may be asked whether these are special properties of hypothalamic neurons which they show because they are specially involved in the control of motivational responses, or whether this degree of specificity and type of modulation are general properties which are evident throughout sensory systems. In one respect it would be inefficient if motivational modulation were present far peripherally, because this would imply that sensory information was being discarded without the possibility for central processing. A subjective correspondent of such a situation might be that it might not be possible to taste food, or even to see food, when satiated! It is perhaps more efficient for most of the system to function similarly whether hungry or satiated, and to have a special system (such as the hypothalamus) following sensory processing where motivational state influences responsiveness. Evidence on the actual state of affairs which exists for visual processing in primates in relation to feeding has been summarized above. In contrast, apparently there is at least some peripheral modulation of taste processing in rats (in the nucleus of the solitary tract) (see Scott and Giza, 1992). Evidence is now being obtained for primates on the tuning of neurons in the gustatory pathways, and on whether responsiveness at different stages is influenced by motivation, as follows. These investigations on the gustatory pathways have also been able to show where flavour, that is, a combination of taste and olfactory input, is computed in the primate brain. The gustatory and olfactory pathways, and some of their onward connections, are shown in Fig. 2.4.

The first central synapse of the gustatory system is in the rostral part of the nucleus of the solitary tract (Beckstead, Morse, and Norgren, 1980; Beckstead and Norgren, 1979). The caudal half of this nucleus receives visceral afferents, and it is a possibility that such visceral information, reflecting, for example, gastric distension, is used to modulate gustatory processing even at this early stage of the gustatory system.

In order to investigate the tuning of neurons in the nucleus of the solitary tract, and whether hunger does influence processing at this first central opportunity in the gustatory system of primates, we recorded the activity of single neurons in the nucleus of the solitary tract. To ensure that our results were relevant to the normal control of feeding (and were not due, for example, to abnormally high levels of artificially administered putative satiety signals), we allowed the monkeys to feed until they were satiated, and determined whether this normal and physiological induction of satiety influenced the responsiveness of neurons in the nucleus of the solitary tract, which were recorded throughout the feeding, until satiety was reached. It was found that in the nucleus of the solitary tract, the first central relay in the gustatory system, neurons are relatively broadly tuned to the prototypical taste stimuli (sweet, salt, bitter, and sour) (Scott, Yaxley, Sienkiewicz, and Rolls, 1986a). It was also found that neuronal responses in the nucleus of the solitary tract to the taste of food are not influenced by whether the monkey is hungry or satiated (Yaxley, Rolls, Sienkiewicz, and Scott, 1985).

To investigate whether there are neurons in the primary gustatory cortex in the primate which are more closely tuned to respond to foods as compared to non-foods, and whether hunger modulates the responsiveness of these neurons, we have recorded the activity of

OFC

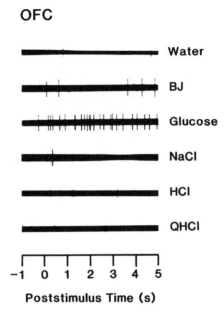

Water

BJ

Glucose

NaCl

HCl

QHCl

−1 0 1 2 3 4 5

Poststimulus Time (s)

Fig. 2.5 Examples of the responses recorded from one caudolateral orbitofrontal taste cortex neuron to the six taste stimuli, water, 20 per cent blackcurrant juice (BJ), 1 M glucose, 1 M NaCl, 0.01 M HCl, and 0.001 M quinine HCl (QHCl). (From Rolls *et al.*, 1990.)

single neurons in the primary gustatory cortex during feeding in the monkey. In the primary gustatory cortex in the frontal operculum and insula, neurons are more sharply tuned to gustatory stimuli than in the nucleus of the solitary tract, with some neurons responding primarily, for example, to sweet, and much less to salt, bitter, or sour stimuli (Scott, Yaxley, Sienkiewicz, and Rolls, 1986*b*; Yaxley, Rolls, and Sienkiewicz, 1990). However, here also, hunger does not influence the magnitude of neuronal responses to gustatory stimuli (Rolls, Scott, Sienkiewicz and Yaxley, 1988; Yaxley, Rolls, and Sienkiewicz, 1988).

A secondary cortical taste area, in the caudolateral orbitofrontal taste cortex of the primate, has recently been discovered, and here gustatory neurons are even more sharply tuned to particular taste stimuli (Rolls and Treves, 1990; Rolls, Yaxley, and Sienkiewicz, 1990) (see Fig. 2.5). In addition to representations of the 'prototypical' stimuli sweet, salt, bitter, and sour, different neurons in this region respond to umami (protein) taste (e.g. glutamate, Baylis and Rolls, 1991), and to a wide range of complex foods (Baylis and Rolls, in preparation). In this region, it is found that the responses of taste neurons to the particular food with which a monkey is fed to satiety decrease to zero (Rolls, Sienkiewicz, and Yaxley, 1989). That is, not only is motivational modulation of taste responses found in this region, but this modulation is sensory-specific (see, e.g. Fig. 2.6).

These results were obtained during normal feeding to satiety, when a comparison was made between the hungry and the satiated condition. The results do not completely eliminate the possibility that at some considerable time into the post-satiety period, some decrease of responsiveness to foods might occur. But even if this does occur, such modulation would not then account for the change in acceptability of food, which of course is seen as the satiety develops, and is used to define satiety. Nor would this modulation be relevant to the decrease in the pleasantness in the taste of a food which occurs when it is eaten to satiety (Cabanac, 1971; Rolls and Rolls, 1977, 1982; Rolls, Rolls and Rowe, 1983; Rolls, Rolls, Rowe and Sweeney, 1981; Rolls, Rowe and Rolls, 1982; Rolls, Rowe, Rolls, Kingston, and Megson, 1981). Thus it appears that the reduced acceptance of food as satiety develops, and the reduction in its pleasantness, are not produced by a reduction in the responses of neurons in the nucleus of the solitary tract or frontal opercular or insular gustatory cortices to gustatory stimuli. (As described above, the responses of gustatory neurons in these areas do not decrease as satiety develops.) Indeed, after feeding to satiety, humans reported that the taste of the food on which they had been satiated tasted almost as intense as when they were hungry, though much less pleasant (Rolls, Rolls, and Rowe, 1983). This comparison is consistent with the possibility that activity in the frontal opercular and insular taste cortices, as well as the nucleus of the solitary tract, does not reflect the pleasantness of the taste of a food, but, rather, its sensory qualities independently of motivational state. On the other hand, the responses of the neurons in the orbitofrontal taste area and in the lateral hypothalamus are modulated by satiety, and it is presumably in areas such as these that neuronal activity may be related to whether a food tastes pleasant, and to whether the human or animal will work to obtain and then eat the food, that is, to whether the food is rewarding.

The present results also provide evidence on the nature of the mechanisms which underlie sensory-specific satiety. Sensory-specific satiety, as noted above, is the phenomenon in which the decrease in the palatability and acceptability of a food which has been eaten to satiety is partly specific to the particular food which has been eaten (Rolls and Rolls, 1977, 1982; Rolls, Rolls, and Rowe, 1983; Rolls, Rowe and Rolls, 1982; Rolls, Rowe, Rolls, Kingston, and Megson, 1981). The results just described suggest that such sensory-specific satiety cannot be largely accounted for by adaptation at the receptor level, in the nucleus of the solitary tract, or in the frontal opercular or insular gustatory cortices, to the food which has been eaten to satiety; otherwise modulation of

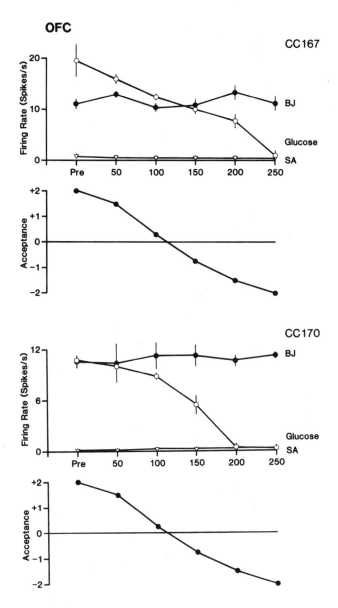

Fig. 2.6 The effect of feeding to satiety with glucose solution on the responses of two neurons in the secondary taste cortex to the taste of glucose and of blackcurrant juice (BJ). The spontaneous firing rate is also indicated (SA). Below the neuronal response data for each experiment, the behavioural measure of the acceptance or rejection of the solution on a scale from +2 to −2 (see text) is shown. The solution used to feed to satiety was 20 per cent glucose. The monkey was fed 50 ml of the solution at each stage of the experiment, as indicated along the abscissa, until he was satiated as shown by whether he accepted or rejected the solution. Pre is the firing rate of the neuron before the satiety experiment started. (From Rolls, Sienkiewicz, and Yaxley, 1989.)

neuronal responsiveness should have been apparent in the recordings made in these regions. Indeed, the findings suggest that sensory-specific satiety is not represented in the primary gustatory cortex. It is thus of particular interest that a decrease in the response of orbitofrontal cortex neurons occurs which is partly specific to the food which has just been eaten to satiety (Rolls, Sienkiewicz, and Yaxley, 1989).

These findings lead to the following proposed neuronal mechanism for sensory-specific satiety (see also Rolls and Treves, 1990). The tuning of neurons becomes more specific for gustatory stimuli through the NTS, gustatory thalamus, and frontal opercular taste cortex. Satiety, habituation and adaptation are not features of the responses here. This is observed (see above). The tuning of neurons becomes even more specific in the orbitofrontal cortex, but here there is some effect of satiety by internal signals such as gastric distension and glucose utilization, and in addition habituation with a time course of several minutes which lasts for 1–2 hours is a feature of the synapses which are activated. Because of the relative specificity of the tuning of orbitofrontal taste neurons, this results in a decrease in the response to that food, but different foods continue to activate other neurons. (For orbitofrontal cortex neurons that respond to two similar tastes before satiety, it is suggested that the habituation that results in a loss of the response to the taste eaten to satiety occurs because of habituation of the afferent neurons or synapses on to these orbitofrontal cortex neurons.) Then, the orbitofrontal cortex neurons have the required response properties, and it is only then necessary for other parts of the brain to use the activity of the orbitofrontal cortex neurons to reflect the reward value of that particular taste. Evidence that the activity of neurons in the orbitofrontal cortex does reflect reward is described below, and includes the evidence that electrical stimulation here produces reward which is like food in that its reward value is attenuated by satiety (Mora, Avrith, Phillips, and Rolls, 1979). One output of these neurons may be to the hypothalamic neurons with food-related responses, for their responses to the sight and/or taste of food show a decrease which is partly specific to a food which has just been eaten to satiety (see above). Another output may be to the ventral and adjoining striatum, which may provide an important link between reward systems and action (see below).

It is suggested that the computational significance of this architecture is as follows (see also Rolls, 1986, 1989; Rolls and Treves, 1990). If satiety were to operate at an early level of sensory analysis, then because of the broadness of tuning of neurons, responses to non-foods would become attenuated as well as responses to foods (and this could well be dangerous if poisonous non-foods became undetectable). This argument becomes even more compelling when it is realized that satiety typically shows some specificity for the particular food eaten, with others not eaten in the meal remaining relatively pleasant (see above). Unless tuning were relatively fine, this mechanism could not operate, for reduction in neuronal firing after one food had been eaten would inevitably reduce behavioural responsiveness to other foods. Indeed, it is of interest to note that such a sensory-specific satiety mechanism can be built by arranging for tuning to particular foods to become relatively specific at one level of the nervous system (as a result of categorization processing in earlier stages), and then at this stage (but not at prior stages) to allow habituation to be a property of the synapses, as proposed above.

Thus information processing in the taste system illustrates an important principle of higher nervous system function in primates, namely, that it is only after several or many stages of sensory information processing (which produce efficient categorization of the stimulus) that there is an interface to motivational systems, to other modalities, or to systems involved in association memory (Rolls, 1987; Rolls and Treves, 1990).

CONVERGENCE BETWEEN TASTE AND OLFACTORY PROCESSING TO REPRESENT FLAVOUR

At some stage in taste processing, it is likely that taste representations are brought together with inputs from different modalities, for example with olfactory inputs to form a representation of flavour. Takagi and his colleagues (Tanabe *et al.*, 1975a,b) have found an olfactory area in the medial orbitofrontal cortex. In a mid-mediolateral part of the caudal orbitofrontal cortex is the area investigated by Thorpe, Rolls, and Maddison (1983) in which are found many neurons with visual and some with gustatory responses. During our recordings in the caudolateral orbitofrontal cortex taste area our impression was that it was different from the frontal opercular and insular primary taste cortices, in that there were neurons with responses in other modalities within or very close to the caudolateral orbitofrontal taste cortex. We therefore investigated systematically whether there are neurons in the secondary taste cortex which respond to stimuli in other modalities, including the olfactory and visual modalities, and whether single neurons in this cortical region in some cases respond to stimuli from more than one modality.

In this investigation of the caudolateral orbitofrontal cortex taste area (Rolls and Baylis, 1994; Rolls, 1989; 1994), we found that of the single neurons which responded to any of these modalities, many were unimodal (taste 47 per cent, olfactory 12 per cent, visual 10 per cent), but were found in close proximity to each other. Some single neurons showed convergence, responding, for example, to taste and visual inputs (17 per cent), taste and olfactory inputs (10 per cent), and olfactory and visual inputs (4 per cent). Some of these multimodal single neurons had corresponding sensitivities in the two modalities, in that they responded best to sweet tastes (e.g. 1 M glucose), and responded more in a visual discrimination task to the visual stimulus which signified sweet fruit juice than to that which signified saline; or responded to sweet taste, and in an olfactory discrimination task to fruit odour. An example of one such bimodal neuron is shown in Fig. 2.7. The neuron responded best among the tastants to NaCl (N), and best among the odours to onion odour (On), and well also to salmon (S). The olfactory input to these neurons was further defined by measuring their responses while the monkey performed an olfactory discrimination task, in which it was possible to show that these neurons could respond to odours with response latencies as short as 150 ms, and had selective responses in that the neurons did not in some cases respond while the monkey performed a visual discrimination task (see Rolls, 1989, Fig. 9). The different types of neurons (unimodal in different modalities, and multimodal) were frequently found close to one another in tracks made into this region (see Fig. 2.8), consistent with the hypothesis that the multimodal representations are actually being

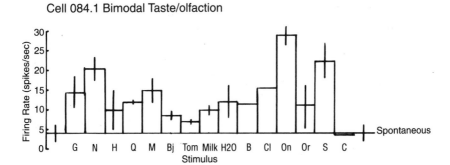

Fig. 2.7 The responses of a bimodal neuron recorded in the caudolateral orbitofrontal cortex. G, 1M glucose; N, 0.1M NaCl; H, 0.01M HCl; Q, 0.001M Quinine HCl; M, 0.1M monosodium glutamate; Bj, 20 per cent blackcurrant juice; Tom, tomato juice; B, banana odour; Cl, clove oil odour; On, onion odour; Or, orange odour; S, salmon odour; C, control no-odour presentation. The mean responses ± se are shown. The neuron responded best to the tastes of NaCl and monosodium glutamate and to the odours of onion and salmon.

formed from unimodal inputs to this region (see also Rolls and Mason, 1991). Further evidence linking these olfactory neurons to the control of responses to food is that in current experiments we (Critchley, Rolls, and Wakeman, 1993) are finding that the responses of these olfactory neurons decrease selectively for the odour of a food with which the monkey is fed to satiety. Thus the responses of these neurons are related to sensory-specific satiety effects for odour. These results show that there are regions in the orbitofrontal cortex of primates where the sensory modalities of taste and olfaction converge; that in many cases the neurons have corresponding sensitivities across modalities; and that the neurons have responses which are related to motivation, in

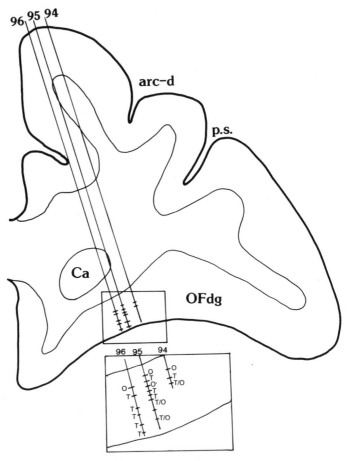

Fig. 2.8 Examples of tracks made into the orbitofrontal cortex in which taste (T) and olfactory (O) neurons were recorded close to each other in the same tracks. Some of the neurons were bimodal (T/O). arc−d, arcuate sulcus; Ca, caudate nucleus; OFdg, orbitofrontal cortex; p.s., principal sulcus.

that they are related to sensory- specific satiety. This may be the part of the primate nervous system where flavour is computed (Rolls and Baylis 1994; Rolls, 1994). In addition, information about the texture of food also influences neurons in this region (Critchley *et al.*, 1993).

The convergence of visual information on to neurons in this region not only allows associations to be learned between the sight of a food and its taste and smell, but may also provide the neural basis for the well-known effect which the sight of a food has on its perceived taste.

FUNCTIONS OF THE AMYGDALA AND TEMPORAL CORTEX IN FEEDING

Bilateral damage to the temporal lobes of primates leads to the Kluver–Bucy syndrome, in which lesioned monkeys, for example, select and place in their mouths non-food as well as food items shown to them, and repeatedly fail to avoid noxious stimuli (Aggleton and Passingham, 1982; Baylis and Gaffan, 1991; Jones and Mishkin, 1972; Kluver and Bucy, 1939). Rats with lesions in the basolateral amygdala also display altered food selection, in that they ingest relatively novel foods (Borsini and Rolls, 1984; Rolls, E.T. and Rolls, B.J., 1973), and do not learn to avoid ingesting a solution which has previously resulted in sickness (Rolls, B.J. and Rolls, E.T., 1973). (The deficit in learned taste avoidance in rats may be due to damage to the insular taste cortex, which has projections through and to the amygdala—Dunn and Everitt, 1988.) The basis for these alterations in food selection and in food-related learning are considered next (see also Rolls, 1990*b*, 1992*b*).

The monkeys with temporal lobe damage have a visual discrimination deficit, in that they are impaired in learning to select one of two objects under which food is found, and thus fail to form an association between the visual stimulus and reinforcement correctly (Gaffan, 1992; Jones and Mishkin, 1972). Gaffan, Gaffan and Harrison (1988), and Gaffan and Harrison (1987) have shown that the tasks which are impaired by amygdala lesions in monkeys typically involve a cross-modal association from a previously neutral stimulus to a primary reinforcing stimulus (such as the taste of food), consistent with the hypothesis that the amygdala is involved in learning associations between stimuli and primary reinforcers (see also Gaffan, 1992; Gaffan, Gaffan, and Harrison, 1989). Further evidence linking the amygdala to reinforcement mechanisms is that monkeys will work in order to obtain electrical stimulation of the amygdala, and that single neurons in the amygdala are activated by brain-stimulation reward of a number of different sites (Rolls, 1975; Rolls, Burton, and Mora, 1980).

The Kluver–Bucy syndrome is produced by lesions which damage the cortical areas in the anterior part of the temporal lobe and the underlying amygdala (Jones and Mishkin, 1972), or by lesions of the amygdala (Aggleton and Passingham, 1981; Gaffan, 1992; Weiskrantz, 1956), or of the temporal lobe neocortex (Akert *et al.*, 1961). Lesions to part of the temporal lobe neocortex, damaging the inferior temporal visual cortex and extending into the cortex in the ventral bank of the superior temporal sulcus, produce visual aspects of the syndrome, seen, for example, as a tendency to select non-food as well as food items (Weiskrantz and Saunders, 1984). Anatomically, there are connections from the inferior temporal visual cortex to the amygdala (Herzog and van Hoesen, 1976), which in turn projects to the hypothalamus (Nauta, 1961), thus providing a route for visual information to reach the hypothalamus (see Amaral *et al.*, 1992; Rolls, 1981*b*, 1990*b*, 1992*b*). This evidence, together with the evidence that damage to the hypothalamus can disrupt feeding (see Clarke *et al.*, 1991; LeMagnen, 1992; Winn *et al.*, 1984, 1990), thus indicates that there is a system which includes visual cortex in the temporal lobe, projections to the amygdala, and further connections to structures such as the lateral hypothalamus, which is involved in behavioural responses made on the basis of learned associations between visual stimuli and primary (unlearned) reinforcers such as the taste of food (see Fig. 2.4). Given this evidence from lesion and anatomical studies, the contribution of each of these regions to the visual analysis and learning required for these functions in food selection will be considered using evidence from the activity of single neurons in these regions.

Recordings were made from single neurons in the inferior temporal visual cortex while rhesus monkeys performed visual discriminations, and while they were shown visual stimuli associated with positive reinforcement such as food, with negative reinforcement such as aversive hypertonic saline, and neutral visual stimuli (Rolls, Judge, and Sanghera, 1977). It was found that during visual discriminations inferior temporal neurons often had sustained visual responses with latencies of 100–140 ms to the discriminanda, but that these responses did not depend on whether the visual stimuli were associated with reward or punishment (in that the neuronal responses did not alter during reversals, when the previously rewarded stimulus was made to signify aversive saline, and the previously punished stimulus was made to signify reward) (Rolls, Judge, and Sanghera, 1977). The conclusion, that the responses of inferior temporal neurons during visual discriminations do not code for whether a visual stimulus is associated with reward or punishment, is also consistent with the findings of Gross, Bender, and Gerstein (1979), Jarvis and Mishkin (1977), Ridley, Hester and Ettlinger (1977), and Sato *et al.* (1980). Further, it was found that inferior temporal neurons did not respond only to food-related visual stimuli, or only to aversive stimuli, and were not dependent on hunger, but, rather, that in many cases their responses depended on physical aspects of the stimuli such as shape, size, orientation, colour, or texture (Rolls, Judge, and Sanghera, 1977).

These findings thus indicate that the responses of neurons in the inferior temporal visual cortex do not reflect the association of visual stimuli with reinforcers such as food. Given these findings and the lesion evidence described above, it is thus likely that the inferior temporal cortex is an input stage for this process. The next structure on the basis of anatomical connections (see Fig. 2.4) is the amygdala, and this is considered next.

In recordings made from 1754 amygdaloid neurons, it was found that 113 (6.4 per cent), of which many were in a dorsolateral region of the amygdala known to receive directly from the inferior temporal visual cortex (Herzog and van Hoesen, 1976), had visual responses which in most cases were sustained while the monkey looked at effective visual stimuli (Sanghera, Rolls, and Roper-Hall, 1979). The latency of the responses was 100–140 ms or more. The majority (85 per cent) of these visual neurons responded more strongly to some stimuli than to others, but physical factors which accounted for the responses, such as orientation, colour and texture, could not usually be identified. It was found that 22 (19.5 per cent) of these visual neurons responded primarily to foods and to objects associated with food, but for none of these neurons did the responses occur uniquely to food-related stimuli, in that they all responded to one or more aversive or neutral stimuli. Further, although some neurons responded in a visual discrimination task to the visual stimulus which indicated food reward, but not to the visual stimulus associated with aversive saline, only minor modifications of the neuronal responses were obtained when the association of the stimuli with reinforcement was reversed in the reversal of the visual discrimination. Thus even the responses of these neurons were not invariably associated with whichever stimulus was associated with reward (see, further, Rolls, 1992b). A comparable population of neurons with responses apparently partly but not uniquely related to aversive visual stimuli was also found (Sanghera, Rolls, and Roper-Hall, 1979).

Amygdala neurons with responses which are probably similar to these have also been described by Nishijo *et al.* (1988), Ono *et al.* (1980), Ono *et al.* (1989), and Ono and Nishijo (1992). When Nishijo *et al.* (1988) tested four amygdala neurons in a simpler relearning situation than reversal, in which salt was added to a piece of food such as a water melon, the neurons' responses to the sight of the water melon appeared to diminish. However, in this task it was not clear whether the monkeys continued to look at the stimuli during extinction. It will be of interest in further studies to investigate whether in extinction evidence can be found for a rapid decrease in the neuronal responses to visual stimuli formerly associated with reward, even when fixation of the stimuli is adequate (see Rolls, 1992*b*).

Wilson and Rolls (1994; see also Rolls, 1992*b*) extended the analysis of the responses of these amygdala neurons by showing that while they do respond to (some) stimuli associated with primary reinforcement, they do not respond if the reinforcement must be determined on the basis of a rule (such as stimuli when novel are negatively reinforced, and when familiar are positively reinforced). This is consistent with the evidence that the amygdala is involved when reward must be determined, as normally occurs during feeding, by association of a stimulus with a primary reinforcer such as the taste of food, but is not involved when reinforcement must be determined in some other ways (see Gaffan, 1992; Rolls, 1992*b*). In the same study (Wilson and Rolls, 1994), it was shown that these amygdala neurons that respond to food can also respond to some other stimuli while they are relatively novel. It is suggested that it is by this mechanism that when relatively novel stimuli are encountered, they are investigated, for example by being smelled and then placed in the mouth, to assess whether the new stimuli are foods (see Rolls, 1992*b*).

The failure of this population of amygdala neurons to respond only to reinforcing stimuli, and the difficulty in reversing their responses, are in contrast with the responses of certain populations of neurons in the caudal orbitofrontal cortex and in a region to which it projects, the basal forebrain, which do show very rapid (in one or two-trials) reversals of their responses in visual discrimination reversal tasks (Thorpe, Rolls and Maddison, 1983; Wilson and Rolls, 1990; see below). On the basis of these findings, it is suggested that the orbitofrontal cortex is more involved than the amygdala in the rapid readjustments of behavioural responses made to stimuli when their reinforcement value is repeatedly changing, as in discrimination reversal tasks (Rolls, 1986*b*, 1990*b*; Thorpe *et al.*, 1983). The ability to flexibly alter responses to stimuli based on their changing reinforcement associations is important in motivated behaviour (such as feeding) and in emotional behaviour, and it is this flexibility which, it is suggested, the orbitofrontal cortex adds to a more basic capacity which the amygdala implements for stimulus- reinforcement learning (Rolls, 1990*b*).

These findings thus suggest that the amygdala could be involved at an early stage of the processing by which visual stimuli are associated with reinforcement, but that neuronal responses here do not code uniquely for whether a visual stimulus is associated with reinforcement. Neurons with responses more closely related to reinforcement are found in areas to which the amygdala projects, such as the lateral hypothalamus, substantia innominata, and ventral striatum. Thus in the anatomical sequence inferior temporal visual cortex to amygdala to lateral hypothalamus/substantia innominata and ventral striatum, there is evidence that neuronal responses become more relevant through these stages, as a result of learning, to the control of feeding, so that finally there are neurons in, for example, the lateral hypothalamus and substantia innominata with responses which occur only to stimuli which the organism has learned are food or signify food and to which it is appropriate when hungry to initiate feeding (see Fig. 2.4).

FUNCTIONS OF THE ORBITOFRONTAL CORTEX IN FEEDING

Damage to the orbitofrontal cortex alters food preferences, in that monkeys with damage to the orbitofrontal cortex select and eat foods which are normally rejected (Baylis and Gaffan, 1991; Butter, McDonald, and Snyder, 1969). Their food choice behaviour is very similar to that of monkeys with amygdala lesions (Baylis and Gaffan, 1991). Lesions of the orbitofrontal cortex also lead to a failure to correct feeding responses when these become inappropriate. Examples of the situations in which these abnormalities in feeding responses are found include (i) extinction, in that feeding responses continue to be made to the previously reinforced stimulus, (ii) reversals of visual discriminations, in that the monkeys make responses to the previously reinforced stimulus or object, (iii) Go/Nogo tasks, in that responses are made to the stimulus which is not associated with food reward, and (iv) passive avoidance, in that feeding responses are made even when they are punished (Butter, 1969; Iversen and Mishkin, 1970; Jones and Mishkin, 1972; Tanaka, 1973; see also Fuster, 1989; Rosenkilde, 1979). (It may be noted that, in contrast, the formation of associations between visual stimuli and reinforcement is less affected by these lesions than by temporal lobe lesions, as tested during visual discrimination learning and reversals—Jones and Mishkin, 1972).

To investigate how the orbitofrontal cortex may be involved in feeding and in the correction of feeding responses when these become inappropriate, recordings were made of the activity of 494 orbitofrontal neurons during the performance of a Go/Nogo task, reversals of a visual discrimination task, extinction, and passive avoidance (Thorpe, Rolls, and Maddison, 1983). First, neurons were found which responded in relation to the preparatory auditory or visual signal used before each trial (15.1 per cent), or non-discriminatively during the period in which the discriminative visual stimuli were shown (37.8 per cent). These neurons are not considered further here. Second, 8.6 per cent of neurons had responses which occurred discriminatively during the period in which the visual stimuli were shown. The majority of these neurons responded to whichever visual stimulus was associated with reward, in that the stimulus to which they responded changed during reversal. However, six of these neurons required a combination of a particular visual stimulus in the discrimination *and* reward in order to respond. Further, none of this second group of neurons responded to all the reward-related stimuli including different foods which were shown, so that in general this group of neurons coded for a combination of one or several visual stimuli *and* reward. Thus information that particular visual stimuli had previously been associated with reinforcement was represented in the responses of orbitofrontal neurons. Third, 9.7 per cent of neurons had responses which occurred after the lick response was made in the task to obtain reward. Some of these responded independently of whether fruit juice reward was obtained, or aversive hypertonic saline was obtained in trials on which the monkey licked in error or was given saline in the first trials of a reversal. Through these neurons, information that a lick had been made was represented in the orbitofrontal cortex. Other neurons in this third group responded only when fruit juice was obtained, and thus through these neurons information that reward had been given on that trial was represented in the orbitofrontal cortex. Such neurons reflect the taste of the liquid received, and are in a part of the orbitofrontal cortex which is close to, and probably receives inputs from, the secondary taste cortex (Rolls, 1989; Rolls *et al.*, 1990). Other neurons in this group responded when saline was obtained when a response was made in error, or when saline was obtained in the first few trials of a reversal (but not in either case when saline was simply placed in the mouth), or when reward was not given in extinction, or when food was taken away instead of being given to the monkey, but did not respond in all these situations in which reinforcement was omitted or punishment was given. Thus through these neurons task-selective information that reward had been omitted or punishment given was represented in the responses of these neurons.

These three groups of neurons found in the orbitofrontal cortex could together provide for computation of whether the reinforcement previously associated with a particular stimulus was still being obtained, and generation of a signal if a match was not obtained. This signal could be partly reflected in the responses of the last subset of neurons with task-selective responses to non-reward or to unexpected punishment. This signal could be used to alter the monkey's behaviour, leading, for example, to reversal to one particular stimulus but not to other stimuli, to extinction to one stimulus but not to others, etc. It could also lead to the altered responses of the orbitofrontal differential neurons found as a result of learning in reversal, so that their responses indicate appropriately whether a particular stimulus is now associated with reinforcement.

Thus the orbitofrontal cortex contains neurons which appear to be involved in altering behavioural responses when these are no longer associated with reward or become associated with punishment. In the context of feeding, it appears that without these neurons the primate is unable to suppress his behaviour correctly to non-food objects, in that altered food preferences are produced by orbitofrontal damage (Butter *et al.*, 1969). It also appears that without these neurons the primate is unable to correct his behaviour when it becomes appropriate to break a learned association between a stimulus and a reward such as food (Jones and Mishkin, 1972). The orbitofrontal neurons could be involved in the actual breaking of the association, or in the alteration of behaviour when other neurons signal that the connection is no longer appropriate. As shown here, the orbitofrontal cortex contains neurons with responses which could provide the information necessary for, and the basis for, the unlearning. This type of unlearning is important in enabling animals to alter the environmental stimuli to which motivational responses such as feeding have previously been made, when experience shows that such responses have become inappropriate. In this way they can ensure that their feeding and other motivational responses remain continuously adapted to a changing environment.

The more rapid reversal of neuronal responses in the orbitofrontal cortex, and in a region to which it projects, the basal forebrain (Thorpe, Rolls, and Maddison, 1983; Wilson and Rolls, 1990), than that in the amygdala suggests that the orbitofrontal cortex is more involved than the amygdala in the rapid readjustments of behavioural responses made to stimuli when their reinforcement value is repeatedly changing, as in discrimination reversal tasks (Rolls, 1986, 1990*b*; Thorpe *et al.*, 1983). The ability to alter flexibly responses to stimuli based on their changing reinforcement associations is important in motivated behaviour (such as feeding) and in emotional behaviour, and it is this flexibility which, it is suggested, the orbitofrontal cortex adds to a more basic capacity which the amygdala implements for stimulus-reinforcement learning (Rolls, 1986; Rolls, 1990*b*). The great development of the orbitofrontal cortex in primates, yet the similarity of its connections to those of the amygdala, and its connections with the amygdala, lead to the suggestion that in evolution, and as part of continuing corticalization of functions, the orbitofrontal cortex has come to be placed hierarchically above the amygdala, and is especially important when rapid readjustment of stimulus-reinforcement associations is required (see Rolls, 1990*b*). This suggestion is also consistent with the indication that whereas in rodents sub-cortical structures such as the amygdala and hypothalamus have access to taste information from the precortical taste system, the same does not occur in primates; and that some precortical processing of taste in relation to the control of feeding occurs in rodents (see above and Scott and Giza, 1993). In contrast, there is great development and importance of cortical processing of taste in primates, and it is very appropriate that the orbitofrontal cortex area just described is found just medial to the secondary taste cortex, which is in primates in the caudolateral orbitofrontal cortex. It appears that close to this orbitofrontal taste cortex the orbitofrontal cortical area just described develops and receives inputs from the visual association cortex (inferior temporal cortex), the olfactory (pyriform) cortex, and probably from the somatosensory cortex, so that reward associations between these different modalities can be determined rapidly.

FUNCTIONS OF THE STRIATUM IN FEEDING

Damage to the nigro-striatal bundle, which depletes the striatum of dopamine, produces aphagia and adipsia associated with a sensori-motor disturbance in the rat (Marshall, Richardson, and Teitelbaum, 1974; Stricker, 1984; ; Stricker and Zigmond, 1976; Ungerstedt, 1971). Moreover, many of the brain systems implicated in the control of feeding, such as the amygdala and orbitofrontal cortex, have projections to the striatum, which could provide a route for these brain systems to lead to feeding responses (Mogenson *et al.*, 1980; Rolls and Johnstone, 1992; Rolls and Williams, 1987*a*; Williams *et al.*, 1993). In order to analyse how striatal function is involved in feeding, the activity of single neurons is being recorded in different regions of the striatum (see Fig. 2.9) during the initiation of feeding and during the performance of other tasks known to be affected by damage to particular regions of the striatum (see Rolls, 1979, 1984, 1986; Rolls and Johnstone, 1992; Rolls and Williams, 1987*a*), as follows.

In the *head of the caudate nucleus* (Rolls, Thorpe, and Maddison, 1983), which receives inputs particularly from the prefrontal cortex, many neurons responded to environmental stimuli which were cues to the monkey to prepare for the possible initiation of a feeding response. Thus, 22.4 per cent of neurons recorded responded during a cue given by the experimenter that a food or non-food object was about to be shown, and fed, if food, to the monkey. Comparably, in a visual discrimination task made to obtain food, 14.5 per cent of the neurons (including some of the above) responded during a 0.5 s tone/light cue which preceded and signalled the start of each trial. It is suggested that these neurons are involved in the utilization of environmental cues for the preparation for movement, and that disruption of the function of these neurons contributes to the akinesia or failure to initiate movements (including those required for feeding) found after depletion of dopamine in the striatum (Rolls, Thorpe, and Maddison, 1983). Some other neurons (25.8 per cent) responded if food was shown to the monkey immediately prior to feeding by the experimenter, but the responses of these neurons typically did not occur in other situations in which food-related visual stimuli were shown, such as during the visual discrimination task. Comparably, some other neurons (24.3 per cent) responded differentially in the visual discrimination task, to for example the visual stimulus which indicated that the monkey could initiate a lick response to obtain food, yet typically did not respond when food was simply shown to the monkey prior to feeding. The responses of these neurons thus occur to particular stimuli which indicate that particular motor responses should be made, and are thus situation-specific, so that it is suggested that these neurons are involved in stimulus-motor response connections. In that their responses are situation-specific, they are different from the responses

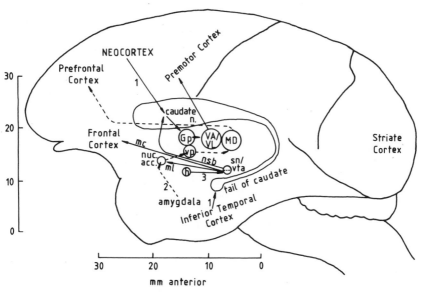

Fig. 2.9 Some of the striatal and connected regions in which the activity of single neurons is described shown on a lateral view of the brain of the macaque monkey. Gp, globus pallidus; h, hypothalamus; Sn, substantia nigra, pars compacta (A9 cell group), which gives rise to the nigro-striatal dopaminergic pathway, or nigro-striatal bundle (nsb); vta, ventral tegmental area, containing the A10 cell group, which gives rise to the mesocortical dopamine pathway (mc) projecting to the frontal and cingulate cortices and to the mesolimbic dopamine pathway (ml), which projects to the nucleus accumbens (nuc acc).

of the hypothalamic neurons described above with visual responses to the sight of food (Rolls, Thorpe, and Maddison, 1983). It is thus suggested that these neurons in the head of the caudate nucleus could be involved in relatively fixed feeding responses made in particular, probably well-learned, situations to food, but do not provide a signal which reflects whether a visual stimulus is associated with food, and on the basis of which any response required to obtain the food could be initiated. Rather, it is likely that the systems described above in the temporal lobe, hypothalamus, and orbitofrontal cortex are involved in this more flexible decoding of the food value of visual stimuli.

In the *tail of the caudate nucleus*, which receives inputs from the inferior temporal visual cortex, neurons were found which responded to visual stimuli such as gratings and edges, but which showed habituation which was rapid and pattern-specific (Caan, Perrett, and Rolls, 1984). It was suggested that these neurons are involved in orientation to patterned visual stimuli, and in pattern-specific habituation to these stimuli (Caan, Perrett, and Rolls, 1984). These neurons would thus appear not to be directly involved in the control of feeding, although a disturbance in the ability to orient normally to a changed visual stimulus could indirectly have an effect on the ability to react normally.

In the *putamen*, which receives from the sensori-motor cortex, neurons were found with activity which occurred just before mouth or arm movements made by the monkey (Rolls *et al.*, 1984). Disturbances in the normal function of these neurons might be expected to affect the ability to initiate and execute movements, and thus might indirectly affect the ability to feed normally.

The *ventral striatum*, which includes the nucleus accumbens, the olfactory tubercle (or anterior perforated substance of primates), and the islands of Calleja, receives inputs from limbic structures such as the amygdala and hippocampus, and from the orbitofrontal cortex, and projects to the ventral pallidum (see, further, Groenewegen *et al.*, 1991). The ventral pallidum may then influence output regions by the subthalamic nucleus / globus pallidus / ventral thalamus / premotor cortex route, or via the mediodorsal nucleus of the thalamus / prefrontal cortex route (Heimer *et al.*, 1982). The ventral striatum may thus be for limbic structures what the neostriatum is for neocortical structures, that is, a route for limbic structures to influence output regions. There is evidence linking the ventral striatum and its dopamine input to reward, for manipulations of this system alter the incentive effects which learned rewarding stimuli have on behaviour (Everitt and Robbins, 1992; Robbins and Everitt, 1992).

Because of its possible role as an output structure for the amygdala and orbitofrontal cortex to enable learned associations between previously neutral stimuli and rewards such as food to influence behaviour, we have analysed the activity of neurons in the ventral striatum of the behaving monkey (Rolls and Williams, 1987b, 1987a; Williams *et al.*, 1993). A number of different types of neuronal response were found. One population of neurons was found to respond to visual stimuli of emotional or motivational significance, that is, to stimuli which have in common the property that they are positively or negatively reinforcing (Rolls, 1990b). (Reinforcers are stimuli which, if their occurrence, termination, or omission is made contingent upon the making of a behavioural response, alter the future emission of that response.) The responses of an example of a neuron of this type are shown in Fig. 2.10. The neuron increased its firing rate to the S− on non-food trials in the visual discrimination task, and decreased its firing rate to the S+ on food reward trials in the visual discrimination task. The differential response latency of this neuron to the reward-related and to the saline-related visual stimulus was approximately 150 ms (see Fig. 2.10), and this value was typical.

Of the neurons which responded to visual stimuli that were rewarding, relatively few responded to all the rewarding stimuli used. That

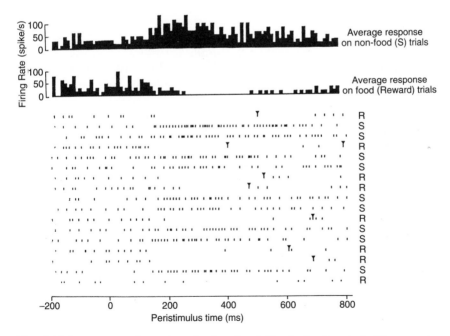

Fig. 2.10 Responses of a neuron in the visual discrimination task. The neuron decreased its firing rate to the S+ on food reward trials, and increased its firing rate to the S− on non-food trials. Rastergrams and peristimulus time histograms are shown. T, touch behavioural response.

is, only few (1.8 per cent) ventral striatal neurons responded both when food was shown and to the positive discriminative stimulus, the S+, in a visual discrimination task. Instead, the reward-related neuronal responses were typically more context- or stimulus-dependent, responding, for example, to the sight of food but not to the S+ which signified food (4.3 per cent), differentially to the S+ or S− but not to food (4.0 per cent), or to food if shown in one context but not in another context. Some other neurons (1.4 per cent) responded to aversive stimuli. These neurons did not respond simply in relation to arousal, which was produced in control tests by inputs from different modalities, for example by touching the leg.

These neurons with reinforcement-related responses represented 13.9 per cent of the neurons recorded in the ventral striatum, and may receive their inputs from structures such as the amygdala, in which some neurons with similar responses are found (Rolls, 1992*b*; Sanghera, Rolls, and Roper-Hall, 1979).

In that the majority of the neurons recorded in the ventral striatum did not have unconditional sensory responses, but instead the response typically depended on memory, for whether the stimulus was recognized, or for whether it was associated with reinforcement, the function of this part of the striatum does not appear to be purely sensory. Rather, it may provide one route for such memory-related and emotional and motivational stimuli to influence motor output. This is consistent with the hypothesis that the ventral striatum is a link for learned incentive (e.g. rewarding) stimuli (see, e.g., Everitt and Robbins, 1992), and also for other limbic-processed stimuli such as faces and novel stimuli, to influence behaviour (Mogenson *et al.*, 1980; Rolls, 1984*b*, 1989*a*, 1990*a*; Rolls and Johnstone, 1992; Rolls and Williams, 1987*a,b*; Williams *et al.*, 1993). The role of the ventral striatum in feeding may thus be to provide a route for learned incentive stimuli such as the sight of food to influence behavioural responses such as approach to food.

Synthesis: the functions of the striatum in feeding and reward

These neurophysiological studies show that in different regions of the striatum neurons are found which may be involved in orientation to environmental stimuli, in the use of such stimuli in the preparation for and initiation of movements, in the execution of movements, in stimulus–response connections appropriate for particular responses made in particular situations to particular stimuli, and in allowing learned reinforcers, including food, to influence behaviour. Because of its many inputs from brain systems involved in feeding and from other brain systems involved in action, the striatum may provide a crucial route for signals which have been decoded through sensory pathways and limbic structures, and which code for the current reward value of visual, olfactory, and taste stimuli, to be interfaced in an arbitration mechanism, to produce behavioural output. The issue then arises of how the striatum, and more generally the basal ganglia, might operate to perform such functions.

We can start by commenting on what functions must be performed in order to link the signals that control feeding to action. It has been shown above that through sensory pathways, representations of objects in the environment are produced. These are motivation-independent, and are in, for example, the primary taste cortex and the inferior temporal visual cortex in primates (see Fig. 2.4). After this stage, the sensory signals are interfaced to motivational state, so that the signals in, for example, the orbitofrontal cortex reflect not only the taste of the food, but also whether the monkey is hungry. The sensory signals are also passed in these structures (e.g. the orbitofrontal cortex and amygdala) through association memories, so that the outputs reflect whether a particular stimulus has been previously, and is still, associated with a primary reward. (This process will include conditioned effects from previous ingestion which reflect the energy obtained from the food, sickness produced by it, etc.) These neurons thus reflect the reward value of food, and neurons in this system can be driven by visual, olfactory, and/or taste stimuli. Now, it is of fundamental importance that these reward-related signals should not be interfaced directly to feeding movements, such as chewing. (Brainstem systems which perform such functions in a limited way may assist in the execution of feeding movements later in the feeding sequence.) Instead, what is required is that the food-related reward signals should enter an arbitration mechanism, which takes into account not only the other rewards (with their magnitude) that are currently available, but also the cost of obtaining each reward.

The proposal is developed at the conceptual level elsewhere that the basal ganglia perform this function (Rolls, 1984; Rolls, 1994; Rolls and Johnstone, 1992; Rolls and Williams, 1987a). The striatum receives the appropriate signals for this function, including not only information from limbic structures and the orbitofrontal cortex about rewards available; and cognitive information from the association areas of the cerebral cortex; but also inputs from the motor, premotor, somatosensory, and parietal cortical areas which provides information about action and movements. The hypothesis is that the striatum, followed by the globus pallidus and substantia nigra, provide a two-stage system for bringing these signals together. Such convergence is implied and provided for by the dendritic organization of the basal ganglia (Percheron *et al.*, 1984; Rolls, 1984; Rolls and Johnstone, 1992; Rolls and

Williams, 1987*a*). By virtue of such anatomy, the basal ganglia would allow in its output stages signals indicating that food was available, was currently rewarding, and that the costs of obtaining it were not too high as indicated perhaps by frontal cortical inputs, to be combined with, for example, signals from parietal and premotor areas reflecting what position in space is being visually fixated, and actions or movements being made to approach that position in space. These signals might well lead to the activation of individual neurons as a result of previous repeated co-occurrence, and associated synaptic modification in the basal ganglia. The output of such neurons would then indicate that actions should be made to approach and obtain rewarding targets in the environment. If a signal arrived in the basal ganglia from another cortical or limbic area (indicating, for example, that a novel visual stimulus had appeared), then lateral inhibitory connections and the competitive interactions it makes possible within the striatum would lead to interruption of feeding, and would implement an arbitration system (see, further, Rolls, 1984; Rolls and Johnstone, 1992; Rolls and Williams, 1987*a*). It is suggested that part of what is implemented in this way is a relatively simple interface between sensory and action systems, in that the signals reaching the striatum about reward need only signify that reward is available, with the details about where it is being implied, for example, by which position in space is being visually fixated, and is the current subject of attention. Limiting sensory analysis in this way allows the reward signal, reflecting the output of the 'what' system in perception, to be linked unambiguously with the output of the 'where' system in perception (see Rolls, 1992*a*, p. 18; Rolls, 1991), and this is part of what simplifies the interface between systems that specify which targets in the environment should be the targets for action, and the systems which lead to action. The action system in this case can be general-purpose, in that it can be organized to perform general purpose operations (which are not different for each type of goal object or reward), to approach and acquire the objects in space which are currently the focus of attention. (Of course, if the object that is the object of attention is associated with punishment, as shown by inputs carried by other neurons from limbic structures, then the basal ganglia should access or 'look up' operations learned previously that will lead to withdrawal from the current focus of attention.) The ways in which reward systems provide for an interface to action systems, and in which the basal ganglia may operate to map signals into actions, are discussed more fully elsewhere (Rolls, 1984; Rolls, 1990*b*; Rolls, 1994; Rolls and Johnstone, 1992; Rolls and Williams, 1987*a*). These ideas do need a great deal of development, but are addressing some of the crucial current questions in understanding how brain systems involved in decoding rewards, including food reward, are interfaced to action systems to produce, for example, feeding. It is likely that understanding the functions of the basal ganglia will be crucial in understanding these issues.

SUMMARY AND CONCLUSIONS

(1) Investigations in non-human primates have provided evidence that the lateral hypothalamus and adjoining substantia innominata are involved in the control of feeding, for there is a population of neurons in these regions which respond to the sight and/or taste of food if the organism is hungry. The responses of these neurons may reflect the rewarding value or pleasantness of food, for stimulation in this region can mimic the reward value of food. These neurons may also be on a route for forebrain-decoded stimuli, such as the sight of food, to produce autonomic responses, such as salivation and insulin release.

(2) It has been found that although after satiation with one food these hypothalamic neurons no longer respond to that food, they may still respond at least partly to other foods which have not been eaten. Following this finding, it has been shown that sensory-specific satiety is an important determinant of human food intake, and that, associated with this, variety is an important factor in determining the amount of food eaten.

(3) A route for information about which visual stimuli are foods to reach the hypothalamus is provided by temporal lobe structures such as the inferior temporal visual cortex and amygdala, with the amygdala being important for learning which visual stimuli are foods.

(4) The orbitofrontal cortex contains a population of neurons which appear to be important in correcting feeding responses as a result of learning. Its functions are closely related to those of the amygdala, but especially in primates, it may be able to implement a more rapid system for constantly updating associations between stimuli and primary reinforcers.

(5) Activity in the taste pathways up to and including the primary taste cortex of primates reflects what the taste is. After this, in the secondary taste cortex (part of the orbitofrontal cortex), activity in the gustatory system reflects motivational state, and thus the reward value of the taste.

(6) In the orbitofrontal cortex, there is also an olfactory processing region in which olfactory responses similarly reflect motivational state. In this region, some convergence between olfactory and taste signals occurs. The flavour of food may thus be computed here.

(7) The striatum contains neural systems which are important for the initiation of different types of motor and behavioural responses, including feeding. It is suggested that it may be crucial in bringing together food reward signals with information from many parts of the cerebral cortex which are required for the initiation of actions.

REFERENCES

Aggleton, J. P. and Passingham, R. E. (1981). Syndrome produced by lesions of the amygdala in monkeys (Macaca mulatta). *Journal of Comparative and Physiological Psychology*, **95**, 961–77.

Aggleton, J.P. and Passingham, R.E. (1982). An assessment of the reinforcing properties of foods after amygdaloid lesions in rhesus monkeys. *Journal of Comparative and Physiological Psychology*, **96**, 71–7.

Akert, K., Gruesen, R.A., Woolsey, C.N., and Meyer, D.R. (1961). Kluver–Bucy syndrome in monkeys with neocortical ablations of temporal lobe, *Brain*, **84**, 480–98.

Amaral, D.G., Price, J.L., Pitkanen, A., and Carmichael, S.T. (1992). Anatomical organization of the primate amygdaloid complex, ch. 1, pp. 1–66 in *The Amygdala* (ed. J.P.Aggleton). Wiley-Liss, New York.

Anand, B.K. and Brobeck, J.R. (1951). Localization of a feeding center in the hypothalamus of the rat. *Proceedings of the Society of Experimental Biology and Medicine*, **77**, 323–4.

Aou, S., Oomura, Y, Lenard, L., Noshino, H., Inokuchi, A., Minami, T, and Misaki, H. (1984). Behavioral significance of monkey hypothalamic glucose-sensitive neurons. *Brain Research*, **302**, 69–74.

Baylis, L.L. and Gaffan, D. (1991). Amygdalectomy and ventromedial prefrontal ablation produce similar deficits in food choice and in simple object discrimination learning for an unseen reward. *Experimental Brain Research*, **86**, 617–22.

Baylis, L.L. and Rolls, E.T. (1991). Responses of neurons in the primate taste cortex to glutamate. *Physiology and Behavior*, **49**, 973–9.

Beckstead, R.M. and Norgren, R. (1979). An autoradiographic examination of the central distribution of the trigeminal, facial, glossopharyngeal, and vagal nerves in the monkey. *Journal of Comparative Neurology*, **184**, 455–72.

Beckstead, R.M., Morse, J.R., and Norgren, R. (1980). The nucleus of the solitary tract in the monkey: projections to the thalamus and brainstem nuclei. *Journal of Comparative Neurology*, **190**, 259–82.

Borsini, F. and Rolls, E.T. (1984). Role of noradrenaline and serotonin in the basolateral region of the amygdala in food preferences and learned taste aversions in the rat. *Physiology and Behavior*, **33**, 37–43.

Burton, M.J., Rolls, E.T., and Mora, F. (1976). Effects of hunger on the responses of neurons in the lateral hypothalamus to the sight and taste of food. *Experimental Neurology*, **51**, 668–77.

Butter, C.M. (1969). Perseveration in extinction and in discrimination reversal tasks following selective prefrontal ablations in Macaca mulatta. *Physiology and Behavior*, **4**, 163–71.

Butter, C.M., McDonald, J.A., and Snyder, D.R. (1969). Orality, preference behavior, and reinforcement value of non-food objects in monkeys with orbital frontal lesions. *Science,* **164**, 1306–7.

Caan, W., Perrett, D.I., and Rolls, E.T. (1984). Responses of striatal neurons in the behaving monkey. 2. Visual processing in the caudal neostriatum. *Brain Research,* **290**, 53–65.

Cabanac, M. (1971). Physiological role of pleasure. *Science,* **173**, 1103–7.

Cabanac, M. and Duclaux, R. (1970). Specificity of internal signals in producing satiety for taste stimuli. *Nature,* **227**, 966–7.

Cabanac, M. and Fantino, M. (1977). Origin of olfacto-gustatory alliesthesia: Intestinal sensitivity to carbohydrate concentration? *Physiology and Behavior,* **10**, 1039–45.

Clark, J.M., Clark, A.J.M., Bartle, A., and Winn, P. (1991). The regulation of feeding and drinking in rats with lesions of the lateral hypothalamus made by N-methyl-D-aspartate. *Neuroscience,* **45**, 631–40.

Critchley, H.D., Rolls, E.T., and Wakeman, E.A. (1993). Orbitofrontal cortex responses to the texture, taste, smell and sight of food. *Appetite,* **21**, 170.

Divac, I. (1975). Magnocellular nuclei of the basal forebrain project to neocortex, brain stem, and olfactory bulb. Review of some functional correlates. *Brain Research,* **93**, 385–98.

Dunn, L. T. and Everitt, B. J. (1988). Double dissociations of the effects of amygdala and insular cortex lesions on conditioned taste aversion, passive avoidance, and neophobia in the rat using the excitotoxin ibotenic acid. *Behavioural Neuroscience,* **102**, 3–23.

Dunnett, S.B., Lane, D.M., and Winn, P. (1985). Ibotenic acid lesions of the lateral hypothalamus: comparison with 6-hydroxydopamine-induced sensorimotor deficits. *Neuroscience,* **14**, 509–18.

Everitt, B.J. and Robbins, T.W. (1992). Amygdala-ventral striatal interactions and reward-related processes, pp. 401–430 in *The amygdala* (ed. J.P. Aggleton). Wiley, Chichester.

Ewart, W. (1993). Hepatic and other parenteral visceral afferents affecting ingestive behaviour. In *The neurophysiology of ingestion* (ed. D.A. Booth). Pergamon Press, Oxford.

Fuster, J.M. (1989). *The prefrontal cortex,* 2nd edn, Raven Press, New York.

Gaffan, D. (1992). Amygdala and the memory of reward, ch. 18, pp. 471–83 in *The amygdala* (ed. J.P.Aggleton). Wiley- Liss, New York.

Gaffan, D. and Harrison, S. (1987) Amygdalectomy and disconnection in visual learning for auditory secondary reinforcement by monkeys. *Journal of Neuroscience,* **7**, 2285–92.

Gaffan, E. A., Gaffan, D., and Harrison, S. (1988). Disconnection of the amygdala from visual association cortex impairs visual reward-association learning in monkeys. *Journal of Neuroscience,* **8**, 3144–50.

Gaffan, D., Gaffan, E. A., and Harrison S. (1989) Visual-visual associative learning and reward-association learning in monkeys: the role for the amygdala. *Journal of Neuroscience,* **9**, 558–64.

Gallistel, C.R. and Beagley, G. (1971). Specificity of brain-stimulation reward in the rat. *Journal of Comparative and Physiological Psychology,* **76**, 199–205.

Gibbs, J., Maddison, S.P., and Rolls, E.T. (1981). The satiety role of the small intestine in sham feeding rhesus monkeys. *Journal of Comparative and Physiological Psychology,* **95**, 1003–15.

Grill, H.J. and Norgren, R. (1978). Chronically decerebrate rats demonstrate satiation but not bait shyness. *Science*, **201**, 267–9.

Groenewegen, H.J., Berendse, H.W., Meredith, G.E., Haber, S.N., Voorn, P., Wolters, J.G., and Lohman, A.H.M. (1991) Functional anatomy of the ventral, limbic system-innervated striatum, pp. 19–60 in *The mesolimbic dopamine system: from motivation to action* (ed. P.Willner and J.Scheel-Kruger). Wiley, Chichester.

Gross, C.G., Bender, D.B., and Gerstein, G.L. (1979). Activity of inferior temporal neurons in behaving monkeys, *Neuropsychologia*, **17**, 215–29.

Grossman, S.P. (1967). *A textbook of physiological psychology*. Wiley, New York.

Grossman, S.P. (1973). *Essentials of physiological psychology*. Wiley, New York.

Heimer, L., Switzer, R.D., and van Hoesen, G.W. (1982). Ventral striatum and ventral pallidum. Additional components of the motor system ? *Trends in Neuroscience*, **5**, 83–7.

Heimer, L. and Alheid, G.F. (1990). Piecing together the puzzle of basal forebrain anatomy. In *The basal forebrain: Anatomy to function* (eds. T.C. Napier, P.W.Kalivas, and I.Hanin). Plenum, New York.

Herzog, A.G. and van Hoesen, G.W. (1976). Temporal neocortical afferent connections to the amygdala in the rhesus monkey, *Brain Research*, **115**, 57–69.

Hoebel, B.G. (1969). Feeding and self-stimulation. *Annals of the New York Academy of Science*, **157**, 757–78.

Iversen, S.D. and Mishkin, M. (1970). Perseverative interference in monkey following selective lesions of the inferior prefrontal convexity. *Experimental Brain Research*, **11**, 376–86.

Jarvis, C.D. and Mishkin, M. (1977). Responses of cells in the inferior temporal cortex of monkeys during visual discrimination reversals. *Social Neuroscience, Abstract*, **3**, 1794.

Jones, B. and Mishkin, M. (1972). Limbic lesions and the problem of stimulus-reinforcement associations. *Experimental Neurology*, **36**, 362–77.

Kievit, J. and Kuypers, H.G.J.M. (1975). Subcortical afferents to the frontal lobe in the rhesus monkey studied by means of retrograde horseradish peroxidase transport, *Brain Research*, **85**, 261–6.

Kluver, H. and Bucy, P.C. (1939). Preliminary analysis of functions of the temporal lobes in monkeys. *Archives of Neurological Psychiatry*, **42**, 979–1000.

LeDoux, J. E., Iwata, J., Cicchetti, P., and Reis, D. J. (1988). Different projections of the central amygdaloid nucleus mediate autonomic and behavioral correlates of conditioned fear. *Journal of Neuroscience*, **8**, 2517–29.

Le Magnen, J. (1992). *Neurobiology of feeding and nutrition*. Academic Press, San Diego, CA.

Marshall, J.F., Richardson, J.S., and Teitelbaum, P. (1974). Nigrostriatal bundle damage and the lateral hypothalamic syndrome. *Journal of Comparative and Physiological Psychology*, **87**, 808–30.

Mei, N. (1993). Gastrointestinal chemoreception and its behavioural role. Ch. 4, pp. 47–56, in *The neurophysiology of ingestion* (ed. D.A. Booth). Pergamon Press, Oxford.

Mogenson, G.J., Jones, D.L., and Yim, C.Y. (1980). From motivation to action: functional interface between the limbic system and the motor system. *Progress in Neurobiology*, **14**, 69–97.

Mora, F., Rolls, E.T., and Burton, M.J. (1976). Modulation during learning of the responses of neurons in the hypothalamus to the sight of food, *Experimental Neurology*, **53**, 508–19.

Mora, F., Avrith, D.B., Phillips, A, G., and Rolls, E.T. (1979). Effects of satiety on self-stimulation of the orbitofrontal cortex in the monkey. *Neuroscience Letters*, **13**, 141–5.

Nauta, W.J.H. (1961). Fiber degeneration following lesions of the amygdaloid complex in the monkey. *Journal of Anatomy*, **95**, 515–31.

Nauta, W.J.H. and Domesick, V.B. (1978). Crossroads of limbic and striatal circuitry: Hypothalamonigral connections, pp. 75–93 in *Limbic mechanisms* (eds. K.E. Livingston and O. Hornykiewicz). Plenum, New York.

Nishijo, H., Ono, T., and Nishino, H. (1988). Single neuron responses in amygdala of alert monkeys during complex sensory stimulation with affective significance. *Journal of Neuroscience*, **8**, 3570–83.

Olds, J. (1977). *Drives and reinforcements: Behavioral studies of hypothalamic Functions*. Raven Press, New York.

Ono, T., Nishino, H., Sasaki, K., Fukuda, M., and Muramoto, K. (1980). Role of the lateral hypothalamus and amygdala in feeding behavior. *Brain Research Bulletin*, **5**, Suppl. 4, 143–9.

Ono, T., Tamura, R., Nishijo, H., Nakamura, K., and Tabuchi, E. (1989). Contribution of amygdala and LH neurons to the visual information processing of food and non-food in the monkey. *Physiology and Behavior*, **45**, 411–21.

Ono, T. and Nishijo, H. (1992). Neurophysiological basis of the Kluver–Bucy syndrome: responses of monkey amygdaloid neurons to biologically significant objects, ch. 6, pp. 167–90 in *The amygdala* (ed. J.P. Aggleton). Wiley-Liss, New York.

Oomura, Y and Yoshimatsu, H. (1984). Neural network of glucose monitoring system. *Journal of the Autonomic Nervous System*, **10**, 359–72.

Percheron, G., Yelnik, J., and Francois, C. (1984). The primate striato-pallido-nigral system: an integrative system for cortical information. In *The basal ganglia: Structure and function* (eds. J.S. McKenzie, R.E. Kemm and L.N. Wilcox), pp. 87–105. Plenum, New York.

Ridley, R.M., Hester, N.S., and Ettlinger, G. (1977). Stimulus- and response-dependent units from the occipital and temporal lobes of the unanaesthetized monkey performing learnt visual tasks. *Experimental Brain Research*, **27**, 539–52.

Ritter, S. (1986). Glucoprivation and the glucoprivic control of food intake, ch. 9, pp. 271–313 in *Feeding behavior: Neural and humoral controls* (eds. R.C. Ritter, S.Ritter, and C.D.Barnes). Academic Press, New York.

Robbins, T.W. and Everitt, B.J. (1992). Functions of dopamine in the dorsal and ventral striatum. *Seminars in the Neurosciences*, **4**, 119–28.

Rolls, B.J. (1990). The role of sensory-specific satiety in food intake and food selection, ch. 14, pp. 197–209 in *Taste, experience, and feeding* (eds. E.D. Capaldi and T.L. Powley). American Psychological Association, Washington, DC.

Rolls, B.J. and Hetherington, M. (1989). The role of variety in eating and body weight regulation, ch. 3, pp. 57–84 in *Handbook of the psychophysiology of human eating* (ed. R.Shepherd). Wiley, Chichester.

Rolls, B.J. and Rolls, E.T. (1973). Effects of lesions in the basolateral amygdala on fluid intake in the rat. *Journal of Comparative and Physiological Psychology*, **83**, 240–47.

Rolls, B.J., Rolls, E.T., Rowe, E.A., and Sweeney, K. (1981). Sensory specific satiety in man. *Physiology and Behavior*, **27**, 137–42.

Rolls, B.J., Rowe, E.A., Rolls, E.T., Kingston, B., Megson, A., and Gunary, R. (1981). Variety in a meal enhances food intake in man. *Physiology Behavior*, **26**, 215–21.

Rolls, B.J., Rowe, E.A. and Rolls, E.T. (1982). How sensory properties of foods affect human feeding behavior. *Physiology and Behavior*, **29**, 409–17.

Rolls, B.J., Van Duijenvoorde, P.M., and Rowe, E.A. (1983). Variety in the diet enhances intake in a meal and contributes to the development of obesity in the rat. *Physiology and Behavior*, **31**, 21–7.

Rolls, B.J., van Duijenvoorde, P.M., and Rolls, E.T. (1984). Pleasantness changes and food intake in a varied four course meal. *Appetite*, **5**, 337–48.

Rolls, E.T. (1975). *The brain and reward*. Pergamon Press, Oxford.

Rolls, E.T. (1976). The neurophysiological basis of brain-stimulation reward, pp. 65–87 in *Brain-stimulation reward* (eds. A.Wauquier and E.T.Rolls). North-Holland, Amsterdam.

Rolls, E.T. (1979). Effects of electrical stimulation of the brain on behavior, pp. 151–169 in *Psychology surveys*, Vol. 2 (ed. K. Connolly). George Allen and Unwin, Hemel Hempstead, UK.

Rolls, E.T. (1981a). Processing beyond the inferior temporal visual cortex related to feeding, memory, and striatal function, ch. 16, pp. 241–69 in *Brain mechanisms of sensation* (eds. Y. Katsuki, R. Norgren, and M. Sato). Wiley, New York.

Rolls, E.T. (1981b). Central nervous mechanisms related to feeding and appetite, *British Medical Bulletin*, **37**, 131–4.

Rolls, E.T. (1982). Feeding and reward, pp. 323–337 in *The neural basis of feeding and reward* (eds. B.G.Hoebel and D. Novin). Haer Institute for Electrophysiological Research, Brunswick, Maine.

Rolls, E.T. (1984). Activity of neurons in different regions of the striatum of the monkey, pp. 467–493 in *The basal ganglia: Structure and function* (eds. J.S. McKenzie, R.E. Kemm, and L.N. Wilcox). Plenum, New York.

Rolls, E.T. (1986). Neuronal activity related to the control of feeding, ch. 6, pp. 163–190 in *Feeding behavior: Neural and humoral controls* (eds. R.C. Ritter, S. Ritter, and C.D. Barnes). Academic Press, New York.

Rolls, E.T. (1987). Information representation, processing and storage in the brain: analysis at the single neuron level, pp. 503–540 in *The neural and molecular bases of learning* (eds. J.-P. Changeux and M. Konishi). Wiley, Chichester.

Rolls, E.T. (1989). Information processing in the taste system of primates. *Journal of Experimental Biology*, **146**, 141–64.

Rolls, E.T. (1990a). Functions of different regions of the basal ganglia, ch. 5, pp. 151–184 in *Parkinson's disease* (ed. G.M. Stern). Chapman and Hall, London.

Rolls, E.T. (1990b). A theory of emotion, and its application to understanding the neural basis of emotion. *Cognition and Emotion*, **4**, 161–90.

Rolls, E.T. (1991). Neural organisation of higher visual functions. *Current Opinion in Neurobiology*, **1**, 274–8.

Rolls, E.T. (1992a). Neurophysiological mechanisms underlying face processing within and beyond the temporal cortical visual areas. *Philosophical Transactions of the Royal Society*, **335**, 11–21.

Rolls, E.T. (1992b). Neurophysiology and functions of the primate amygdala, ch. 5, pp. 143–165 in *The amygdala*, (ed. J.P. Aggleton). Wiley-Liss, New York.

Rolls, E.T. (1993). Neurophysiology and cognitive functions of the striatum. *Revue neurologique*, in press.

Rolls, E.T. (1994). Central taste anatomy and physiology. In *Handbook of clinical olfaction and gustation* (ed. R.L. Doty). Marcel Dekker, New York.

Rolls E.T. and Baylis, L.L. (1994). Gustatory, olfactory and visual convergence within the primate orbitofrontal cortex. *Journal of Neuroscience*, in press.

Rolls, E.T. and Johnstone, S. (1992). Neurophysiological analysis of striatal function, ch. 3, pp. 61–97 in *Neuropsychological disorders associated with subcortical lesions* (eds. G.Vallar, S.F.Cappa, and C.Wallesch). Oxford University Press, Oxford.

Rolls, E.T. and Mason, R. (1991). Convergence of olfactory and taste inputs in the primate orbitofrontal cortex: modification by learning. *European Journal of Neuroscience, Supplement*, **4**, 88.

Rolls, E.T. and Rolls, B.J. (1973). Altered food preferences after lesions in the basolateral region of the amygdala in the rat. *Journal of Comparative and Physiological Psychology*, **83**, 248–59

Rolls, E.T. and Rolls, B.J. (1977). Activity of neurones in sensory, hypothalamic, and motor areas during feeding in the monkey, pp. 525–49 in *Food intake and chemical senses* (eds. Y.Katsuki, M.Sato, S.F.Takagi and Y.Oomura). University of Tokyo Press, Tokyo.

Rolls, E.T. and Rolls, B.J. (1982). Brain Mechanisms involved in feeding, ch. 3, pp. 33–62 in *Psychobiology of human food selection* (ed. L.M. Barker). AVI Publishing, Westport, CT.

Rolls, E.T. and Treves, A. (1990). The relative advantages of sparse versus distributed encoding for associative neuronal networks in the brain. *Network*, **1**, 407–21.

Rolls, E.T. and de Waal, A.W.L. (1985). Long-term sensory-specific satiety: evidence from an Ethiopian refugee camp. *Physiology and Behavior*, **34**, 1017–20.

Rolls, E.T. and Williams, G.V. (1987*a*). Sensory and movement-related neuronal activity in different regions of the primate striatum, pp. 37–59 in *Basal ganglia and behavior: Sensory aspects and motor functioning* (eds. J.S. Schneider and T.I. Lidsky). Hans Huber, Bern.

Rolls, E.T. and Williams, G.V. (1987*b*). Neuronal activity in the ventral striatum of the primate, pp. 349–356 in *The basal ganglia II—Structure and function—Current concepts* (eds. M.B. Carpenter and A. Jayamaran). Plenum, New York.

Rolls, E.T., Burton, M.J. and Mora, F. (1976). Hypothalamic neuronal responses associated with the sight of food, *Brain Research*, **111**, 53–66.

Rolls, E.T., Judge, S.J., and Sanghera, M.K. (1977). Activity of neurons in the inferotemporal cortex of the alert monkey. *Brain Research*, **130** 229–38.

Rolls, E.T., Sanghera, M.K. and Roper-Hall, A. (1979). The latency of activation of neurons in the lateral hypothalamus and substantia innominata during feeding in the monkey. *Brain Research*, **164**, 121–35.

Rolls, E.T., Burton, M.J., and Mora, F. (1980). Neurophysiological analysis of brain-stimulation reward in the monkey, *Brain Research*, **194**, 339–57.

Rolls, E.T., Rolls, B.J., and Rowe, E.A. (1983). Sensory-specific and motivation-specific satiety for the sight and taste of food and water in man. *Physiology and Behavior*, **30**, 185–92.

Rolls, E.T., Thorpe, S.J., and Maddison, S.P. (1983). Responses of striatal neurons in the behaving monkey. 1. Head of the caudate nucleus. *Behavioural Brain Research*, **7**, 179–210.

Rolls, E.T., Thorpe, S.J., Boytim, M., Szabo, I., and Perrett, D.I. (1984). Responses of striatal neurons in the behaving monkey. 3. Effects of iontophoretically applied dopamine on normal responsiveness. *Neuroscience*, **12**, 1202–12.

Rolls, E.T., Murzi, E., Yaxley, S., Thorpe, S.J., and Simpson, S.J. (1986). Sensory-specific satiety: food-specific reduction in responsiveness of ventral forebrain neurons after feeding in the monkey. *Brain Research*, **368**, 79–86.

Rolls, E.T., Scott, T.R., Sienkiewicz, Z.J., and Yaxley, S. (1988). The responsiveness of neurones in the frontal opercular gustatory cortex of the macaque monkey is independent of hunger. *Journal of Physiology*, **397**, 1–12.

Rolls, E.T., Sienkiewicz, Z.J., and Yaxley, S. (1989). Hunger modulates the responses to gustatory stimuli of single neurons in the caudolateral orbitofrontal cortex of the macaque monkey. *European Journal of Neuroscience*, **1**, 53–60.

Rolls, E.T., Yaxley, S., and Sienkiewicz, Z.J. (1990). Gustatory responses of single neurons in the orbitofrontal cortex of the macaque monkey. *Journal of Neurophysiology*, **64**, 1055–66.

Rosenkilde, C.E. (1979). Functional heterogeneity of the prefrontal cortex in the monkey: a review. *Behaviour and Neural Biology*, **25**, 301–45.

Russchen, F.T., Amaral, D.G., and Price, J.L. (1985). The afferent connections of the substantia innominata in the monkey, Macaca fascicularis. *Journal of Comparative Neurology*, **242**, 1–27.

Sanghera, M.K., Rolls, E.T., and Roper-Hall, A. (1979). Visual responses of neurons in the dorsolateral amygdala of the alert monkey. *Experimental Neurology*, **63**, 610–26.

Saper, C.B., Loewy, A.D., Swanson, L.W., and Cowan, W.M. (1976). Direct hypothalamo-autonomic connections. *Brain Research*, **117**, 305–12.

Saper, C.B., Swanson, L.W., and Cowan, W.M. (1979). An autoradiographic study of the efferent connections of the lateral hypothalamic area in the rat. *Journal of Comparative Neurology*, **183**, 689–706.

Sato, T., Kawamura, T., and E.Iwai (1980). Responsiveness of inferotemporal single units to visual pattern stimuli in monkeys performing discrimination. *Experimental Brain Research*, **38**, 313–19.

Scott, T.R., Yaxley, S., Sienkiewicz, Z.J., and Rolls, E.T. (1986). Taste responses in the nucleus tractus solitarius of the behaving monkey. *Journal of Neurophysiology*, **55**, 182–200.

Scott, T.R., Yaxley, S., Sienkiewicz, Z.J., and Rolls, E.T. (1986). Gustatory responses in the frontal opercular cortex of the alert cynomolgus monkey. *Journal of Neurophysiology*, **56**, 876–90.

Scott, T.R. and Giza, B.K. (1993). Gustatory control of ingestion. Ch. 7, pp. 99–117 in *The neurophysiology of ingestion* (ed. D.A. Booth). Pergamon Press, Oxford.

Spiegler, B.J. and Mishkin, M. (1981). Evidence for the sequential participation of inferior temporal cortex and amygdala in the acquisition of stimulus-reward associations. *Behavioural Brain Research*, **3**, 303–17.

Stellar, E. (1954). The physiology of motivation. *Psychological Review*, **61**, 5–22.

Stricker, E.M. (1984). Brain monoamines and the control of food intake. *International Journal of Obesity*, **8**, Suppl. 1, in press.

Stricker, E.M. and Zigmond, M.J. (1976). Recovery of function after damage to central catecholamine-containing neurons: a neurochemical model for the lateral hypothalamic syndrome. *Progress in Psychobiology and Physiological Psychology*, **6**, 121–88.

Swash, M. (1989). John Hughlings Jackson: a historical introduction, ch. 1, pp. 3–10 in *Hierarchies in neurology: A reappraisal of a Jacksonian concept* (eds. C. Kennard and M. Swash). Springer, London.

Tanabe, T., Yarita, H., Iino, M. Ooshima, Y., and Takagi, S.F. (1975a). An olfactory projection area in orbitofrontal cortex of the monkey. *Journal of Neurophysiology*, **38**, 1269–83.

Tanabe, T., Iino, M., and Takagi, S.F. (1975b). Discrimination of odors in olfactory bulb, pyriform-amygdaloid areas, and orbitofrontal cortex of the monkey. *Journal of Neurophysiology*, **38**, 1284–96.

Tanaka, D. (1973). Effects of selective prefrontal decortication on escape behavior in the monkey. *Brain Research*, **53**, 161–73.

Thorpe, S.J., Rolls, E.T., and Maddison, S. (1983). Neuronal activity in the orbitofrontal cortex of the behaving monkey. *Experimental Brain Research*, **49**, 93–115.

Ungerstedt, U. (1971). Adipsia and aphagia after 6–hydroxydopamine induced degeneration of the nigrostriatal dopamine system. *Acta Physiologica Scandinavica*, **81** (Suppl. 367), 95–122.

Weiskrantz, L. (1956). Behavioral changes associated with ablation of the amygdaloid complex in monkeys, *Journal of Comparative and Physiological Psychology*, **49**, 381–91.

Weiskrantz, L. and Saunders, R.C. (1984). Impairments of visual object transforms in monkeys. *Brain*, **107**, 1033–72.

Williams, G.V., Rolls, E.T., Leonard, C.M., and Stern, C. (1993). Neuronal responses in the ventral striatum of the behaving macaque. *Behavioural Brain Research*, **55**, 243–52.

Wilson, F.A.W. and Rolls, E.T. (1990). Neuronal responses related to reinforcement in the primate basal forebrain. *Brain Research* **502**, 213–31.

Wilson, F.A.W. and Rolls, E.T. (1994). The primate amygdala and reinforcement: a dissociation between rule-based and associatively-mediated memory revealed in amygdala neuronal activity (in preparation).

Winn, P., Tarbuck, A., and Dunnett, S.B. (1984). Ibotenic acid lesions of the lateral hypothalamus: comparison with electrolytic lesion syndrome. *Neuroscience*, **12**, 225–40.

Winn, P., Clark, A., Hastings, M., Clark, J., Latimer, M., Rugg, E., and Brownlee, B. (1990). Excitotoxic lesions of the lateral hypothalamus made by N-methyl-d-aspartate in the rat: behavioural, histological and biochemical analyses. *Experimental Brain Research*, **82**, 628–36.

Yaxley, S., Rolls, E.T., Sienkiewicz, Z.J., and Scott, T.R. (1985). Satiety does not affect gustatory activity in the nucleus of the solitary tract of the alert monkey. *Brain Research*, **347**, 85–93.

Yaxley, S., Rolls, E.T. and Sienkiewicz, Z.J. (1988). The responsiveness of neurones in the insular gustatory cortex of the macaque monkey is independent of hunger. *Physiology and Behavior*, **42**, 223–29.

Yaxley, S., Rolls, E.T., and Sienkiewicz, Z.J. (1990). Gustatory responses of single neurons in the insula of the macaque monkey. *Journal of Neurophysiology*, **63**: 689–700.

3

Brainstem orosensorimotor mechanisms and the neural control of ingestive behaviour

H. Philip Zeigler

INTRODUCTION

Animals control their intake by varying the frequency of ingestive responses to food and water and by generating topographically distinct eating and drinking movement patterns. A hungry animal responds with eating behaviour to orosensory cues identifying food; a thirsty one with drinking responses to stimuli signifying water. However, responsiveness to food and water may vary in the absence of corresponding variations in external stimuli. That is, sensory input is necessary, but not sufficient for the elicitation of eating and drinking behaviours. Thus the generation of ingestive behaviour requires the integration of interoceptive inputs related to metabolic homeostasis and exteroceptive inputs from orosensory structures. There is now considerable evidence that such integration involves brainstem mechanisms which function to modulate the oromotor systems mediating eating and drinking. The delineation of these modulatory mechanisms represents a central problem in the study of ingestive behaviour.

We may conceive of three general research strategies for the study of brain mechanisms of ingestion. A *sensory* strategy focuses upon the stimulus properties which elicit and direct eating and drinking, identifies the afferent systems involved, and works forward to trace the central projections of the relevant afferents. A *motor* strategy focuses upon the relevant movement patterns, and works backwards from the periphery towards the centre, beginning with the 'final common path' structures controlling the patterning of ingestive movements. A *central* strategy focuses upon interneuronal groups located at some remove from either afferent or efferent structures, utilizing lesion or stimulation techniques or manipulation of putative neurotransmitters.

Now, since the same neurotransmitters are found in a wide variety of structures, their ability to modulate behaviours must involve an interaction between transmitter properties and those of the neural circuits within which they operate (Harris-Warwick and Marder, 1991). Central strategies provide little information as to the nature of those circuits. Indeed, from the standpoint of functional circuit-tracing, central strategies are problematic, since they tend to leave us stranded in the middle of the brain, with no precise links to either afferent or efferent mechanisms. Moreover, the use of a central strategy has tended, unfortunately, to reinforce a conceptual dichotomy between 'sensorimotor' and 'motivational' mechanisms, and has generated a concentration on central (putatively 'motivational') structures, to the neglect of sensory and motor processes. I would submit that the resulting *hypothalamocentrism* which has characterized much research in this area, has not advanced our understanding of ingestive behaviour to an extent commensurate with the research effort expended (Gallistel, 1980; Zeigler, 1983, 1985).

The present review reflects a convergence of sensory and motor strategies, and is particularly appropriate for the study of ingestive behaviour. Ingestive movement patterns are relatively stereotyped, their organization may be characterized at appropriate levels of spatio-temporal resolution, and the afferent systems eliciting and patterning the behaviours may be identified. A focus on sensorimotor mechanisms thus provides starting points for the identification of primary and secondary sensory pathways and nuclei, of motor and premotor neurons and, ultimately, for a functional analysis of neuronal circuitry linking sensory and motor mechanisms at lower brainstem levels.

For control of oromotor behaviours in the rat—the preparation of choice for most investigators—two sensory systems are pre-eminent: the trigeminal and the gustatory. Trigeminal primary afferents (N V) innervate mechanoreceptors distributed throughout the orofacial region, as well as within the oral cavity. They are associated, in many cases, with specialized sensory structures such as the vibrissae, furry buccal pads and rhinarium, as well as with the jaw muscles and the temporomandibular joint. With the exception of muscle receptors (innervated by displaced ganglion cells located in the trigeminal mesencephalic nucleus) the cell bodies of trigeminal primary afferents are located within the trigeminal (Gasserian) ganglion. Gustatory afferents innervate receptor cells which form distinct, spatially discrete aggregates at a number of intraoral and extraoral locations, including the anterior and posterior tongue, the anterior (hard) and posterior (soft) palates, the larynx, and pharynx. Input from these receptors is conveyed to the brainstem by branches of the VIIth (Facial: Chorda Tympani, Greater Superfical Petrosal), IXth (Glossopharyngeal) and Xth (Vagus: Pharyngeal, Superior Laryngeal) cranial nerves. However, it is important to note that both fungiform and filiform (gustatory) receptors of the anterior tongue are also innervated by the lingual branch of the trigeminal nerve (Suemune *et al.*, 1992). Trigeminal sensorimotor mechanisms control the initial component of the consummatory sequence—the jaw-opening response. Gustatory mechanisms provide a final 'gating' for ingestion, based upon the sensory properties of the food, that is, its *palatability* (Grill and Berridge, 1985).

OROMOTOR BEHAVIOURS AND THE SENSORY CONTROL OF INGESTION IN THE RAT

The oromotor portion of the rat's ingestive sequence begins with contact of the object by the oral region and continues with jaw and tongue movements until the food or water is removed from the oral cavity. During the initial period of perioral contact, there is a flow of trigeminal orosensory input, which continues into the intraoral portion of the sequence to be joined by gustatory inputs from taste receptors on the tongue and within the oral cavity.

Detailed analysis of the response to food or water presented, shown in Fig. 3.1(a), indicates that the ingestive sequence begins with the rat's snout tilted towards the floor so that its rhinarium is below the level of the pellet *and its mouth is completely closed*. As the snout advances, it is elevated, brushing the frontal perioral hairs across the surface of the food pellet, and bringing the rhinarium opposite to and parallel with the pellet. The snout is then brought forward and upward, bringing the upper lip line into contact with the pellet edge. This forward movement overlaps with the initiation of mouth opening. It continues until the pellet is within the oral cavity and concludes with the initiation of jaw closure. In drinking, as in eating, the mouth is closed during the period of approach to the sipper tube, and remains closed until some time after perioral contact. The fact that jaw opening does not occur during the approach phase of eating or drinking, but always follows a relatively prolonged (Fig. 3.1(b)) period of perioral contact, suggests that the jaw-opening phase of ingestion is elicited not by distal (visual, olfactory) stimuli but by proximal (somatosensory) inputs from the perioral region.

Once past the lips, the acceptance or rejection of solids or liquids may elicit highly stereotyped (*taste-reactivity*) response patterns which have been characterized as ingestive or aversive sequences (Fig. 3.2) based upon their consequences. Ingestive responses (which include rhythmic jaw movements, tongue protractions, paw licking) are elicited by intraoral infusions of glucose, sucrose, and isotonic sodium chloride, varying in freqency and/or amplitude with tastant concentration. Aversive responses (including gapes, chin rubs, head shakes, and

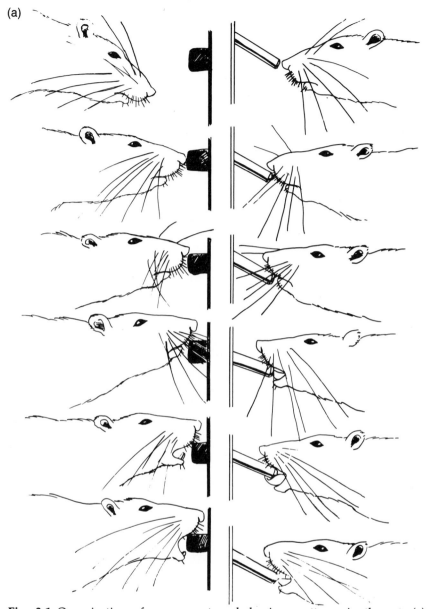

Fig. 3.1 Organization of consummatory behaviour patterns in the rat. (a) Topography of the eating (left) and drinking (right) response sequences; a schematic representation based upon photographic analysis. (b) (*overleaf*) Temporal relations among ingestive behaviour phases in three normal rats (open bars, approach; dotted bars, perioral contact; closed bars, mouth opening/tongue protrusion). (c) (*overleaf*) Effects of trigeminal orosensory deafferentation upon the organization of the rat's ingestive behavior sequence. Conventions as in (b). Note the prolonged duration of perioral contact and the absence of the mouth-opening and tongue-protrusion phases. (From Zeigler *et al.* 1984. Copyright 1984 by the American Psychological Association. 1984. Reprinted by permission).

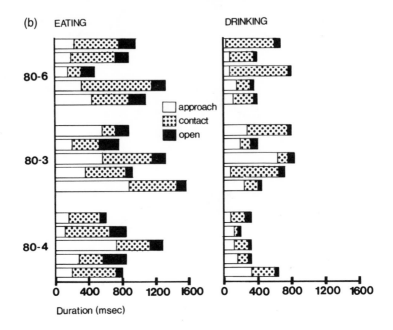

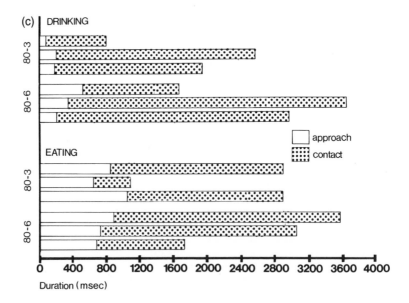

(b) **Behavioral Responses to Different Tastes**

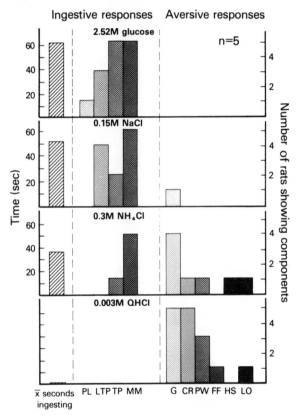

Fig. 3.2 Analysis of taste-reactivity patterns in the rat. (a) Ingestive responses elicited by intraoral infusions of various tastants (see below). Ingestive responses include rhythmic mouth movements (MM), tongue protrusions (TP), lateral tongue protrusions (LTP) and paw licking (PL). Aversive responses include gapes (G), chin rubs (CR), head shakes (HS), paw wipes (PW), forelimb flailing (FF) and locomotion (LO) (not shown). (b) Taste-reactivity profiles. Ingestive and aversive response profiles elicited by oral infusions of four different taste stimuli: abbreviations as above. (From Grill and Berridge, 1985; reprinted with permission).

forelimb flailings) may be elicited by such tastants as quinine and caffeine (Grill and Norgren, 1978a). The specificity of tastant effects upon the elementary ingestive components strongly suggests a controlling role for gustatory stimuli, but does not exclude a contribution from somatosensory afferents, with which the oral cavity is also richly endowed. It is important to note that taste-elicited oromotor responses may be modulated by both associative and motivational variables (e.g. deprivation, sodium depletion, conditioned taste aversions: Grill and Berridge, 1985). Comparable modulation has not yet been demonstrated for the trigeminally elicited jaw-opening response, but informal observation suggests that its probability is reduced in the satiated animal.

THE OROSENSORIMOTOR SYSTEM: AFFERENT AND EFFERENT PATHWAYS AND BRAINSTEM NUCLEAR STRUCTURES

The organization of the neural structures controlling the oromotor apparatus reflects a basic tripartite groundplan, common to all vertebrates, and consisting of orosensory, oromotor, and internuncial components, located at lower brainstem levels (Ten Donkelaar, 1990). Primary gustatory afferents project, ipsilaterally, and in a rostral to caudal sequence, upon the nucleus of the solitary tract (nTS). The majority of trigeminal primary afferents project, also ipsilaterally, upon a column of second-order neurons comprising the trigeminal brainstem nuclear complex (TBNC). In recent years, the use of more sensitive tracing methods has demonstrated a substantial projection of primary trigeminal afferents upon 'non-trigeminal' structures, including nTS (where it overlaps gustatory terminal fields), as well as upon the lateral (parvocellular) reticular formation (Hamilton and Norgren, 1984; Jacquin, Semba, Rhoades, and Egger, 1982; Marfurt and Rajchert, 1991).

Orosensory processing by the solitary nucleus

The orosensory projection upon nTS reflects the fact that the mouth contains receptors sensitive to both gustatory and somatosensory inputs; the latter including tactile, thermal, and nociceptive stimuli. That projection is organized orotopically, such that the rostral portion of nTS receives primary afferent terminations from oral, pharyngeal and laryngeal gustatory and somatosensory receptors; its caudal portion receives inputs from receptors in more distal regions of the alimentary tract. Physiological studies confirm the restriction of taste responses primarily to neurons in the rostral portion of nTS. They indicate that the organization of specific taste sensitivities of those neurons is also orotopic, that is, the sensitivity of a central neuron corresponds to that of the peripheral fibres innervating the receptive field from which the nTS response is elicited.

Given the known distribution of trigeminal orosensory projections, it is not surprising that nTS is also the recipient of somatosensory inputs from the oral cavity. These inputs appear to originate from intra-oral rather than orofacial regions. Thus corneal and infraorbital regions have little or no representation within nTS, while the tongue and palate have a substantial nTS projection. This pattern of distribution accounts for the fact that nTS contains at least three classes of neurons: those exclusively responsive to (i) gustatory, or (ii) somatosensory, generally tactile, stimuli, and (iii) those responsive to both modalities.

For the gustatory population, physiological studies suggest a considerable degree of spatial convergence, that is, the activity of a single unit may be modulated by stimuli applied to spatially discrete regions, for example, the anterior tongue and the nasoincisor ducts Convergence is greater between the loci within the anterior or posterior oral cavity than between anterior and posterior oral cavities Many gustatorily responsive nTS neurons are also responsive to somatosensory (tactile, thermal) stimuli. However, since gustatory primary afferents are themselves known to respond to somatosensory stimulation it is unclear whether the dual responsiveness of nTS neurons simply reflects the peripheral situation, or represents an actual convergence, at nTS levels, of inputs from two distinct modalities. Interestingly, the degree of relative responsiveness of nTS neurons to gustatory vs somatosensory stimuli varies with their location. Neurons whose receptive fields lie in the anterior oral cavity are significantly more responsive to taste than to somatosensory stimuli; those representing more caudal peripheral areas (e.g. the epiglottis) are likely to be equally responsive to both modalities. These more caudal neurons appear to be involved in detecting the *presence* of sapid stimuli rather than discriminating between them (Travers and Norgren, 1986; Travers, Norgren, and Akey, in preparation; Sweazy and Bradley, 1989).

Although the number of exclusively gustatory or somatosensory neurons appears to be approximately equal, they are not intermingled but form distinct, though overlapping, distributions in rostral nTS. Physiological studies suggest that taste-responsive neurons dominate the rostral and medial sub-divisions of this region, to be gradually replaced, in its caudal and lateral sub-divisions, by somatosensory neurons. The representation of these somatosensory neurons displays an orotopy which parallels that exhibited by gustatory neurons, with the anterior oral cavity represented anterior and lateral to the posterior oral cavity. The distribution of intraoral gustatory and somatosensory

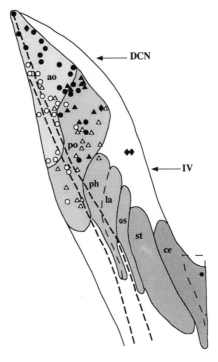

Fig. 3.3 Schematic representation of the alimentary tract within the nucleus of the Tractus Solitarius, to indicate the projection of orosensory and viscerosensory afferents. The diagram is viewed in the horizontal plane: rostral = top; medial = right. DCN indicates the level of nST that is coincident with the caudal limit of the dorsal cochlear nucleus; IV indicates where the medial border of nST merges with the IVth ventricle. Successively more caudal regions represent successively more caudal alimentary tract structures: anterior (ao) and posterior (po) oral cavities; pharynx (pH) and larynx (la); oesophagus (es), stomach (st) and caecum (ce). The outline of the nucleus is modified from Hamilton and Norgren (1984). The orosensory representation was derived from experiments in which gustatory or mechanical stimuli were applied to ao or po and unit responses recorded in nTS. Circles and triangles represent cells that responded maximally to ao or po stimulation. Filled and open symbols represent cells that responded, respectively, only to gustatory or mechanical stimulation. Diamonds represent gustatory cells which responded only to whole mouth stimulation. The representations of the remainder of the alimentary tract are based upon the anterograde tracing studies of Altschuler and his colleagues (e.g. Altschuler *et al.*, 1989) and Norgren and Smith (1988), as well as the neurophysiological data of Sweazy and Bradley (1988,1989), on the location of epiglottal chemosensitive neurons. The representations of the pharynx and larynx are separated only by a dotted line because they overlap greatly in peripheral injection-tracing experiments. (Reprinted with permission from S. P. Travers, 1994. Copyright CRC Press Inc., Boca Raton, FL.)

inputs within the rostral portion of nTS is illustrated in Fig. 3.3, which also relates the orosensory representation to that of progressively more caudal (viscerosensory) structures within the alimentary system of the rat (Altschuler *et al.*, 1989, 1991; Norgren and Smith, 1988; Sweazy and Bradley, 1988, 1989; S.P. Travers, 1994).

Orosensory processing by the trigeminal brainstem nuclear complex

The trigeminal system may be the most generalized of all cranial nerve systems, and is well developed in vertebrates from fish to man. This phylogenetic ubiquity reflects the importance of stimuli from the orofacial region and the pattern of trigeminal innervation suggests at least three functional specializations: analysis of extraoral stimuli during exploration, characterization of intraoral stimuli, and control of the jaw.

The primary afferent fibres mediating these functions travel in the trigeminal sensory root, bifurcating at their entrance into the brainstem to form ascending and descending trigeminal tracts. Fibres in the ascending tract project rostrally to terminate upon cells in the principal trigeminal nucleus (PrV); those in the descending tract project caudally, descending variable distances to terminate upon cells in one or more of the sub-divisions of the spinal trigeminal (SpV) nucleus (pars oralis, interpolaris and caudalis). The orofacial representation is mapped onto TBNC cells in an inverted somatotopic organization in the transverse plane, with the snout facing medially. Although trigeminal primary afferents innervate the entire orofacial region, including cornea, orbital and suprorbital regions and dura, the representation of the vibrissae and the oral cavity dominate the projection at all levels of TBNC.

In the rat, each TBNC sub-nucleus contains a population of neurons which vary in their receptive field locations, sub-modality (touch, temperature, nociception, vibrissa movement), adaptation properties, thresholds, connectivity patterns, and targets. A primary distinction is between projection and local circuit neurons. In each nucleus, some percentage of the neurons have axons which terminate in extranuclear structures (e.g. spinal cord, thalamus, cerebellum, superior colliculus) and which may be antidromically activated from these loci. In contrast, cells designated as 'local circuit' neurons do not respond to such stimulation and have axons terminating in inter-sub-nuclear and adjacent reticular structures. Within each nucleus, neurons may also be classified with respect to their degree of spatial and/or intramodality convergence, for example, responsiveness to stimulation of a single vibrissa, to several vibrissae, or to multiple receptor organs (vibrissa, teeth, skin). Finally, the distinction between high- and low-threshold units is assumed to be related to nociceptive vs non-nociceptive processing. There appears to be a correlation between the morphology and projection target of a TBNC neuron, as determined by intracellular injection/reconstruction techniques, and its response properties and projection status, as demonstrated, respectively, by unit recording and antidromic stimulation techniques (e.g. Jacquin *et al.*, 1986, 1988, 1989, 1990). While most types of neuron are represented in each TBNC nucleus, the relative proportions of each type may differ for each nucleus. Such differences between nuclear populations, *though relative rather than categorical*, may have functional implications.

For example, most PrV neurons have small soma, with small dendritic trees and no local branching. The preponderance of PrV units are driven primarily by vibrissal stimulation, have low thresholds, small receptive fields, and minimal (single-vibrissa) convergence. They project, preferentially, upon the ventrobasal nucleus, a thalamic relay to cortical somatosensory areas. In contrast, the oral cavity is heavily represented in the SpV oralis, and neurons in this nucleus and Spv interpolaris have more extensive dendritic trees, receptive fields characterized by intra-modality convergence (vibrissa, skin, tooth, gums), and project preferentially to cerebellum and mid-brain areas (Fig. 3.4). Based upon their population characteristics, the 'lemniscal' properties of PrV neurons suggest a discriminative function in the vibrissal mapping of the extra-oral environment. In contrast, the properties of oralis and interpolaris

––––

Fig. 3.4 Low- and high-magnification reconstructions of a trigeminothalamic neuron that responded to all the vibrissae circled on the diagram. Its axon (arrows) gave off collaterals to interpolaris (SpVi, parvicellular reticular formation (RPC), sub-nucleus principalis (PrV, not shown), and the dorsal midbrain. Its responses to high-frequency shocks, delivered at two times threshold, to the trigeminal (V) ganglion, thalamus, tectum, and PrV are shown in A, B, E, and H, respectively. Collision of a ganglion-evoked orthodromic spike with antidromically activated spikes from the thalamus (C), tectum (F), and PrV (I) are also shown. Collision recovery at longer interstimulus intervals is shown in D, G, and J. In K, spikes elicited from the thalamus and tectum are shown. At shorter interstimulus intervals (L), the tectum-evoked spike is obliterated by the thalamic-evoked spike, thus illustrating collision of axon branches. In M, it can be seen that two spikes can be produced by two shocks delivered to the tectum at an equivalent interstimulus interval. In A–M, arrows denote the beginning of the shock artefact. Sustained deflection of selected vibrissae resulted in rapidly adapting responses, as shown in N–Q (S.O. = supraorbital sinus hair; A.T. = auriculotemporal sinus hair). R illustrates the lack of a response to intervening guard hair deflection. The post-penetration responses of this cell to C1 vibrissa deflection are shown in S. T illustrates the membrane potential shift exhibited when the electrode was retracted. (From Jacquin, Mooney and Rhoades, 1986; reprinted with permission.)

suggest an involvement in the control of oromotor responses, elicited and guided by inputs from the perioral and intraoral areas.

Brainstem motor systems and the control of oromotor behaviours

Efferent control of the oromotor apparatus is mediated by a system of cranial motor neurons which are organized into discrete facial, trigeminal, hypoglossal, and ambiguus motor nuclei, innervating, respectively, the muscles of the vibrissae, jaw, tongue, hyoids, and

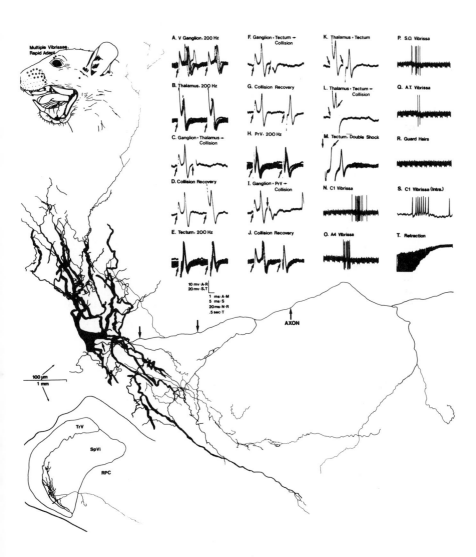

pharynx. These motoneuron pools provide a substrate for 'final common path mechanisms' of 'whisking', jaw opening and closing, mastication, licking, and swallowing. Many of these oromotor nuclei receive inputs relayed directly from second-order trigeminal and gustatory brainstem nuclei, but they also receive a substantial and highly organized input from brainstem 'premotor' regions (Ter Horst *et al.*, 1991; Travers and Norgren, 1983).

nTS originates a descending efferent projection which terminates in the lateral (parvocellular) reticular formation. This region contains premotor and local circuit connections with cranial motor nuclei for the jaw, tongue, and pharyngeal muscle groups involved in such ingestive responses as licking, chewing, and swallowing. The organization of afferent connections to nTS exhibit a kind of *intraoral* 'musculotopy', that is nTS sub-nuclei projecting upon premotor neurons innervating a specific alimentary structure (e.g. the oesophagus) receive their afferent input from receptors in that same structure. Thus, the complex but orderly relationship between intraoral inputs, sensory modality and differential responsiveness illustrated, for nTS, in Fig. 3.3 is likely to be of functional significance in the sensory control of the alimentary sequence.

A first step in linking anatomy and behaviour is the correlation of specific ingestive response patterns with specific patterns of orofacial muscle activity. Travers and Norgren (1986) correlated taste-reactivity responses with oromotor muscle activity patterns by recording electromyographic activity during the ingestion and rejection of intraorally delivered sapid solutions. Licking, the ingestive response to water, saline, or sucrose, was characterized by a rhythmic alternation of activity in the genioglossus (tongue protruder), and styloglossus, (tongue retractor) muscles, with jaw opening (digastric) activity in phase with tongue protrusion. The same pattern was seen for both water and sapid solutions, the latter affecting primarily the duration of individual licking bouts. The rejection response involved a reorganization of the activity pattern in those same muscles, such that jaw-opening and tongue retraction were now in phase (Fig. 3.5). Thus the shift from ingestion to rejection behaviour involves modulation of the duration and timing of activity in the same muscle groups ('motor program switching': Harris-Warwick and Marder, 1991).

As noted earlier, jaw opening, the first phase of the ingestive sequence, is elicited by perioral, rather than intraoral stimuli and mediated by the trigeminal sensory system. Trigeminal inputs may influence oromotor activity relatively directly, via connections with motoneurons or interneurons in the V (jaw) motor nucleus or indirectly via secondary trigeminal projections upon the adjacent lateral reticular formation (Nozaki *et al.*, 1983; Taylor, 1990). The most direct examples of motor control involve the (monosynaptic) jaw-closing and (disynaptic) jaw-opening reflexes. The former, analogous with the spinal myotatic (stretch) reflex, involves sensory ganglion cells in the trigeminal mesencephalic nucleus which receive primary afferent input from spindles in the closer muscles and, in conjunction with other intraoral and perioral afferents, elicits a jaw closing reflex. The jaw-opening reflex (JOR) may be elicited both by high-intensity (nociceptive) or low-intensity stimulation of trigeminal sensory nerve branches (Dubner *et al.* 1978; Lund, Appenteng, and Seguin, 1982). In the former case it may function as a protective response to excessive mechanical stimulation of extraoral structures during biting or chewing. That the JOR may have an appetitive function when elicited by low-threshold afferents is suggested by the observation that it is the earliest cranial reflex in the mammalian fetus (Humphrey, 1970). Both reflexes are important components of the ingestive final common path, and may be viewed as the fundamental behavioural units from which the ingestive sequence is assembled.

The experiments summarized in Fig. 3.1 suggested that perioral somatosensory (trigeminal) inputs play an important role in eliciting the jaw-opening component of the ingestive sequence. The areas involved were defined more precisely, and their relation to the JOR was clarified in a study of reflex responses to stimulation of the rat's orofacial region (Zeigler *et al.*, 1984). Using evoked activity in the mylohyoid nerve as an index of jaw-opener (digastric) muscle responsiveness, thresholds for the elicitation of this reflex to tactile and electrical stimuli were determined. The most effective sites for elicitation of the JOR by tactile stimulations tended to cluster about the region of the upper lip and superior portions of the oral cavity. For this region, less than 1 g of mechanical displacement by a von Frey hair was often sufficient to elicit the JOR in these anaesthetized preparations. The critical involvement of this region for elicitation of jaw opening in the intact rat was later confirmed in the deafferentation studies reviewed below.

OROSENSORY DEAFFERENTATION AND INGESTIVE BEHAVIOUR IN THE RAT

The contribution of the orosensory systems to ingestive behaviour may be assessed by manipulation of chemosensory or somatosensory properties of food, by reversible elimination of the normal orosensory consequences of ingestion (intragastric infusion), or by surgical disruption of orosensory inputs (deafferentation). While the first two paradigms have been extremely informative, the deafferentation procedure allows us to discriminate more precisely between the contributions

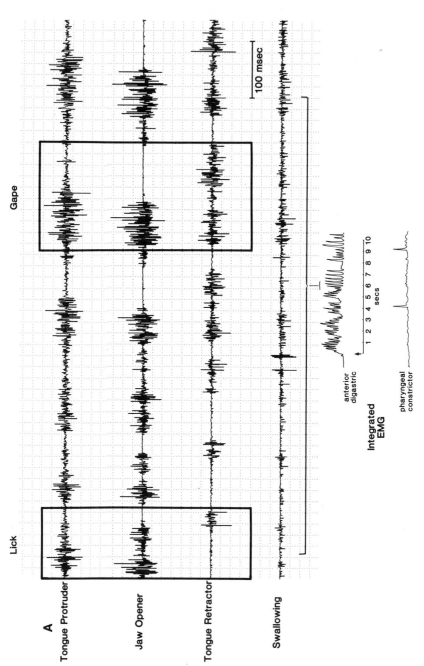

Fig. 3.5 Electromyographic (EMG) activity from jaw, tongue and pharyngeal muscles of a rat during the licking of 0.3 M sucrose solution from a water bottle spout. A single lick cycle is outlined. (From Travers and Norgren, 1986. Copyright 1986 by the American Psychological Association. Reprinted with permission.)

of trigeminal and gustatory inputs, as well as among the various afferent sub-divisions of the two systems. Moreover, the analysis of deafferentation effects provide a foundation for subsequent studies of the contribution of gustatory or trigeminal structures at various levels of the neuraxis.

Effects of gustatory deafferentation

In assessing orosensory contributions to ingestion the nature of the testing instrument used is a critical variable. Thus, while it has long been known that some tastants (e.g. sucrose) facilitate ingestion while others (e.g. quinine) inhibit it, studies using standard two-bottle preference tests reported only minor effects of gustatory deafferentation upon the relative (24-hour) intakes of water vs one of a small number of tastants (Akaike *et al.*, 1965; Pfaffman, 1952; but see Grill *et al.*, 1987). Recently, Grill and his colleagues used both the two-bottle preference test, and a taste-reactivity measure of oromotor responses to assess the effects of gustatory deafferentation upon ingestive and aversive responses to a variety of tastants. The chorda tympani (CT) and glossopharyngeal (GP) nerves were sectioned, singly or in combination, a procedure which denervates about 80 per cent of the rat's complement of oropharyngeal taste buds, and has been shown to disrupt a broad range of taste sensitivities.

The most important finding was the striking disparity between the two bottle preference and oromotor response measures of ingestive behaviour. Combined CT+GP deafferentation did not significantly affect relative intakes of three preferred tastants (sucrose, glycine, isotonic saline) and had only minor effects upon intake of the normally avoided stimuli (magnesium chloride and hypertonic saline). Intraorally delivered taste stimuli in deafferented rats were effective in eliciting the normal complement of ingestive and aversive response components (gapes, chin rubs, tongue extensions, protrusions), and their topography appears normal. However, the coherent pattern of oromotor responses elicited by these stimuli in intact rats was significantly disrupted by gustatory deafferentation. For example, in normal rats, the frequency of aversive responses to quinine increases, and latency to reject the solution decreases with tastant concentration, and this response pattern was significantly disrupted after gustatory deafferentation. Deafferentation also reduced the total number of ingestive responses and eliminated the concentration-dependent increases in oromotor reactivity to intraorally applied sucrose and glycine, even though glycine and sucrose preference measures were unaffected by the procedure. The reduced taste reactivity of the deafferented animal was most explicitly indicated by the observation that 'in the absence of CT and GP nerve input, rats respond to these stimuli as they would to infusions of water, they allow the fluid to drip passively out of the mouth' (Grill and Schwartz, 1992, p. 113).

These findings, while implying a critical role for gustatory stimuli in eliciting oromotor responses under short-term testing conditions, provide no data as to gustatory deafferentation effects upon long-term food and water intake in the rat. Jacquin (1983) provided such data in a study involving combined section of CT, GP and the pharyngeal branch of the vagus. In addition to body weight, he monitored water intake and ingestion of a variety of foods, including pablum, mash, soft and hard pellets, and rat chow.

Although there were no apparent impairments in consummatory responses to food and water, effects upon both food and water intake were evident. Deafferented rats exhibited a significant reduction in body weight and solid food intake, and took almost three times as long as shams to recover free-feeding weight (see also Grill and Schwartz, 1992, Fig. 1). There was an obvious interaction between diet palatability and intake, such that intake was high and weight gain rapid with sweetened pablum but not with rat chow mash. An initial period of adipsia was significantly greater than that of controls, and recovered experimental rats drank significantly less water than shams during a 24-hour period of food deprivation. These reductions in intake probably reflect the reduced contribution of gustatory inputs to the elicitation and maintenence of oromotor ingestive responses. Conversely, the extent to which intake recovers, as well as the general level at which intake is maintained in the recovered animal, is likely to reflect the contribution of the other main group of orosensory afferents—the trigeminal system.

Effects of trigeminal orosensory deafferentation

The nature of that contribution was explored in a series of deafferentation studies by Zeigler and his colleagues (Jacquin and Zeigler, 1983, 1984; Jacquin, Harris, and Zeigler, 1982; Miller, 1981, 1984; Miller and Teates 1984, 1985; Zeigler, Semba, and Jacquin, 1984; summarized in Zeigler, Miller, and Jacquin, 1985). The magnitude and the extent of the disruptions revealed by these studies was quite unexpected, especially by contrast with the reported effects of gustatory deafferentation.

The array of deficits seen after trigeminal orosensory deafferentation, and characterized as the 'trigeminal syndrome', was produced by interruption of a relatively restricted set of trigeminal orosensory inputs, since the deafferentation procedures interrupted *only* afferents from the intraoral and perioral regions. Gustatory afferents were spared, as were trigeminal afferents from the vibrissae, the tongue, jaw joint, and muscle spindle receptors, and, of course, the trigeminal motor nerve. The trigeminal rat appears deceptively normal: alert, and with no obvious deficits of posture or movement, orienting appropriately to visual stimuli and displaying a well-oriented placing response (forepaw extension) to vibrissal stimulation. It is capable of biting, licking, chewing, and swallowing in response to *intraoral* stimuli, such as liquid food or insertion of a Q tip, and forceful, well-directed biting may also be elicited by *extraoral* stimuli, such as tail-pinch or paw-pinch.

Trigeminal orosensory deafferentation produces a pervasive array of deficits related to the organization of consummatory behaviours, responsiveness to food and water, the quantitative control of intake, the regulation of body weight, dietary self-selection behaviour, and the acquisition or maintenance of food- or water-reinforced instrumental behaviours. Indeed, the deficits in the sensorimotor and motivational control of ingestive behavior which characterize the trigeminal syndrome are comparable in magnitude to those seen after lateral hypothalamic lesions. The nature and extent of those deficits are described, briefly, below.

Consummatory behaviours

In contrast to the ease with which biting and licking could be produced by *intraoral* stimuli, orosensory deafferentation reduced the ease with which oromotor behaviours could be elicited by *perioral* stimuli. In the immediate post-operative period, approaches to the food were hesitant and incomplete. Although the initial orientation of the snout and lower lip was normal, neither mouth opening nor tongue extension occurred. Alternative modes of ingestion were often attempted, and, if successful, were rapidly acquired and perfected. For example, the rat might grasp the sipper tube with both paws, turn the head 90° and push the upper lip against the tube. Ingestion of mash might be facilitated by pushing the snout through the mash so as to immerse the entire perioral region, or by 'scooping'—a behaviour in which a small amount of mash was taken up in the paw, lifted to the lips and pushed through the teeth, eliciting weak lapping movement and minimal mouth opening. The recovery of solid food and water intake was accompanied by the return of periorally elicited mouth opening and biting, and by the replacement of 'scooping' by oral grasping behaviour.

Formal analysis of ingestive sequences videotaped during the first few post-operative days, revealed that while the approach phase of the sequence was unchanged, the perioral contact phase was markedly prolonged and the jaw opening/tongue protrusion phases were often absent (Fig. 3.1 (c)). Under these conditions, the rat behaved as if 'fixed' in the contact phase, continually rubbing its snout against the chow block or sipper tube, but eventually aborting the ingestive sequence.

The magnitude of this deficit and its persistence was a function of the extent of the deafferentation.

Food and water intake and the regulation of body weight   When offered only rat or cat chow pellets and water, the deafferented rat exhibited an aphagia so persistent that, without intervention, starvation was inevitable. When offered, in addition, an array of highly palatable foods (e.g. pablum, rat chow mash, soft cat chow), the magnitude and persistence of the disruption in food intake were a joint function of the locus and extent of the sections and the sensory properties of the diet. However, even with unlimited access to highly palatable diets, deafferented rats lost considerable weight and did not recover their pre-operative weights within a 40-day post-operative observation period (Fig. 3.6).

Water intake in these subjects was also depressed. However, since food and water intake are interdependent in the rat, it is possible that the reduced intake of the trigeminal rat was due to the reduction in solid food intake and the increased proportional intake of semiliquid foods. However, when the water intake of deafferented rats was compared with that of yoked-for-food controls, there were persistent differences between the groups. Controls did not show the immediate adipsia of the deafferented subjects. Post-operatively, they decreased their intake gradually and showed substantial water intake ten days or more before the deafferented rats. Thus trigeminal orosensory deafferentation disrupts water as well as food intake.

Effects upon the regulation of body weight were suggested by the observation that, although deafferented rats lost weight at normal rates, recovery of the lost weight was retarded for significant periods, even after the rats were no longer exhibiting consummatory deficits and were ingesting substantial amounts of solid food. However, these animals had undergone a prolonged period of reduced food and water intake, and such treatments have been shown to depress the levels at which weight is subsequently regulated (Armstrong et al., 1980). To clarify this issue we compared the weight regulation of deafferented subjects with that of yoked-for-food intake controls. Yoking was continued until the deafferented rats began to ingest chow pellets at pre-operative levels, at which point the control rat was unyoked and both members of the pair were given access only to chow pellets and water. As Fig. 3.7 indicates, the control rats continued to increase weight during the 30-day observation period, while the weight of the deafferented rats came to asymptote at significantly lower levels. Since other data indicate that recovered trigeminal rats respond appropriately to a *short-term* period of deprivation, the data presented in Fig. 3.7 suggest a persistent reduction, in the *long-term* level of body weight regulation in the trigeminal animal.

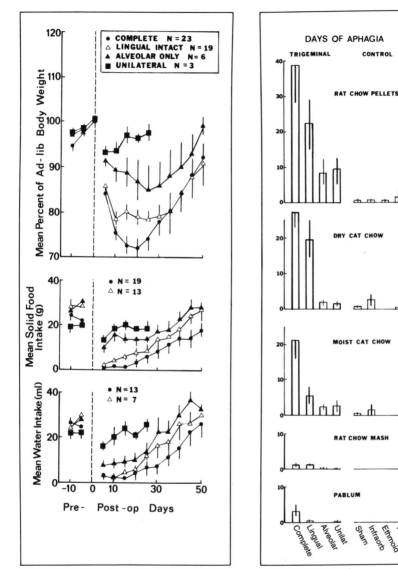

Fig. 3.6 Effects of trigeminal deafferentation on food and water intake in the rat: Interaction with sensory properties of the food. Left: solid food and water intake and body weight following varying degrees of orosensory deafferentation. Right: days of aphagia as a joint function of diet type and surgical treatment: complete = bilateral orosensory deafferentation; lingual = complete, with lingual nerve intact; alveolar = section of inferior and posterior superior alveolar nerves; infraorb. = infraorbital nerve section; ethmoid = ethmoid nerve section; teeth = clipped to avoid incisor overgrowth. (From Jacquin and Zeigler, 1983. Copyright 1983 by the American Psychological Association. Reprinted with permission.)

Responsiveness to food and water   Given the obvious disruption of consummatory behaviour in the trigeminal animals, especially in the immediate post-operative period, it was important to clarify the extent to which their reduced food and water intake was a consequence of their sensorimotor impairment or reflected a reduction in responsiveness. Responsiveness to water was measured using a standard drinkometer circuit to dissociate discrete licking movements from total time spent in contact with the sipper tube—a measure of thirst. Responsiveness to food was assessed by monitoring the frequency and duration of 'scooping' responses (paw extension, grasping and retraction) to mash presented in a feedometer which prevented oral access. In both situations, rats with bilateral section of the trigeminal motor or hypoglossal nerves served as oromotor controls.

As Fig. 3.8 indicates, subjects with oromotor lesions ingest water, albeit, inefficiently, despite their severe impairments, while intake is almost completely abolished for prolonged periods in the trigeminal orosensory animal. The oromotor controls, although they obtained little or no water, made vigorous and repeated attempts to drink over the

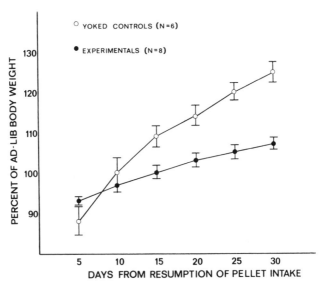

Fig. 3.7 Trigeminal deafferentation: Effects upon long term body weight: Data were recorded starting with the day on which a subject resumed eating rat chow pellets. Six of the subjects had previously served as 'yoked' intake controls (open circles). Note that even though the control group starts at a slightly lower weight, it continues to increase weight during the 30-day period, while the deafferented group (closed circles, N=8) asymptotes at a significantly lower weight. (From Jacquin and Zeigler, 1983. Copyright 1983 by the American Psychological Association. Reprinted with permission.)

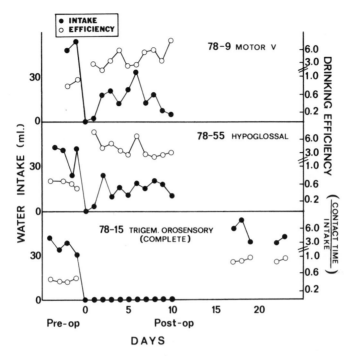

Fig. 3.8 Effects of orosensory deafferentation upon water intake and drinking efficiency. Intake (filled circles) and drinking efficiency (open circles) in three representative subjects with either oromotor (motor V or hypoglossal nerve) or orosensory denervations. A reduction in drinking efficiency is indicated by an increase in the contact time/intake ratio. Note the presence of intake in both oromotor controls, despite reduced efficiency, and its absence for 10 days in the orosensory group.

ten day post-operative period, while the orosensory animals made few responses and ingested little or no water.

A comparable effect with respect to food was shown in subjects trained, pre-operatively, to obtain their total daily intake by 'scooping' wet mash (Fig. 3.9). Thus, the hypoglossal animal, although it was unable to ingest the mash brought to the mouth by 'scooping', dramatically increased the number and duration of scooping bouts during this period, until eventually it was spending up to ten hours per day in scooping behaviour. In contrast, the trigeminal orosensory animal reduced both the frequency and the duration of its feeding bouts over the first post-operative week. When body weight fell to life-threatening values, there was a marked increase in bout duration sufficient to restore body weight to about 85 per cent of *ad lib*, and to maintain it at, *but not above* that level for more than two months post-operatively. Thus, even when obtaining palatable food did not involve an oromotor behaviour, the responsiveness of the orosensory subjects was not sufficient to sustain the slight increase in 'scooping' activity required to recover their *ad lib* body weight.

Dietary self-selection behaviour   Under natural conditions, the rat selects from a variety of food sources with different nutritional compositions, organizing its feeding patterns so as to meet both its caloric and nutritional needs. Whatever mechanisms are involved in translating metabolic conditions into selective ingestive behaviour, the sensory properties of the food must be important sources of control, so that the trigeminal orosensory system may be expected to play a mediating role. To assess that role, Miller (1984; Miller and Teates, 1985) offered rats unlimited access to high protein and protein-free carbohydrate diets, which also differed in their texture. Normal rats rapidly acquire intake patterns which maintain stable protein/carbohydrate ratios and consistent growth. They do so by making fine, quantitative adjustments of intake on a day-to-day basis. These adjustments are lost in the deafferented animals, whose selection patterns are extraordinarily variable, and might include extreme preferences for either of the diets. Moreover, even though they do eventually recover almost normal protein intake, their ability to adjust dietary self-selection to metabolic requirements is severely impaired. For example, normal (or surgical control) rats respond to a period of food deprivation by immediate and compensatory increases in intake from the high-protein diet. Such increases are delayed in 'recovered' trigeminal rats, and do not involve maximum utilization of the available protein. Similarly, normal rats adjust rapidly to intragastric infusions of protein or carbohydrate suspensions by an appropriate compensatory decrease in the intake only of the 'surplus' nutrient, while trigeminal animals compensate only for the caloric value of the 'surplus' rather than its nutrient composition. Such impairments suggest that while a combination of post-ingestional mechanisms and non-trigeminal (e.g. gustatory) inputs may contribute to the recovery and long-term maintenance of body weight in the 'trigeminal' animal, they are insufficient to guide the precise and fairly rapid daily adjustments which mediate normal dietary self-selection behaviour.

Trigeminal deafferentation and operant behaviour   Unlike consummatory responses, which, like reflexes, are presumed to be under the direct control of stimulus factors, the acquisition and maintenance of food or water-reinforced instrumental responses is assumed to reflect the operation of motivational mechanisms (Teitelbaum, 1977).

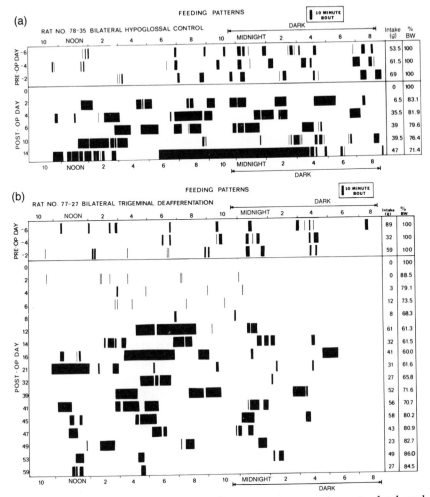

Fig. 3.9 Trigeminal deafferentation: effects upon responsivess to food and feeding behaviour ('scooping') patterns. Animals obtained total daily intake (chow mash) by a forelimb scooping response. Each bout of 'scooping' is represented by a vertical bar, whose width is proportional to bout duration. Daily food intake and body weight (as percentage of *ad lib* weight) are shown in the right two columns. (a) Effects of hypoglossal nerve section (tongue inactivation). Note that although this rat has a profound motor impairment which prevents ingestion of food, responsiveness, as measured by the frequency and duration of scooping bouts, is high on post-operative day 2 and increases dramatically with weight loss. (b) Effects of complete orosensory deafferentation. Note that, despite the absence of a motor impairment, responsiveness is low for the first post-operative week. Although bout duration increases as weight decreases, it eventually asymptotes at a level which maintains body weight at about 85 per cent of its *ad lib* level. (From Jacquin and Enfiejiam, 1982; Copyright 1982 by the Haer Institute. Reprinted with permission.)

To test the hypothesis that trigeminal orosensory deafferentation disrupts motivational as well as sensorimotor mechanisms, we examined deafferentation effects upon an instrumental (lever-pressing) response, reinforced either by food, water, or intracranial electrical stimulation. In some animals denervation was carried out in two stages, with the first (unilateral) procedure serving as a control.

Unilateral deafferentation had little or no effect upon previously acquired lever-pressing responses in either food- or water-reinforced subjects. However, for both reinforcers, bilateral deafferentation was followed by severe and persistent reductions in lever pressing which were evident within the very first minutes of the first session. Moreover, response rates remained low even after a reinforcement was generated by the animal, and reinforcers delivered by the experimenter were frequently ignored. A variety of control procedures suggested that deafferentation effects did not reflect reductions in the amount of food obtained, or difficulties in ingestion. Even when food or water was ingested, it did not increase the probability of lever pressing. That is, trigeminal deafferentation appears to reduce the *incentive* value of food and water as reinforcers of instrumental behaviours.

Deafferented subjects did not behave like extinction controls, who were very active and made large numbers of lever presses in the absence of reinforcement. Instead, deafferented subjects often fell asleep in the test chamber within a few minutes after the start of the session, despite the fact that they were being tested at between 65 per cent and 85 pre cent of their free-feeding weights. In subjects followed for several weeks post-operatively, the return of lever pressing parallelled the return of responsiveness to the reinforcer. However, performance in these animals was quite variable even a month or more post-operatively. Thus trigeminal deafferentation severely disrupts performance of an operant task *whose execution does not require a trigeminally mediated response* (Jacquin and Zeigler, 1984).

Interestingly, trigeminal deafferentation does *not* disrupt lever pressing reinforced by electrical stimulation of the brain, through electrodes which support stimulus-bound feeding, *even in subjects so unresponsive to food and water as to require daily intubation* (Jacquin, Harris, and Zeigler, 1982). Indeed, these subjects consistently exhibited significant increases in lever pressing reinforcd by brain stimulation. At the very least, this finding casts doubt upon the generally held assumption that hunger, thirst, and electrical stimulation of the brain share common neural substrates. Perhaps more important, the operant conditioning experiments support the hypothesis that trigeminal orosensation makes a critical contribution to both the sensorimotor and motivational control of ingestive behaviour.

BRAINSTEM SUBSTRATES FOR OROSENSORIMOTOR MODULATION

Ingestive movement patterns—jaw opening, mastication, licking, and swallowing—share common oromotor nuclei and efferent pathways to the orofacial musculature. Thus, the observation that they can be elicited in the decerebrate rat (Berntson and Micco, 1976) implies that the sensorimotor circuitry mediating these oromotor patterns is organized at brainstem levels. However, in the normal animal, unlike the decerebrate (Grill and Norgren, 1978*b*), ingestive movement patterns may be controlled by 'motivational' variables, so as to be congruent with both the sensory properties of the nutrients and the bodily economy of the animal. Such control implies the existence of mechanisms for modulating the responsiveness of these circuits and coordinating their activity The increased responsiveness of the food- or water-deprived or sodium-depleted animal, exemplifies the former mechanism. The shift from eating to drinking responses or from ingestion to rejection responses exemplifies the latter, since it involves the imposition of different forms of neural organization upon the same 'final common path' structures. Both mechanisms imply the existence of anatomical connections between brainstem oromotor nuclei and more rostral structures (e.g. the hypothalamus) involved in the control of metabolic homeostasis. A variety of anatomical and physiological studies in the rat have suggested that the pontomedullary parvocellular reticular formation (PCRt) may provide a substrate for the integration of viscerosensory and orosensory inputs and the modulation of oromotor systems mediating ingestive behaviours (reviews in Holstege, 1991; Luiten *et al.*, 1987; Ter Horst *et al.*, 1991).

PCRt extends from the rostral medulla to the level of the trigeminal nucleus caudalis, and is divisible into rostral and caudal portions, exhibiting different patterns of afferent and efferent connections. Its rostral portion (rPCRt), receives inputs from trigeminal and gustatory receptors in the perioral region, the oral cavity, and the jaw muscles, and originates *bilateral* projections upon trigeminal brainstem sensory (Principal V, Spinal V, Mesencephalic V), interneuronal (supratrigeminal, intertrigeminal), and motor nuclei, as well as upon nuclei innervating facial, tongue, pharyngeal, and laryngeal muscles (facial, hypoglossal, and ambiguus nuclei). rPCRt projections upon trigeminal brainstem *sensory* nuclei terminate upon those areas of PrV and SpV innervated by primary afferents from oral and perioral areas functionally related to ingestive jaw-opening movements. rPCRt projections to orofacial *motor* nuclei are arranged topographically such that projections to motoneurons innervating functionally related muscle groups originate within the same PCRt regions. Thus motoneurons mediating jaw-closing and tongue retraction movements (which occur together during eating and drinking) originate from more rostral parts of rPCRt; those mediating jaw-opening and tongue protraction movements from more caudal rPCRt. Such patterns of functional organization suggest a role for rPCRt in the modulatory control of orosensorimotor mechanisms.

This hypothesis is consistent with the results of physiological studies indicating a role for parvocellular reticular neurons in the control of swallowing (Jean, 1990), mastication and rhythmic ingestive responses (Chandler and Tal, 1986; Hiraba et al., 1988; Nozaki et al., 1993), orofacial movements (Siegel and Tomaszewski, 1983), and the facilitation of jaw-opening and closing reflexes (Minkels et al., 1991).

Caudal PCRt receives a substantial projection from hypothalamic nuclei and, projects, in turn, upon brainstem autonomic nuclei such as the nucleus ambiguus and the dorsal motor nucleus of the vagus. The two divisions are linked by reciprocating connections. Ter Horst et al. (1991) have hypothesised that caudal PCRt is involved in controlling metabolic homeostasis, while rostral PCRT controls orofacial ingestive musculature. Fig. 3.10 illustrates the organization of PCRt in relation to neural circuitry related to metabolic and orosensorimotor control.

CONCLUSIONS

Following Lashley's (1938) discussion of motivational mechanisms, a number of theorists have proposed that internal states influence an animal's behaviour by modulating its responsiveness to external stimuli (Flynn, 1967; Gallistel, 1980; Pfaff, 1980). While the proposition is intuitively appealing, supporting evidence with respect to ingestive behaviour is sparse, in part because the historical focus on central (hypothalamic) structures led to a neglect of sensorimotor processes. The analysis of putative modulatory mechanisms requires quantitative characterization of the consummatory response, delineation of the sensory and motor nuclei and pathways mediating the response, and identification of CNS loci which could mediate such modulation. The characterization of ingestive response patterns elicited (intraorally) by gustatory and (periorally) by trigeminal somatosensory inputs (Grill and Norgren, 1978; Zeigler et al., 1984) was an important first step in this analysis. The recent development of sophisticated anatomical tracing techniques has made possible delineation of the relevant orosensorimotor circuitry, as well as the identification of putative modulatory substrates. Physiological experiments in intact, behaving preparations (e.g. Travers and Jackson, 1992) are now required to link brainstem anatomy to ingestive behaviour.

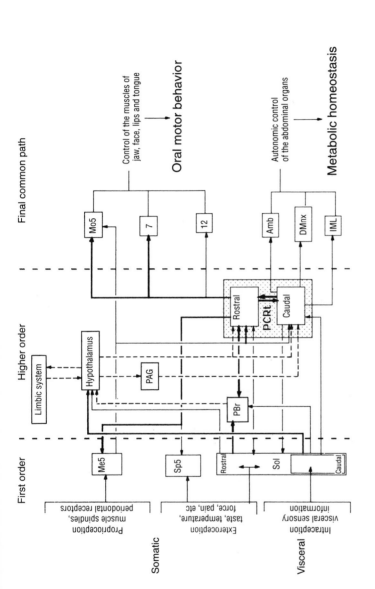

Fig. 3.10 Summary schematic diagram showing the efferent connections of the parvocellular reticular formation (PCRt) for the regulation of oromotor behavior and metabolic homeostasis. Specific pathways related to the limbic system, visceral sensory, and somatic sensory nuclei. Abbreviations: Amb, nucleus ambiguus; DMnX, dorsal vagal motor nucleus; IML, intermediolateral cell column; Me5, trigeminal mesencephalic nucleus; Mo 5, 7, 12, trigeminal, facial, and hypoglossal nuclei; PAG, periacqueudctal grey; PBr, parabrachial nuclei; Sol, nucleus of the Tractus Solitarius; Sp5, spinal trigeminal nucleus. (After Ter Horst *et al.*, *Neuroscience*, **40**, 735–58, Copyright 1991, with kind permission from Pergamon Press Ltd, Oxford, UK.)

ACKNOWLEDGEMENTS

Supported by Grant MH-08366, Research Scientist Award MH-00320, and by the Biopsychology Program, Hunter College (CUNY). I am grateful to Dr Susan Travers for making available a review of central gustatory processing (Travers, S. P., 1993) upon which I have drawn shamelessly. I thank Dr Joseph Travers for his helpful comments on an earlier draft of the manuscript. More extensive reviews of some of the topics considered in this chapter may be found in Grill and Berridge (1985), Travers *et al.* (1987), Travers, (1991), Zeigler, (1983), Zeigler, Jacquin and Miller, (1985) and Zeigler, (1991).

REFERENCES

Aikaike, N., Hiji, Y., and Yamada, K. (1965). Taste preference and aversion in rats following denervation of the chorda tympani and the IXth nerve. *Kunamoto Medical Journal*, **18**, 108–9.

Altschuler, S. M., Bao. X., Bieger, D., Hopkins, D. A., and Miselis, R. R. (1989). Viscerotopic representation of the upper alimentary tract in the rat: sensory ganglia and nuclei of the solitary and spinal trigeminal tracts. *Journal Comparative Neurology*, **283**, 248–68.

Altschuler, S.M., Ferenci, D.A. Lynn, R.B., and Miselis, R.R. (1991). Representation of the cecum in the lateral dorsal motor nucleus of the vagus nerve and commissural subnucleus of the nucleus tractus solitarii in rat. *Journal of Comparative Neurolofy*, **304**, 261–74.

Armstrong, S. Coleman, G., and Singer, G. (1980). Food and water deprivation: changes in rat feeding, drinking and body weight. *Neuroscience and Biobehavioral Reviews*, **4**, 377–402.

Berntson, G. G. and Micco, D.J. (1976). Organization of brainstem behavioral systems. *Brain Research Bulletin*, **1**, 471–83.

Chandler, S. H. and Tal, M. (1986). The effects of brain stem transections on the neuronal networks responsible for rhythmical jaw muscle activity in the guinea pig. *Journal of Neurophysiology* **6**, 1831–42.

Dubner, R., Sessle, B. J., and Storey, A. T. (1978). *The neural basis of oral and facial functions*. New York: Plenum.

Flynn, J. P. The neural basis of aggression in cats. In D. C. Glass (ed.) (1967). *Neurophysiology and emotion*. Rockefeller University Press, New York, pp. 40–59.

Gallistel, C. R. (1980). *The organization of action: A new synthesis.*, Erlbaum, Hillsdale, NJ.

Grill, H. J. and Berridge, K. (1985). Taste reactivity as a measure of the neural control of palatability. In J. Sprague and A. N. Epstein (eds.), *Progress in psychobiology and physiological psychology*, Vol. 11, Academic Press, New York, pp.1–61.

Grill, H. J. and Norgren, R. (1978a). The taste reactivity test: I. Mimetic responses to gustatory stimuli in neurologically normal rats. *Brain Research*, **143**, 263–279.

Grill, H. J. and Norgren, R. (1978*b*). The taste reactivity test: II. Mimetic responses to gustatory stimuli in thalamic and chronic decerebrate rats. *Brain Research*, **143**, 281–97.

Grill, H. J. and Schwartz, G. J. (1992). The contribution of gustatory nerve input to oral motor behavior and intake-based preference. II. Effects of combined chorda tympani and glossopharyngeal nerve section in the rat. *Brain Research*, **573**, 105–13.

Grill, H. J., Spector, A. C., Schwartz, G. J., Kaplan, J. M., and Flynn, F. W. (1987). Evaluating taste effects on ingestive behavior. In F. M. Toates and N. E. Rowland (Eds.), *Feeding and drinking*, Elsevier, New York, pp. 151–88.

Grill, H. J., Schwartz, G. J., and Travers, J. B. (1992). The contribution of gustatory inputs to oral motor behavior and intake-based preference. I. Effects of chorda tympani or glossopharyngeal nerve section in the rat. *Brain Research*, **573**, 95–104.

Hamilton, R. B. and Norgren, R. (1984). Central projections of gustatory nerves in the rat. *Journal of Comparative Neurology*, **222**, 560–77.

Harris-Warwick, R. M. and Marder, E. (1991). Modulation of neural networks for behavior. *Annual Review of Neuroscience*, **14**, 39–57.

Hiraba, K. Taira, M., Sahara, Y., and Nakamura, Y. (1988). Single unit activity in bulbar reticular formation during food ingestion in chronic cats. *Journal of Neurophysiolology*, **60**, 1333–49.

Holstege, G. (1991). Descending motor pathways and the spinal motor system: Limbic and non-limbic components. In G. Holstege (ed.), *Progress in brain research*, Vol. 87, New York: Elsevier, pp. 307–421.

Humphrey, T. (1970). Reflex activity in the oral and facial area of the human fetus. In J. F. Bosma (Ed.), *Second symposium on oral sensation and perception*. Charles C. Thomas, Springfield, IL., pp. 195–223.

Jacquin, M. F. (1983). Gustatory deafferentation and ingestive behavior in the rat. *Behavioral Neuroscience*, **97**, 98–109.

Jacquin, M.F. and Enfiejian, H. (1982). Trigeminal mediation of a fractional anticipatory goal response. In B. Hoebel and D. Novin, (eds.) *The neural basis of feeding and reward*. The Haer Institute, Brunswick, Maine, pp. 85–96.

Jacquin, M. F. and Zeigler, H. P. (1983). Trigeminal orosensation and ingestive behavior in the rat. *Behavioral Neuroscience*, **97**, 62–97.

Jacquin, M. F. and Zeigler, H. P. (1984). Trigeminal denervation and operant behavior in the rat. *Behavioral Neuroscience*, **98**, 1004–22.

Jacquin, M. F. and Rhoades, R. W. (1990). Structure and response properties of cells in trigeminal subnucleus oralis. *Somatosensory and Motor Research*, **7**, 265–88.

Jacquin, M. F., Golden, J., and Panneton, W. M. (1988). Structure and function of 'barrel' precursor cells in trigeminal nucleus principalis. *Developmental Brain Research*, **43**, 309–14.

Jacquin, M. F, Harris, R., and Zeigler, H. P. (1982). Dissociation of hunger and self-stimulation by trigeminal deafferentation in the rat. *Brain Research*, **244**, 53–58.

Jacquin, M. F., Mooney, R. D., and Rhoades, R. W. (1986). Morphology, response properties and collateral projections of trigemino-thalamic neurons in brainstem subnucleus interpolaris of rat. *Experimental Brain Research*, **61**, 457–68.

Jacquin, M. F., Semba, K. Rhoades, R. W., and Egger, M. D. (1982). Trigeminal primary afferents project bilaterally to dorsal horn and ipsilaterally to cerebellum, reticular formation and cuneate, solitary, supratrigeminal and vagal nuclei. *Brain Research*, **246**, 285–91.

Jean, A. (1990). Brainstem control of swallowing: localization and organization of the central pattern generator for swallowing. In A. Taylor (ed.), *Neurophysiology of the jaws and teeth*, Macmillan, London, pp. 294–321.

Lashley, K. S. (1938). The experimental analysis of instinctive behavior. *Psychological Review*, **45**, 445–71.

Luiten, P.G.M., Ter Horst, G. J., and Steffens, A. B. (1987). The hypothalamus, intrinsic connections and outflow pathways to the endocrine system in relation to the control of feeding and metabolism. *Progress in Neurobiology*, **28**, 1–54.

Lund, J. P., Appenteng, K., and Seguin, J. J. (1982). Analogies and common features in the masticatory and speech control systems. In S. Grillner (ed.), *Speech motor control*, Wenner-Gren Center International Symposium Series, Vol. 36. Pergamon Press, Oxford pp. 231–45.

Marfurt, C. M. and Rajchert, D. M. (1991). Trigeminal primary projections to 'non-trigeminal' areas of the rat central nervous system. *Journal of Comparative Neurology*, **303**, 489–511.

Miller, M. G. (1981). Trigeminal deafferentation and ingestive behavior in rats. *Journal of Comparative and Physiological Psychology*, **95**, 252–69.

Miller, M. G. (1984). Oral somatosensory factors and dietary self-selection in rats. *Behavioral Neuroscience*, **98**, 416–23.

Miller, M.G. and J.F. Teates, (1984). Oral somatosensory factors in dietary self-selection after food depivation and supplementation in rats. *Behavioral Neuroscience*, **98**, 424–34.

Miller, M.G. and Teates, J.F. (1985). Acquisition of dietary self-selection in rats with normal and impaired oral sensation. *Physiology and Behavior*, **34**, 401–8.

Minkels, R. F., Juch, P. J. W., Ter Horst, G. J., and van Willigen, J. D. (1991). Projections of the parvocellular reticular formation to the contralateral trigeminal mesencephalic nucleus. *Brain Research*, **547**, 13–21.

Norgren, R. and Smith, G. P. (1988). Central distribution of subdiaphragmatic vagal branches in the rat. *Journal of Comparative Neurology*, **273**, 207–11

Nozaki, S., Enomoto, S., and Nakamura, Y. (1983). Identification and input output properties of bulbar reticular neurons involved in the cerebral cortical control of trigeminal motoneurons in cats. *Experimental Brain Research*, **49**, 363–72.

Pfaff, D. (1980). *Estrogens and brain function*. Springer, New York.

Pfaffmann, C. (1952). Taste preference and aversion following lingual denervation. *Journal of Comparative and Physiological Psychology*, **45**, 393–400.

Siegel, J. and Tomaszewski, K. S. (1983). Behavioral organization of the reticular formation: Studies in the unrestrained cat. I. Cells related to axial, limb, eye and other movements. II. Cells related to facial movements. *Journal of Neurophysiology*, **50**, 696–723.

Suemune, S., Nishimori, T., Hosoi, M., Suzuki, Y., Tsuru, H., Kawata, T., Yamauchi, K., and Maeda, N. (1992) Trigeminal nerve endings of lingual mucosa and musculature of the rat. *Brain Research*, **586**, 162–5.

Sweazy, R. D. and Bradley, R. M. (1988). Responses of lamb nucleus of the solitary tract neurons to chemical stimulation of the epiglottis. *Brain Research*, **439**, 195–210.

Sweazy, R. D. and Bradley, R. M. (1989). Responses of neurons in the lamb nucleus tractus solitarius to stimulation of the caudal oral cavity and epiglottis with different stimulus modalities. *Brain Research*, **480**, 133–50.

Taylor, A. (ed.) (1990). *Neurophysiology of the teeth and jaws*. The Macmillan Press, London.

Teitelbaum, P. (1977). Levels of integration of the operant. In W. K. Honig and J. E. R. Staddon (eds.), *Handbook of operant behavior*, Prentice-Hall, New York, pp. 7–27.

Ten Donkelaar, H.J. (1990). Comparative aspects. In W.R. Klemm and R.P. Vertes (eds.), *Brainstem mechanisms of behavior*. Wiley, New York, pp. 199–237.

Ter Horst, G. J., Copray, J. C. V. M., Liem, R. S. B., and van Willigen, J. D. (1991). Projections from the rostral parvocellular reticular formation to pontine and medullary nuclei in the rat: Involvement in autonomic regulation and orofacial motor control. *Neuroscience*, **40**, 735–58.

Travers, J. B. (1991). Drinking: hindbrain sensorimotor neural organization. In D. J. Ramsay and D. A. Booth (eds.), *Thirst: Physiological and psychological aspects*. Springer-Verlag, New York, pp. 258–75.

Travers, J. B. and Jackson, L. M. (1992). Hypoglossal neural activity during licking and swallowing in the awake rat. *Journal of Neurophysiology*, **67**, 1171–84.

Travers, J. B. and Norgren, R. (1983). Afferent projections to the oral motor nuclei in the rat. *Journal of Comparative Neurology*, **220**, 280–98.

Travers, J. B. and Norgren, R. (1986). Electromyographic analysis of the ingestion and rejection of sapid stimuli in the rat. *Behavioral Neuroscience*, **100**, 544–55.

Travers, J. B., Travers, S. P., and Norgren, R. (1987). Gustatory neural processing in the hindbrain, *Annual Review of Neuroscience*, **10**, 595–632.

Travers, S. P. (1994). Orosensory processing in neural systems of the nucleus of the solitary tract. In S. Simon and S. Roper (eds.), *Mechanisms of taste transduction*, chapter 13, CRC Press, Boca Raton, in press.

Travers, S. P., Norgren, R., and Akey, L. Functional organization of orosensory responses in the nucleus of the solitary tract. In preparation.

Zeigler, H. P. (1983). The trigeminal system and ingestive behavior. In E. Satinoff and P. Teitelbaum (eds.), *Handbook of behavioral neurobiology: Motivation*. Plenum Press, New York, pp. 265–328.

Zeigler, H. P. (1991). Drinking in mammals: functional morphology, orosensory modulation and motor control. In D. J. Ramsay and D. A. Booth (eds.), *Thirst: Physiological and psychological aspects*. Springer-Verlag, New York, pp. 241–257.

Zeigler, H. P., Miller, M. G. and Jacquin, M. F. (1985). Trigeminal orosensation and ingestive behavior in the rat. In J.M. Sprague and A. N. Epstein (eds.), *Progress in psychobiology and physiological psychology*, Vol. 11, Academic Press, New York, pp. 63–196.

Zeigler, H. P., Semba, K., and Jacquin, M. F. (1984). Trigeminal reflexes and ingestive behavior in the rat. *Behavioral Neuroscience*, **98**, 1023–38.

4

Role of the digestive afferents in food intake regulation

N. Mei

INTRODUCTION

The determination of feeding behaviour involves numerous and complex mechanisms (Booth, 1992; Le Magnen, 1983; Morley, 1987). Recent investigations have emphasized the role of neural mechanisms in the regulation of food intake. This is partly due to significant progress in the field of digestive sensory physiology (Grundy and Scratcherd, 1989; Mei, 1985). Despite these recent advances many points remain to be elucidated:

(1) What are the exact origins of pre-absorptive neural signals (mouth, oesophagus, stomach, small intestine)?
(2) What is the relative importance of these signals in comparison with other neural signals (visual, hepatic, central signals)?
(3) What is the role of neural sensory mechanisms in comparison with other mechanisms (metabolic and humoral)?
(4) What are the possible interactions between neural, humoral, and metabolic mechanisms?

This chapter attempts to answer these questions with special reference to digestive afferents.

ORIGIN OF SENSORY INFORMATION

The different sensory signals can be classified into several categories according to their origin: the cephalic, the digestive, the hepatic, the serosal, and the central signals. In addition, these signals fall into external and internal types on the one hand, and into pre-absorptive (cephalic and digestive) and post-absorptive (hepatic, central) signals, on the other hand (Table 4.1).

Table 4.1 Origin and classification of different neural sensory signals probably involved in food intake control

Origin	Afferent type		
Cephalic area	visual olfactory gustatory periodontal	} External	} Pre-absorptive
Digestive system	oesophageal gastric intestinal	} Internal	
Abdomen (GI tract excepted)	hepatic abdominal (dorsal wall)		} Post-absorptive
CNS	hypothalamic: VMH, LH bulbar: NTS, area postrema		

The cephalic signals

In general when speaking about cephalic signals, people mean visual and olfactory signals. In fact, many other sensory structures are involved. In addition to gustatory signals, particular attention must be paid to dental signals since periodontal receptors deliver a variety of messages during mastication about the intensity and direction of forces exerted on the crown of the teeth (Cash and Linden, 1988; Mei et al., 1975). Furthermore, these afferents project extensively on the hypothalamic regions (ventromedial hypothalamus: VMH, lateral hypothalamus: LH) which are involved in food intake (Trub and Mei, 1991).

The digestive signals

The extensive use of single-fibre and microelectrode techniques have made it possible to investigate the sensory signals originating in the digestive tract. In our laboratory we developed the latter method because it was more suitable for studying the visceral afferents in general (Mei, 1983, 1985). Contrary to the classical idea, the sensory signals generated by the digestive system are very abundant. Moreover, most of them are elicited during normal conditions (digestion), which is consistent with current data about the richness of visceral sensory neurones and endings (see above). They may be classified into four categories, as represented in Fig. 4.1:

(1) signals relating to mechanical changes of the digestive wall: contraction and distension due to the passage of the bolus;
(2) signals relating to the chemical and physical properties of nutrients which are absorbed;
(3) signals relating to the chemical environment of receptors, namely the presence of neuropeptides and hormones (Substance P: SP, Cholecystokin: CCK, for example) released during digestion;
(4) signals produced under pathophysiological conditions (pain): strong stretching of viscus, and release of nociceptive substances.

Contrary to what was formerly believed, these sensory signals are carried by numerous fibres that mainly travel in the vagal nerves. Actually, the sensory fibres represent around 75 per cent of the total nerve population in both humans and animals (Grundy and Scratcherd, 1989; Mei et al., 1980; Paintal, 1973). The underevaluation of the ratio of sensory fibres to motor fibres may be explained by the high proportion of unmyelinated fibres in the visceral nerves (80 per cent for example, in the vagal nerves) which were not clearly visible using light microscopy (Mei et al., 1980).

We need to know whether the digestive sensory signals originate from only one type of ending, the polymodal receptors, or from various endings, the specific receptors. In the present state of the art, it is accepted that several types of receptors exist in the digestive tract. Some are rather specific, such as the true chemoreceptors and thermo-receptors, while others, such as certain mucosal receptors, belong to the polymodal type. Between these two kinds of receptors, there are intermediate receptors which include the mechanoreceptors exhibiting

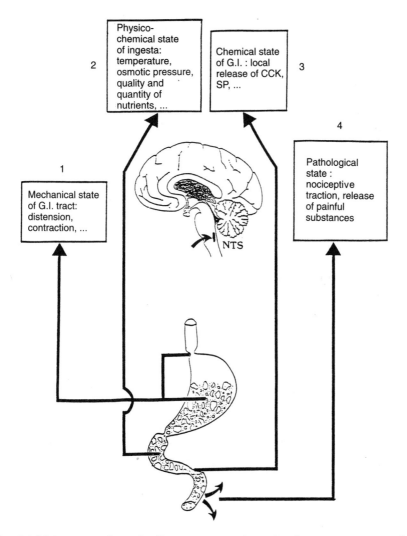

Fig. 4.1 Main types of vagal afferents coming from the digestive system and reaching the brain (NTS).

a chemosensitivity towards neuropeptides and hormones (see above).

The existence of such a functional diversity may seem surprising in the face of the simplicity and uniformity of the morphology of visceral sensory endings. Actually, they include free nerve-endings with few terminal branches. However, more complex formations may be encountered in the visceral area (Fig. 4.2). One may mention, for example, the Pacinian corpuscles located in the mesentery and the pseudo-taste-buds constituted by special enterocytes (caveolated cells) associated with nerve terminals (Newson *et al.*, 1982; Young and Levin, 1989). In fact, the functional specialization of the digestive sensory receptors results from several mechanisms. These include:

(1) changes in ion permeability of the membrane leading to the production of generator potentials (mechanoreceptors);
(2) binding of stimulating substances on specific membrane receptors (true chemoreceptors);
(3) changes in concentration of Ca^{2+} in nerve terminals (chemo-sensitivity of mechanoreceptors, Mei *et al.*, 1992).

Therefore, at least two mechanisms may co-exist in the same receptor, even though it has a simple structure.

The hepatic signals

Glucoreceptors have been revealed in the hepatic area (Niijima, 1982). Unlike intestinal glucoreceptors, the hepatic receptors fire when the glucose concentration decreases. In addition, osmoreceptors sensitive to variations of the osmotic pressure in the hepatic circulation have been described (Niijima, 1969).

The serosal signals

The dorsal wall of the abdominal cavity contains thermoreceptors capable of detecting small changes in internal temperature (Rawson and Quick, 1972; Riedel, 1976).

The central signals

Many experiments, including those involving the destruction or stimu-lation (local administration of glucose, electrical stimulation) of VMH and LH nuclei, have suggested the existence of central receptors. In fact, two types of cells have been described so far: (i) the VMH glucoreceptor neurones which are activated by glucose and inhibited by insulin, and (ii) the LH glucose-sensitive neurones whose activity is depressed by glucose and increased by insulin (Himmi *et al.*, 1988; Oomura, 1980; Oomura *et al.*, 1974). More recently, the existence of glucoreceptors

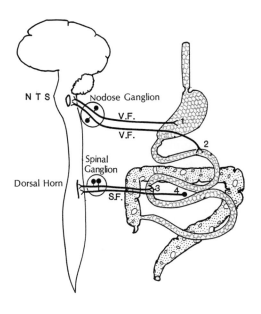

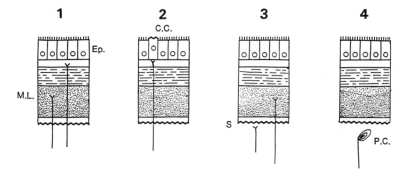

Fig. 4.2 Schematic representation of pathways and origin of the digestive sensory neurones. The vagal fibres (VF) originate from the digestive wall (mucosa and muscular layers: ML); Ep: ephithelial cells. The relevant endings correspond in general to free endings (1). However some nerve terminals are associated with special enterocytes the so-called caveolated cells (CC). The splanchnic fibres (SF) are connected to receptors located either in muscular layers or in serous membrane (S) (3); in the latter case endings are free endings or Pacinian corpusles (PC) (4).

was reported in the nucleus tractus solitarius: NTS (Mizuno and Oomura, 1984; Yettefti *et al.*, 1992) and in the area postrema (Adachi and Kobashi, 1985).

PUTATIVE ROLES OF DIGESTIVE AFFERENTS IN FOOD INTAKE REGULATION

Despite the tremendous complexity of mechanisms involved in alimentary behaviour (Le Magnen, 1983), various experiments performed both on humans and animals suggest the participation of digestive sensory information in the regulation of food intake. Many studies are based on bypass experiments, which allow the determination of the role of each part of the digestive tract. In other experiments, the effects of section, destruction, or stimulation of the nervous system are examined in terms of food intake or maintenance of body weight. It is difficult to ascertain the role of a particular type of afferent, because it generally acts in association with other mechanisms. This is especially so in humans, where numerous social and conditioning factors greatly influence eating. Moreover, the digestive afferents may play a role *per se*, or indirectly via their involvement in the regulation of digestive motility and homeostasis. The sensory messages may be involved in short-term or long-term mechanisms. We will examine these different aspects.

It was formerly thought that pre-absorptive signals might be implicated in the regulation of alimentary behaviour. Unfortunately, the exact site (gastric versus intestinal in particular) and the type (mechanoreceptors versus chemoreceptors, for example) of the relevant receptors were only speculative. The recent electrophysiological data mentioned above, as well as the results supplied by perfusion, bypass, or nerve section experiments (Blundell, 1991; Forbes, 1992; Morley, 1987), clearly indicate that no single input is responsible for triggering or stopping alimentary behaviour, but, rather, several inputs (cephalic, gastric, intestinal, and hepatic) are involved simultaneously. According to circumstances (degree of hunger, hedonic and organoleptic qualities of meals especially), however, one particular kind of afferent may play a preponderant role. Digestive signals may also act indirectly through mechanisms involving both the control of motility and of homeostasis. Current ideas on this aspect are summarized in Fig. 4.3.

Direct involvement of digestive afferents

Short-term mechanisms

The triggering of food intake (hunger) seems to depend mainly on metabolic changes in cells, including deprivation of glucose. This

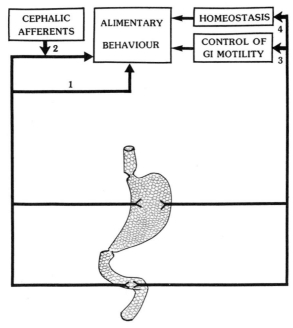

Fig. 4.3 Neural mechanisms involved in alimentary behaviour regulation and triggered by the digestive afferents. 1: direct effect on the CNS; 2: direct effect on the CNS in association with cephalic afferents; 3: indirect effect through the control of gastrointestinal (GI) motility; 4: indirect effect through the control of metabolic homeostasis.

behaviour is induced by changes occurring in the hypothalamic region (LH), which contains sensors capable of detecting such changes (Le Magnen, 1983; Oomura, 1980). However, since the activity of these centres depends on visceral information, digestive receptors might also be involved. Recent observations suggest that the onset of hunger may be influenced by chemical stimulation of the small intestine: for example, the infusion of lipid solutions into the human duodenum reduces both the sensation of hunger before a meal and its rate of ingestion (Read, 1992; Welch *et al.*, 1988). In addition, the rapid stimulation of any kind of digestive endings triggers anticipatory reflexes (Nicolaïdis, 1978) that potentiate humoral and metabolic reactions involved in digestion. For example, the intestinal glucoreceptors induce an insulin release through the vagal pathway (Mei *et al.*, 1981). Finally the contractions occurring during hunger produce sensory messages that increase the drive to eat (Mei, 1992).

During meals, the rich information delivered from the digestive tract (stomach and small intestine) modifies progressively the palatability of food induced by cephalic afferents (Cabanac and Fantino, 1977) and therefore contributes to reducing hunger.

The digestive afferents are also implicated in the arrest of food intake, since satiety occurs before metabolic changes affect the cells (recovery of glucose storage in particular). The intestinal chemoreceptors probably play the major role because they provide information on the quality and quantity of each absorbed nutrient (glucose in particular). Modern thinking, however, suggests that all the receptors are implicated whatever their location (gastric versus intestinal) or their function (mechanosensitive versus chemosensitive or thermosensitive).

Long-term mechanisms

Learning and conditioning mechanisms which determine alimentary behaviour require qualitative and quantitative information on nutrients from the cephalic region (palatability of nutrients), as well as from the digestive region and the 'milieu interieur' (nutritive value of absorbed nutrients). The hepatic and the gastrointestinal receptors which provide this kind of information probably play the major role. It has been shown that section of hepatic nerve branches leads to a change in diet selection by rats (Langhans *et al.*, 1989). In this case, portal glucose can act as an unconditioned stimulus for the acquisition of a learned food preference (Tordoff and Friedman, 1986). This phenomenon could be produced either via the direct activation of receptors and/or via the release of CCK. This hormone is considered to be an important factor in alimentary behaviour regulation because it exerts a complex action including contraction of digestive muscle, slowing down of gastric emptying, direct activation of sensory nerve endings and a central effect on memory processes (see, in particular Flood *et al.*, 1987; Mei, 1992; Shillabeer and Davison, 1987; Silver *et al.*, 1989).

Indirect involvement of digestive afferents

Mechanisms involved in digestive motility

Digestive afferents of any kind (mechanosensitive, chemosensitive, thermosensitive) play an important role in food intake regulation through the motor coordination of the alimentary tract. Thus all the intestinal receptors participate in the regulation of gastric emptying (Melone *et al.*, 1991).

Mechanisms involved in homeostasis

As previously mentioned, intestinal glucoreceptors induce a rapid increase of insulin secretion, via the vagal pathway (Mei *et al.*, 1981). Both the hepatic and the intestinal glucoreceptors contribute to the regulation of blood glucose maintenance through control of glucose storage by the liver (Niijima, 1989). Therefore, these afferents may intervene in alimentary behaviour since the glucose metabolism constitutes an important factor both in hunger and in satiety.

CONCLUSION

The current data provided by a large range of appropriate techniques highlight the striking complexity of sensory signals originating from the digestive tract. These signals, chiefly produced under physiological conditions, represent the main source of pre-absorptive information involved in food intake regulation. They are elicited in different kinds of endings regarding their location (mucosa, muscular layers, or serous membrane of any part of the digestive tract). Although the role of each type of afferent (gastric or intestinal, muscular or mucosal, mechanosensitive or chemosensitive, etc.) is not yet known, it is currently thought that the digestive sensory information is largely involved in mechanisms controlling short-term and long-term regulation of food intake. The digestive sensory signals act directly or indirectly through mechanisms that they control (gastric emptying, regulation of insulin, and glucose, levels in particular), separately or in connection with other afferents (visual, gustatory, olfactory, and dental afferents). Despite their simple structure, the digestive sensory endings display several mechanisms responsible for transduction. Further experiments are needed, however, to determine the characteristics of these mechanisms exactly, in comparison with those involved in other sensory receptors. The morphofunctional particularities of digestive sensory innervation, as well as its prominent and complex role in digestion, explain the current interest of both researchers and clinicians in this topic.

REFERENCES

Adachi, A. and Kobashi, M. (1985). Chemosensitive neurons within the area postrema. *Neuroscience Letters*, 55, 137–40.

Blundell, J. (1991). Pharmacological approaches to appetite suppression. *Trends in Pharmacological Sciences*, 12, 147–57.

Booth, D.A. (1992). Integration of internal and external signals in intake control. *Proceedings of the Nutrition Society*, 51, 21–8.

Cabanac, M. and Fantino, M. (1977). Origin of olfacto-gustatory alliesthesia: intestinal sensitivity to carbohydrate concentration. *Physiology and Behavior*, 18, 1039–45.

Cash, R.M. and Linden, R.W.A. (1988). The distribution of mechanoreceptors in the periodontal ligament of the mandibular canine tooth of the cat. *Journal of Physiology* (London), 330, 439–47.

Flood, J.F., Smith, J., and Morley, E. (1987). Modulation of memory processing by cholecystokinin: dependence on the vagus nerve. *Science*, **236**, 832–4.

Forbes, J.M. (1992). Metabolic aspects of satiety. *Proceedings of the Nutrition Society*, **51**, 13–19.

Grundy, D. and Scatcherd, T. (1989). Sensory afferents from the gastrointestinal tract. In *Handbook of physiology. Section 6: The gastrointestinal system*, pp. 593–620. American Physiological Society, New York.

Himmi, T., Boyer, A., and Orsini, J.C. (1988). Changes in lateral hypothalamic neuronal activity accompanying hyper- and hypoglycemias. *Physiology and Behavior*, **44**, 347–354.

Langhans, W., Kunz, U., and Scharrer, E. (1989). Hepatic vagotomy increases consumption of a novel-tasting diet presented immediately after surgery. *Physiology and Behavior*, **46**, 671–8.

Le Magnen, J. (1983). Body energy balance and food intake: a neuroendocrine regulatory mechanism. *Physiological Reviews*, **63**, 314–86.

Mei, N. (1983). Sensory structures in viscera. In *Progress in sensory physiology* (ed. D. Ottoson), Springer-Verlag, Berlin, pp. 1–42.

Mei, N. (1985). Intestinal chemosensitivity. *Physiological Reviews*, **65**, 211–37.

Mei, N. (1992). The intestinal chemosensitivity. In *Advances in the innervation of the gastrointestinal tract*, Holle G.E. and Wood J.D. (eds.), Excerpta Medica, Amsterdam, pp. 273–84.

Mei, N., Condamin, M., and Boyer, A. (1980). The composition of the vagus nerve of the cat. *Cell Tissue Research*, **209**, 423–31.

Mei, N., Arlhac, A., and Boyer, A. (1981). Nervous regulation of insulin release by the intestinal vagal glucoreceptors. *Journal of the Autonomic Nervous System*, **41**, 351–63.

Mei, N., Hartman, F., and Roubien, R. (1975). Caractéristiques fonctionnelles des mécanorécepteurs des ligaments dentaires chez le chat. *Journal de Biologie Buccale*, **3**, 29–39.

Mei, N., Lucchini, S., Garnier, L., and Michelucci, M.H. (1992). Nouvelles données sur la chémosensibilité des mécanorécepteurs gastro-intestinaux. *Archives Internationales de Physiologie de Biochimie et de Biophysique*, **100**, A 104.

Melone, J. and Mei, N. (1991). Intestinal effects of the products of lipid digestion on gastric electrical activity in the cat. Possible involvement of vagal intestinal receptors sensitive to lipids. *Gastroenterology*, **100**, 380–7.

Mizuno, Y. and Oomura, Y. (1984). Glucose responding neurons in the nucleus tractus solitarius of the rat: *In vitro* study. *Brain Research*, **307**, 109–16.

Morley, J.E. (1987). Neuropeptide regulation of appetite and weight. *Endocrine Reviews*, **8**, 256–87.

Newson, B., Ahlman, H., Dahlström, A., and Nyhus, L.M. (1982). Ultrastructural observations in the rat ileal mucosa of possible epithelial 'taste cells' and submucosal sensory neurons. *Acta Physiologica Scandinavica*, **114**, 161–4.

Nicolaïdis, S. (1978). Rôle des réflexes anticipateurs oro-végétatifs dans la régulation hydrominérale et énergétique. *Journal de Physiologie* (*Paris*), **74**, 1–29.

Niijima, A. (1969). Afferent discharges from osmoreceptors in the liver of the guinea-pig. *Science*, **166**, 1519–20.

Niijima, A. (1982). Glucose-sensitive afferent fibres in the hepatic branch of the vagus nerve in the guinea-pig. *Journal of Physiology* (*London*), **332**, 315–23.

Niijima, A. (1989). Nervous regulation of metabolism. *Progress in Neurobiology,* **33**, 135–47.

Oomura, Y. (1980). Input–output organization in the hypothalamus relating to food intake behavior. In *Handbook of the hypothalamus,* Vol. 2, P.J. Morgane and J. Panksepp (eds.), M. Dekker, New York, pp. 557–620.

Oomura, Y., Ooyama, H., Sugimori, M., Nakamura, T., and Yamada, Y. (1974). Glucose inhibition of the glucose-sensitive neurones in the rat lateral hypothalamus. *Nature,* **247**, 284–6.

Paintal, A.S. (1973). Vagal sensory receptors and their reflex effects. *Physiological Reviews,* **53**, 159–226.

Rawson, R.O. and Quick, K.P. (1972). Localisation of intra-abdominal thermoreceptors in the ewe. *Journal of Physiology (London),* **222**, 665–77.

Read, N.W. (1992). Role of gastrointestinal factors in hunger and satiety in man. *Proceedings of the Nutrition Society,* **51**, 7–11.

Riedel, W. (1976). Warmth receptors in the dorsal abdominal wall of the rabbit. *Pflügers Archiv,* **361**, 205–6.

Shillabeer, G. and Davison, J.S. (1987). Endogenous and exogenous cholecystokinin may reduce food intake by different mechanisms. *American Journal of Physiology,* **253**, R379–82.

Silver, A.J., Flood, J.F., Song, A.M., and Morley, J.E. (1989). Evidence for a physiological role for CCK in the regulation of food intake in mice. *American Journal of Physiology,* **256**, R646–52.

Tordoff, M.G. and Friedman, M.I. (1986). Hepatic portal glucose infusions decrease food intake preference. *American Journal of Physiology,* **251**, R192–6.

Trub, M. and Mei, N. (1991). Effects of periodontal stimulation on VMH neurones in anesthetized rats. *Brain Research Bulletin,* **27**, 29–34.

Welch, I.Mc .L., Sepple, C., and Read, N.W. (1988). Comparisons of the effect of infusion of lipid into the jejunum on eating behaviour and satiety in man. *Gut,* **29**, 306–11.

Yettefti, Y., El Ouazzani, T., Himmi, T., and Perrin, J. (1992). Etude électrophysiologique et immunocytochimique d'une région du bulbe postérieur sensible aux hyperglycémies modérées. *Archives Internationales de Physiologie de Biochimie et de Biophysique,* **100**, A 135.

Young, A. and Levin, R.J. (1989). The rat distal ileum has a reduced absorptive and secretary capacity compared with proximal ileum—is it to facilitate its chemosensing function? *Quarterly Journal of Experimental Physiology,* **74**, 561–3.

5

Small objects of desire: the recognition of appropriate foods and drinks and its neural mechanisms

D.A. Booth, E.L. Gibson, Anne-Marie Toase, and R.P.J. Freeman

INTRODUCTION

A person's or an animal's desire to eat a piece of food and/or to have a drink is normally a highly skilled cognitive performance. Those familiar with such objects as an apple or a piece of chocolate instantly recognize them as deliciously edible materials. A regular purchaser of a brand of beer knows that what comes from the barrel or bottle is not just potable but highly desirable when it's time for a drink.

The appetite for food and drink is often more capacious, though. What is then desired is a collection of several items in a larger, more complex object, sometimes called a dish, which may be the whole or part of a meal or of a course in a meal. Only certain sets of materials are recognized by human adults as proper meals. Some items of food and drink are more appropriate than others to include in a certain dish or meal.

The cognitive approach to ingestive behaviour is based on this concept of recognizing certain materials as objects of greater or lesser desire, often indeed contingently on the context of other materials, social and physical environment, and bodily state. As we shall see, the theory of recognition mechanisms in the mind (conscious and subconscious) is capable of being applied at any level of analysis, from the patterns of information extracted from stimulation of a specific type of sensory receptor by a foodstuff to the historical concept of the appropriate menu, ambience, and guest list for a birthday party or religious festival.

MAKING A MEAL OF IT

A meal is an elaborate social construct. The collation of materials into a dish, and even the arrangement of items on the plate, can reflect strong cultural determinants. Indeed, it has been said that social background is most clearly identifiable from a person's food preferences.

Meals are more, too, than complex, purely physicochemical objects or combinations of materials. A meal can also have symbolic meaning and serve interpersonal functions, for example in hospitality, celebrations, and indeed everyday caring for a household. Even the routine occasions for eating and drinking are fitted to personally habitual and culturally meaningful physical or interpersonal contexts, such as time of day or season of the year and what sort of other person is present or how many others there are. High-quality strawberry ice-cream served as the main course would be an insult and probably quite repulsive except to an unsophisticated child.

The social structuring and occasioning of meals in Western cultures have been studied to some extent by historians, anthropologists, and sociologists (e.g. Mennell, Murcott, and van Otterloo, 1992; Murcott, 1983). The eating and drinking occasions on which we spend almost a fifth of our waking lives (Booth, 1987a) have yet, however, to engage the research interest of any body of psychologists in mainstream areas such as visual object recognition or episodic and semantic memory. Indeed, the scientific study of causal processes within an individual's eating of a meal has hardly begun, even in food research or nutrition (Booth, Freeman and Lähteenmäki, 1991).

Deciding what to eat and drink in a meal

The social conventions for meal sizes and timings may be adapted to the average physiological requirements within a culture (Booth and Mather, 1978), subject to constraints on when people can get together to eat (and perhaps prepare the meal). Nevertheless, research has been unduly confined to measuring total dietary 'intake' (that is the weights of foods of known composition) at meals or even over fixed periods of time that may not relate to eating occasions. Moreover, the common practice in human nutrition is to estimate daily food intakes and throw away data on the, often crucial, differences between meals throughout the day.

Even the measurement of food intake at a meal disregards the processes by which people or other animals recognize items of food and drink and decide whether and what to eat or drink next. So, it is not relevantly objective to measure intakes of nutrients or of the estimated yield of energy to metabolism, rather than the factors that change food selection from moment to moment. Also, the usual data on food choices or intakes over periods of more than a minute or so are likely to miss these changes in ingestive decision dynamics as the meal approaches, progresses and recedes into the past. Such limited observational data preclude the elucidation of the actual causal factors sensed in the foodstuffs and in the wider ecological and physiological contexts. It is the behavioural expression of the cognitive processing of these factors as they change that results in the amounts of foods and nutrients that are cumulatively ingested on an occasion and across occasions over a day (Booth, 1972, 1980).

Other primates readily learn to recognize the attractions and satisfactions of a source of calories having a particular appearance and taste (Burton, Rolls, and Mora, 1976) or of the flavours given to more or less concentrated syrups of glucose polymers (Booth and Grinker, 1993). In other words, food is not just liked for eating; it is also expected to be nutritious, hunger-satisfying, or filling.

These two lines of research also opened up some of the neural processes at the basis of eating choices during meals. Firstly, shortly after the first demonstration of caloric conditioning of preferences in mammals (Booth, Lovett, and McSherry, 1972), learned food-specific recognition neurones were found on diencephalic pathways in the monkey that habituated out in the same way as ingestion of the preferred food did during the meal (Burton et al., 1976; Rolls, this volume). Secondly, the learned control of meal size according to the glucose-polymer level in a specific menu, achieved both by rats (Booth and Davis, 1973) and by people (Booth, Lee, and McAleavey, 1976), depends on a low level of adrenergic arousal in a region of the anterior hypothalamus (Gibson and Booth, 1986b; Matthews, Gibson, and Booth, 1985). Both these sets of neurones are presumably on pathways from the limbic and neocortical regions that integrate sensory information through learned network connections (Rolls, 1989, 1993).

Those behavioural analyses indicate minimally complex ways in which our humble commensal the rat can acquire the ability to make complicated choices among food materials that are nutritionally adaptive. The rat's cognitive skills with foodstuffs are most clearly seen, although with many idiosyncrasies, when a long-term choice is given between sufficiently palatable artifical diets that are equally calorific and adequate in vitamins and minerals but either rich or poor in protein content (Baker, Booth, Duggan, and Gibson, 1987; Booth, 1974; Leathwood and Ashley, 1983). The 'search images' for food in many vertebrate species are probably at least fine-tuned by learning about nutrients, although there is behavioural and neurophysiological evidence that quite complex perceptual integration is achieved without learning in some invertebrates (Simpson et al., 1991).

This means, as we shall see in detail below, that intakes or ratings of recognizable foodstuffs do not assess 'satiety' for calories or 'selection' among nutrients such as protein, carbohydrate, and fat. Post-ingestional satiety mechanisms or nutrient-specific motivation cannot be measured in people or experimental animals without factoring out perceptions of, and beliefs about, the dietary materials whose energy or macronutrient contents have been calculated or prepared.

LEARNED APPETITES AND SATIETIES

A cognitive–perceptual approach to ingestive behaviour was initiated 20 years ago with evidence for learning from the nutritional after-effects of eating, both to like a particular level of sweetness or of other food qualities and also to control the amount in a meal on a particular menu. Post-ingestional effects of foodstuffs associatively conditioned both sensory preference/aversion and sensory–visceral interaction in overall appetite and satiation.

These phenomena were substantiated first in laboratory rats on experimental diets (preference: Booth, 1974; Booth, Lovett, and McSherry, 1972; Booth and Simson, 1971; Booth, Stoloff, and Nicholls, 1974; Simson and Booth, 1973; satiety: Booth, 1972, 1977, 1980; Booth and Davis, 1973; Gibson and Booth, 1989). The work was then extended to people eating more or less normal foods (Booth, Lee, and McAleavey, 1976; Booth, Mather, and Fuller, 1982; Booth and Toase, 1983). Evidence for the same sort of learning of amount to eat on an occasion has also been obtained from monkeys (Booth and Grinker, 1993) and from young children (Birch and Deysher, 1985, 1986, and other experiments reviewed by Birch, 1990). Nutritionally conditioned sensory preferences have since been demonstrated in rats by many groups (reviewed by Booth, 1985; see also Sclafani, 1990). Flavour preferences have been conditioned by carbohydrate and by fat in toddlers (Birch, McPhee, Steinberg, and Sullivan, 1990) and by protein in adults (Gibson, Wainwright, and Booth, 1992).

Nutritional evaluation

The experiments in adult human beings, as well as in monkeys and rats, showed that the appropriateness of eating a particular food can be recognized relative to the state of bodily depletion or repletion. As a result of past learning, the momentary strength of desire for a piece of that food depends on the emptiness or fullness of the digestive tract (Gibson and Booth, 1989).

This brings out a crucial difference between learned appetite and unlearned influences on behaviour, such as ingestion, that has been neglected by all branches of research, including even psychology. The disposition to consume foods, that is, hunger, depends on how much is in the stomach but, to the extent that control of eating has been learned, it also depends on each food that is available, to the extent that the signals from the stomach have been reinforced by eating that food. In contrast, despite two decades of evidence for learned appetite for food, most people still think of hunger and satiety as being proportional to the emptiness and fullness of the stomach, perhaps added to the palatability of the given food. Gibson and Booth (1989) confirmed the truth of the interpretation given to the early data (Booth and Davis, 1973), that a liking for a food flavour that had been acquired when the gut was full disappeared when the gut was empty (Fig. 5.1(a)), rather than being amplified, as has traditionally been assumed. It is a particular level of distension that has been conditioned to facilitate ingestion of that flavour.

In other cases, where inhibition has been conditioned with nutrient in the digestive tract (e.g. Gibson and Booth, 1987), one must therefore allow for the possibility that the cue is a particular level of distension. This is the simplest explanation of the fact that some of us some of the time feel satisfied at the end of a meal while there is far less in the stomach than may be needed to obtain a clear sensation of fullness on other occasions. We (and the rats) recognize our visceral state as being sufficiently similar to the degree of fullness from that menu that avoided any discomfort or overfullness.

The desire for food is generally assumed to have its physiological basis in the fuel that its ingestion yields to tissues, although there is a remarkable dearth of direct evidence. There is some evidence for some nutrient-specific appetites, although this is also very limited.

It has been suggested that mammals learn to distinguish sources of water from sources of food soon after weaning (Booth, 1979; Hall, 1991) and can learn throughout life which food made more demands on water balance than others (Fitzsimons and Le Magnen, 1969). Despite that, the neuroscientists of thirst are apparently unshakably certain that recognition of water when needed is an innate skill, despite their mystification as to the adequate stimulus (Norgren, 1991) and the absence of any ontogenic evidence for water-specific selection during a deficit specifically of water (Booth, 1991b; Hall, 1991).

Hunger can be suppressed via oxidation of the carbon in carbohydrate, fat, alcohol, or protein (Langhans and Scharrer, 1992) or their actions on receptors in the gut (Read, 1992), but the craving for energy (if that is hunger's physiological objective) may not usually distinguish between carbohydrate and fat or other energy sources. Nevertheless, different energy substrates may act to varying extents on different detector systems. For example, rats seems to vary around the clock in the proportions of carbohydrate and fat (as well as of protein)

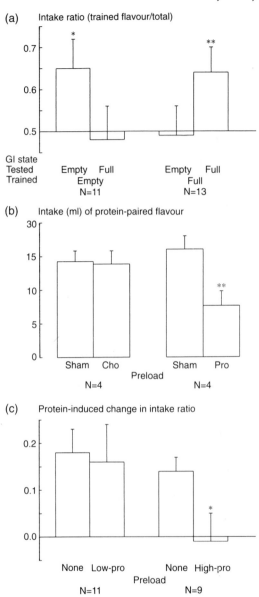

Fig. 5.1 Generalization gradients for somatic stimuli. (a) Dependency of calorically conditioned flavour preference in rats on the level of gastrointestinal distension in which the conditioning occurred. (From Gibson and Booth, 1989.) (b) and (c) Dependency of protein-conditioned flavour acceptance on the lack of protein intake during which learning was induced (b) in rats (from Gibson and Booth, 1986) and (c) in people (data summarized by Gibson *et al.*, 1992). Learned preference is shown by an increase in the ratio of intake of the flavour previously paired with protein to total intake (intake ratio).

that they select, and the dietary selections are modulated by central injection specifically to drug and site (Leibowitz *et al.*, 1985). So it may be possible to establish carbohydrate-specific and fat-specific appetites by learning.

There is no solid evidence to back the widespread presumption that sweetness is an innate signal for calories. Indeed, it has been suggested instead that sugars are super-releasers by which plants exploit a mammalian reflex whose real function is to prevent infants from spitting out what otherwise might be highly aversive nitrogenous compounds in mother's milk (Booth, 1990). After weaning, such a reflex would be vestigial. Unfortunately for the teeth of modern children (and of commensal pets and vermin) and the waistlines of adults, sucrose and other sugars have become cheap enough to provide longlasting portable food items for nibbling away from meals: these objects are desired when novel because they stimulate the ingestive reflex and then cravings for their sweetness, crispness, or creaminess, and other sensory characteristics, are reinforced as the items become familiar.

Besides water and calories, there is remarkably little firm evidence for nutrient-specific appetites (or satieties)—that is to say, ingestion (or rejection) that is evaluated in the light of nutrient-specific bodily states as well as nutrient-specific sensory cues from foodstuffs. There is a taste-facilitated innate sodium appetite in rats, that is, sodium deficit increases the desire for salty tastes, independently of learning. Evidence for a need-dependent avidity for saltiness in people, learned or unlearned, remains inconclusive, however (Beauchamp, 1987; Huggins *et al.*, 1992).

There is certainly a learned protein-specific appetite in the rat (Baker *et al.*, 1987; Gibson and Booth, 1986a): rats learn to like a taste, smell or texture in the presence of an incipient amino acid deficit when those sensory and metabolic cues have been paired even just once with rectification of that deficit (Fig. 5.1(b)). Omission of protein from a single meal is sufficient to set up both the motivating bodily cue of depletion and the associatively reinforcing effect of repletion. In people, just a low-protein breakfast provides all the metabolic signals necessary to acquire and perform the recognition processes of a protein-specific appetite at lunchtime (Fig. 5.1(c); Gibson *et al.*, 1992 and submitted).

Social and emotional values

The desire for familiar items of food and drink has social bases as well as nutritional ones. Rodents' eating can be socially reinforced and informed (Galef and Wigmore, 1983). Young children switch their preferences to the foods that their playmates (Birch, 1980) or heroes (Lowe, 1992) are eating. Young people of all ages like to drink what their friends are drinking. Certain foods and drinks have symbolic values: it does not feel right to many people to give a toast with a non-alcoholic drink.

Furthermore, an object of ingestive desire can be set up by personal emotional experience.

Many drinks and some foods are taken as tonics or medicaments. The toning up may be social, such as alcohol to raise the party spirits or a cup of tea to refresh a visitor. The benefit may be intellectual, to help one concentrate on a mental task. Some constituents may indeed act on the brain, although probably mildly and non-specifically. This encourages the sociability or mental effort that the occasion calls for. Thus, a stronger and more specific effect is created by an autosuggestive process and becomes expected of that drink in that situation (Booth, French, and Gatherer, 1992).

More obviously, affluent societies generate conflict between social and nutritional values of food. A source of fuel is also a source of stigma. The pleasures of eating conflict with the dangers to shape. The naughtiness of the 'naughty but nice' chocolate eclair may make it even nicer. Certainly, restraining oneself from eating a food regarded as a danger to a socially approved bodily shape will increase the craving for that food and make the temptation harder to resist. (This at least is one likely process; see Jansen, this volume, for other possibilities.) As a result, a dieter is sooner or later liable to lapse when food is readily available and will start eating the very thing that should be avoided. The pleasures of eating, its short-term countering of anxiety and guilt about the eating, and the nutrients to cover the self-deprivation will all reinforce future eating of such foods, perhaps especially when in the same emotional and physiological state. With repetition, the binge will become larger or at least feel more and more out of control.

This is not to suggest that convenience foods can be blamed for eating disorders, any more than pubs and off-licences can be blamed for alcoholism. The marketing of foods and drinks with an explicit or implicit promise of weight loss and an attractive shape, such as 'diet' drinks, 'slim' meal replacements and even small or fat-reduced meal portions when called 'lean', has some responsibility for unsuccessful dieting, however, just as the advertising of (also 'slim') low-tar cigarettes for young women must take the blame for subsequent increases in respiratory cancer and cardiovascular disease. (Appetites for nicotine and other drugs, and indeed for the pleasures of sex, are considered in other chapters in this book; they should all be susceptible to this cognitive approach.)

FOOD RECOGNITION PERFORMANCE

An appetite for food and drink is therefore a desire to ingest small objects or pieces of materials that have acquired personal significance from familiarity, nutritional benefit, and social and emotional value. Eating and drinking normally follow from recognizing edible or potable materials as foods or drinks that are appropriate to the situation. That is, these small objects of desire, a piece of food or a mouthful of a drink, are often thoroughly contextualized. Hunger and thirst (the appetites specifically for foods and drinks, respectively) are driven by the momentary palatability of what is in the mouth in context of items on the plate and a current physiological state of incipient deficit, and a social and physical environment where such eating and/or drinking is meaningful.

Human and other mammalian ingestive appetite is thus a sophisticated cognitive performance, even when it is habitual and non-deliberative. Information from the patterns of stimulation provided by foods and contexts is signalled over channels that transform the information into selective movements and acts. This viewpoint provides powerful methods for qualitative and quantitative investigation of the causal processes involved in ingestive behaviour, first at the cognitive level but, on that basis, then at the physiological level and at the cultural level, too. The neural bases of human appetite for food and drink must involve integration within and among sensory modalities and with linguistic information and then the relay of the output from those food recognition networks to the sensorimotor control of sucking, chewing, and swallowing, as well as to behaviour instrumental in bringing food to the mouth.

The basic principle of the cognitive approach is that strength of appetite depends on the closeness of the current situation to the learned object and context of desire (Fig. 5.2). A food item is more likely to be sought and ingested the less discriminable the whole situation is for the eater from the combination of stimuli at levels to which maximum facilitation of ingestion has been learned (Booth, 1977, 1986; Booth, Thompson, and Shahedian, 1983). In other words, appetite for food (and indeed any other form of learned motivation) declines in proportion to the distance from maximum motivation to eat. The strength of the learned reaction is proportional to the situation's similarity to the ideal configuration of features of the object of desire in its context.

This recognition of dissimilarity between a test stimulus and the learned stimulus is what psychologists of learned behaviour call a stimulus generalization decrement (Shepard, 1957): the further apart

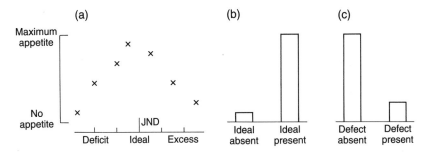

Fig. 5.2 The appetite triangle, quantitative and categorial: the strength of appetite or desire declines with the size of difference of a feature of the object from the individual's ideal. (a) Notional data showing graded decrements in appetite with increasing deficit or excess in strength of the feature. (b) Presence and absence of a feature in the ideal object, for example normally flavoured versus unflavoured. (c) Presence and absence of a feature foreign to the ideal object, for example a food taint, an inappropriate context, or some other defect.

the test and learned stimuli are in their parameters, the less the learned response generalizes to the test stimulus; the more weakly it is evoked. Some appetizing features of a food can deviate from ideal in being too strong or too weak, for example its saltiness or hardness. This gives a peaked generalization or similarity function, familiar as the inverted U of the hedonic curve. However, if we can scale the stimulus feature in a way that gives a linear decline in generalization or similarity, we can then describe the characteristics of this elemental cognitive process in appetite as an isosceles triangle (Fig. 5.2, left-hand graph). Where the maximum or minimum conceivable level of a feature of the food or appetitive context is ideal (maximally motivating), then only one limb of the appetite triangle exists (Fig. 5.2, middle and right-hand histograms). Indeed, if a stimulus may only be present or absent, or two qualitatively distinct stimuli are compared, then only the peak and one base of the appetite triangle can exist (although responses may distribute themselves along that limb if the discrimination is probabilistic).

This may seem a rather mechanical analysis of the pleasures of eating and drinking. Yet it merely takes seriously the assumption that would be made by any science that the people or animals involved in such experiences and activities are systems of causal processes (Booth, 1991*a*). The cognitive aspect of ingestive behaviour is the causally effective transformation of information by an eater, as distinct from the physical aspect of mechanical forces, electrical charges, and chemical reactions in brain and environment and from the exchange of money, supply of foods, and arrangements for company at meals in societal systems.

Empirical basis

We now turn to a few specific examples of objects of ingestive desire, from the most atomic category of a taste to the most contextualized and multifactorial situation of an item in a meal. One piece of evidence will be considered for each of these levels of cognitive processing in the appetite for food.

DESIRE FOR A PARTICULAR LEVEL OF A TASTE

The innate reaction to sweetness is to ingest the material more enthusiastically the more strongly it tastes of sucrose. This is the output from a brainstem reflex that also produces licking and smacking the lips and a slight smile in human infants (taken by some as a sign of pleasure, as distinct from ingestive facilitation, although this can be questioned—see Booth, 1991b). In the first experiments to demonstrate caloric conditioning of flavour preferences (Booth, Lovett, and McSherry, 1972), it was found that rats could be trained to prefer whatever level of sweetness was associated with more calories. Indeed, an aversion could be conditioned to the stronger of two sweet tastes if it was associated with the discomfort produced by drinking a concentrated sugar solution. Thus a rat could be trained to prefer a lower sweetness over a higher one, the reverse of the innate preference.

As a result of learning, therefore, palatability is not a fixed property of the food, nor is it a graded property of the strength of flavouring, any more than learned hunger or satiety are graded properties of visceral cues. This was in fact demonstrated by equally old results showing that flavour and fullness together could acquire control of ingestion (Booth, 1972; Booth and Davis, 1973): the desire for the flavour depends on the degree of fullness.

Again, the point is that the learning is to recognize a particular level of sweetness as most appropriate to eat or reject, just as a particular level of gastric distension might be learned to be appropriate to stop eating or a certain level of gastrointestinal motility triggered by emptiness might be learned as appropriate to start eating. Indeed, internal and external cues at particular levels are also likely to have become appropriate to eating or stopping, perhaps on certain foods only. For example, awareness that the clocks are saying about 1 p.m. may be highly appetizing and yet, not only is 11.30 a.m. less so, but also 2.30 p.m. is a time of less hunger: an important trick in fasting is to get past mealtimes without succumbing. Someone used to leaving a little on the plate may be happiest to stop eating with that amount there, and not to eat it all up, rather than to leave a greater amount. After breakfast cereal for lunch, people do not feel so satisfied in mid-afternoon as after a normal lunch menu (Kramer *et al.*, 1992).

Quantitative implications

The most appropriate sweetness, time, or gastric stretch is remembered and compared with whatever is present. If it is similar enough, then the learned response will to some degree generalize to that situation and the person or animal will be somewhat disposed to act accordingly (Fig. 5.2).

This psychological distance between the object of strongest desire and the one that is on offer should therefore be inversely proportional to the strength of the appetite, at least so long as the distance is not too great for the similarity to be plausible. There is indeed a linear decline in an individual's food preference both above and below the personally preferred level of taste (Booth *et al.*, 1983; Conner *et al.*, 1988) or texture (Booth and Conner, 1991). Moreover, the slopes are numerically the same while, of course, being opposite in sign (Conner, 1991; Conner and Booth, 1992).

That is to say, the traditional lopsided inverted U of the hedonic curve is an artefact. The effects of influences on pleasure, when measured properly in psychological distances (that is, scaled in just noticeable differences, JNDs) in a real piece of behaviour (by one person, not fogging the picture by grouping data), form the inverted V of the 'appetite triangle' (Booth, 1986; Fig. 2).

This cognitive element in appetite provides a quantitative theory that can handle interactions between features, including contextualization of appetite and faults in design of meals or ambience. When a food flavour combines with a contextual factor, for example, the responses to that two-dimensional integration lie on the surface of a cone. If a contextual factor is held constant at an imperfect level, then the triangle or cone will be truncated. Nevertheless, any two levels of an influence on appetite that differ in their distance from the ideal point will produce a difference in response that reflects the underlying symmetrically peaked function. These principles of multidimensional appetite are now illustrated by the results of experiments on human eating.

PHYSIOLOGICALLY APPROPRIATE FOOD-SPECIFIC SATIATION

First we shall consider a piece of qualitative evidence for the integration of food stimuli with visceral states in recognizing the context in which to stop eating: as a result of learning, different flavour qualities become liked in the categorially distinct states before and after a meal (Booth and Toase, 1983). This study showed that people can acquire flavour preferences that depend on how full they feel, just like rats (Booth and Davis, 1973; Gibson and Booth, 1989) and monkeys (Booth and Grinker, 1993). In addition, the results indicated that aspects of a person's eating habits further modulate this joint recognition of dietary and visceral cues.

Two groups of female campus staff were taken through a one-trial learning design that had been adapted from the previous demonstrations of conditioned desatiation and conditioned appetite in animals (Booth, 1977, 1980) and people (Booth et al., 1976, 1982). From the earlier results, it was predicted that, when a person was full, the effects of dilute carbohydrate would condition a greater liking than would those of a concentrated solution of glucose polymers, because the latter were liable to create oversatiation which can condition a flavour aversively in the full state (Gibson and Booth, 1986b). In contrast, concentrated glucose polymers before a meal should condition a greater preference than dilute carbohydrate does (Booth et al., 1972, 1982; Booth and Davis, 1973) and this, too, can be configured with the empty state of the gut into a food-appetite Gestalt (Gibson and Booth, 1989).

One set of women ($N = 40$), including non-dieters and successful and unsuccessful dieters, was trained on four successive days 30 minutes before a standard version of their normal lunch; another set ($N = 24$), also dieters and non-dieters, was trained 30 minutes after (Fig. 5.3). For each main group, there were two training days on which participants were required to eat a 100 ml portion of yoghurt. In one training session, a participant ate a cartonful of yoghurt that had been flavoured with an unusual mixture of two types of fruit and spiked with glucose polymers to make it extra-rich in readily digested carbohydrate (CHO). On the other training day, she ate the same amount of yoghurt but it was differently flavoured and had been thickened with calorie-free cellulose gum to make it low in CHO but similar to the high-CHO version to look at and feel. In each group, half the women had the high-CHO yoghurt on the first training day and half on the second. Also, as many women had a particular flavour in the high-CHO yoghurt as had it with low-CHO.

The effects of training on appetite were measured by comparing ratings of the pleasantness of eating a spoonful of each of the two flavours of yoghurt on the day before the two training days with ratings on the day after training, both before and after lunch in both sets of participants. To rate a flavour, a spoonful was eaten of a mixture of equal volumes of high- and low-CHO versions and a line marked between 'not at all pleasant for me to eat right now' and 'as pleasant to eat as I can

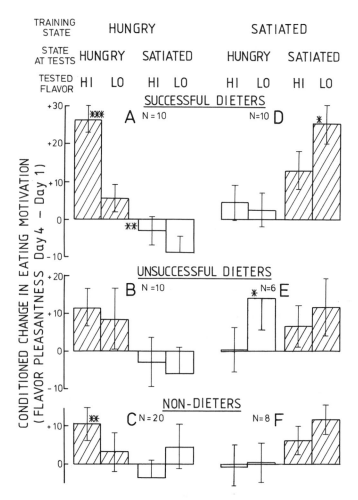

Fig. 5.3 Increases in the pleasantness of flavours of a single yoghurt mixture after their association during depletion ('hunger', before lunch: panels A–C) or repletion ('satiety', after lunch: panels D–F) with the effects of disguised high- or low-carbohydrate (CHO) versions of the yoghurt, in relatively successful (panels A and D) or unsuccessful (panels B and E) female dieters or non-dieters (panels C and F). ***$p<0.01$, **$p<0.02$, *$p<0.05$. Data summarized by Booth and Toase (1983) and Booth (1985).

imagine' (later scored from zero to 100). The conditioning of an increase in pleasantness would be seen as a rise in the rating score from Day 1 to Day 4 (the ordinates in Fig. 5.3). In an overall analysis of the group trained and tested before lunch, there was clearly the expected increase in pleasantness score of the high-starch flavour, mean difference = 8.6, SE of difference = 3.0, paired $t(39) = 2.87, p < 0.01$ (sub-groups A, B, and C, Fig. 5.3). Conversely, the group trained after lunch acquired more of an appetite for the low-starch flavour in their state at that time, overall mean increase = 7.6, $SE = 3.3$, t (23) = 2.32, $p < 0.05$.

Furthermore, these increases in liking for the flavoured yoghurt associated with the optimum degree of repletion were perceptually integrated with the state in which they were acquired. The pleasantness rating did not recognize the object of desire when the flavour was tested on the opposite side of lunch to that in which appetite had been trained (Fig. 5.3). The expected generalization decrement between lunchtime-related states for the group trained before lunch was confirmed by a mean difference of 9.4, difference $SE = 4.0$, paired $t(39) = 2.36$, one-tailed $p < 0.025$. In the set of women trained after lunch, the lack of similarity in state gave a mean pleasantness difference of 9.9, $SE = 5.7$, $t(23) = 1.76$, $p < 0.05$ (one-tailed). These means represent the heights of the appetite triangles acquired by the individuals under each sort of training condition; no other comparisons provide a measure of a mechanism theoretically involved and so an overall ANOVA would be an invalidly exploratory strategy.

Thus, the control of the pleasantness change by the flavour difference was statistically as complete as that by the visceral difference and it was also not dissimilar numerically (Booth, 1985). That is to say, after such perceptual learning, satiety and hunger are as completely under oral control as under visceral control. This is of the nature of multifeature object recognition or configural learning: the effects of cues are not additive and, indeed, recognition may be absolutely dependent on each of them. The standard notion of satiety subtracting from palatability is therefore unrealistic to normal appetite, in so far as it has been learned (Booth, 1977, 1987a). This also exposes the fallacy of using the caloric intakes resulting from choices among familiar foods in efforts to measure either the satiating power or the stable palatability of a material. Yet this was the practice in dietary investigations of both people and experimental animals before the importance of learning in normal appetite was demonstrated. Extraordinarily enough, this practice has become more frequent over the last decade and is even offered as a standard technique for research into satiety. No inhibitory or facilitatory process on food or drink choice or intake can be measured without identifying separately the momentary sensory, physiological, and ecological influences on the cognitive integration that controls the observed dietary behaviour.

Learned satiation in dieting

After the end of the satiety-conditioning experiment (Booth and Toase, 1983), each participant completed a dietary restraint questionnaire (Herman and Polivy, 1980), reported her maximum body weight and her personal target for weight, and was weighed on a beam scale. The median score for restraint was 15 and those scoring higher were classified as dieters. These dieters were sub-classified as successful or unsuccessful according to whether they had lost more or less than half the difference between their reported maximum and target weights.

Successful dieters showed the strongest and most complete recognition of food flavour and nutritional state. The high-CHO flavour increased in preference more than the low-CHO flavour did in the group trained before lunch, as predicted (Fig. 5.3, top far left-hand panel). The reverse happened in the successful dieters in the group trained after lunch (Fig. 5.3, top far right-hand panel). Moreover, these conditioned flavour preferences in the successful dieters depended entirely on the internal state at testing (Fig. 5.3, top centre panels). Non-dieters showed a similar pattern of differential response to both flavouring and visceral status, albeit possibly not so strong (Fig. 5.3, bottom panels). Dieters who had not succeeded in holding weight down as much as halfway to their target did not acquire the configural percepts at all, however (Fig. 5.3, middle four panels). In one group (E), the flavours were conditioned but the response generalized from training state to the untrained state, that is, the pre- and post-lunch states were not discriminated: these women appeared to confuse bodily and episodic signals of hunger and satiety. (One possibility is that their meal was so small that there was little difference). The other group of unsuccessful dieters distinguished between before and after lunch but did not learn different reactions to the two flavours. (Perhaps they were not sufficiently affected by the aftereffects of the training yoghurts because of their eating habits.) These results open the possibility that unsuccessful dieting induces poor desatiation conditioning. Instead or as well, such learning deficits might contribute to difficulties in keeping weight off.

A part of this design has been run in rats with control specifically of visceral state. This was not achieved in the human study because, although the gut was filled by eating a meal, people can also anticipate and remember the amount and time of food ingestion. To exclude such possibilities for rats, Gibson and Booth (1989) tubed them with a non-nutritive fluid to fill the stomach and upper intestine. Just as in the human experiment, the liking for CHO-paired flavour depended on reinstating the trained visceral state (Fig. 5.1(a)). Since rats can therefore learn to recognize fullness and emptiness of the gut, we can be sure that people are capable of learning the sensations that are induced or prevented by distension and the foods that are appropriate to eat when full or empty. Nevertheless, it should be noted that human studies of gastrointestinal control of hunger and satiety sensations and visceral control of the desire for particular foods have yet to succeed in dissociating out the effects of memory and expectation (Booth, 1989, 1992*a*).

Conditioned satiety and emotional eating

Relative preferences or aversions can be conditioned to flavours combined with visceral cues. That is, when an aversion is controlled by internal cues produced as a result of ingestion earlier in a meal, we have a food-specific conditioned satiety.

It turns out that we have a lead into the neural bases of this sort of learned satiation. The neurotransmitter noradrenaline has long been known to have a dramatic effect on food intake in rats. When agonists to a sub-class of adrenergic receptors are injected close to the paraventricular nucleus in the rostral hypothalamus of the sated rat, the animal takes a meal (Booth, 1967) and a rat that is already eating consumes more than it does after control injection (Ritter and Epstein, 1975). This effect is widely thought to be some interference with the satiating effects of eating. Certainly no effects on unlearned or learned sensory preferences or aversions have been found that could explain this increased intake; rather, learned sensory control of eating towards the end of the meal is implicated (Matthews *et al.*, 1985).

The effect is not on satiety generally, though, nor on the strong post-ingestional signals produced by the meal that the rat eats after control injection (Gibson and Booth, 1986*b*). When, however, this meal-eliciting injection is tested on a conditioned fullness-dependent flavour aversion in rats, the noradrenaline in this location completely disrupts the learned recognition of the appropriateness of the conjunction of the food and the bodily state to the stopping of eating (Gibson and Booth, 1987).

Nutrient-specific satiation?

In this experiment on aversion-blockade by hypothalamic noradrenaline, the digestive tract was filled with concentrated glucose polymers, not non-nutritive fluid as in Gibson and Booth's (1989) demonstration of mechanoreceptor cues in appetite/satiety conditioning (Fig. 5.1(a)).

Therefore, the visceral cues could have arisen from glucoreceptors as well as, or instead of, mechanoreceptors. Indeed, natural satiation might also be conditioned to chemospecific stimulation of the gut wall. If so, rats brought up on laboratory chow, which is predominantly starch, could well have learned food aversions that depend on intestinal glucoreceptor stimulation. Then the conditioned satiation will be specific to meals including familiarly formulated starch products or sugars containing glucose (such as sucrose). Also, its disruption by noradrenaline would tend to increase the size of meals on carbohydrate-rich diets selectively, a sort of carbohydrate-specific appetite that is limited to the later parts of meals. Carbohydrate selectivity of noradrenaline-elicited meals has indeed been observed (Leibowitz *et al.*, 1985).

Learning of nutrient-specific appetite has been clearly demonstrated in rats (Fig. 5.1(b); Baker *et al.*, 1987; Gibson and Booth, 1986*a*) and people (Fig. 5.1(c)) but, from the time required after protein administration for the signal of lack of protein to be removed, intestinal chemoreception is not involved in that case and the signals probably arise in the brain (Booth and Stribling, 1978). Nevertheless, such demonstrations of nutrient-specific dietary selection and intake require complete control and measurement of the sensory qualities of the foodstuffs used. Protein-high and protein-low (or low and high calorie, or whatever nutrient is being investigated) diets must not differ in any cues that might have innate or learned significance that is unrelated to the differences in their metabolic effects after ingestion. It is therefore not reasonable to look for evidence of nutrient-specific motivation in the intakes of familiar foodstuffs differing in nutrient contents. It is simply bogus to present the intakes of nutrients in the foods chosen from a familiar diet as evidence of nutrient selection or as nutrient intakes that are under the control of the eater.

A mechanism of emotional overeating?

This intake-eliciting synaptic field in the rostral hypothalamus is one highly localized projection of an adrenergic part of the 'arousal' system that ascends from the brainstem into the forebrain (Leibowitz, 1978). The evidence above shows that release of noradrenaline at these synapses stops the learned integration of information about the diet and the body from controlling ingestive behaviour. The post-synaptic neurones must therefore be on a pathway from olfactory afferents that has converged with a pathway from visceral receptors via some associative neurones, perhaps in limbic or neocortex. These hypothalamic neurones are so greatly inhibited or facilitated by the noradrenaline that they can no longer transmit the information that the appetite-suppressing coincidence of the flavour and state of the digestive tract has reoccurred. In psychological language, one of the effects of general arousal, in the rat at least, is to mask recognition of the circumstances in which a loss of interest in eating has been learned.

This opens up the intriguing possibility of a neural mechanism for emotional overeating. When someone's ascending adrenergic pathways are sufficiently activated, the normal learned 'boundaries' on intake could be overwhelmed. The emotions are not merely distracting attention from satiety: transmission of the conditioned satiation complex into behaviour is blocked.

SENSORILY AND SEMANTICALLY APPROPRIATE CONTEXT

Finally, we return to quantitative analysis and consider objects of desire having features which are not physical in the sense that tastes, tummies, and times of day are. These features include concepts attributed to foodstuffs (including sensory descriptions, as distinct from the percepts behind them). They are symbolic representations of the foods or drinks, either in the linguistic sense or in the cultural sense, for example as a sign of hospitality or celebration.

The above evidence provides qualitative support for the position that learned appetite depends on closeness of the whole situation to ideal levels of the sensory and somatic features influencing the disposition to ingest. A decade ago, we developed a quantitative version of this cognitive approach to appetite. This was because we had begun to tackle the problem of formulating palatable foods (Booth et al., 1983) which required measurement of cognitive performance, not just categorial demonstrations of its structure.

The food item or meal that is most desired by a person in a particular situation can only be specified if we relate the strength of the desire to eat to the quantities of the materials in a mouthful and of the conceptual attributes attached to that food in that context (externally and internally); see Figs 5.3 and 5.5. Such research into the recognition of high quality in foods and drinks has, moreover, provided the incentive and opportunity to develop in a new way the basic theory and methodology for analysis of cognitive processes and indeed the performance of any system. These principles go back a century or more in psychology, to the notions of dimensions of mind and of measuring them in just noticeable differences. The novelty is to gather the data and complete their analysis in one person at a time, before seeking to generalize. The resulting individualized multidimensional discrimination theory and analysis has been paralleled by other developments in the quantitative psychology of recognition and similarity (cf. Ashby and Perrin, 1988; Macmillan and Creelman, 1991) but these have been based largely on analyses of grouped data, which, rather paradoxically, has long been the norm in the science of individual minds.

We conclude with some examples of such quantitative evidence for the integration of the sweet taste with other material percepts and with socially based conceptual dimensions, namely calorific value attributed to the sweetener. Once again, people differing in eating habits differ in what they identify as the most desirable material to ingest.

Sensory context

Amino acids are often sweet, or bitter, or both. One of the commonest amino acids, both within proteins and in free form, is glutamic acid, which has two carboxyl groups and tastes very sour; its monosodium salt still tastes a bit sour but is also sweet and bitter, too. The most abundant mineral ion in animal and plant tissues is Na^+. Thus flesh foods and vegetables, especially when cooked, are liable to taste salty, sweet, bitter, and sour in the proportions that arise from their contents of sodium and glutamate as well as other salts and amino acids.

A pure solution of monosodium glutamate (MSG) indeed has a crude chicken-like flavour (Lovett and Booth, 1970). MSG is well-known for its use as a flavouring in Chinese food. Too much MSG spoils the taste but at lower levels it can improve the flavour of a dilute meat broth or boiled vegetables. Indeed, some delicacies in the Japanese diet contain quite high levels of glutamate and/or the similarly tasting 5'-ribonucleotides inosine and guanosine monophosphates (IMP and GMP), broken down from plant or animal tissue RNA. So, MSG can be used to improve the flavour of more mundane foods to the Japanese palate. The Japanese word for deliciousness has been used in the term 'umami' to promote this taste by the brewers of MSG.

We are testing the hypothesis that some English people have learned to recognize a mixture of tastes of sodium and glutamate that recurs in many foods eaten in the main courses of meals. These foods are known in British English as 'savoury'. So we examined the effects of various levels of MSG on the rated closeness of the savoury taste to the individual eater's preference in mouthfuls of chicken soup: this person's liking for the taste was closely controlled by MSG concentration ratios (Fig. 5.4(a)). (Ratios of tastant concentrations are usually equally discriminable, that is, give a constant value of the just noticeable difference (JND), and so the logarithm of concentration is likely to be a good scale of psychological distance, that is, to give a linear dissimilarity function as in Fig. 5.2.) Then we varied the levels of sodium chloride, sucrose, citric acid, and caffeine independently in mixtures of the four compounds in mouthful samples of the soup and again got this person to rate how close to ideal was the savoury taste, and also the salty, sweet, sour, and bitter tastes. We found that a four-dimensional combination of the JND-scaled distances of the four tastants from each of their ideal levels accounted for savoury ratings at

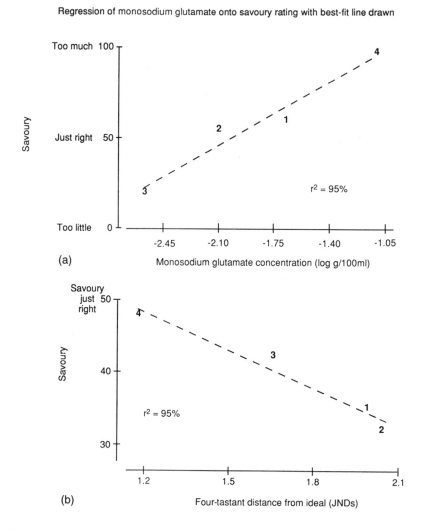

Fig. 5.4 Differences from the individual assessor's ideal for savoury taste in sample mouthfuls of a chicken soup containing different concentrations of (a) monosodium glutamate or (b) sodium chloride, sucrose, citric acid and caffeine: r^2 square of regression coefficient, that is, proportion of variance in response accounted for by the JND-scaled levels of solute or solutes.

least as well as did MSG levels (Fig. 5.4(b)). In other words, this person was able to make an integral judgment as to how far the proportions of the four tastants in a sample departed from the complex taste that she recognized as typical of a savoury food.

Moreover, only some people were able, like this person, to recognize a savoury taste in these samples. Some other English people apparently had not learned to integrate proportions of the simple tastes into a complex integral percept of savouriness.

It should be noted that the experimental design for this discrimination measurement does not have to include a sample that exactly mimics the taste of MSG. It has been claimed that MSG is a fifth basic taste because statistically based multidimensional scaling of response similarities separates it from classic tastants and a wide variety of mixtures of them, even when the attempt is made to equate total intensities. However, this additive statistical patterning of raw responses does not adequately represent the cognitive processes in discrimination space that are actually involved in recognition of a taste or any other eating motivator.

Nevertheless, our resolution of the savoury taste of MSG into a mixture of four classic tastants does not preclude the existence of a fifth type of receptor. The ribonucleotides are supposed to act synergistically on some MSG taste ratings but this has yet to be examined on JND scales. GMP potentiates firing in neural units from some taste receptors sensitive to MSG (Faurion, 1991). Fish are richly endowed with amino acids receptors and there is some neurophysiological evidence for a distinct glutamate receptor in mice (Ninomiya and Funakoshi, 1989). However, MSG would be expected to elicit neural responses from receptors sensitive to sucrose as well as from those for sodium and, no doubt, the less well understood sour and bitter receptors, too. Thus, demonstrating a distinct glutamate receptor in mammals may depend on differences in intracellular mediation of neural response (Brand *et al.*, 1991).

Social context

Our desire for a comestible is also affected by the culturally derived attributions we make to it. These are values that we believe are supported by eating the food. The attributes may be represented by the company in which we eat or the social nature of the occasion, such as champagne at a wedding meal. Some attributes can be made explicit by messages that the food supplier attaches to the food item by advertising, pricing and words or pictures on the packaging. As an initial example of quantitative integration of a socially significant semantic attribute with a material characteristic, we have examined the role of the named calorie content of the sweetener on the level of sweetness that is recognized as being appropriate for an orange-flavoured drink. Again, the person's habitual attitude to foods and drinks was hypothesized to modulate the integration of features. Someone who preferred to avoid calories and chose 'diet' drinks might prefer an orangey taste that was less sweet when it was believed to be sugar than when the sweetener was labelled as being low in calories (Booth, 1988). Conversely, someone who often took a drink in part to ward off hunger would prefer the sugar version and might perhaps want it to be sweeter than the unhelpful low-calorie version. These possibilities can be investigated by the use of sugar in all the test drinks but briefing assessors that some of them may contain a low-calorie sweetener and then labelling some samples with the name of such a sweetener that has a good sugar-like taste.

In a substantial sample of young people, the hypothesis about diet drink users was better supported than the one about sugar users (R.P.J. Freeman and D.A. Booth, unpublished data). Nevertheless, individuals could be found who illustrated both effects. A young woman who professed to always choose diet drinks preferred the sugar-labelled drinks with less sugar (Fig. 5.5(a)), while another who always chose the traditional sugar-containing versions preferred more sugar in the sugar-labelled samples (Fig. 5.5(b)).

All the same, the recognition processes had the same form for the two women. Both interpreted the sweetener label in terms of the total calories provided by the drink so labelled and they thought about the meaning of the sweetness, presumably in the same terms, rather than their preference being driven by the taste as such, consciously or sub-consciously (Freeman and Booth, in preparation). In both cases, too, the effects on preference of the sugar level and the sweetener label acted in separate dimensions in discrimination space (choice lay on the hypotenuse) but at the same time acted on the same dimension (additively). Presumably, therefore, the sweetener name and the sweetness intensity were distinct features of the drink but they also had a feature in common, probably relating to the caloric content of the drink, or possibly to its danger to the teeth, its naturalness, or its safety.

Somatic context

A gastric and intestinal psychophysics of human desires to eat or not to eat is ready to emerge (Read, 1992; Robinson, 1989). So, there is now the prospect that the integration of external and internal signals in hunger and its satiation, illustrated qualitatively above (Fig. 5.3), will also be elucidated by discrimination measurement (Booth, 1987*b*, 1992).

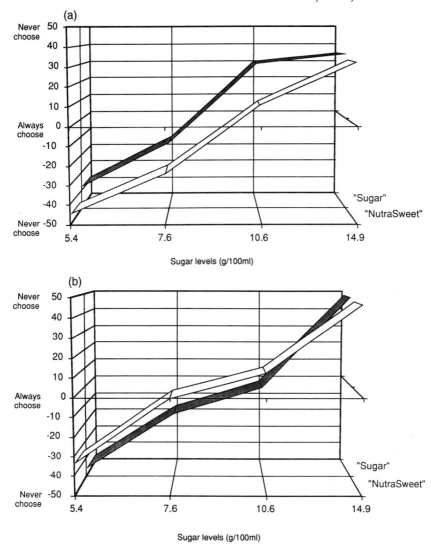

Fig. 5.5 Relationships between degree of preference for an orange-drink sample and both sugar concentration and sweetener label ('low-calorie' or 'sugar') for (a) a user of 'diet' drinks, and (b) a user of sugar drinks.

CONCLUSION

The appetite for food and drink, or indeed any learned motivation or habitual behaviour, can be qualitatively or quantitatively measured as the behavioural disposition in response to the JND-scaled multidimensional distance of the current situation from the individual's for that object of desire. Where the individual's decision-making processes form a network (Booth, 1992b; Glymour *et al.*, 1987), this approach can be used to characterize each integration node in the net.

REFERENCES

Ashby, F.G. and Perrin, N. (1988). Towards a unified theory of similarity and recognition. *Psychological Review*, **95**, 124–50.

Baker, B.J., Booth, D.A., Duggan, J.P., and Gibson, E.L. (1987). Protein appetite demonstrated: learned specificity of protein-cue preference to protein need in adult rats. *Nutrition Research*, **7**, 481–7.

Beauchamp, G.K. (1987). The human preference for excess salt. *American Scientist*, **75**, 27–33.

Birch, L.L. (1990). The control of intake in young children: the role of learning. In E.D. Capaldi and T.L. Powley (eds.), *Taste, experience and feeding*, pp. 116–35. American Psychological Association, Washington DC.

Birch, L.L. (1980). Effects of peer models' food choices and eating behaviors on preschoolers' food preferences. *Child Development*, **51**, 489–96.

Birch, L.L. and Deysher, M. (1985). Conditioned and unconditioned caloric compensation: evidence for self-regulation of food intake by young children. *Learning and Motivation*, **16**, 341–55.

Birch, L.L. and Deysher, M. (1986). Caloric compensation and sensory-specific satiety: evidence for self-regulation of food intake in young children. *Appetite*, **7**, 323–31.

Birch, L.L., McPhee, L., Steinberg, L., and Sullivan, S. (1990). Conditioned flavor preferences in young children. *Physiology and Behavior*, **47**, 501–5.

Booth, D.A. (1967). Localization of the adrenergic feeding system in the rat diencephalon. *Science*, **158**, 515–17.

Booth, D.A. (1972). Conditioned satiety in the rat. *Journal of Comparative and Physiological Psychology*, **81**, 457–71.

Booth, D.A. (1974). Acquired sensory preferences for protein in diabetic and normal rats. *Physiological Psychology*, **2**, 344–8.

Booth, D.A. (1977). Appetite and satiety as metabolic expectancies. In Y. Katsuki, M. Sato, S.F. Takagi, and Y. Oomura (eds.), *Food intake and chemical senses*, pp. 317–30. University of Tokyo Press.

Booth, D.A. (1979). Is thirst largely an acquired specific appetite? *Behavioral and Brain Sciences*, **2**, 103–4.

Booth, D.A. (1980). Conditioned reactions in motivation. In F.M. Toates and T.R. Halliday (eds.), *Analysis of motivational processes*, pp. 77–102. Academic Press, London.

Booth, D.A. (1985). Food-conditioned eating preferences and aversions with interoceptive elements: learned appetites and satieties. *Annals of New York Academy of Sciences*, **443**, 22–37.

Booth, D.A. (1986). Objective measurement of influences on food choice. *Appetite*, **7**, 236–7.

Booth, D.A. (1987a). Cognitive experimental psychology of appetite. In R.A. Boakes, M.J. Burton, and D.A. Popplewell (eds.), *Eating habits*, pp. 175–209. Wiley, Chichester.

Booth, D.A. (1987*b*). Objective measurement of determinants of food acceptance: sensory, physiological and psychosocial. In J. Solms, D.A. Booth, R.M. Pangborn, and O. Raunhardt (eds.), *Food acceptance and nutrition*, pp. 1–27. Academic Press, London.

Booth, D.A. (1988). Relationships of diet to health: the behavioral research gaps. In C.H. Manley and R.E. Morse (eds.), *Healthy eating—a scientific perspective*, pp. 39–76. Allured, Wheaton, IL.

Booth, D.A. (1989). Mood- and nutrient-conditioned appetites. Cultural and physiological bases for eating disorders. *Annals of New York Academy of Sciences*, **575**, 122–35.

Booth, D.A. (1990). Learned role of tastes in eating motivation. In E.D. Capaldi and T.L. Powley (eds.), *Taste, experience and feeding*, pp. 179–94. American Psychological Association, Washington, DC.

Booth, D.A. (1991*a*). Learned ingestive motivation and the pleasures of the palate. In R.C. Bolles (Ed.), *The hedonics of taste*, pp. 29–58. Erlbaum, Hillsdale NJ.

Booth, D.A. (1991*b*). Influences on human drinking behaviour. In D.J. Ramsay and D.A. Booth (eds.), *Thirst: physiological and psychological aspects*, pp. 52–72. Springer-Verlag, London.

Booth, D.A. (1992*a*). Integration of internal and external signals in satiety. *Proceedings of the Nutrition Society*, **51**, 21–8.

Booth, D.A. (1992*b*). Towards scientific realism in eating research. *Appetite*, **19**, 56–60.

Booth, D.A. and Conner, M.T. (1991). Characterisation and measurement of influences on food acceptability by analysis of choice differences: theory and practice. *Food Quality and Preference*, **2**, 75–85.

Booth, D.A. and Davis, J.D. (1973). Gastrointestinal factors in the acquisition of oral sensory control of satiation. *Physiology and Behavior*, **11**, 23–9.

Booth, D.A. and Grinker, J.A. (1993). Learned control of meal size in spontaneously obese and nonobese bonnet macaque monkeys. *Physiology and Behavior*, **53**, 51–7.

Booth, D.A. and Mather, P. (1978). Prototype model of human feeding, growth and obesity. In D.A. Booth (ed.), *Hunger models: computable theory of feeding control*, pp. 279–322. Academic Press, London.

Booth, D.A. and Simson, P.C. (1971). Food preferences acquired by association with variations in amino acid nutrition. *Quarterly Journal of Experimental Psychology*, **23**, 135–45.

Booth, D.A. and Stribling, D. (1978). Neurochemistry of appetite mechanisms. *Proceedings of the Nutrition Society, London*, **37**, 181–91.

Booth, D.A. and Toase, A.M. (1983). Conditioning of hunger/satiety signals as well as flavour cues in dieters. *Appetite*, **4**, 235–6.

Booth, D.A., Conner, M.T., and Marie, S. (1987). Sweetness and food selection: measurement of sweeteners' effects on acceptance. In J. Dobbing (ed.), *Sweetness*, pp. 143–160. Springer-Verlag, London.

Booth, D.A., Freeman R.P.J., and Lähteenmäki, L. (1991). Likings for complex foods and meals. *Appetite*, **17**, 156.

Booth, D.A., French, J.A., and Gatherer, A.J.H. (1992). Personal benefits from postingestional actions of dietary constituents. *Proceedings of the Nutrition Society*, **51**, 335–41.

Booth, D.A., Lee, M., and McAleavey, C. (1976). Acquired sensory control of satiation in man. *British Journal of Psychology*, **67**, 137–47.

Booth, D.A., Lovett, D., and McSherry, G.M. (1972). Postingestive modulation of the sweetness preference gradient in the rat. *Journal of Comparative and Physiological Psychology*, **78**, 485–512.

Booth, D.A., Mather, P., and Fuller, J. (1982). Starch content of ordinary foods associatively conditions human appetite and satiation, indexed by intake and eating pleasantness of starch-paired flavours. *Appetite*, **3**, 163–84.

Booth, D.A., Stoloff, R., and Nicholls, J. (1974). Dietary flavor acceptance in infant rats established by association with effects of nutrient composition. *Physiological Psychology*, **2**, 313–19.

Booth, D.A., Thompson, A.L., and Shahedian, B. (1983). A robust, brief measure of an individual's most preferred level of salt in an ordinary foodstuff. *Appetite*, **4**, 301–12.

Brand, J.G., Teeter, J.H., Kumazawa, T., Huque, T., and Bayley, D.L. (1991). Transduction mechanisms for the taste of amino acids. *Physiology and Behavior*, **49**, 899–904.

Burton, M.J., Rolls, E.T., and Mora, F. (1976). Effects of hunger on the responses of neurons in the lateral hypothalamus to the sight and taste of food. *Experimental Neurology*, **51**, 669–77.

Conner, M.T. (1991). Sweetness and food selection. In S. Marie and J.R. Piggott (eds.), *Handbook of sweeteners*, pp. 1–32. Blackie, Glasgow.

Conner, M.T. and Booth, D.A. (1992). Combining measurement of food taste and consumer preference in the individual: reliability, precision and stability data. *Journal of Food Quality*, **15**, 1–17.

Conner, M.T., Haddon, A.V., Pickering, E.S., and Booth, D.A. (1988). Sweet tooth demonstrated: individual differences in preference for both sweet foods and foods highly sweetened. *Journal of Applied Psychology*, **73**, 275–80.

Faurion, A. (1991). Are umami taste receptors structurally related to glutamate CNS receptor sites? *Physiology and Behavior*, **49**, 905–12.

Fitzsimons, J.T. and Le Magnen, J. (1969). Eating as a regulatory control of drinking. *Journal of Comparative and Physiological Psychology*, **67**, 273–83.

Galef, B.G. and Wigmore, S.W. (1983). Transfer of information concerning distant food in rats: a laboratory investigation of the 'information centre' hypothesis. *Animal Behaviour*, **31**, 748–58.

Gibson, E.L. and Booth, D.A. (1986a). Acquired protein appetite in rats: dependence on a protein-specific need state. *Experientia*, **42**, 1003–4.

Gibson, E.L. and Booth, D.A. (1986b). Feeding induced by injection of norepinephrine near the paraventricular nucleus is suppressed specifically by the early stages of strong postingestional satiety in the rat. *Physiological Psychology*, **14**, 98–103.

Gibson, E.L. and Booth, D.A. (1987). Paraventricular noradrenaline injection modulates learned integration of visceral satiety signals and dietary stimuli. *Neuroscience Letters*, Supplement 29, S97.

Gibson, E.L. and Booth, D.A. (1989). Dependence of carbohydrate-conditioned flavor preference on internal state in rats. *Learning and Motivation*, **20**, 36–47.

Gibson, E.L., Wainwright, C.J., and Booth, D.A. (1992). Disguised protein in lunch after low-protein breakfast conditions preference for protein-paired flavor during protein lack. *Appetite*, **19**, 183.

Glymour, C., Scheines, R., Spirtes, P., and Kelly, K. (1987). *Discovering causal structure*, Academic Press, New York.

Hall, W.G. (1991). The ontogeny of drinking. In D.J. Ramsay and D.A. Booth (eds.), *Thirst: physiological and psychological aspects*, pp. 35–52. Springer-Verlag, London.

Herman, C.P. and Polivy, J. (1980). Restrained eating. In A.J. Stunkard (ed.), *Obesity*, pp. 208–25. W.B. Saunders, Philadelphia.

Huggins, R.L., Di Nicolantonio, R., and Morgan, T.O. (1992). Preferred salt levels and salt taste acuity in human subjects after ingestion of untasted salt. *Appetite*, **18**, 111–19.

Kramer, F.M., Rock, K., and Engell, D. (1992). Effects of time of day and appropriateness on food intake and hedonic ratings at morning and midday. *Appetite*, **18**, 1–13.

Langhans, W. and Scharrer, E. (1992). Metabolic control of eating. *World Review of Nutrition and Dietetics*, **70**, 1–67.

Leathwood, P.D. and Ashley, D.V.M. (1983). Strategies of protein selection by weanling and adult rats. *Appetite*, **4**, 97–112.

Leibowitz, S.F. (1978). Paraventricular nucleus: a primary site mediating adrenergic stimulation of feeding and drinking. *Pharmacology Biochemistry and Behavior*, **8**, 163–75.

Leibowitz, S.F., Weiss, G.H., Yee, F., and Tretter, J.B. (1985). Noradrenergic innervation of the paraventricular nucleus: specific role in control of carbohydrate ingestion. *Brain Research Bulletin*, **14**, 561–7.

Lovett, D. and Booth, D.A. (1970). Four effects of exogenous insulin on food intake. *Quarterly Journal of Experimental Psychology*, **22**, 406–19.

Lowe, C.F. (1992). Influence of advertising on children's food preferences. British Association for Advancement of Science, Annual Meeting, Southampton.

Macmillan, N.A. and Creelman, C.D. (1991). *Detection theory: a user's guide*. Cambridge University Press, New York.

Matthews, J.W., Gibson, E.L., and Booth, D.A. (1985). Norepinephrine-facilitated eating: reduction in saccharin preference and conditioned flavor preferences with increase in quinine aversion. *Pharmacology Biochemistry and Behavior*, **22**, 1045–52.

Mennell, S., Murcott, A., and van Otterloo, A.H. (1992). The sociology of food: eating, diet and culture. *Current Sociology*, **40**, 1–152.

Murcott, A. (ed.) (1983). *The sociology of food and eating*. Gower, Aldershot.

Ninomiya, Y. and Funakoshi, M. (1989). Peripheral neural basis for behavioral discrimination between glutamate and the four basic taste substances in mice. *Comparative Biochemistry and Physiology A*, **92**, 371–6.

Norgren, R. (1991). Sensory detection of water. In D.J. Ramsay and D.A. Booth (eds.), *Thirst: physiological and psychological aspects*, pp. 221–31. Springer-Verlag, London.

Read, N.W. (1992). Role of gastrointestinal factors in hunger and satiety in man. *Proceedings of Nutrition Society, London*, **51**, 7–11.

Ritter, R.C. and Epstein, A.N. (1975). Control of meal size by central noradrenergic action. *Proceedings of National Academy of Sciences (US)*, **72**, 3740–3.

Robinson, P.H. (1989). Gastric function in eating disorders. *Annals of New York Academy of Sciences*, **575**, 456–65.

Rolls, E.T. (1989). Parallel distributed processing in the brain: implications of the functional architecture of neuronal networks in the hippocampus. In

R.G.M. Morris (ed.), *Parallel distributed processing*, pp. 286–308. Clarendon Press, Oxford.

Rolls, E.T. (1993). Central neural systems controlling ingestion in primates. In D.A. Booth (ed.) *Neurophysiology of appetite*, pp. 137–69 Pergamon Press, Oxford.

Sclafani, A. (1990). Nutritionally based learned flavor preferences in rats. In E.D. Capaldi and T.L. Powley (eds.), *Taste, experience and feeding*, pp. 139–56. American Psychological Association, Washington, DC.

Shepard, R.N. (1957). Stimulus and response generalization: a stochastic model relating generalization to distance in psychological space. *Psychometrika*, **22**, 325–45.

Simson, P.C. and Booth, D.A. (1973). Olfactory conditioning by association with histidine-free or balanced amino acid loads. *Quarterly Journal of Experimental Psychology*, **25**, 354–9.

Simpson, S.J., James, S., Simmonds, M.S.J., and Blaney, W.M. (1991). Variation in chemosensitivity and the control of dietary selection behaviour in the locust. *Appetite*, **17**, 141–54.

6

Human male sexuality: appetite and arousal, desire and drive

R. J. Levin

INTRODUCTION

Human beings undertake sexual activity for two primary reasons, to procreate (reproductive sex) and to give themselves pleasure (recreational sex). It does not take much calculating, using an average family of two to three children and the limited number of coital encounters needed to beget each child (probably 10–20), to realize that most people's heterosexual coital activity during their lifetime, at least in the western world, is for recreation rather than procreation. A study in Sweden showed that only about 2 per cent of sexual activity was performed with the conscious purpose of procreation (Linner, 1972). Thus in its essence, human sexual motivation should simply be for pleasure and (rarely!) for procreation. However, the simplicity, if it ever really existed even for primal man, has become corrupted and overlaid with many other factors. In any human society, men and women can want and even have sex for a host of motives (Neubeck, 1974). Coitus is undertaken not only for pleasure and procreation but also to degrade, control and dominate, to punish and hurt, to overcome loneliness or boredom, to rebel against authority, to establish one's sexuality, or one's achieving sexual competence (adulthood), or to show that sexual access was possible (to 'score'), for duty, for adventure, to obtain favours such as a better position or role in life, or even for a livelihood. Similarly, other sexual activities such as oral genital sex can be used to avoid coitus, as an act of degradation, or to give and receive pleasure, and, not least, as an expression of love!

The present account of human sexuality is limited to that of the human male. The reason for this is two-fold. First, human male sexuality is an easier behaviour to analyse and model in detail than that of the female and, second, there is far more factual material available in the literature for the male. Although many of the factors of the model will be common to both male and female sexuality a number will be inappropriate (namely, the emission and ejaculation processes). Modelling human female sexuality, as has been done for the male, is a challenge for the future.

The heuristic models

Two heuristic models are employed (Figs. 6.1 and 6.2), where the major physiological and psychological features involved in the sexual arousal of the human male are identified in the framework of a flowchart. In order to facilitate the referencing of the features of the main model in Fig. 6.1, with its many complex interacting pathways, all relevant aspects are assigned a number which is given boldface in parentheses, where appropriate, in the text. Specific pathways are described by a linked chain of numbers, thus the influence of aggression (**43**) on sexual arousal (**23**) would be designated (**43–30–23**).

The terminology of human sex and sexuality

Psychological terms to describe many basic human mental states or particular aspects of the human psyche have been notoriously difficult to define accurately, although they are used extensively. Simple words such as emotion, drive, motivation, consciousness, appetite, pleasure, interest do not describe simple phenomena, and often tortuous definitions are attempted to try to be comprehensive. Superimposed on these difficulties when discussing human sex and sexuality is the added problem of a clearly agreed terminology. Numerous words are employed to describe particular aspects of our sexuality and these have been subjected to scientific fashion. The terms, moreover, are often difficult to define accurately despite their frequent use both in the technical literature and even in everyday life. The lexicon includes sexual identity, sexual interest, sexual impulse, sexual desire, sexual arousal, sexual arousability, sexual excitement, sexual excitability, sexual fantasy, libido, sexual motivation, sexual drive, sexual appetite, sexual feelings, sexual gratification, sex guilt, sexual preference, sexual scripting, and sexuality. Terms such as reproductive urge or imperative have also been used but have become outmoded. Interestingly, the occasional use of the vernacular has been employed by some writers who find that the more technical terms do not always convey the subtleties of sexual feeling. Examples are 'turned on' for being sexually aroused, 'horny' or 'randy' for having sexual desire (Neubeck, 1974; Stoller, 1976), 'scoring' for obtaining sexual access (usually coitally with a female) merely for the sense of achievement (pleasure) gained from obtaining the access and 'mood' (namely, I'm in/not in the mood for sex). Different terms are sometimes used indiscriminately by authors, suggesting that they think they characterize identical concepts. Does this mean that libido, sexual desire, sexual excitement, sexual appetite,and sexual drive have no distinguishing features and that they all describe the same brain mechanisms? Money (1961) regarded sexual drive and libido as synonymous with sexual desire while Kaplan (1979) believed that 'sexual desire is an appetite or drive which is produced by the activation of a specific neural system in the brain' (p. 9). Everitt and Bancroft (1992) in their review on the similarities and differences in the sexual mechanisms of man and rodents recently stated that 'to make an operational distinction between sexual desire and sexual excitement quickly comes to grief. When does desire become excitement? Is a sexual thought or fantasy a stimulus or a response, or both?' Some of these problems are discussed in the following sections in relation to a number of the various terms from the above list, especially those that are used in the heuristic model (Fig. 6.1).

SEXUAL DESIRE

What is sexual desire? Some authors have been at pains to argue that it is clearly different from sexual arousal. Sexual desire is an attitude toward an object while sexual arousal is a state with specific feelings, usually attached to the genitals. There can be sexual arousal without sexual desire and sexual desire without arousal. A man or a woman can become sexually excited despite having little or no desire to be so; in some situations they may be actually disgusted by their own sexual arousal, especially if they think it inappropriate. However, if sexual arousal is to be easily effected and enjoyed, it is beneficial to first have sexual desire. Indeed, a major criticism of the original Masters and Johnson (1966) EPOR model (the acronym EPOR comes from the phases of their human sexual responses namely, Excitement, Plateau, Orgasm, and Resolution (Levin,1980)) was that it ignored the desire phase of human sexual response. Kaplan (1979) tagged this phase at the beginning of the EPOR model to create a DEOR (Desire, Excitement, Orgasm, and Resolution) model. She reported that women coming for sex therapy treatment could suffer from a lack of sexual desire; they were simply not interested in becoming sexually aroused or undertaking the sexual arousal of another human despite the fact that that human might be their significant other (husband or partner). Goldberg (1973) had previously reported on men with an absent sexual desire. Hypoactive sexual desire has been classified as a separate and distinct sexual disorder in diagnostic nosology (American Psychiatric Association, 1987). Many definitions of sexual desire exist in the literature, coloured

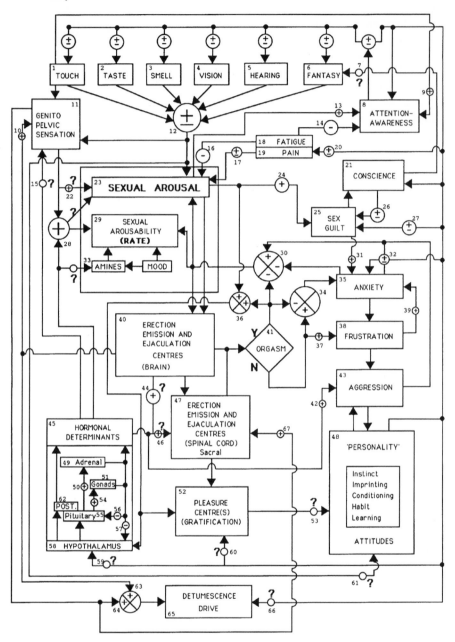

Fig. 6.1 A flow chart model of sexual man. The numbers refer to specific aspects of the model and are used in the text for easy reference. The question marks above empty open circles indicate that the effect of the pathway is unknown, those above open circles with positive or negative signs indicate the likely effect of the path. See text for further details.

by the author's background or subject allegiance. Goldman (1977) defined it simply as 'a desire for contact with another person's body and for the pleasure which such contact produces' (p. 268). Unfortunately, as Shaffer (1978) pointed out, there are many situations where one person desires body contact with another yet the desire is not sexual (a parent hugging a child or friends shaking hands). In his philosophical discourse he argued that sexual desire differs markedly from the standard case of desire in that the important feature of sexual desire is that it is directed towards an object but, interestingly, the cause of the desire is not necessarily the object of desire (an erotic drawing can activate sexual desire but the desire is not for the drawing). Sexual desire, he maintains, is like feelings of longing, craving, yearning, hungering, or thirsting, which are all connected with the concept of satisfaction, unlike emotions. Sartre (1966) remarked about sexual desire that the 'desire is not a desire of doing.The "doing" is after the event, is added onto the desire from outside.' Sexual desire possesses the concept that something should occur (Shaffer, 1978, p. 178). Leiblum and Rosen (1988) regarded sexual desire as a 'subjective feeling state that may be triggered by both internal and external cues and may or may not result in overt sexual behaviour' (p. 5). Zilbergeld and Ellison (1980) regarded sexual desire (and sexual interest), idiosyncratically, as a category that 'refers exclusively to frequency, how often a person wants to have sex'. No other author has directly equated the frequency of wanting sex exclusively with sexual desire or interest.

From this brief overview of the concepts of sexual desire by different workers it is clear that its characterization is not simple. No definition will satisfy all disciplines entirely. An attempted working definition is that sexual desire is normally an activated, unsatisfied mental state of variable intensity created by external (via the sensory modalities (**1–5**), Fig. 6.1) or internal (fantasy, memory, cognition (**6 and 48**) Fig. 6.1) stimuli that induces a feeling of a need or want to partake of sexual activity (usually with the object of the desire) to satisfy the need.

SEXUAL AROUSAL (**23**)

While most humans experience sexual arousal and usually know when they are sexually aroused or not, it is far from easy to define what sexual arousal is. At first this difficulty appears ridiculous, for surely if a man has an erect penis and a women has a lubricating vagina then they must be sexually aroused? In this case the answer is obviously yes, they are clearly sexually aroused at the genital level but they need not necessarily be sexually aroused in their minds. For if the man's erect penis happens to be in the state of erection a few moments after he has just ejaculated and had an orgasm he is actually not likely to be sexually aroused in his mind, as ejaculation and orgasm discharge sexual arousal before the activation of the neural circuit for erection is discharged. Thus sexual arousal can apply to a number of human systems that have some independence and is thus a multicomponent concept. Bancroft (1971) usefully employed the analysis of Lacey (1967) to characterize human sexual arousal into three components: a central arousal, a non-genital peripheral arousal, and a genital arousal. Normally, these three components are usually associated but they can occur independently of one another (see Levin and Wagner, 1987). Such independence can lead to sexual dysfunction. Walen and Roth (1987) defined sexual arousal as a product of perception and evaluation of events that leads in turn to further cognitive appraisal. Let us use another example to show some of the inherent difficulties with our sexual terminology. When does sexual interest become sexual desire or sexual arousal? Take the scenario of a woman in front of a young man. She suddenly bends down to pick up a dropped book and the thin material of her dress is pulled tight over her buttocks showing the outline of her skimpy panties. The man's interest can change immediately from general observation that she exists to one of sexual interest in her buttocks activated by the now disclosed, but previously hidden, underwear. If the thought pathway is allowed to develop, his now sexual interest can be instantly converted into sexual desire for the woman because her buttocks now make her appear sexually alluring. When she straightens up and turns around, allowing him to see that she is extremely attractive and then smiles at him, the desire can change to sexual arousal, leading even to genital arousal. The whole scenario may take but a second or two (see Fig. 6.2 for the flow chart systems activation of this scenario). While the transitions between sexual interest, desire, and arousal are obviously fuzzy as they partially merge into one another, yet, as shown previously, the scenario reveals that the terms do define distinct (mental) entities. Moreover, if, when she turns round, he thinks that she is unattractive or downright ugly, his sexual desire or arousal could turn to sexual disgust. In case the described scenario is criticized as sexist, the defence is that, in general men, rather than women, are more aroused by seeing a visual image and are relatively immune from the effects of distraction to visual erotic stimuli, unlike women (Przybyla and Byrne, 1984). Interestingly, it does not seem to matter too much whether this is reality or a photograph, drawing, painting, or video of the opposite sex; sexual arousal can still take place. The erotic and pornographic industry rests on this bedrock fact! An obvious question is why is there this difference? Symons (1987) argues that there is an evolutionary explanation, 'the male can potentially impregnate a female at almost no cost to himself, hence selection favored the basic male

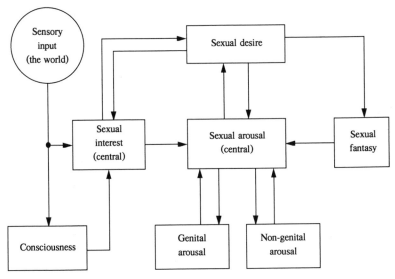

Fig. 6.2 A flow chart indicating the possible interrelationships between sexual interest, desire, arousal, and fantasy. Central sexual arousal activates genital arousal and non-genital arousal (increases in blood pressure, heart rate, respiration, muscle tension). The sensory input from the world is constantly monitored. That which is of sexual interest will perhaps be acted upon immediately while other less important features of sexual interest can pass into consciousness (or awareness and then memory) without direct or immediate activation. See text for details.

tendency to become sexually aroused by the sight of females. Human females, on the other hand, invest a substantial amount of energy and incur serious risks by becoming pregnant, hence selection favoured the basic female tendency to become sexually aroused tactually by favoured males. Women who become sexually aroused simply by the sight of males (like men do at the sight of women) would risk being randomly impregnated and would gain nothing reproductively but would lose a great deal' (p. 102). The concept of the female having the larger 'parental investment' in her pregnancy was first suggested by Trivers (1972).

Models of human sexual arousal

For many years the only full accounts of human sexual responses had to be gleaned from erotic writings and pornographic descriptions but the detailed validity of these was always suspect. In the early part of the century, models of human sexual arousal appeared in the 'sexual hygiene' literature. These were of varying degrees of sophistication which began to utilize as their core the psychophysiological changes that underlie the behaviour patterns. Early attempts used a graphical display of the hypothetical sexual excitement level against time during coitus, characterizing selected portions of the continuous curve as the behaviour pattern during initial excitement or arousal, the curve peaking at orgasm and then returning back to normal (van de Velde, 1926). Kinsey *et al.* (1953) added a variety of physiological phenomena to the model such as cardiovascular and genital responses. Wenger, Jones, and Jones (1956) proposed a general model of the activation of the autonomic nervous system to account for the sequential nature of human sexual physiological responses culminating in orgasm. They discussed the concept that particular emotional behaviours had a typical pattern of autonomic nervous system activation. For sexual excitement, they proposed a triphasic model. In the early excitement phase the parasympathetic system dominates but as excitement mounts, the sympathetic dominates at ejaculation and orgasm and then subsides allowing the parasympathetic to be dominant again, perhaps even more so than previously. Lack of ability to verify the various dominances experimentally prevented this model from becoming popular. Masters and Johnson (1966) clearly built their model of human sexual response on the graphical framework of the early models, but they completely ignored the pre-initiative or desire phase. They characterized the sexual arousal curve against time into four sequential phases (Excitement, Plateau, Orgasmic, and Resolution). Its apparent didactic simplicity and easy applicability to both men and women, and to homosexual or heterosexual arousal, allowed it to dominate sexology and, to many, it became unquestionable dogma rather than a descriptive attempt to formalize human sexual behaviour into a comprehensive pattern. While there has been criticism of certain aspects of the model (see Hoon, 1979; Levin, 1980; Robinson, 1976) it is still used extensively. Tiefer (1992) has recently criticized the model from the point of view of her feminist and social constructionist ideas of human sexuality (Tiefer, 1987). The section on sexual scripts and lovemaps deals with some of these social constructionist concepts of human sexuality. An influential model of male sexual arousal came about from Beach's (1956) work on animal (mainly rat) sexual responses. He separated the sexual responses into a 'sexual arousal mechanism (SAM)' and an 'intromission and ejaculatory mechanism (IEM)'. The main function of the SAM is to 'increase the male's sexual excitment to such a pitch that the copulatory threshold is attained' (p. 20). The SAM can be activated by visual, olfactory, tactile, or cognitive stimuli. The second mechanism (IEM) then came into operation during the mounting and intromission and gave rise to bringing the animal up to and then beyond the threshold for ejaculation. The IEM is activated by impulses that promote clonic contractions of the ejaculatory system. He described how various factors could affect the

SAM and the IEM separately, allowing the possibility of ejaculation occurring without erection (Beach, Westbrook, and Clemens 1966). It is often thought that Beach created this dual nature model of sexual arousal. In fact he quotes both Moll (1897) and Ellis (1936) as having pointed out that human sexual behaviour could be divided into two phases: a 'contrection drive' (involving a combination of inborn and learned reactions to sensory stimulation) leading to the establishment of body contact and physical stimulation and then a 'detumescence drive' that leads to sexual orgasm.

SEXUAL AROUSABILITY (29)

Sexual arousal is a state, while sexual arousability (or excitability) is a rate (Whalen 1966). Bancroft (1977) defined it as 'the facility to respond to sexual stimuli with an increase in arousal'. As this is not an easy thing to measure, perhaps a better way of regarding it is the speed with which a person becomes sexually aroused. If we were to try and measure it in the laboratory objectively we could use latency such as like the time taken to have a full erection, or become lubricated, or to reach a maximum increase in heart rate, or obtain an orgasm (Levin and Wagner, 1985). When a person says that they are easily sexual aroused, that means their arousability is high and the time taken for the previous measures would be correspondingly short, while if they are difficult to arouse sexually then their arousability is low and the time taken would become correspondingly long. Sexual arousability has links with sexual interest. If one has no sexual interest at a particular time then arousability is likely to be low; increasing sexual interest enhances arousability. Confusion between the various terms can easily occur and arousal is often used as if it were synonomous with arousability (Zilbergeld and Ellison, 1980). Arousability has gradually replaced the older term excitability just as sexual arousal has replaced sexual excitement. Sexual arousability is certainly influenced by the hormonal status (45–28) of an individual, especially in relation to sex steroids (49, 51). Whalen (1966) proposed that arousability was conditionable.

LIBIDO, SEX APPETITE, SEX MOTIVATION AND SEX DRIVE

Libido

A variety of terms exist to characterize why people are sexually active or the principle that governs their sexual behaviour. A simple theory was that people sought to optimize pleasure, the hedonic theory of motivation (Wundt 1893). In 1877 Freud attempted to define the principle by using the term 'libido' (from the latin word for desire) which he defined as the 'quantitatively variable force which could serve as a measure of processes and transformation occurring in the field of sexual excitation' (Freud, 1977, pp. 138–9). It was distinguished from the energy that underlined general mental processes, existed in a finite quantity, was easily displaceable, or repressed, and could be sublimated or diverted into behaviour that was not obviously sexual. The libido, or sexual impulse, was practically the core of virtually all human motivation. It thus underlies art, science, music, aggression, etc. In later developments, the hedonic theory was modified by Freud; pleasure was now seen as deriving from a diminution of the stimulus. The sexual impulse underlying human motivation was only pleasurable if it could be reduced. Human beings were always trying to reduce, consciously or unconsciously, what could be described as 'libidinal tension' (Evans, 1989, p. 88).

Sexual appetite

Beach (1956) argued that 'what is commonly confused with a primary drive associated with sexual deprivation is in actuality sexual appetite, and this has little or no relation to biological or physiological needs' and that 'sexual appetite is a product of experience, actual or vicarious'. Hardy (1964) reviewed previous work that presented the idea that human sexual activity was governed by a drive reduction state. He concluded from his analysis that the 'overwhelming proportion of the variance in human sexual motivation and behaviour is not explicable in terms of some biological need or tension, however conceived'. He proposed an appetitional theory of human sexual motivation. It was based on the concept that motives that are learned in association with affective experiences must, in order to be complete, describe those conditions which produce affective change in the first place. Briefly, in the formation of the constitutional base of the sexual appetite Hardy suggested that the random exploration of the body by the infant's hands leads to finding the genitals which on mild local stimulation is 'innately pleasurable' but that unless preventive action is taken an 'undue amount of time is spent stimulating the genital organs', then 'the pleasure accompanying genital stimulation (arousal) continues throughout life as an affective base for motivational development. Many stimuli, once neutral, may become associated with it, as a consequence functioning as cues leading to genital arousal, even in the absence of the tactile stimulation itself' (p. 7). Hardy then applied the appetitional theory to a number of aspects of the personal and social management of sexuality, namely premarital sexual relations, masturbation, control of sexual appetite, and sexual compatability in marriage. Remarkably, the tenor of this section of the paper deteriorates into a morality campaign. It can perhaps be judged by such phrases as 'appetitional theory suggests a set of recommendations for the control of lust during the premarital period', or 'some degree of social control of blatant obscenity is probably required' or 'sex is often indulged in as a substitute for a reasonably satisfying life in other areas'! Margoshes and Litt (1965) were highly critical of the attempt by Hardy to regard human sexuality as primarily an appetite rather than in terms of a 'drive reduction, homeostatic disequilibrium, endocrine secretion or instinctual libido'. They tried to show that where Hardy differed from Freud, he was either demonstrably incorrect or made ethical rather than scientific judgments. They also pointed out that, for many appetites, such as that for food or drink, repeated satiations leads to them becoming dulled and that this also happens to many married men, yet their 'sexual drive becomes stronger than ever with regard to other women'. Hardy, on the other hand, wrote that 'once this erotic arousal has occurred, bringing powerful excitement in its wake, the desire to repeat and continue the experience is greatly enhanced, thus the sexual appetite is increased' (p. 11). Tiefer (1992) remarked that the concept of sexual appetite has never caught on in sexology.

Rosen (1992) reviewed the effects of recreational and illicit drug usage on sexual desire. Increased 'sexual appetite' is said to occur with marihuana users but the mechanism(s) of action is unknown; some suggest that it is the expectations of users and the influence of the social setting, some mention release of inhibitions, while others report enhanced tactile sensitivity and changed perception of time. Cocaine is also said to enhance 'sexual desire' (also sensuality and to delay orgasm), but long-term chronic use frequently leads to its loss. The opiate narcotics (morphine, heroin, and methadone) appear to be potent suppressors of sexual desire and responsiveness. It should be noted that most studies on illicit drug use rely on reports from recovering addicts with few control groups. The reliability of the data is thus suspect.

SEX MOTIVATION AND SEX DRIVE

Whalen (1966) reviewed the concept of human sexual motivation. He felt that the two dimensions of human sexuality that comprised sexual motivation were sexual arousal (23) and sexual arousability (29), a state and a rate. Sexual arousal is influenced by all sensory modalities touch (1), taste (2), smell (3), vision (4) and hearing (5). Individuals become conditioned (by habit based on practice?) to respond to selected arousal stimuli. Whalen proposed that arousability, too, was determined by learning and by the physiological state of the organism. The latter included the hormonal determinants of arousability (45), mainly androgens from the testes (51) and adrenals (49), and the second determinant, the feedback of sexual activity on subsequent arousal (41–30–29). Evidence for the latter is seen immediately after ejaculation in the human male. It is extremely difficult to excite another ejaculation and, even when the erection has subsided, the induction of another needs a lot more stimulus for it to to be created than did the initial erection. Whalen rejected the appetitional theory of sexual motivation propounded by Hardy (1964) because Hardy could not conceive of human sexual motivation in terms of a 'biological need or tension'. Drive is the term used by many psychologists to describe the internal stimulation behind a behaviour pattern or activity. It has an extensive history and has strong supporters and detractors for its continued use (Bindra, 1980; Deutsch, 1979; Morgan, 1979). Sex drive has been employed extensively in the older literature to describe the underlying physiological or biological force behind human sexuality (Kirkendall, 1961). Beach (1956) argued that the sex drive was clearly different from the hunger drive and thirst drive because you did not die from being deprived of sex (but while this is obviously true for the individual the species would die out if sex deprivation were universal!). Many authors have replaced sex drive with the more fashionable sex motivation.

Factors affecting human sex motivation

Many factors influence human sexual motivation; some are obvious and clear-cut, others less so. In general it is extremely difficult, if not impossible, to know the sexual motivation of any human unless they are willing to tell you, and even then they can lie about it. As Freud (1910, p. 41) colourfully wrote 'People are in general not candid over sexual matters, they do not show their sexuality freely, but to conceal it wear a heavy overcoat of a tissue of lies, as though the weather were bad in the world of sexuality.' What is often taken as the sexual motivation of a person is actually that person's sexual behaviour. The assumption is often made that a person's sexual behaviour is equivalent to their motivation. A dramatic example of this is in the classic Japanese film *Rashomon* (1950). Set in mediaeval Japan, the wife of a Japanese nobleman is apparently raped by a bandit in front of her husband and three other characters. This is the obvious conclusion that the viewer first draws but as the story unfolds the 'rape' scene is retold visually through the eyes of each of the participants and the viewer begins to see that each of the characters has a different motivation for undertaking their portrayed behaviour. The initially obvious 'rape' becomes far from clear-cut, as one possibility is that the wife wishes to humiliate the husband by her sexual activity with the bandit. Did she encourage him purposely? Of course it is possible that in a number of situations motivation and behaviour actually do correspond. For most observers, however, it is not possible to be certain that they do.

FACTORS AFFECTING SEXUAL ACTIVITY

Some of the major factors influencing sexual activity are illustrated in the wheel shown in Fig. 6.3. Many of these, if not all, will also have an effect, albeit indirectly, on human sexual motivation. A brief explanation of each of the factors is given below.

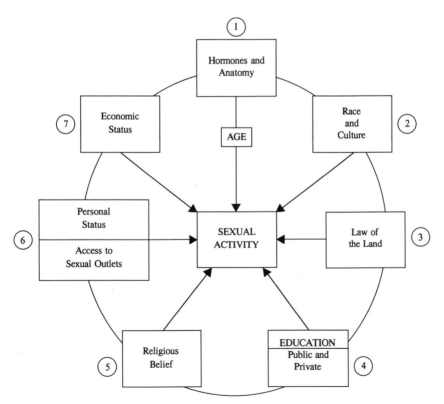

Fig. 6.3 Major factors affecting human sexual activity. See text for details.

Hormones and anatomy interacting with age

The level and type of hormones present, especially the steroid sex hormones, will influence not only the various sexual structures dependent on their secretion (internal and external genitals, breasts) but also the responsiveness (sexual arousability, see preceding section) of the person to passive and active sexual behaviour (Gooren, Fliers, and Courtney, 1990). Clearly, age will also play a role, not only in terms of the levels and type of hormones secreted (in pre-puberty, puberty, maturity, and during senescence) but also in terms of the other factors which are influenced by age such as personal and economic status and education.

Race and culture

Races, and the cultures they have created, show remarkably different attitudes and responses to human sexual behaviour. The extremes that are always employed to illustrate the spectrum are shown by the Grand Valley Dani, a few thousand people who live in Irian Jaya in Indonesia, and the Mangaians, the Polynesian inhabitants of Mangaia, a southern Cook Island in central Polynesia in the South Pacific. The Dani have been said to be unique in that they have the lowest level of sexual interest and activity yet described (Heider, 1976). Dani men do not often behave sexually nor apparently does sex have much interest for them. The parents of a Dani child refrain from coitus with each other from the time the child is born until it is about five years old. As far as Heider (1976) could ascertain, no other sexual outlet was used by the Dani parents during the long post-partum sexual abstinence period, nor could he observe any signs of unhappiness or stress during the abstinence period. In contrast is the Mangaian sexual behaviour. Mangaian couples have regular coitus up to the onset of labour and may resume it within a few days of delivery, although the usual wait is three months (Marshall, 1971). A Mangaian male has coitus in the single room of a hut inhabited by 5–15 family members of all ages while his daughter makes love with a different suitor each night in the same room. Remarkably, this all takes place without anyone noticing; they appear to look in the other direction. Despite this sexual licence to western eyes, Mangaian men are horrified at the way Europeans casually expose their penises during the process of urination. Thus humans basically equipped with the same genital structures, and presumably hormonal status, develop totally different sets of attitudes, values, and behaviour patterns in relation to genitals and sexual activity. The Dani's lack of sexual interest and behaviour has been used to argue against the concept that humans, especially the male, are driven by a biological imperative (see sexual drive above) to constantly seek sexual outlets. If, however, there is such a drive, then the Dani appear to be unique in having learnt the art of inhibiting it without unhappiness!

Law of the land

Public and private sexual activity, or, more accurately, access to sexual activity (Bullough, 1976), is governed by the law of the land. The extent of the law's interference in the individual's right to behave sexually as he or she wishes depends on the country and often on its dominant religion. Modern, westernized democracies try to balance the rights of consenting individuals to practise the sexual behaviour of their desires within the demands of its society to ensure the safety and well-being of its citizens. This, of course, is nearly an impossible task, for one person's pleasure is another person's perversion and ultimately who is to decide what is the acceptable behavioural line to be drawn for the safety of society? In a recent law case in England, the police prosecuted a number of men who undertook sadistic acts that were requested for by consenting masochist male 'victims', although no complaints were made to the authorities by the (presumably) satisfied consenting masochists. Most, if not all, countries, have an age of consent; sexual activity with a child under this age is illegal. Sexual activity with children, even if undertaken in the context of 'loving paedophilia' or maintained simply by photographs or fiction (O'Carroll, 1980) is abhorred in many societies. It is the mental corruption of the innocent child that fuels society's wish to punish the offenders. The paedophile has become a despised sexual offender and even has to be protected in prison from other inmates. In some countries homosexual behaviour is forbidden while in others it is accepted, especially among consenting adults. Certain states in the United States of America have laws that make oral genital sexual contacts illegal, even between consenting adults. The list of examples that can be quoted where the law tries to govern sexual behaviour is endless.

Education – public and private

Kinsey, Pomeroy, and Martin (1948) collected data that showed that public (high school, college) education appeared to be a significant factor in influencing sexual behaviour. The males that entered into high school but did not progress further than the tenth grade were more sexually active than those who did. The single males who had the lowest frequency of total sexual outlet (behaviour) were those who went to college (p. 337). However, the highest frequency of masturbation was among those who went to college. Among the occupational classes, members of the professional group were the ones who masturbated the most. Nocturnal emissions occurred most frequently among the males who went to college. Interpretation of this type of data is dangerous because so many factors can create the differences observed. Kinsey *et al.* commented that the frequency of nocturnal emissions showed some correlation with the level of erotic responsiveness of an individual. Boys from the lower levels were not so often aroused erotically as those from the upper educational levels. The upper-level male was aroused by a considerable variety of sexual stimuli while the lower-level male was less often aroused by anything except physical contact in coitus. It was felt that the higher degree of eroticism in the upper-level males may be due to their greater capacity to visualize situations which are not immediately apparent. They were the consumers of erotic literature, objects, and pictures, none of which were significant sources for the lower-level males. Private education involves factors such as buying and reading books and magazines, obtaining objects and pictures (videotapes and audiotapes), and debating and arguing with friends and one's peer group about sexual subjects. Contact with a wide range of upper-level educated people will broaden an individual's horizons and thus enlarge the sexual domain for the upper-level males.

Religious belief

Kinsey *et al.*'s data showed that when the total sexual outlet was used the sexually least active individuals in any age or educational group were the Orthodox Jews, then the devout Catholics, and then the active Protestants. While strict Orthodox Jews and Catholics differ in many religious practices, they both adhere to the reproductive philosophy of sexual activity. Basically, if the sexual activity undertaken cannot allow the union of the sperm with the egg then it is not acceptable behaviour. This means that masturbation either by oneself or by one's sexual partner, coitus interruptus, contraception, oral genital contacts and coitus during menstruation are all forbidden activities. Non-religious people may or may not accept some of these restrictions but, clearly, their decisions for choice will not come from a religious directive.

Personal status—access to sexual outlets

It is obvious that one's personal status can have a large bearing on a person's access to sexual outlets. A soldier with leave before going into a war zone will accept and perhaps pay for sexual activity with a woman in case he is killed in battle. A schoolboy or schoolgirl at a single-sex boarding school is likely to have masturbation and homosexual contacts as their only outlets, at least during term time. A newly bereaved widow is suddenly cut off from heterosexual activity with her husband; if she is highly sexed she must resort to masturbation until the socially acceptable grieving period is over. A host of such scenarios can be created where the personal status of the individual greatly influences access to sexual outlets.

Economic status

Individuals' economic status can play a role in influencing their sexual behaviour. Money can buy sexual activity, possibly unobtainable with a current partner (via prostitution or the sex industry), or provide access to recreational sexual activity that is unobtainable in one's own country (via world travel), or allow a variety of sexual partners because the person can afford to spend money lavishly on the selected individuals.

SEXUAL IDENTITY OR GENDER

An important aspect of personality (48) is sexual identity or gender. This is the knowledge that one is a male or a female, although other identities (hermaphrodite) are possible (Money, 1988). Some think it is prenatally determined (Zuger, 1970), while others often regard it as being learned in childhood. A number of learning theories (conditioning, behaviourism, psychoanalytic theory, cognitive approaches, social learning theory) have been proposed to be central to the development of a human's sexual identity, but no single one is acceptable to all critics (McConaghy, 1987; Money and Ehrhardt, 1972; Money, Hampson and Hampson, 1957). Money and Ehrhardt (1972) and Diamond (1965) emphasize the interaction between prenatal factors and nurture (environmental factors), a view supported by Bancroft (1977).

SEXUAL SCRIPTS AND LOVEMAPS

The concept that human sexual activity is powered by a biological drive has been unattractive to a number of authors. Gagnon and Simon (1973) proposed that human sexual conduct involved an organized cognitive schema that they called a 'script' which was needed by the subjects to recognize a potentially sexual situation, and that such recognition involved a complex interaction between persons and the context rather than to a simple response to sexual stimuli and, furthermore, the sexual conduct activated was negotiated through the context rather than being driven by some internal state. It was argued that 'scripts are involved in learning the meaning of internal states, organizing the sequences of specifically sexual acts, decoding novel situations, setting the limits on sexual responses and linking meanings from nonsexual aspects of life to specifically sexual experiences' (p. 17). Many aspects of human sexual conduct are easily explainable using the notion of scripts, for example the control of visual access to our bodies by posture and forms of clothing (Levin, 1975) rather than drives, but this does not preclude that some drives may be influenced, if not partially controlled, by scripts. More recently, Gagnon (1991) described the extended formulation of the concept of sexual scripting in a negative form: 'Without the proper elements of a script that defines the situation, names the actors, and plots the behavior, nothing sexual is likely to happen ... The script is what connects feelings of desire and pleasure or disgust and disintegration with the bodily activities associated with physical touching and physical signs of arousal.' (p. 6) According to Gagnon (1991), sexual scripts can be assigned to three levels: (i) the intrapsychic—on the level of mental life, broadly involving future plans, guides for current action, etc; (ii) the interpersonal—the level of social interaction; and (iii) the cultural scenario—instructional guides that exist at the level of collective life (society's mores?). As is to be expected from his social environmentalist approach, Gagnon (1991) reduces the importance of the biological sexual drive and strongly advocates sexual scripting and its application to a host of sexual behaviours, the interpretation of physiological events relevant to sexual arousal, pleasure and climax. Another way to describe the script activation of human sexual conduct was formulated by Money (1986, 1988), regarded by many as an important theoretician of human sexuality and a prolific inventor of terms to describe its intricacies. His scripts are lovemaps that induce or augment a person's 'sexuoerotic' arousal. He defined a lovemap as 'a personalized, developmental representation or template in the mind and in the brain that depicts the idealized lover and the idealized program of sexuoerotic activity with that lover as projected in imagery and ideation, or actually engaged in with that lover' (Money, 1986, 1988). A lovemap is rated as normophilic on the basis of what is ideologically defined by those with ideological authority as sexuoerotically normal and acceptable. Ideological norms vary historically, regionally, and by community. Lovemaps may be incomplete or insufficient (hypophilic), too dominant or pervasive (hyperphilic), or too peculiar and divergent from a given norm (paraphilic). According to Money (1988), everyone has a personal lovemap with a repository (credenda) and a memorandum or readout of things to do (agenda). One's sexual credenda is 'a memorandum of the complete inventory of imagery and ideation, separated or interconnected as in the story line or drama of a dream or fantasy,' (that can) 'either induce or augment personal sexuoerotic arousal, heightening its intensity and facilitating the achievement of orgasm' (Money 1988). He relates credenda to agenda in the same way as a rehearsal is related to an actual dramatic performance; one precedes and then becomes the other. Interestingly, Gagnon (1991) makes no mention of lovemaps despite the fact that they are very similar to his sexual scripts. Both sexual scripts and lovemaps would reside in the personality, attitude box (**48**) of the model (Fig. 6.1), being achieved by imprinting, conditioning, habit, and learning.

McConaghy (1987) has critically discussed the view that 'all sexual behaviour is learned' (p. 326), and argued that many of its proponents, coming from a sociological allegiance, gave no consideration to the possibility that biological factors could be interacting with social factors to produce the behaviours. He illustrates a number of areas of sexual development and behaviour where past research findings of the apparent lack of importance of biological factors needs be reexamined to include genetic, biological, and prenatal hormonal factors.

INNATE SEX DRIVE OR ORIENTATION

Children, in their upbringing, are so subjected to the wants and wishes of others (parents, schooling, society) that it is impossible to find out if there are any instinctive or innate aspects of human sexuality. However, there are two rare cases where a child has apparently been brought up from a very young age in the absence of normal contacts with other humans and with no educational or socializing milieu. The first case is that of the 'wild boy' named Victor, who wandered out of the woods into a village in France on 9 January, 1800. He was naked, had no speech, showed no toilet training and did not relate to or understand the humans who captured him. No parents ever came to claim him. Jean-Marc Itard tried to teach Victor to speak and wrote reports about this aspect of his attempted education but he also described his sexual development briefly. When he was about 17 his long awaited puberty arrived. He had severe behavioural problems with women, as Itard wrote: 'Several times I have watched him in a group of women seek to calm his tenseness by sitting down next to one and squeezing her hand, her arms and her knees. Continuing these bizarre caresses, he would feel his unruly desires grow stronger instead of disappear. Then, seeing no way out of his uncomfortable emotions, he would change mood completely. He would push away the woman he had first sought out and go through the same process with another' (Shattuck, 1980). Clearly, there was a residue of sexual drive or motivation in Victor but it was obviously vestigial and he had no method of expressing it correctly, namely, the sexual scripts or lovemaps were not available (see above section). Victor never learned to speak or to form any but the most basic social attachments. The second case is that of Genie. Her mother was blind and terrified that her husband would kill her if she did not go along with his child-hating behaviour. The father did not want children so when the first one was born he banished her into the garage where she died of exposure. Genie, the fourth child, was apparently confined to her bedroom with a baby's potty seat attached by a harness to her bottom. She was beaten for making a noise so did not speak and rarely heard speech. She was fed subsistance rations with the minimum of attention. Her days were spent in the harness and her nights sewn up in a sleeping bag until she was 14 when her mother finally left the house and took Genie with her. Susan Curtiss (1977), a psychologist, worked with Genie to teach her to talk. She also reported on the effects of her puberty. Genie told her of a crush she had on her school bus driver, a Mr B. She blushed when his name was mentioned and covered her face. She also said 'Mr B. hand. Mr.B. have hand. Mr.B. hand tickle vulva. Finger tickle vulva. Genie vulva.' These were fantasies as no such behaviour had ever happened (it should be noted in passing that 'vulva' was a surprising word for Genie to have been taught or have known considering her background). It thus appears that puberty activated her to target her sexual desires on a male rather than on her female psychologist, while Victor's desires were targetted on women. The likelihood is that the hormonal changes at puberty activated innate behaviour patterns, albeit primitive and crude ones. While these fascinating cases should not be overinterpreted, they perhaps suggest that humans may have innate sexual orientations or drives.

EXPERIMENTAL APPROACHES TO STUDYING SEXUAL BRAIN FUNCTION

A number of experimental approaches have been used to study the functions of specific parts of the brain. These are listed in Table 6.1 with a brief description of their effects. Some of the techniques have been applied to try to evaluate the sexual functioning of the brain both in animals and in humans. While there have been a large number of studies in animals the number in humans is extremely limited. The one obvious advantage in brain studies with humans is that humans can tell the investigator their mental state before, during, and after the treatment because practically all the experimental brain procedures are conducted in conscious subjects.

Table 6.1 Experimental approaches to studying brain function in humans and animals (after Collins, 1991)

Brain procedure	Species	Effects
Epileptic focus	Human	Possible evoked or blockade of site function
Lesion analysis	Human and animal	Loss/change in mental state and/or behaviour after site destroyed
Stimulating electrodes	Animal and human	Evoked behaviour or mental state indicates possible site functions
Injection via cannula	Animal and human	Elicits mental and behavioural changes
Recording electrodes	Animal and human	Changes in neuronal function during performed activity suggests site involved
Metabolic mapping	Human and animal	Changes in regional blood flow and energy metabolism
Magnetic stimulation	Human	Stimulate selective brain areas to induce motor changes

BRAIN 'PLEASURE CENTRES' (52)

Olds (1956) discovered that animals would work to be electrically stimulated in some parts of their brains. He proposed that there was a specialized brain circuit for reward and called the sites where it occurred 'pleasure centres'. Later, Olds (1972) rescinded the concept as being premature, believing that the electrical stimulation was of fibres rather than neurons, thus the site of stimulation was not necessarily the site where the nervous impulses take on the subjective experience of pleasure. Pleasure centres became anathema in neurophysiology. Wise (1980), however, argued that, with minor modifications, the concept of pleasure centres still provided a useful paradigm. Much pharmacological evidence suggests dopamine involvement in reward function, while the fibres of the ascending dopamine systems have their highest concentration in the median forebrain bundle, the best site for self-stimulation, as reported by Olds. Wise (1980) proposed that the 'dopamine synapse is the "pleasure centre", which Olds originally thought was in the lateral hypothalamus' (p. 93). According to Wise 'the dopamine synapse qualifies as a reasonable candidate for the site in the brain where the hedonic impact of the sensory message is first associated with the sense impressions of the external events which constitute natural rewards' (p. 95). Despite some later criticism by Arbuthnott (1980), the critical and unique role that dopamine plays in reward was upheld by Wise (1980*a*). The 'pleasure centres' (**52**) in the present heuristic model (Fig. 6.1) should not be taken as evidence that such 'centres' exist but should be accepted in the terms of Wise's proposal as a model device to indicate that at sites somewhere in the brain, the sensory messages involved in sexual arousal and orgasm must be translated into the feeling of pleasure. In relation to the previous discussion the unique studies of Heath (1972) are more than relevant. He inserted brain elecrodes into a young male adult suffering from temporal lobe epilepsy and chronic depression characterized by an inability to experience pleasure. The subject responded with pleasure only when electrical stimulation was applied to the septal site of electrode implantation (not to the other sites). When he was equipped with a device that allowed him to self-stimulate he stimulated the septal region repeatedly. On one occasion he stimulated his septal region 1200 times, on another 1500, and on a third 900 times (during three hour sessions). He reported 'feelings of pleasure, alertness,and warmth (goodwill); he had feelings of sexual arousal and described it as a compulsion to masturbate' (p. 7).

Epileptic focus

Each temporal lobe consists partly of limbic system structures—the amygdala and hippocampus. Sexual functioning is partly related to these structures so epileptic foci in the temporal lobe can affect sexual functioning. The commonest finding in temporal lobe epilepsy is hyposexuality, a lack of sexual drive and impotence which may occur in males (Hierons and Saunders, 1966). The treatment of removing the focus by brain surgery (Blumer and Walker, 1967) can sometimes lead to gross hypersexuality (Blumer, 1970), as can bilateral removal of the temporal lobes (Freeman, 1973; Terzian and Ore, 1955). It is often claimed that the condition resembles the hypersexuality said to be displayed in rhesus macaques on removal of both temporal lobes (Klüver and Bucy, 1939). Beach (1967) has pointed out, however, that this widely quoted monkey experiment and its conclusions is flawed because the sexual behaviour of the animals before the lesions was not established as a pre-operative norm so that the post-operative changes are difficult to identify and interpret.

Lesion analysis in human males

A controversial treatment has been utilized by a number of workers in order to reduce criminal sexual behaviour, namely, making lesions in the brains of sexual offenders. Roeder, Orthner, and Muller (1972) made stereotaxic lesions in the ventral medial hypothalamic nucleus (nucleus of Cajal) in ten cases of sexual deviation. About three-quarters of the nucleus was damaged. This improved three cases of uncontrollable paedophilic homosexuality, three cases of homosexuality, and a further three results were unsatisfactory. Bilateral lesions in the tenth patient were said to have cured him of intractable exhibitionism. In general, sexual potency was weakened but preserved after unilateral lesion but abolished after bilateral lesions.The selectivity of the operation was attested by the lack of effect on sperm counts or changes in the levels of adrenocortical or gonadal hormones. Dieckman, Hassler, Horn, and Schneider (1975) reported that when part of the hypothalamus of the sub-dominant hemisphere that was regarded as the sexual behaviour centre, together with smaller sections of the hormonal centre, were removed, sexual drive was clearly reduced in a follow-up of from seven to 40 months. Meyers (1961, 1962) reported a complete loss of sexual interest and erectile capability after lesions in the ansa lenticularis which were undertaken to relieve abnormal motor behaviour.

Lesions in the hypothalamus (mPOA/AHA) in animals

In practically all animals, lesions in the medial preoptic/anterior hypothalamic area of the brain (mPOA/AHA) induce reductions in sexual responses. Heimer and Larsson (1966–7) were the first to report that large electrolytic lesions in the mPOA/AHA abolished copulatory behaviour in the male rat but that partial lesions were without effect. This work has been the starting point for a number of investigations of the role of the mPOA/AHA in sexual activity which have been recently reviewed by Everitt and Bancroft (1992). It appears that the lesions cause a block in the performance of the reflexive acts of mounting and copulation, but the male rats still show interest in oestrus females. In fact, their excitement over them can apparently be channelled into purposeless motor acts. The male rats thus appear to be sexually aroused but are unable to perform. Slimp, Hart, and Goy (1978) found that mPOA/AHA lesions in the male rhesus monkey severely impaired coitus with female rhesus monkeys, but the males could still masturbate to ejaculation as frequently as control animals. Thus the area controls the ability to copulate rather than to ejaculate. In this context it is interesting to speculate how those who decry a biological basis for sexual behaviour would report on the lesioned monkeys. Would a social interactionist argue that the lesioned males did not have the sexual script(s) for the coital performance ? (see section on sexual scripts and lovemaps) or would they argue that this is where the programmes of the sexual scripts are stored? The effects of similar lesions in humans are not known. Parallels with the human condition of psychogenic erectile dysfunction, where a man can experience normal sexual desire and be able to masturbate but cannot obtain a serviceable erection during sexual activity with his partner, have been suggested (Everitt and Bancroft, 1992, p. 87).

Electrical stimulation of the brain

Indwelling electrodes have been inserted into the brains of patients suffering from epilepsy, dyskineas, or intractable pain, for diagnostic and therapeutic purposes. During electrical stimulation of the brain via these electrodes, specific intracerebral areas have been found to evoke sensations that are described as pleasurable. The term usually encompasses a wide range of affects such as happiness, delight, joy, gratification, satisfaction, euphoria, and elation (Delgado, 1976). However, despite many thousands of brain stimulations remarkably few descriptions of evoked sexual pleasure have been forthcoming. Penfield and Jasper (1954) stimulated a great part of the medial and lateral cortex in man but never elicited signs or symptoms of a sexual nature. Evoked sexual pleasure by septal stimulation has been described by two subjects who were stimulated electrically in this area (Heath, 1972; Heath et al., 1974; Moan and Heath, 1972). Heath (1972) commented in the paper that previous stimulations of the septal site induced a sexual motive state but this was never reported for other sites despite the fact that it created pleasant feelings. Bechtereva et al. (1975) reported that in one epileptic patient who was stimulated in the right thalamic centre median, positive sexual sensations were felt, while Crow and Cooper (1972) described a patient who had sexual sensations when a point in the cingulate region was stimulated. Sem-Jacobson (1968) reported that two of his male patients (each suffering from psychiatric disorders) described responses related to sex in the course of depth EEG examinations. One said 'it is pleasant, it is like a sexual pleasure. no smell. no taste. I feel it in the whole body.' Subsequent further stimulation was stopped at this time. The second subject liked the stimulation and asked for more. It culminated in him wetting the bed and ejaculating (orgasm) with flushing and breathing. The electrodes were located in 'the anterior part of the brain the posterior part of the frontal lobe, two cm from the midline'. It is unfortunate that Sem-Jacobson (1968) felt ethically, during brain stimulation, that in any area that aroused sexual behaviour 'it was not necessary nor justified to analyse in detail the various aspects of the responses'. Hence the crudity and near practical absence of any details in the descriptions.

In the context of human brain studies, mention must be made of the classic investigations of Maclean (1976) on the localization of sexual function in squirrel and rhesus monkeys. He showed that there were a number of sites where electrical stimulation by implanted electrodes produced erection or ejaculation. The sites included the preoptic region, lateral hypothalamus, tegmentum, and anterior part of the cingulate gyrus (Maclean and Ploog, 1962).

Intracerebral cannula injections

In a unique set of experiments, which were strongly criticized by some sections of the medical press (Anonymous, 1972), Heath (1972) injected,via intracerebral cannula implanted in the septal regions, acetylcholine (400 μg) in the case of a male and acetylcholine and levarterenol bitartrate (150 μg) in a female. Both were suffering from psychomotor seizures and in the case of the 60-year-old male this condition was accompanied with dysphoria. In the male (B10), acetylcholine induced 'strong pleasure feelings and a sexual motive state but it did not culiminate in orgasm (p. 15). The patient said he had never before experienced such intense feelings of pleasure (in sharp contrast to his dysphoria).' The injections in the 34-year-old woman resulted in an elevation 'in mood and heightened awareness' and 'involved the development of sexual motive state and in most instances, within another 5–10 minutes, culminated in repetitive orgasms' (p. 12). The orgasmic state was apparently confirmed by questioning the subject and observing her 'sensuous appearance and movements' (p. 12).The injections were carried on for over four months and appeared to inhibit her convulsions. The fact that both cholinergic (acetylcholine) and adrenergic (levarterenol) could induce sexual excitement to orgasm from the same brain area suggests that arousal can occur either by excitatory activation (cholinergic) or by suppressing an inhibitory path (adrenergic).

Recording electrodes

Heath (1972) recorded electroencephalographic data (EEG) from in-dwelling intracerebral electrodes in two patients while they were intensely sexually aroused. In the case of the male, EEGs were obtained once with arousal induced by masturbation culminating in orgasm and once through heterosexual coitus. With the female patient, recordings were obtained during intracerebral pharmacological induction of sexual arousal to orgasm; the details of this pharmacological stimulation have been described in the preceding section. While spikes and slow waves with superimposed fast activity were seen at orgasm in the septal region, less dramatic changes were also seen in the amygdala, thalamic nuclei, and deep cerebellar nuclei.

Recording brain electrical activity by external electrodes on the scalp during sexual arousal to orgasm has been accomplished in a number of studies (Cohen, Rosen, and Golden, 1976; Graber, Rohrbaugh, Newlin, Varner, and Ellingson, 1985; Heath, 1972; Mosavich and Tallaferro, 1954), but the specificity of the records are confounded by movement artefacts thus creating serious difficulties of interpretation. Moreover, as little significant change appears to have been obtained from the records (Heath, 1972), they have not added any new insights into brain activity during arousal or orgasm.

Metabolic mapping

An increased activity in specific brain sites can be shown by the technique of metabolic mapping. In this technique any increase in brain site metabolism due to increased nervous activity can be revealed. It has not as yet been used for a full study on human sexual arousal.

Magnetic stimulation

By stimulating with an intense magnetic field over the brain and spinal cord, selected areas can be activated and the muscle(s) controlled can be monitored. At present this technique has been applied to the study of pelvic muscle function (Herdmann, Bielefeldt and Enck 1991) but has not yet been used to try to activate genital sexual muscle function.

ANDROGENS AND MALE SEXUAL BEHAVIOUR (49, 51)

Androgens are the major sex steroids of the human male. They are produced mainly in the testes (51), secreted into the plasma as testosterone and androstenedione, and are carried in the plasma mainly bound to testosterone binding globulin. The free androgen in the plasma, some 4 per cent of the total, is the active principle. Only about 2 per cent of the total androgens are produced in the adrenal cortex (49).

The consensus opinion about the effects of castration, an operation that has been used either as a punishment or for religious reasons for thousands of years, is that after puberty it results in diminished sexual activity and erectile dysfunction, but there is a large variability in individual responses. Some individuals can maintain sexual activity and interest for years after their orchidectomy. A modern series of castrations was undertaken for medico-legal reasons in Norway (Bremer, 1959). Evaluated changes in the sexual function of 157 cases (but unfortunately not against a control group) showed that two-thirds had a complete loss of sexual drive and activity within the first year of the operation. A number of individuals, however, retained the capacity for coitus for more than ten years after their castration. It is thought that adrenal androgens (**49**), previous sexual experience, sexual partner availability, and the individual's expectations of the effects all play a role in the final response to testicular loss.

Over the years the involvement of androgens in human male sexual behaviour has been reviewed numerous times (Bancroft, 1977, 1980, 1989; Bermant and Davidson, 1974; Everitt and Bancroft, 1992; Ford and Beach, 1965; Kinsey, Pomeroy, Martin, and Gebhard 1953; Schiavi and White, 1976). In hypogonadal men, or castrated adults, replacement and removal of testosterone gives rise to a restoration and then a decline of sexual interest and sexual activity (Davidson, Camargo, and Smith, 1979; O'Carroll, Shapiro, and Bancroft, 1985; Skakkebaek, Bancroft, Davidson, and Warner 1981). Changes in behaviour were assessed by using daily log recordings by the subjects of their sexual activity, experiences, and sexual interest such as frequencies of erections, coitus, and masturbation. Sexual thoughts and the accompanying feeling of excitment were increased by androgen replacement (Skakkabaek *et al.*, 1981).

As androgens are clearly involved in the maintenance of male sexual behaviours antiandrogens should inhibit androgen-dependent sexual drive. Neuman (1977) reviewed studies with cyproterone acetate, a synthetic steroid that is antiandrogenic, progestational, and antigonadotrophic. Antiandrogenic activity is the result of competitive androgen antagonism at target organ sites. With sexually naïve rats the compound suppressed their sexual motivation but with sexually experienced rats no inhibition was discernible. Clinical trials of the compound for hypersexuality and sexual deviation were begun in 1966. It was effective in the treatment of hypersexuality. First there was loss of libido, then the capacity to erect decreased, and, finally, orgasmic capability disappeared. Antiandrogen treatment does not have any influence on the direction of the sexual drive, only on its force.

Androgen effects on the brain (45–28–29; 45–33–29)

Despite the fact that androgens clearly affect human male sexual behaviour, sadly at present, there is very little concrete evidence for any specific action on the particular brain mechanisms involved. The influence of androgens on erectile function, however, can be interpreted, according to Everitt and Bancroft (1992) to indicate that there are at least two controlling systems in the brain. One is androgen-dependent and subserves sexual arousability and desire. It is claimed that its activity can be measured by monitoring spontaneous erections during sleep as nocturnal penile tumescence (abbreviated as NPT) is impaired in men with loss of sexual desire due to non-hormonal causes (Bancroft, 1988). The other system is androgen-independent and involves the erectile response to visual stimuli. The evidence for postulating the two systems comes from the fact that the spontaneous erections that arise during sleep (NPT) are androgen-dependent as they are impaired in states of androgen insufficiency but can be restored by androgen replacement (Cunningham, Karacan, Ware, Lantz, and Thornby, 1982; Kwan, Greenleaf, Mann, Crapo, and Davidson, 1983). The erections in response to visual erotic stimuli, however, persist in hypogonadal men and are not altered by androgen replacement (Bancroft and Wu, 1983; Kwan *et al.*, 1983).

BRAIN NEUROTRANSMITTERS AND MALE SEXUAL ACTIVITY (33, 52)

Most animal data, and the sparse human data available, suggest that monoaminergic neurotransmitters dopamine, nor-adrenaline, and 5–hydroxytryptamine (5-HT or serotonin) are involved in sexuality (see Rosen (1992) and Everitt and Bancroft (1992) for references). In rodent work, dopamine agonists enhance male sexual behaviour and antagonists inhibit it. In humans, apomorphine, a dopamine agonist, enhances the number of spontaneous erections in normal males and in men with pyschogenic erectile dysfunction. The dopamine antagonist, benperidol, appears to reduce human sexual behaviour and has been used clinically to control deviant behaviour in certain patients (Rosen, 1992). Yohimbine (an alpha-2 antagonist) appears to be helpful in improving erectile dysfunction (Rosen, 1992). In some cases of men who complain of a poor quality of orgasm with no sexual gratification (52), alpha-2 antagonists such as yohimbine and Idazoxan appear to enhance the quality of the orgasm, making it pleasureable again despite the unpleasant side effects that can occur with the drugs (Qureshi and Levin, 1992). Central serotonergic mechanisms have been proposed as inhibitory factors in the control of rodent sexual drive (Foreman, Hall, and Love, 1989), but the possible role of serotonin in human sexuality is confusing (Everitt and Bancroft, 1992; Rosen, 1992). Different serotonergic drugs have been claimed to have prosexual effects, increasing sexual desire in both male and female patients. Serotonin reuptake inhibitors have also been said to cause yawning and spontaneous erections and orgasms in some patients. Other studies, however, have reported anorgasmia with such drugs. The different results cannot as yet be explained and may well be due to the choice of human who is given the drug; their brain systems may be very different although they may present initially with apparently the same mental conditions.

While androgens and brain amines influence male human sexual behaviour separately there do not seem to be any studies on the effects of androgens on brain amines (**45–33**). It is highly likely that there will be interactions between the latter and that this is perhaps one way in which androgens influence sexual behaviour.

PATHWAYS THROUGH THE MODEL OF SEXUAL MAN

The heuristic model shown in Fig. 6.1 characterizes sexual man as a 'positive feedback—negative feedback, relaxation oscillator'. The relaxation oscillation occurs because there is a build up of sexual arousal (**23**) which finally activates a discharge of activity through the emission and ejaculation centres (**40, 47**) to the pleasure centres (**52**). When this happens, it inhibits (**41–30–29–23**) sexual arousal and arousability for a finite time (Masters and Johnson, 1966). After a variable period (dependent on age, intensity, and novelty of arousing stimuli), the inhibition wears off and the system can be charged up again to allow a further discharge. It should be stressed strongly that this heuristic model has been developed to attempt to show some of the dynamic basic interactions of known psychological and physiological features of human sexuality in a single flow chart. The reality of man's sexual behaviour is, of course, infinitely more complex.

A brief tour through the flow chart model

The central feature of the model is sexual arousal (**23**), the state, and sexual arousability (**29**), the rate (Whalen, 1966). These are influenced by a variety of paths. Inputs from the senses: touch (**1**), taste (**2**), smell (**3**), vision (**4**) and hearing (**5**) can either enhance or decrease (**12**) sexual arousal and also genito-pelvic sensation (**11**). The activation of sexual arousal at a particular threshold, varying for the individual and at different times, will activate (**13**) 'attention-awareness' (**8**) to sexual matters and this can augment or depress the modalities.

Touch (**1**), the haptic sense, is a very important stimulus for sexual attention/awareness (**8**) and so has its own path to activate (**9**). Fatigue (**18**) reduces attention/awareness (**8**) and sexual arousal (**16**). Pain is more complex in that it can enhance or reduce (**16**) sexual arousal. Genito-pelvic sensation (**11**), enhanced by the output from the erection centre (**40**), activates the detumescence drive (**65**) to reduce the erection. It also appears to be an important component for the maintenance of sexual desire/libido. Men with complete spinal transections gradually lose the wish to partake of sexual activity (Money, 1960). Hormonal determinants (**45**), especially androgens from the adrenal cortex (**49**) and the gonads (**51**), affect sexual arousal (**23**) and sexual arousability (**29**) the latter probably via changes in brain amines (**33**) (Everett, 1975). These can also be altered by mood. The hormonal determinants can affect the centres for erection, emission, and ejaculation in the spinal cord (**47**) and may (**15**) influence genito-pelvic structures (blood flow, nerves, end organs?) and thus sensory input from the area. In relation to aggression (**43**), the androgen components (**49, 51**) are known to increase (**42**) aggressive tendencies (Meyer-Bahlburg, Boon, Sharma, and Edwards, 1974). Other types of hormones from the posterior pituitary (**62**), such as oxytocin and vasopressin, can also be increased through activation of the hypothalamus (**58**) by sexual arousal (**23**), before (**36**) and by orgasm (**41–36**).Their possible role(s) in male sexual mechanisms are unknown (Davidson, 1991; Gooren, 1991). The 'output' of the sexual arousal (**23**) activates the erection, emission, and ejaculation centres in the brain (**40**) and spinal cord (**47**). If orgasm occurs (**Y, 41**), then there will be an inhibition (Masters and Johnson, 1966) of sexual arousability and arousal (**41–30–29–23**) and an activation of the pleasure centres (**36–52**) creating sexual gratification.

The 'personality/attitudes' (**48**) is a hypothetical complex that summates all aspects that go to make up the 'behavioural core' and consciousness (ego?) of a human being; it is the 'self' part of being. It is not simply personality, as it can be influenced or modified by factors such as learning, conditioning, habit forming, together with other possible such as like imprinting and instinct. It will influence the manner by which pain (**19**) is treated (**20**), as it can be used to enhance or inhibit sexual arousal. The pleasure and gratification (**52**) (Wise, 1980) from sexual arousal (**23–36–52**) feeds back (**53**) into the 'personality/attitudes' (**48**) as a reward. Normally, this feedback will be an enhancing factor, positively influencing learning, habit, and conditioning. However, the 'personality-attitudes' (**48**) will feed back to the pleasure centre (**52**) as the habits, learning, imprinting, and conditioning influence the acceptance, appreciation, and facilitation of sexual pleasure (Byrne and Schulte, 1990). It is also possible that the 'personality/attitudes' (**48**) influences hormonal outputs via the hypothalamus (**59**) in terms of the emotional balance of the personality/attitudes (**48**). Stress, for example, could act via the personality/attitudes (**48**) to depress androgen output from the testes via the hypothalamus (Kreuz, Rose, and Jennings, 1972).

If the level of sexual arousal (**23**) induced is unable to activate the ejaculation centres (**40, 47**) and the system fails to take the orgasm path, then the non-orgasmic path (**N, 41**) becomes dominant. This path can increase fustration (**37–38**) and anxiety (**34–35**). Anxiety (**35**) can inhibit sexual arousal (**23**) (Masters and Johnson, 1966) or it can enhance it (**30**) (Beck and Barlow, 1984), depending how the 'personality/attitudes' (**48**) gates (**32**) the anxiety path to sexual arousal. Frustration (**38**) has its own enhancing feedback (**39**) on to anxiety (**39**), while the output path of frustration (**38**) to aggression (**43**) (Zillman, 1984) can influence the personality/attitudes (**48**) core.Aggression (**43**) in the form of anger is known as an enhancer (**30**) of sexual arousal (**23**) and arousability (**29**) (Barclay, 1969; Maclean, 1962). Indeed, according to the psychoanalyst Stoller (1976), sexual excitement is normally generated by and enhanced by hostility (overt or hidden). Sex guilt (**25**) is activated (**24**) by sexual arousal (**23**) which in turn can create (**31**) anxiety (**35**) (Byrne and Sheffield, 1965). Sex guilt (**25**) activates conscience (**21**) (Friedman, 1970) and conscience (the sense of right or wrong) can either inhibit or enhance the guilt (**25**). Conscience (**21**) is influenced by the personality/attitudes (**48**). Conscience can also call up (**7**) fantasy (**6**) which may be used to enhance or depress the sexual arousal (**23**). Fantasy (**6**) can itself be activated or suppressed by the personality/attitudes (**48**).

THE FINAL WORDS

This short review on selected aspects of human male sexuality clearly reveals our lack of knowledge, sometimes about the most simple of things (namely, defining sexual states and conditions). Progress occurs, however, on the biological front with the application of new techniques for assessing brain and genital function. Advances are now being made in analysing brain functions at the tissue level by analysing the release of transmitters using chronoamperometry, at the cellular level by application of molecular techniques (*in situ* hybridization, DNA and RNA analysis, and cloning), while new agonists and antagonists are being created to activate or block selective pathways in neural tissue (Everitt and Bancroft, 1992). With these new methodologies and the new physical techniques of measuring and imaging brain function in the human subject the future looks promising for the biological characterization and evaluation of many aspects of human male sexuality.

ADDENDUM

Sexual dimorphism of the human brain

In a number of male and female animals there are known qualitative and quantitive sex differences in brain form referred to as sexual dimorphism (see Tobet and Fox 1992 for references). Structural differences between male and female brains is a contentious subject as such differences have been postulated but most of the findings, apart from the larger relative size of the male brain, have remained unconfirmed on reevaluation (Hofman and Swaab 1991). Allen and Gorski (1990), however, reported that the volume of the posteromedial region of the bed nucleus of the stria terminalis, located in the basal part of the brain, was 2.5 times larger in males than in females. According to Hofman and Swaab (1991), this region corresponds to an area in the bed nucleus of rodents that concentrates gonadal steroids and is involved in aggressive and sexual behaviour, and gonadotrophin secretion. It may be that the hormones influence the structures in humans as well as in rodents. Hofman and Swaab (1989) themselves found that the medical preoptic area in the hypothalamus was 2.2 times larger in males than females and that the area had a sex-dependent pattern of growth and decay varying with age. Even more contentious than the possible sexual dimorphism of the human male and female brains is the postulated difference in the suprachiasmatic nucleus between heterosexual men's brains and in homosexual men who died from AIDS (Le Vay 1991, Swaab and Hofman 1990). These reports aroused great controversy especially as Le Vay (1991) concluded that the differences observed suggested that sexual orientation could have a biological substrate. The observations, however, are complicated by a number of uncontrolled factors, some of which are discussed by Tobet and Fox (1992), such as that the differences may be a result of rather than a cause of sexual orientation. It appears that more controlled studies are needed before acceptable conclusions can be made about structure and function in the human brain.

REFERENCES

Allen, L. S. and Gorski, R. A. (1990). Sex differences in the bed nucleus of the stria terminalis of the human brain. *Journal of Comparative Neurology*, **302**, 697–706.

American Psychiatric Association. (1987). *Diagnostic and statistical manual of mental disorders*, 3rd edn., rev., American Psychiatric Association, Washington, DC.

Anon. (1972). Studies on orgasm (Editorial). *British Medical Bulletin.* **1**, 644.

Arbuthnott, G. W. (1980). The dopamine synapse and the notion of 'pleasure centres' in the brain. *Trends in Neuroscience*, **3**, 199–200.

Bancroft, J. (1971). The application of psychophysiological measures to the assessment and modification of sexual behaviour. *Behaviour Research and Therapy*, **9**, 119–30.

Bancroft, J. (1977). The relationship between hormones and sexual behaviour in humans. In *Biological determinants of sexual behaviour*, (ed. J.B. Hutchison), pp. 494–519. Wiley, Chichester.

Bancroft, J. (1980). Endocrinology of sexual function. *Clinic in Obstetrics and Gynaecology*, **7**, 253–81.

Bancroft, J. (1988). Reproductive hormones and male sexual function. In *The Handbook of Sexology* (ed. J.M.A. Sitsen), vol. VI. The pharmacology and endocrinology of sexual function, pp,. 297–315. Elsevier, Amsterdam.

Bancroft, J. (1989). *Human sexuality and its problems*. 2nd edn. Churchill Livingstone, Edinburgh.

Bancroft, J. and Wu, F. C. W. (1983). Changes in erectile responsiveness during androgen therapy. *Archives of Sexual Behaviour*, **12**, 59–66.

Barclay, A. M. (1969). The effect of hostility on physiological and fantasy responses. *Journal of Personality*, **37**, 651–67.

Beach, F. A. (1956). Characteristics of masculine 'sex drive'. In *Nebraska Symposium on Motivation*, (ed. M. Jones), pp. 1–32. University of Nebraska Press, Lincoln.

Beach, F. A. (1967). Cerebral and hormonal control of reflexive mechanisms involved in copulatory behaviour. *Physiological Reviews*, **47**, 289–316.

Beach, F.A., Westbrook, W.H., and Clemens, L.G. (1966). Comparisons of the ejaculatory response in men and animals. *Psychosomatic Medicine*, **28**, 749–63.

Bechtereva, N., Kambarova, D. K., Smirnov, V. M., and Shandurina, A. N. (1975). Using the brain's latent abilities for therapy: chronic intracerebral electrical stimulation. In *Neurosurgical treatment in psychiatry, pain and epilepsy*, (eds. W. H. Sweet, S. Obrador, and J. Marin-Rodriguez), pp. 581–613. University Park Press, Baltimore.

Beck, J. G. and Barlow, D. H. (1965). Current conceptualization of sexual dysfunction: a review and an alternative perspective. *Clinical Psychology Review*, **4**, 363–78.

Beck, J.G., and Barlow, D.H. (1986). The effects of anxiety and attentional focus on sexual responding. 1. Physiological patterns in erectile dysfunction. *Behaviour Research and Therapy*, **24**, 9–17.

Bermant, G. and Davidson, J. M. (1974). *Biological bases of sexual behaviour*; pp. 123–77. Harper and Row, New York.

Bindra, D. (1980). What shall replace drive? *Trends in Neuroscience*, **3**, 24–5.

Blumer, D. (1970). Hypersexual episodes in temporal lobe epilepsy. *Journal of Nervous and Mental Diseases*, **126**, 1099–1106.

Blumer, D. and Walker, A. E. (1967). Sexual behaviour in temporal lobe epilepsy. A study of the effects of temporal lobectomy on sexual behaviour. *Archive of Neurology (Chicago)*, **16**, 37–43.

Bremer, J. (1959). *Asexualization, a follow up study of 244 cases*. Macmillan, New York.

Bullough, V. L. (1976). *Sexual variance in society and history*. Wiley, New York.

Byrne, D. and Schulte, L. (1990). Personality dispositions as mediators of sexual responses. In *Annual Review of Sex Research*, (ed. J. Bancroft), Volume 1, pp. 93–117. The Society for the Scientific Study of Sex Inc., Iowa.

Byrne, D. and Sheffield, J. (1965). Response to sexually arousing stimuli as a function of repressing and sensitising defences. *Journal of Abnormal Psychology*, **70**, 114–18.

Cohen, H.D., Rosen, R.C., and Golden, L. (1976). Electroenceohalographic laterality changes during human sexual orgasm. *Archives Sexual Behaviour*, **5**, 189–99.

Collins, R. C. (1991). Basic aspects of fundamental brain metabolism. In *Ciba Foundation Symposium 163* (eds. D. J. Chadwick and J. Whelan), pp. 6–16. Wiley, Chichester.

Crow, H. J. and Cooper, R. (1972). Stimulation, polarization and coagulation using intracerebral implanted electrodes during investigation and treatment of psychiatric and other disorders. *Medical Progress and Technology*, 1, 91–102.

Cunningham, G. R., Karacan, I., Ware, J. C., Lantz, C. D., and Thornby, J. I. (1982). The relationship between serum and prolactin levels and nocturnal penile tumescence. *Journal of Andrology*, 3, 241–47.

Curtiss, S. (1977). *Genie. a psycholinguistic study of a modern day 'wild child'.* Academic Press, New York.

Davidson, J. M., Camargo, C. A. and Smith, E. R. (1979). Effects of androgens on sexual behaviour of hypogondal men. *Journal of Clinical Endocrinology and Metabolism*, 48, 955–8.

Davidson, J.M. (1991–2). Important questions and trivial answers in the physiology of climax. In *Proceedings First International Conference on Orgasm, New Delhi* (eds., P. Kothari and R. Patel), pp. 57–62. VRP, Bombay.

Delgado, J. M. R. (1976).—New orientations in brain stimulation in man. In *Brain stimulation-reward.* (eds. A. Warquier and E. T. Rolls), pp. 281–503. North-Holland, Amsterdam.

Deutsch J. A. (1979). Drive-another point of view. *Trends in Neuroscience*, 2, 242–4.

Diamond, M. (1965). A critical evaluation of the ontogeny of human sexual behaviour. *Quarterly Review of Biology*, 40, 147–75.

Dieckmann, G., Hassler, R., Horn, H-J., and Schneider, H. (1975). Die behandlung sexueller gewalttater stereotakitsche hypothamatomie. *Sexual Medizin*, 9, 545–51.

Ellis, H. (1936). *Studies in the psychology of sex.* Random House, New York.

Evans, P. (1989). *Motivation and emotion.* Routledge, London.

Everett, G. M. (1975). Role of biogenic amines in the modulation of aggressive and sexual behaviour in animals and men. In *Sexual behaviour—pharmacology and biochemistry*, (eds. M. Sandler and G. L. Gessa), pp. 81–4. Raven Press, New York.

Everitt, B. J. and Bancroft, J. (1992). Of rats and men: the comparative approach to male sexuality. In *Annual Review of Sex Research* (ed. J. Bancroft), Volume 2, pp. 77–118. The Society for the Scientific Study of Sex Inc., Iowa.

Ford, C. S. and Beach, F. A. (1965). *Patterns of sexual behaviour.* Methuen, London.

Foreman, M. M., Hall, J. L., and Love, R. L. (1989). The role of 5HT-2 receptors in the regulation of sexual performance of male rats. *Life Sciences*, 45, 263–70.

Freeman, W. (1973). Sexual behaviour and fertility after frontal lobotomy. *Biological Psychiatry*, 6, 97–104.

Freud, S. (1910). Five lectures on psychoanalysis. In *The standard edition of the works of S. Freud* (ed. and trans. J. Strachey), Vol.11. Hogarth Press, London.

Freud, S. (1977). On sexuality. In *Three essays on the theory of sexuality and other works.* The Pelican Freud Library, Vol. 7 (ed. A. Richards), Penguin Books, London.

Friedman, J.J. (1970). Conscience and its relation to sex. *New York Journal of Medicine*, 70, 2323–7.

Gagnon, J. H. (1991). The explicit and implicit use of the scripting perspective in sex research. In *Annual Review of Sex Research*, (ed. J. Bancroft), Vol. 1, pp. 1–43. The Society for the Scientific Study of Sex Inc., Iowa.

Gagnon, J. H. and Simon, W. (1973). *Sexual conduct.* Aldine, Chicago.

Goldberg, M. (1973) Absence of sexual desire in men. *Medical Aspects of Human Sexuality*, **7**, 13–32.

Goldman, A. H. (1977). Plain sex. *Philosophy and Public Affairs*, **6**, 267–87.

Gooren, L. (1991). Hormones and orgasm, orgasm and hormones. In *Proceedings of the First International Conference on Orgasm, New Delhi* (eds. P. Kothari and R. Patel), pp. 35–47. VRP, Bombay.

Gooren, L., Fliers, E., and Courtney, K. (1990). Biological determinants of sexual orientation. In *Annual Revue of Sex Research* (ed. J. Bancroft), Vol. 1, pp.175–96. The Society for the Scientific Study of Sex Inc., Iowa.

Graber, B., Rohrbaugh, J. W., Newlin, D. B., Varner, J. L., and Ellingson, R. J. (1985) EEG during masturbation and ejaculation. *Archives of Sexual behaviour*, **14**, 491–503.

Hardy, K. R. (1964). An appetitional theory of sexual motivation. *Psychological Review*, **71**, 1–23.

Heath, R .G. (1972). Pleasure and brain activity in man. *Journal of Nervous and Mental Disease*, **154**, 3–18.

Heath, R. G, Cox, A. W., and Lustick, I. S. (1974). Brain activity during emotional states. *American Journal of Psychiatry*, **131**, 858–62.

Heider, K. G. (1976). Dani sexuality; a low energy system. *Man (NS)*, **11**, 188–201.

Heimer, L. and Larsson, K. (1966–7). Impairment of mating behaviour in male rats following lesions in the preoptic-anterior hypothalamic continuum. *Brain Research*, **3**, 248–63.

Herdmann, J., Pielefeldt, K., and Enck, P. (1991). Quantification of motor pathways to the pelvic floor in humans. *American Journal of Physiology*, **260**, G720–3.

Hierons, R., and Saunders, M. (1966). Impotence in patients with temporal lobe lesions. *Lancet*, **2**, 61–64.

Hofman, M. A. and Swaab, D. F. (1989). The sexually dimorphic nucleus of the preoptic area in the human brain: a comparative morphometric study. *Journal of Anatomy*, **164**, 127–43.

Hofman, M. A. and Swaab, D. F. (1991). Sexual dimorphism of the human brain: myth and reality. *Experimental Clinical Endocrinology*, **98**, 161–70.

Hoon, P. W. (1979) The assessment of sexual arousal in women. *Progress in Behaviour Modification*, **7**, 1–61.

Kaplan, H. (1979). *Disorders of sexual desire*. Simon and Schuster, New York.

Kinsey, A. C., Pomeroy, W. D. and Martin, C. E. (1948). *Sexual behaviour in the human male*. W. B. Saunders, Philadelphia.

Kinsey, A. C., Pomeroy, W. D., Martin, C. E., and Gebhard, P. H. (1953). *Sexual behaviour in the human female*. W. B. Saunders, Philadelphia.

Kirkendall, L. A. (1961). Sex drive. In *The Encyclopedia of Sexual Behaviour*. (eds. A. Ellis and A. Abarhanel), pp. 939–48. Hawthorn Books, New York.

Klüver, H. and Bucy, P. C. (1939). Preliminary analysis of the temporal lobe in monkeys. *Archives of Neurology and Psychiatry*, **42**, 979–1000.

Kreuz, L. E., Rose, R. M., and Jennings, R. (1972). Suppression of plasma testosterone levels and psychological stress. *Archives of General Psychiatry*, **26**, 479–82.

Kwan, M., Greenleaf, W. J., Mann, J., Crapo, L., and Davidson, J. M. (1983). The nature of androgen action on male sexuality; a combined laboratory and self-report study in hypogonadal men. *Journal of Clinical Endocrinology and Metabolism*, **57**, 557–62.

Lacey, J. I. (1967). Somatic response patterning and stress; some revisions of activation theory. In *Psychological stress* (eds. M. H. Appley and R. Trumbull), pp. 14–37. Appleton-Century-Crofts, New York.

Leiblum, S. R. and Rosen, R. C. (1988). *Sexual desire disorders*. Guilford, New York.

Le Vay, S. (1991). A difference in hypothalamic structure between heterosexual and homosexual men. *Science*, **253**, 1034–7.

Levin, R. J. (1975). Facets of female behaviour supporting the social script model of human sexuality. *Journal of Sex Research*, **11**, 348–52.

Levin, R. J. (1980). The physiology of sexual function in women. *Clinics in Obstetrics and Gynaecology*, **7**, 213–252.

Levin, R. J. and Wagner, G. (1985). Orgasm in the laboratory—Quantitative studies on duration, intensity, latency and vaginal blood flow. *Archives of Sexual Behaviour*, **14**, 439–49.

Levin, R. J. and Wagner, G. (1987). Self-reported central sexual arousal without vaginal arousal—duplicity or veracity revealed by objective measurement. *Journal of Sex Research*, **23**, 540–4.

Linner, B. (1972). *Sex and society in Sweden*. Harper and Row, New York.

Maclean, P. D. (1962). New findings relevant to the evolution of psychosexual functions of the brain. *Journal of Nervous and Mental Diseases*, **135**, 289–301.

Maclean, P. D. (1976). Brain mechanisms of elemental sexual functions. In *The sexual experience* (eds. B. T. Sadock, H. I. Kaplan, and A. M. Freeman), pp. 119–27. William and Wilkins, Baltimore.

Maclean, P. D. and Ploog, D. W. (1962). Cerebral representation of penile erection. *Journal of Neurophysiology*, **25**, 29–55.

Margoshes, A. and Litt, S. (1965). Sexual appetite and sexual drive. *Psychological Reports*, **16**, 713–9.

Marshall, D. S. (1971). Sexual behaviour on Mangaia. In *Human sexual behaviour (variations in the ethnographic spectrum)* (eds. D. S. Marshall and R. C. Suggs), pp. 103–62. Basic Books, New York.

McConaghy, N. (1987). A learning approach. In *Theories of human sexuality* (eds. J. H. Geer and W. T. O'Donohue), pp. 287–333. Plenum Press, New York.

Masters, W.H. and Johnson, V. E. (1966). *Human sexual response*. Churchill Livingstone, London.

Meyer-Bahlburg, H. F. L., Boon, D. A., Sharma, M., and Edwards, J. A. (1974) Aggressiveness and testosterone measures in man. *Psychosomatic Medicine*, **36**, 269–74.

Meyers, R. (1961). Evidence of a locus of the neural mechanisms of libido and penile potency in the septo-fornico-hypothalamic region of the human brain. *Transactions of the American Neurological Association*, **86**, 81–5.

Meyers, R. (1962). Three cases of myoclonus alleviated by bilateral ansotomy, with a note on post operative alibido and impotence. *Journal of Neurosurgery*, **19**, 71–81.

Moan, C. E. and Heath, R.G. (1972). Septal stimulation for the initiation of heterosexual behaviour in a homosexual male. *Journal of Behavioral Therapy and Experimental Psychiatry*, **3**, 23–30.

Moll, A. (1897). *Untersuchungen über die libido sexualis*. Fischer, Berlin.

Money, J. (1960). Phantom orgasms in the dreams of paraplegic men and women. *Archives of General Psychiatry*, **3**, 373–82.

Money, J. (1961). Components of eroticism in man: 1. The hormones in relation to sexual morphology and sexual desire. *Journal of Nervous and Mental Disease*, **132**, 239–48.

Money, J. (1986), *Lovemaps: clinical concepts of sexual/erotic health and pathology, paraphilia, and gender transposition in childhood, adolescence, and maturity.* Irvington, New York.

Money, J. (1988). *Gay, straight and in between—the sexology of erotic orientation.* Oxford University Press, New York.

Money, J. and Ehrhardt, A. K. (1972). *Man & woman boy & girl.* The Johns Hopkins University Press, Baltimore.

Money, J., Hampson, J. G. and Hampson, J. L. (1957). Imprinting and the establishment of gender role. *Archives of Neurology and Psychiatry*, **77**, 333–6.

Morgan, M. J. (1979). The concept of drive. *Trends in Neuroscience*, **2**, 240–2.

Mosavich, A. and Tallaferro, A. (1954). Studies on EEG and sex function orgasm. *Diseases of the Nervous System*, **15**, 218–20.

Neubeck, G. (1974). The myriad motives for sex. In *Sexual behaviour—current issues* (ed. L. Gross), pp. 89–97. Spectrum, Flushing.

Neumann, F. (1977). Pharmacology and potential use of cyproterone acetate. *Hormone and Metabolism Research*, **9**, 1–13.

O'Carroll, T. (1980). *Paedophilia the radical case.* Peter Owen, London.

O'Carroll, R. E., Shapiro, C., and Bancroft, J. (1985). Androgens, behaviour and nocturnal erections in hypogonadal men; the effect of varying the replacement dose. *Clinical Endocrinology*, **23**, 527–38.

Olds, J. (1956). Pleasure centres in the brain. *Scientific American*, **195**, 105–16.

Olds, J. (1972). The central nervous system and the reinforcement of behaviour. In *Current status of physiological psychology* (eds. D. Singh and C. T. Morgan), pp.141–54. Brooks/Cole, Monterey.

Penfield, W. and Jasper, H. (1954). *Epilepsy and the functional anatomy of the human brain.* Little Brown, Boston.

Przyblya, D. P. J. and Byrne, D. (1984). The mediating role of cognitive processes in self reported sexual arousal. *Journal of Research in Personality*, **18**, 54–63.

Qureshi, M. J. H. and Levin, R. J. (1991–2). Alpha-2 blockers and the treatment of male sexual dysfunction—3 case studies. In *The Proceedings of the First International Conference on Orgasm, New Delhi* (eds. P. Kothari and R. Patel), pp. 205–7. VRP, Bombay.

Rashomon (1950). Japanese film directed by Akira Kurosawa. In *Japanese films*, B.B. Buehrer (1990), pp. 43–7. St James Press, Chicago.

Robinson, P. (1976). *The modernization of sex.* Harper and Row, New York.

Roeder, F., Orthner, H., and Muller, D. (1972). The stereotaxic treatment of pedophilic homosexuality and other sexual deviations. In *Psychosurgery* (eds. E. Hitchcock, L. Laitinen, and K. Vaernet), pp. 87–111. Charles C. Thomas, Springfield, Illinois.

Rosen, C.R. (1992). Alcohol and drug effects on sexual response; human experimental and clinical studies. In *Annual review of sex research.* (ed., J. Bancroft), pp. 119–79. The Society for the Scientific Study of Sex Inc., Iowa.

Sartre, J-P. (1966). *Being and Nothingness* (Hazel E. Barnes, trans.), pp. 501. Washington Square Press, New York.

Schiavi, R. C. and White, D. (1976). Androgens and male sexual function; a review of human studies. *Journal of Sex and Marital Therapy*, **2**, 214–28.

Sem-Jacobsen, C. W. (1968). *Depth-electrographic stimulation of the human brain and behaviour.* Charles C. Thomas, Springfield, Illinois.

Shaffer, J. A. (1978). Sexual Desire. *The Journal of Philosophy*, **75**, 175–8.

Shattuck, R. (1980). *The forbidden experiment; the story of the wild boy of Aveyron.* Farrar, Straus, and Giroux, New York.

Skakkebaek, N. E., Bancroft, J., Davidson, D. W., and Warner, P. (1981). Androgen replacement with oral testosterone undecanoate in hypogonadal men; a double-blind controlled study. *Clinical Endocrinology,* **14**, 49–67.

Slimp, J. C., Hart, B. L., and Goy, R. W. (1978). Heterosexual, autosexual and social behaviour of adult male rhesus monkeys with medial preoptic-anterior hypothalamic lesions. *Brain Research,* **142**, 105–22.

Stoller, R. J. (1976). Sexual excitement. *Archives of General Psychiatry,* **33**, 899–909.

Swaab, D. F. and Hofman, M. A. (1990). An enlarged suprachiasmatic nucleus in homosexual men. *Brain Research,* **537**, 141–8.

Symons, D. (1987). An evolutionary approach. Can Darwin's view of life shed light on human sexuality? In *Theories of human sexuality.* (eds. J. H. Geer and W. T. O'Donohue), pp. 91–125. Plenum Press, New York.

Terzian, J., and Ore, G. D. (1955). Syndrome of Kluver and Bucy reproduced in man by bilateral removal of the temporal lobes. *Neurology,* **5**, 373–80.

Tiefer, L. (1987). Social constructionism and the study of human sexuality. In *Sex and gender* (eds. P. Shaver and C. Hendricks), pp. 70–94. Sage, Beverly Hills.

Tiefer, L. (1992). Historical, scientific, clinical and feminist criticism of 'The Human Sexual Response Cycle' model. In *Annual Review of Sex Research* (ed, J. Bancroft), pp. 1–24. The Society for the Scientific Study of Sex Inc., Iowa.

Tobet, S. A. and Fox, T. O. (1992). Sex differences in neuronal morphology influenced hormonally throughout life. in *Handbook of behavioural neurobiology. sexual differentiation.* (eds. A. A. Geall, H. Moltz, and I. L. Ward). Vol. II, pp. 41–83. Plenum, New York.

Trivers, R.L. (1972). Parental investment and sexual selection. In *Sexual selection and the descent of man 1871–1971* (ed. B. Campbell), pp. 136–79. Aldine, Chicago.

Walen, S. R. and Roth, D. (1987). A cognitive approach. In *Theories of human sexuality* (eds. J. H. Geer and W. T. O'Donohue), pp. 335–62. Plenum Press, New York.

Whalen, R. E. (1966). Sexual motivation. *Psychological Review,* **73**, 151–163.

Wise, R. A. (1980). The dopamine synapse and the notion of 'pleasure centers' in the brain. *Trends in Neuroscience,* **3**, 91–5.

Wise, R. A. (1980*a*). 'Yes, but! . . .' a response to Arbuthnott from Roy Wise. *Trends in Neuroscience,* **3**, 200.

Wenger, M, A., Jones F. N., and Jones, M. H. (1956). *Physiological psychology,* pp. 347–8. Constable, London.

Wundt, W. M. (1893). *Grundzuge der physiologischen psychologie.* Engelman, Leipzig.

van de Velde, T. H. (1926). *Ideal marriage:its physiology and technique.* Random House, New York.

Zilbergeld, B. and Ellison, C. R. (1980). Desire discrepancies and arousal problems in sex therapy. In *Principles and practice of sex therapy* (eds. S. R. Leiblum and L. A. Pervin), pp. 65–101. Tavistock, London.

Zillman, D. (1984). *Connections between sex and aggression.* Lawrence Erlbaum Associates, Hillsdale New Jersey.

Zuger, B. (1970). Gender role determination: a critical review of the evidence from hermaphroditism. *Psychosomatic Medicine,* **32**, 449–67.

7

Classical conditioning, drug cues and drug addiction

Steven Glautier

INTRODUCTION

Classical conditioning theory provides a large and rich source of material with which the problem of addiction can be addressed. This chapter describes the way drug use can be thought of in terms of classical conditioning, the ways in which conditioning processes are thought to affect drug taking behaviour, and implications of the analysis for the development of treatments for addiction. The term 'drug use' is used broadly to refer to a whole range of substances including alcohol, nicotine, opiates, amphetamines, and cocaine, and the chapter is aimed primarily at drugs which have abuse potential. The intention is not to provide a review of all studies relevant to these areas but, rather, to provide an overview.

Two key elements in definitions of drug and alcohol dependence are increased motivation to take the drug and increased tolerance to the effects of the drug (e.g. American Psychiatric Association, 1987; Edwards, Arif, and Hodgson, 1981; Edwards and Gross, 1976; World Health Organization, 1988). A scientific explanation and understanding of *both* of these important features of dependence is possible in terms of the models and concepts of conditioning theory. In this chapter, tolerance to the effects of drugs is considered alongside drug use motivation because altered tolerance to various drug effects can affect drug taking.

Before considering the details of conditioning accounts of drug use motivation and tolerance, some typical drug use episodes will be described.

(1) She was sitting at her garden table on a sultry July afternoon about to enjoy a long cold glass of lager. There was a sharp hiss as she opened the bottle. The drink bubbled and overflowed. Before she had finished pouring, condensation had formed on the sides of the

glass. Every sip was crisp, cool, and refreshing. She put her feet up and began to relax as she felt the first effects of the alcohol.

(2) The instant he woke he knew he was going to feel bad. A wave of panic had swept over him as he struggled to fasten the buttons of his shirt. His hands were shaking so much he had a job getting the first drink to his lips without spilling it. Suddenly he felt dizzy, he was going to fall. A few minutes later he had started to sweat as well as shake but had made it down to the kitchen. With both hands he was steadying a bottle of whisky to his lips. A few minutes later he was still shaking but felt calmer, even cheerful. He sat down gratefully clinging on to the bottle.

(3) It had been nearly two weeks since he had stopped smoking. It was all in the past now, or so he thought. He and his girlfriend had just finished a meal to celebrate his birthday and as she lit her customary cigarette he felt a strong impulse to take one from the packet. For a few minutes he resisted. 'It'll ruin your health. You don't need it', he repeated to himself. But her cigarette smelled good and she looked as though she was enjoying inhaling and playing with the smoke. He picked up the packet and lit up. The first draw made him dizzy, slightly drunk, a few puffs later he felt quite calm and contented, enjoying his cigarette.

It is clear from these situations that drug taking episodes have all the elements necessary to promote classical (Pavlovian) conditioning. Various stimuli which precede drug ingestion (e.g. sight of beer, withdrawal anxiety, smell of cigarette smoke) are closely associated with drugs which have powerful biological and psychological effects. Thus, it is easy to see that these stimuli have the potential to acquire conditioned stimulus properties and become cues for drug use. Because conditioned stimuli play a central role in the control of behaviour, then it must follow that stimuli which have been associated with drug use also have the potential to control behaviour.

In the conditioning analysis of drug use adopted in this chapter a drug induced state is conceived of as an unconditioned stimulus (US) which gives rise to various unconditioned responses (UCRs). Stimuli which are associated with these drug USs may acquire conditioned stimulus (CS) properties as a result of classical conditioning. Conditioned responses (CRs) to drug cues have been argued to play a part in drug use motivation. Specifically, when a CS or cue for drug use is encountered, be it the sight of a needle and syringe or withdrawal anxiety, it is proposed that CRs will be elicited which alter (usually increase) the likelihood of drug use. Fig. 7.1 illustrates a typical drug taking episode.

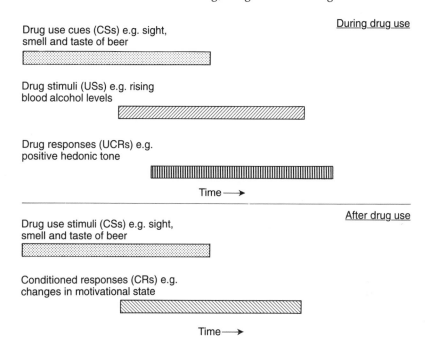

Fig. 7.1 Top half represents the sequence of events in a drug use episode and the bottom half represents the situation after a history of drug use. CSs acquire CR-eliciting capacities as a result of the contingencies present during drug use episodes.

DRUG CUES AND DRUG TAKING

The function of cues accompanying drug taking has had a very high prominence in the behavioural analysis of drug use motivation in recent years. In the above examples the hiss of the bottle opening, the sight of the whisky bottle, the smell of cigarettes, and the withdrawal distress of the alcoholic could all be considered as potential CSs for drug use by virtue of their position with respect to drug ingestion. Three classes of evidence can be used to support the view that drug cues increase the likelihood of drug taking—studies of patterns of drug taking and relapse to drug use amongst people trying to stop using, experimental studies with human subjects, and experimental studies with animals. On its own, each class of evidence has shortcomings. These arise as a result of the methods used in particular investigations, as a result of problems generally associated with the methodology being used, or as a result of some combination of these two things. However, taken together, the convergence of evidence from different studies provides strong support for the view that cues of various sorts can increase drug taking.

Patterns of drug taking and relapse

The conditioning model of drug use being developed requires that patterns of drug use are such that conditioning can occur. At a minimum this means that some stimuli have a higher probability of being followed by drug ingestion than others. The kinds of stimuli which could potentially serve as cues for drug use are many and varied. If smoking occurred at certain times of the day, temporal conditioning may develop; if smoking occurred only in certain rooms, context conditioning may develop; or if smoking occurred only during angry moods, mood conditioning may develop; and so on. Thus, one piece of evidence which would suggest the possibility for drug conditioning would be a non-random distribution of drug taking patterns. With the possibility of conditioning during drug use established, predictions about patterns of relapse follow. Relapse after a period of abstinence should be more likely in some situations than others.

Several studies have examined patterns of drug use and have found that some situations are more likely than others to be antecedents of drug use. With respect to alcohol consumption, for example, Cannon, Leeka, Patterson, and Baker (1990) analysed the relative frequencies of different drinking situations over the last year of drinking in alcoholic subjects using the Inventory of Drinking Situations (Annis, 1982). Using a principal components analysis they found that three factors (unpleasant emotional states, positive emotions and social pressure, and testing personal control) accounted for 43 per cent of the variance in their subject's drinking. Again using alcoholic subjects, Choquette, Hesselbrock, and Babor (1985) asked about the quantity and frequency of drinking in different company (alone, with friends, or with family) and in different settings (alone, in bars, outside, or at sporting events). Among their findings were that drinking occurred more frequently alone and with friends than with family members, and subjects drank in greatest quantities when alone. Also, drinking alone occurred more frequently than in public and greater quantities were consumed than when drinking in bars. Other studies of drinking patterns have supported the view that different situations (moods, contexts, companions, etc.) tend to be associated with different levels and frequencies of alcohol intake (e.g. Deardorff, Melges, Hout, and Savage, 1975; Harford, 1983).

Thus, it may be argued that different situations are likely to be associated with different probabilities and levels of drug use. From this it can be reasoned that the opportunity is present for some situations to acquire CS properties. If conditioning occurs and, as a result, an encounter with a cue increases the likelihood of drug ingestion, then the cue will tend to become more firmly established as a CS. Habitual patterns of drug use may therefore become 'self-perpetuating'. When users attempt to break their habits, the motivational changes which occur during encounters with cues which have effectively become CSs for drug use may undermine their efforts.

Relapse to drug use after a period of abstinence among addicts occurs at a very high rate. Looking across substances Hunt, Barnett, and Branch (1971) found similar rates of relapse among smokers, alcoholics, and heroin addicts. In each of these groups around 60 per cent will have broken abstinence within three months. This kind of finding has led to a great deal of theorizing and research on the nature of the relapse process. Studies of patterns of relapse to drug use in abstinent addicts suggest that the motivational properties of well-established cues are sufficient to have clinical significance.

One particularly well-known model of the relapse process is that described by Marlatt and Gordon (1980, 1985). A central idea in the model is the 'high-risk situation'. High-risk situations can be any set of events or circumstances in which an individual's self-control is threatened. The concept of the high-risk situation is consistent with a conditioning analysis of drug use in that the high-risk situation can be seen as a cue for drug use. Detailed studies by Marlatt and Gordon (1980) of the relapse episodes of alcoholics, smokers, and heroin addicts showed that it was possible to categorize the situations in which people relapse and to rank different categories of situation according to their riskiness. Situations which appeared to precipitate relapse most frequently were negative emotional states (37 per cent), social pressure (24 per cent), and interpersonal conflict (15 per cent).

Many other studies of relapse situations have also been conducted, for example Litman, Stapleton, Oppenheim, Peleg, and Jackson (1983) studied a group of alcoholics; Chaney, Roszell, and Cummings (1982) studied opiate addicts; and Shiffman (1982) studied smokers. These studies broadly replicate the findings of Marlatt and Gordon and support the view that the idea of 'a high-risk situation' is useful to help understand the relapse process.

Experimental studies with human subjects

The second class of evidence which suggests that drug cues may increase drug use motivation is the large body of experimental literature with human subjects. This literature can be sub-divided into three groups. The first, and smallest, group is concerned with experimental analysis of the relapse process itself. The second is concerned with the effects of internal cues which often, although not exclusively, arise from drug effects. Because it is inevitable that a high dose of a drug is preceded by a low dose, early drug effects are especially likely to become

CSs. Effects of this kind are sometimes called priming dose effects. In addition, in dependent users of a drug, the withdrawal phase of drug action is also likely to function as a cue for drug use as the drug will frequently be taken to relieve withdrawal distress. The third group of studies attends to the effects of external cues which precede drug ingestion, for example the sight of a glass of whisky. Although there is no *a priori* reason to suppose that the fundamental process underlying the acquisition of CS properties by internal cues such as early or later drug effects (or indeed mood states) and by external cues differ, the distinction is important. This is because external cues are in a position to play a role in the initiation of a drug use episode whereas the internal cues arising from drug effects relate most clearly to the continuation of an episode once it has begun.

Analysis of relapse

Hodgson (1989) and Abrams, Monti, Carey, Pinto, and Jacobus (1988) have studied the relationship between CRs to drug cues and relapse and the effects of cues on the relapse process. Hodgson describes a study carried out by Coates (1986) in which smokers attempting to quit were instructed to either expose themselves to high-risk situations or avoid high-risk situations. The results were clear cut. The group instructed to expose themselves to cues relapsed more rapidly than the group instructed to avoid cues. At the five-week point fewer than 20 per cent were still abstinent compared to over 80 per cent of the avoidance group. By the 13th week the groups were more alike. There had been no further relapses in the exposure group but the avoidance group's abstinence had fallen to about 30 per cent. This, it was argued by Hodgson, is evidence that cues have powerful effects which need to be considered in order to help people maintain abstinence. Abrams *et al.* (study two) gave a cue exposure test to subjects about to stop smoking. The test involved monitoring psychophysiological and subjective responses to presentation of smoking cues. Out of the 48 subjects completing this test 35 had relapsed at six month follow-up. These subjects had shown greater heart rate increases during the cue exposure test and were more anxious after the test than subjects who were successful abstainers at 6 months.

Internal cues and drug effects

The effect of a dose of alcohol on subsequent motivation to consume alcohol has been the subject of considerable debate as a result of the fact that it is associated with Jellinek's (1952) ideas on loss of control over drinking in alcoholics. At the time Jellinek considered that a single drink would lead an alcoholic into an uncontrollable drinking binge. It is now clear that alcoholic drinking does not necessarily involve complete loss of control (e.g. Mello and Mendelson, 1972). However, it is also clear that under some circumstances consumption of a drug does increase motivation to consume more. A demonstration of this is provided by Funderburk and Allen's (1977) study with alcoholic patients. They gave one of four doses of alcohol over a 13-hour period and then measured motivation to drink eight hours later. Motivation was indexed using an operant task in which subjects pressed a key to earn further drinks. Subjects made increasing numbers of key presses for additional drinks across 0, 16, and 24 oz dose conditions. Key presses dropped off in the 30 oz condition but still remained above the zero dose level. Because of the doses used and the timing of the operant test it is likely that subjects were in a state of acute alcohol withdrawal at the time of testing. It seems, therefore, that this is a test of the effects of drug withdrawal on motivation to drink.

Hodgson, Rankin, and Stockwell (1979) and Stockwell, Hodgson, Rankin, and Taylor (1982) have also demonstrated that doses of alcohol can increase motivation to drink in a speed-of-drinking test. Both of these experiments used doses of alcohol and time intervals between dosing and testing which make it likely that subjects were on the descending limb of the blood alcohol curve at the time of the test. As a result they might also be regarded as tests of the effects of drug withdrawal cues. However, the degree of any withdrawal would have been much less intense than that produced by Funderburk and Allen's (1977) procedures.

Thus, it appears that a dose of alcohol can increase motivation to drink among severely dependent alcoholics, particularly when the effects of the withdrawal state or descending limb of the blood alcohol curve are examined. A further example of the effects of drugs on motivation to consume more of the drug is provided by Jaffe, Cascella, Kumor, and Sherer (1989). Intravenous cocaine users showed increased desire for cocaine 15 minutes after an intravenous bolus of 40 mg of cocaine. The effect was shown in relation to baseline levels and in relation to the effect of placebo (administered double blind) and was abolished by pre-treatment with bromocriptine, a dopamine agonist. In this study, the time course of the effects suggest that it was the initial early drug effect which was important rather than the later withdrawal or descending blood level effect. However, the mechanism by which one dopamine agonist blocks the action of another is unclear at present.

External cues

The analysis of drug effects as internal cues for further drug consumption has a special significance because of its relationship with the clinically important phenomenon of loss of control over drug intake which is considered to affect dependent individuals. External cues which occur before drug ingestion also have a special significance. Since drug effects can only play a part in the regulation of drug use once the drug has been taken, their role in the initiation of an episode of drug use is constrained. Cues which occur before drug ingestion (often, but not exclusively, external), on the other hand, are potentially able to play a part in the initiation of an episode of drug use as well as playing a part during drug use.

Using non-alcoholic subjects Strickler, Dobbs, and Maxwell (1979) found that subjects drinking in bar rooms drank more and sipped their drinks at a greater frequency than when they drank in laboratory situations. Ludwig, Wikler, and Stark (1974) found that alcoholic subjects increased reports of desire to drink and operant lever pressing for further drinks when exposed to the sight and smell of their regular drinks. Interactions between the effects of drug cues and pre-drug cues were also studied. The cueing effects of the drink stimuli were most powerful following a low, rather than a high alcohol dose or placebo priming drink.

Studies comparing alcoholic and non-alcoholic populations have generally found that the presence of alcohol-related stimuli increases reported desire to drink, see, for example, Monti, Binkoff, Abrams, Zwick, Nirenberg, and Liepman (1987). However, a number of studies now exist in which the non-alcoholic subjects have shown the greatest motivational changes in the presence of alcohol cues. Newlin, Hotchkiss, Cox, Rauscher, and Li (1989) noted that, although not significant at the 5 per cent level, their alcoholic subjects reported less desire to drink than their non-alcoholic subjects across different cue conditions. Cooney, Gillespie, Baker, and Kaplan (1987) found that both alcoholics and non-alcoholics reported greater desire to drink following exposure to an alcohol cue as opposed to a neutral cue, but that, overall, non-alcoholics reported greater desire to drink. Using a behavioural measure (lever pressing for alcohol reward) Miller, Hersen, Eisler, Epstein, and Wooten (1974) found that non-alcoholic drinkers worked harder in the presence of alcoholic drink cues whereas alcoholics worked less.

It is not entirely clear how to interpret these findings. If the presence of alcohol cues increases motivation to drink, it might be predicted that alcoholic subjects would show this effect more strongly than non-alcoholics because of their conditioning history. It seems that the presence of alcohol cues can increase reported desire to drink and work for alcohol reward. But when comparisons of alcoholic and non-alcoholic subjects are made the results do not always follow predictions (Drummond, Cooper, and Glautier, 1990). Newlin *et al.* (1989), Cooney *et al.* (1987), and Miller *et al.* (1974) all used alcoholic subjects who were in treatment and speculate that this might be the reason for the discrepant findings. This is one possible explanation, presumably alcoholics in treatment are there because they do not want to drink and/or they may not wish it to be known that they want to drink. Another explanation, suggested by Miller *et al.*, is that alcoholic subjects are not guided by visual cues but show a tendency to drink regardless of cues present or to rely on internal cues arising, for example, from withdrawal states.

Opiate and cocaine addicts have also shown increases in craving for their drugs when exposed to relevant cues. Sherman, Zinser, Sideroff, and Baker (1989) and Childress, McLellan, Ehrman, and O'Brien (1988) presented video tape recordings containing scenes of opiate and cocaine use to opiate and cocaine addicts. Sherman *et al.* (1989) found that heroin-related videos produced more craving among a group of detoxified heroin addicts than did control videos. The heroin-related videos also produced greater reports of withdrawal sickness and a variety of mood changes collectively described as lowered feelings of pleasure and increases in anxiety. Childress *et al.* found that drug-related material produced increases in craving for drugs and decreases in skin temperature among both groups of patients.

Experimental studies with animal subjects

Animal studies add considerably to the evidence provided so far and further strengthen the case that stimuli which have been associated with drug ingestion serve to increase drug use motivation. As with experimental studies using human subjects, attention has been paid to internal as well as external cues in the modification of drug taking and experiments have involved a variety of self-administered drugs. With respect to internal cues, withdrawal states and cues associated with early drug effects have both been shown to play a part. The role of cues for withdrawal and withdrawal itself have been especially amenable to analysis using opiate drugs where injections of the opiate antagonists nalorphine or naloxone can be readily used to produce withdrawal states.

Goldberg, Woods, and Schuster (1969) compared the effects of nalorphine and saline infusions on responding for morphine injections in monkeys. Saline infusions did not affect rate of response, whereas nalorphine produced dramatic increases in response rate. A later study by Goldberg, Hoffmeister, Schlichting and Wuttke (1971) showed that responding could be maintained at high rates if that responding resulted in the termination of a light which had been paired with nalorphine but not saline infusions in morphine-dependent monkeys.

Stewart (1984) and de Witt and Stewart (1981, 1983) have provided demonstrations of the motivational function of early drug effects. If responding for heroin or cocaine reward is first extinguished, it can then be reinstated by small priming doses of the drug. In addition cross-priming has been demonstrated with morphine administration reinstating responses previously rewarded with cocaine.

Context conditioning experiments have also found that external cues can increase drug taking. Hinson, Poulos, Thomas, and Cappell (1986) gave rats extended experience with oral morphine ingestion before subjecting them to a period of abstinence. After abstinence the rats had a series of either morphine or saline injections in a distinctive environment. The amount of morphine solution consumed in the distinctive room or home cage was then tested. Rats which had experienced morphine injections and which underwent the consumption test in the distinctive environment consumed the most. In a similar experiment Krank (1989) measured amounts of alcohol consumed in environments that had either been alcohol CSs or had not. Alcohol consumption was measured after fluid deprivation when the animals were offered either an ethanol solution or water. In one experiment consumption of alcohol was greater in rats for whom the environment had previously been paired with infusions of ethanol than in rats for whom the environment had been paired with saline infusions. However, both of these groups had equal exposure to alcohol and drank less of it than a control group who had no prior alcohol exposure. This suggested prior exposure to alcohol had resulted in a taste aversion.

The fact that self-administered drugs have aversive properties is well known, especially when experience with the drug is limited. In their review, Hunt and Amit (1987) argued that the aversions produced by doses of self-administered drugs such as alcohol, amphetamines, and opiates differ from those produced by emetic agents such as lithium chloride. Self-administered drugs have multiple actions, some of which are aversive and some of which are appetitive. Development of tolerance to the aversive effects of a drug during early experience with it is important in determining the degree to which it, and cues for its delivery, will serve aversive or appetitive functions; see, for example, Berman and Cannon (1974), Cappell and LeBlanc (1975, 1977), and Deutsch and Koopmans (1973). This is one example of a mechanism by which tolerance to drug effects can affect drug taking and this subject will be returned to below.

MECHANISMS OF CUE ACTION

Three principal models of the function of drug cues exist. They all propose that the presentation of drug cues will result in CRs and that these CRs serve to increase the likelihood of drug taking. The models differ in terms of their predictions about the form of CRs. They are predicted to be either like drug withdrawal states or to either resemble or oppose drug effects. Evidence that drug effects and their associated withdrawal states can influence drug intake has been presented. The rationale of the conditioning models presented here is that since drug effects and their associated withdrawal states influence drug use, then CRs which resemble those states will also influence drug use. The operation of drug-opposite CRs may be more complex. Their influence on drug use may arise because of their resemblance to drug withdrawal states or because tolerance to the various effects of the drug is altered by the CRs. The models will be considered in turn.

Conditioned withdrawal symptoms

Wikler (1948) proposed that drug effects were USs and that stimuli which regularly accompanied those USs would acquire CS characteristics. However, the CRs elicited by drug CSs were considered to resemble the adaptive responses to the drug rather than the drug effect itself. By adaptive responses Wikler meant the drug withdrawal state. One of the examples given to illustrate the conditioning of adaptive responses to USs, rather than initial URs, was the elicitation of defensive reactions (the adaptive response) by a bell which is a CS for electric shock. He argued that the immediate effects of the shock US (pain) were not elicited by the bell but that defensive reactions were. Therefore, he expected drug cues to elicit withdrawal states rather than immediate drug effects. A similar analogy was made for the case of appetitive conditioning. Salivation elicited by a cue for food is considered to be the adaptive response to food presentation and elicited in the absence of sensory stimulation accompanying food delivery.

A number of demonstrations in which opiate withdrawal symptoms have been conditioned have now been made. Wikler and Pescor (1967) restricted rats undergoing morphine withdrawal to remain in particular areas of their cages. At other times, before withdrawal began, the rats had free access to all other parts of the cage. Thus, certain areas of the cage were associated with withdrawal whereas other areas were not. When the rats were placed in different areas of their cages (long after cessation of opiate ingestion and subsidence of unconditioned withdrawal) the withdrawal associated areas elicited more 'wet dog shakes' than other areas. Using human methadone addicts O'Brien (1976) provided evidence of withdrawal symptoms being conditioned to the sound of a tone and a peppermint oil smell which overlapped with the subject being given a naloxone injection which precipitated a withdrawal state lasting 15–30 minutes. Symptoms included runny eyes and nose, yawning, gooseflesh, rises in blood pressure and falls in skin temperature.

It should be noted that, while these studies suggest that withdrawal symptoms can be conditioned, the mechanism does not appear to be the same as that originally suggested by Wikler. In both experiments a withdrawal US, rather than an immediate drug effect US, is associated with the CS and the CS then elicits the withdrawal CR. Better support for Wikler's early view would be obtained if a CS paired with drug delivery elicited withdrawal-like states. Some studies have shown that stimuli likely to have been associated with early drug effects can elicit withdrawal-like effects. Powell, Gray, Bradley, Kasvikis, Strang, Barrat, and Marks (1990) and Teasdale (1973) presented slides and injection paraphernalia to detoxified opiate addicts and found increases in subjective reports of withdrawal-like symptoms. These data are more congenial to Wikler's view. However, if addicts are frequently taking their drugs while in withdrawal states then it is possible that syringes, etc., are associated with drug withdrawal or withdrawal relief. A study reported by Kelsey, Aranow, and Matthews (1990) attempted to control the associations between context CSs and withdrawal states/initial drug effects more carefully. During conditioning, rats were exposed to the test contexts for one hour directly after receiving a morphine injection. Because exposure followed the injection so closely the context was not going to be associated with withdrawal. Following a period of abstinence, re-exposure to the training context elicited behaviours seen in withdrawal states: rearing, circling and genital licking (but not wet dog shakes). However, because conditioning trials were done on consecutive days it is possible that there was some pairing of the context and withdrawal states before drug action was fully established. Perhaps the safest interpretation is that any pairing of the context and withdrawal would have been minimal. The short time between the injection and the onset of morphine's effect would be the sole window of opportunity and unlikely to make the context a predictor of withdrawal. It seems likely, then, that withdrawal relief and/or early drug effects were the effective USs.

Thus, in the case of opiates, there is evidence that withdrawal-like CRs can be elicited by cues which have been associated with either a withdrawal US or a drug effect US. With respect to alcohol, there have also been demonstrations of withdrawal-like responses to presentation of stimuli which have been paired with alcohol ingestion. For example, with rat subjects Le, Poulos, and Cappell (1979) found hyperthermic responses to alcohol delivery CSs. With human subjects several studies have shown increases in heart rate and skin conductance on presentation of alcoholic drink cues (Kaplan, Cooney, Baker, Gillespie, Meyer, and Pomerleau, 1985; Kaplan, Meyer, and Stroebel, 1983).

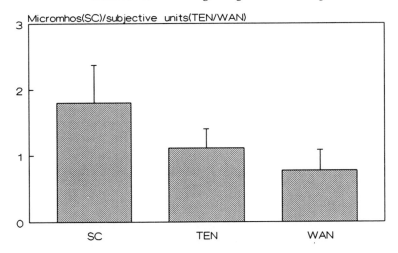

Fig. 7.2 Average difference scores (alcohol cue condition minus neutral cue condition) on skin conductance (SC) feelings of tension (TEN) and desire to drink (WAN). Bars are standard errors and data are based on 31 subjects (all subjects in both alcohol and neutral cue conditions).

All of these are withdrawal-like responses (Sellers and Kalant, 1982). However, the effect of alcohol on heart rate and skin conductance is to raise levels (Niaura, Rosenhow, Binkoff, Monti, Pedraza, and Abrams 1988), so these responses might reflect conditioning of drug effects as well as conditioning of the later adaptive response. Data relating to the subjective and physiological effects of alcohol cue presentation suggest that in alcoholic subjects feelings of anxiety and tension may be elicited (Glautier and Drummond, 1994), a response clearly common in withdrawal. Figure 7.2 shows these physiological and subjective responses to alcohol cues. Measures taken in a neutral cue control condition were subtracted from measures taken in an alcohol cue condition. Skin conductance, feelings of tension, and desire to drink were higher in the alcohol cue condition.

In summary, then, there are several examples of support for the views of Wikler. In the case of alcohol and opiates, experiments with humans and animals have found withdrawal-like responses on presentation of drug CSs. Some difficulties arise in the interpretation of the physiological responses to alcohol cues described here because withdrawal and drug effects are similar on skin conductance and heart rate. Subjective effects of alcohol cue presentation in alcoholic patients, however, resemble the anxiety responses frequently associated with withdrawal states.

Conditioned drug effects

Stewart, de Wit, and Eikelboom (1984), propose that presentation of a drug cue will have similar effects to the administration of the drug rather than the adaptive response to the drug. In other words, CRs to drug cues are drug-like, not drug-withdrawal-like. Their account can also be contrasted with the drive reduction or negative reinforcement accounts of cue function. Rather than cues generating aversive states which are terminated by drug ingestion, cues are thought to activate the same reward pathways in the brain that administration of the drug activates. Experiments in which priming doses of a drug reinstate previously extinguished drug taking suggest that small doses of a drug may, rather than satiate, alter the conditioned incentive value of stimuli which have previously been associated with drug delivery (Stewart, 1984). Thus, there is reinstatement of lever pressing for the drug following a small priming infusion. The lever, which has previously been associated with delivery of the drug, is approached after the extinction of lever pressing when priming doses of the drug are given. Changes in the conditioned incentive value of stimuli associated with drug ingestion (e.g. sight of the lever) following priming doses are considered to be the same as those produced when cues for drug delivery are presented. Approach behaviours, demonstrated in place preference paradigms for instance, are elicited by activation of the same neural pathways that occasion approach and reinstatement of lever pressing in the priming dose paradigm.

There are now a number of demonstrations of responses to drug cues which resemble immediate drug effects and therefore support the model proposed by Stewart *et al.* Krylov (1927, quoted in Pavlov, 1927, p.35) reported that morphine produced nausea, vomiting, and salivation, as did a tone which had been repeatedly paired with the drug. Schwartz and Cunningham (1990) infused rats with morphine through an indwelling catheter and monitored temperature responses to the drug using an implanted telemetry device. One group of rats had the infusion 30 seconds after the onset of a light and white noise cue, whereas the other group experienced the drug 75 minutes after the offset of the cue. They found that both groups of rats responded to morphine infusions with increases in body temperature. The group for which the cue was paired with morphine also responded to the cue with increases in body temperature when the cue was presented without morphine. Presentation of the cue alone in the unpaired group had no such effect.

As noted above, with respect to alcohol cues and human subjects, several studies have shown increases in heart rate and skin conductance on presentation of alcoholic drink cues (Kaplan *et al.*, 1983; Kaplan *et al.*, 1985). However, the effect of alcohol on heart rate and skin conductance is similar to that of withdrawal so these responses might reflect conditioning of immediate drug effects as well as conditioning of the later adaptive response. Drug-like responses to cigarette cues have been found by Abrams, Monti, Carey, Pinto, and Jacobus (1988) and by Abrams, Monti, Pinto, Elder, Brown, and Jacobus (1987). Both studies showed increases in heart rate in response to cigarette cues. Unlike the data for alcoholic subjects mentioned above this effect is unambiguously like the initial effects of nicotine. In contrast, the effect of nicotine withdrawal is to decrease heart rate (Ward, Garvey, and Bliss, 1992; West and Schneider, 1988).

Other examples of drug-like effects come from studies of the subjective effects of placebo administration in human subjects. Saline injections given to opiate addicts can result in euphoric responses. O'Brien (1976) had detoxified addicts who were maintained on cyclazocine, an opiate antagonist, inject themselves with either saline or hydromorphine. Both the subjective reports of the addicts and observer ratings indicated that euphoria was seen following either the saline or the blocked hydromorphine injection. In two experiments Newlin (1985) gave subjects a non-alcoholic beer after leading them to believe it was real beer. In the first experiment he found that 11 out of 68 subjects reported 'easily noticeable' or greater levels of alcohol effects and 8 out of 20 subjects reported 'slightly noticeable' or greater effects in the second experiment. It is clear, however, that in many instances that the instruction about the contents of the drink might be as important as any conditioned associations (Marlatt and Rosenhow, 1980).

Conditioned drug-opposite responses

Siegel and his colleagues, (1975 *et seq.*), have amassed evidence for the view that responses to drug cues will oppose the effects of the drug US (see Siegel, 1989 for a recent and thorough review). The model is like Wikler's in the sense that it is the adaptive response to the drug which is conditioned. However, the response is thought to be opposite in direction to the drug effect (see Solomon and Corbit (1973) for additional discussion of opponent processes) rather than like a drug withdrawal response. Thus, in some instances, where drug effects and drug withdrawal effects are in opposite directions (as in the case of nicotine's effects on heart rate), the predictions of the two models are the same. There is a further similarity with Wikler's model in that both are drive reduction models. Drug-opposite responses are considered to increase the likelihood of drug ingestion because they either resemble or are interpreted as drug withdrawal states and are thus unpleasant and relieved by drug ingestion. Indeed, it has been suggested that so-called 'withdrawal symptoms' might be more properly called drug-opposite preparatory responses (Siegel, 1989; Poulos, Hinson, and Siegel, 1981).

Again, evidence in favour of the model is available from a number of sources. With alcohol USs and rat subjects Le, Poulos, and Cappell (1979) found hyperthermic responses to alcohol delivery CSs in contrast to the unconditioned hypothermic effects of alcohol. This is an instance in which drug effects and drug withdrawal effects are in opposite directions, therefore this evidence supports both conditioned withdrawal and conditioned drug-opposite response models. In the experiment by Newlin (1985) mentioned above, those subjects who reported alcohol effects following consumption of non-alcoholic beer also manifested a drug-opposite physiological response consisting of heart rate and skin conductance falls. McCaul, Turkkan, and Stitzer (1989) reported similar results. Subjects were administered alcohol over the course of four days before a placebo drink was substituted. Skin conductance and heart rate decrease was shown following the placebo challenge.

Classical conditioning and drug tolerance

Drug tolerance exists when a drug's effect on an organism is reduced. The contrast may be between either the responses to the drug shown by different individuals or the responses exhibited by the same individual on different occasions. In the former case tolerance may be due to inherited or acquired characteristics of the individual. In the latter case only acquired characteristics are relevant. As noted in the introduction, drug tolerance has been given prominence in definitions of drug dependence (e.g. American Psychiatric Association, 1987; Edwards and Gross, 1976; Edwards *et al.* 1981; World Health Organization, 1988) alongside increased motivation to take the drug. There are at least two reasons for this. Firstly, the fact that tolerance, physical dependence, and increased motivation to take drugs commonly occur together. This suggests that a common mechanism(s) may be involved in all three phenomena. Secondly, tolerance to a drug's effect may be important in the regulation of drug use. Since the reinforcing and punishing consequences of drug ingestion regulate drug intake, tolerance to these effects must also affect intake. As with drug use motivation, conditioning processes play a role.

One of the key features of Siegel's model is the way in which it integrates findings relating to the motivational functions of drug cues, the form of responses to drug cues and the acquired situational specificity of tolerance to drugs. As well as providing an account of the effects of cues on drug use motivation, conditioning of a drug-opposite response provides a ready means by which the organism can adapt to an impending disturbance in homeostasis and thus manifest tolerance to a drug's effects. There is now a large body of evidence which shows that tolerance to drug effects is determined, to a certain degree, by situational factors (Goudie and Demellweek, 1986; Siegel, 1989 for reviews). One experiment carried out by Siegel, Hinson, and Krank (1978) shows that tolerance to the analgesic effects of morphine is lost if the drug delivery is accompanied by changes in the circumstances of administration, and many other experiments have replicated this basic finding. With human subjects Dafters and Anderson (1982) found that changing the context of alcohol delivery resulted in loss of tolerance to the tachycardic effects of alcohol. Remington, Roberts, and Glautier (in preparation) found that presenting standard doses of alcohol to subjects in a novel vehicle solution (blue peppermint liquid) resulted in greater impairment of cognitive and motor tasks and higher subjective ratings of intoxication than when the alcohol was presented in the usual way (regular beer). Siegel proposes that it is the elicitation of drug-opposite/compensatory responses, described in the preceding section, which accounts for the situational specificity of drug effects. Fig. 7.3 shows the results of this experiment. Performance on cognitive and motor tasks (word search using a grid of jumbled letters and a computerized version of a pursuit rotor task using a mouse pointer)

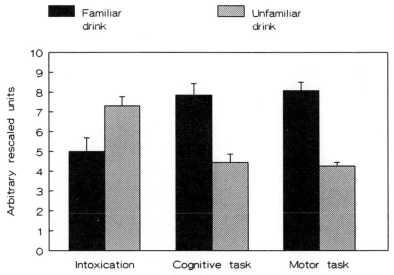

Fig. 7.3 Subjects' performance on a cognitive task (middle panel), on a motor task (right panel) and their ratings of intoxication (left panel) following a standard dose of alcohol presented in either a familiar (FD) or unfamiliar (UD) vehicle drink. Bars are standard errors and the data are based on 20 subjects (ten taking the drink in each presentation mode).

were worse following alcohol in an unfamiliar vehicle drink than in a familiar drink. In addition, subjective ratings of intoxication were higher following the unfamiliar drink.

Siegel proposes that it is the elicitation of drug-opposite/compensatory responses, described in the preceding section, which accounts for the situational specificity of drug effects. Others have proposed that conditioning processes may affect drug tolerance in other ways; opponent processes may not be necessary. Baker and Tiffany (1985) argue that an habituation model based on Wagner's (1976) theorizing provides a better account of the literature on tolerance to drug effects than does Siegel's conditioned opponent model. It is proposed that a priming dose of a drug (self-generated priming) or presentation of cues paired with drug delivery (retrieval generated priming) attenuates processing of a subsequent drug stimulus, the result of which is a reduced drug effect. In other words a surprising dose of a drug will have more of an effect than an expected dose. One of their major objections to opponent process accounts is that often tolerance develops and no opponents are detected when drug CSs are presented. Indeed, responses to drug cues sometimes resemble the drug effect (see above examples). However, the fact that there have been some difficulties in demonstrating compensatory responses is not fatal for Siegel's theorizing. Mackintosh (1987) proposes two 'escape routes' for opponent process theory. Firstly, the effective CS may be early drug effects, in which case placebos would not be elicitors of opponent processes. Secondly, the compensatory reaction may involve a 'blocking' of the drug effect and may not be demonstrable in the absence of the drug. Siegel (1989) has added to these observations by pointing out that the use of different measures may reveal different results because of differences in the sensitivity of the measures. Thus, Krank (1987) found hyperalgesia in response to a saline injection when morphine was expected when a hot-plate, rather than tail-flick, assay was used. Also, tolerance expression can be disrupted by presentation of a novel stimulus (external inhibition) or omission of an expected stimulus. Administration of a placebo may disrupt tolerance because new stimuli are inadvertently added or regular stimuli omitted.

In summary, if conditioning processes can mediate drug tolerance and drug tolerance relates to drug use then there is a further mechanism by which conditioning processes, possibly involving drug-opposite responses, can influence drug use.

CUE EXPOSURE TREATMENT

The evidence outlined above points to the conclusion that drug use CSs may serve to increase drug taking and a number of different mechanisms involving conditioning processes have been proposed to explain how it is that cues come to affect ongoing operant behaviour. These models carry with them the implication that treatment for addiction ought to attempt to reduce the power of these CSs. One method of doing this is to attempt to extinguish the CRs which are elicited by exposure to the CSs by repeated exposure to the CS without allowing drug taking. Somebody who has detoxified will inevitably encounter many drug cues and, in the absence of any steps having being taken to reduce the motivational effects of those cues, then relapse likelihood is increased. This argument was made as long ago as 1948 by Wikler and in recent years there has been growing interest in the development of cue exposure treatment procedures as a method of helping patients deal with cues they will undoubtedly encounter after initial cessation of drug use. These procedures are modelled on the exposure treatments which have been successfully used in the case of phobic and obsessional compulsive disorders. They aim to extinguish CRs to drug cues by repeated presentation of the cue without allowing further drug consumption. As yet there is no convincing evidence for the effectiveness of cue exposure treatments but results from experimental work and clinical trials are encouraging enough to warrant continued research (Drummond, Cooper, and Glautier, 1990).

Four controlled trials of cue exposure treatment with outcome assessment have now been conducted. Raw and Russell (1980) treated smokers, McLellan, Childress, Ehrman, and O'Brien (1986) treated opiate addicts, as did Dawe, Powell, Richards, Gossop, Strang, Marks, and Gray (1993), while Drummond and Glautier (in press) treated alcohol-dependent patients. Of these, only the trial by Drummond and Glautier resulted in a better outcome for the cue exposure treatment group. Cue exposure patients relapsed to drinking just as quickly as relaxation control subjects but did not reinstate heavy drinking to such a great extent as the controls. Thus, at least one trial has shown some indication that treatment outcome was better in the cue exposure rather than control group. Variations in populations and procedures between the trials make it impossible to ascertain exactly why positive results were obtained in only one of these trials. Certainly, given the difficulty of helping patients with addiction, a result such as this should not be dismissed out of hand.

The picture is more encouraging when the results of trials which have focussed on processes during exposure sessions rather than clinical outcome are considered. The studies of clinical applications with alcoholic subjects have involved either resisting the temptation to drink in the presence of drink cues following the consumption of a priming dose, (Laberg and Ellertsen, 1987; Rankin, Hodgson, and Stockwell, 1983), or resisting the temptation to drink in presence of drink cues without prior consumption of a priming dose, (Drummond and Glautier in press). Studies with opiate addicts by Powell *et al.* (1990) and by Powell, Bradley, and Gray (1993) and by Childress, McLellan, Ehrman, and O'Brien (1988) with cocaine addicts have also been undertaken but have focussed solely on exposure to cues without priming dose consumption.

Rankin *et al.* (1983) used a group of severely dependent male alcoholic inpatients. Behavioural testing was done before and after experimental or control treatments. Testing involved taking measures of subjective and physiological state (desire to drink and difficulty in resisting drinks; pulse rate and hand tremor) before and after an alcohol priming dose. Following these measurements subjects were given two further alcoholic drinks and the time taken to consume the drinks was recorded. Experimental treatment involved six sessions in which subjects received a priming dose of alcohol and were then presented with further drinks and asked to pick up, hold, and smell the drink repeatedly while resisting the temptation to drink. Control treatment involved imaginal cue exposure with no priming doses. Control subjects went through the experimental treatment procedure after the control treatment in the fashion of a multiple baseline study.

Both groups showed a reduction in drinking speed on the second behaviour test but this was only significant for the experimental group. However, after the control group went through their experimental procedures they also showed significantly reduced speed of drinking. A reduced desire to drink and difficulty resisting was reported after both experimental conditions but the control group who had the imaginal treatment first showed more reduction in these measures.

Laberg and Ellertsen (1987) also used a group of inpatient alcoholics to examine the effects of six cue exposure sessions on subjective and physiological responses to drink cues. Exposure to alcoholic drink cues or soft drink cues took place after the consumption of an alcoholic or soft drink. The alcohol priming dose condition resulted in increased desire to drink and skin conductance level on day one. The increases in desire to drink were greatest in those whose priming dose was followed by alcoholic drink cue exposure. Similarly, increases in numbers of spontaneous skin conductance fluctuations to drink were greatest in those whose priming dose was followed by alcoholic drink cue exposure. There were reductions in skin conductance level and desire to drink following alcohol priming dose over the course of sessions.

Drummond and Glautier (in preparation) found that alcoholic drink stimuli elicited greater feeling of tension, desire to drink and skin conductance responses when alcoholic drink stimuli were presented (picked up, held, and smelled) when compared to soft drink stimuli. Over the course of treatment both the cue exposure and relaxation control subjects showed reductions in responses to alcohol and soft drink stimuli. Reductions which were specific to the alcohol-related stimuli and experimental group were only seen on one of the subjective measures (feelings of tension).

Powell *et al.*'s (1990 and in press) study with opiate addicts demonstrated a treatment specific effect on subjective ratings of craving in response to drug cues. The subjective experience of craving in response to the presentation of drug-related stimuli was greater than that elicited by the presentation of neutral stimuli. Further, they showed that reported craving in response to the presentation of both kinds of stimulus declined over time to a greater extent for the drug-related stimulus. However, in addition to a control group which received no cue exposure between tests, there were two experimental groups, distinguished by the kinds of cue exposure procedures used (plain extinction vs extinction and rehearsal of negative aspects of drug use), which showed different habituation patterns. The plain exposure group showed a smaller decline in craving to the drug-related stimuli and a larger decline in craving to the neutral stimuli when compared to the rehearsal group.

Cocaine addicts treated by Childress *et al.* (1988) showed greater skin temperature decreases and increases in craving for cocaine after presentation of drug-related stimuli than when neutral stimuli were presented. Again, subjective changes across time were found. No changes in response on the physiological measure were seen though.

A final source of evidence concerning cue exposure treatment comes from Krank and Wall's (1990) animal model of the effects of a cue exposure 'treatment' procedure. Rats were initially trained to lever press for alcohol reward. During two-week abstinences different groups of rats were exposed to cues which had been associated with alcohol delivery. A control group of rats remained in their home cages for the two-week period and had no exposure to any of the alcohol cues. All rats were then returned to the original ethanol exposure conditions and consumption was measured. The level of consumption was inversely related to the degree of exposure to alcohol cues during the abstinence period.

Thus, not only do cues for drug delivery increase drug ingestion in animals but exposure to drug cues without drug consumption reduces their potency. The analogy with exposure treatments for addictions is clear. Because there was an association between the degree of exposure to cues and subsequent reinstatement of drinking, Krank and Wall argue that it is likely that exposure to a broad range of drug cues will be most effective as a treatment procedure.

SUMMARY AND CONCLUSIONS

Drug-taking episodes have all the ingredients necessary to promote the occurrence of classical conditioning. Various stimuli, be they sights, smells, moods, or drug effects, have the potential to become Pavlovian CSs if they are reliably followed by drug effects. Once these stimuli acquire their conditioned properties they increase the likelihood of drug taking behaviour when they are encountered. A number of possible mechanisms have been discussed by which cues might operate. Conditioned withdrawal symptoms, conditioned drug-like responses, conditioned opponent processes, and modulation of drug tolerance are all potential candidates and, currently, all have a reasonable degree of support from the available evidence.

The adoption of a classical conditioning perspective carries with it implications for the treatment of addiction. Exposure to drug cues in the abstinent addict can be 'risky' and may result in increased chances of relapse. Following on from this, treatments geared to weakening the power of cues need to be developed and evaluated. Current evidence shows that failure to deal with cue situations may lead to rapid relapse. However, there is no demonstration of how cue exposure treatments can be conducted to yield substantial clinical benefits, but a number of studies and one clinical trial encourage developments along these lines of research.

Despite the apparent uncertainty as to the mechanisms which under-lie cue action and how best to implement cue exposure treatments, these continue to be active research areas. In the case of mechanisms of cue action, since it is clear that CRs to drug cues can have different forms, there have been some attempts to elucidate factors which influence the form. For instance, Eikelboom and Stewart (1982) have proposed that the site of a drug's action in the nervous system (either on the afferent or efferent arm) is an important determinant of whether or not the observed response to the drug is properly classed as a UR. The fact that some responses may not be URs creates problems when it comes to classifying CRs in relation to the unconditioned effects of the drug. Another approach has been taken by Staiger and White (1988) and Glautier, Drummond, and Remington (1992), who have both found that the manner of cue presentation can influence the apparent directionality of response to alcohol cues. Finally, a more general theory of learning predicts that CRs will resemble later rather than earlier URs and when early and later drug effects oppose, then the CR will apparently be an opponent process (Wagner, 1981). Thus, the task is to specify under what conditions the CR will take on one form or another.

In the case of cue exposure treatments a number of dimensions appear to be worth exploring. These would include the development of active 'coping' strategies for subjects to engage in during cue exposure and manipulations intended to vary the intensity of stimulus exposure. For instance, rehearsal of negative imagery during cue exposure has been explored by Powell *et al.* (in press), while in vivo exposure has been compared with imaginal exposure (Rankin *et al.*, 1983). Other factors such as length and number of exposure sessions, as well as individual differences in response to cue exposure, will undoubtedly need to be studied before firm conclusions can be reached about the overall efficacy of this treatment technique.

ACKNOWLEDGEMENT

I would like to thank Ms Sharon Dawe, Dr Colin Drummond and Professor Griffith Edwards for their helpful comments on a earlier draft of this chapter.

REFERENCES

Abrams, D.B., Monti, P.M., Carey, K.B., Pinto, R.P., and Jacobus, S.I. (1988). Reactivity to smoking cues and relapse: two studies of discriminant validity. *Behaviour Research and Therapy*, **26**, 225–33.

Abrams, D.B., Monti, P.M., Pinto, R.P. Elder, J., Brown, R., and Jacobus, S.I. (1987). Psychosocial stress and coping in smokers who relapsed or quit. *Health Psychology*, **6**, 289–303.

American Psychiatric Association (1987). *Diagnostic and statistical manual of mental disorders* (3rd edn revised). American Psychiatric Association, Washington DC.

Annis, H.M. (1982). *Inventory of drinking situations (IDS-(100))*. Addiction Research Foundation of Ontario, Toronto.

Baker, T.B. and Tiffany, S.T. (1985). Morphine tolerance as habituation. *Psychological Review*, **92**, 78–108.

Berman, R.F. and Cannon, D.S. (1974). The effect of prior ethanol experience on ethanol induced saccharin aversion. *Physiology and Behavior*, **12**, 1041–4.

Cannon, D.S., Leeka, J.K. Patterson, E.T., and Baker, T.B. (1990). Principal components analysis of the inventory of drinking situations: empirical categories of drinking by alcoholics. *Addictive Behaviours*, **15**, 265–9.

Cappell, H. and LeBlanc, A.E. (1975). Conditioned aversion by amphetamine: rates of acquisition and loss of the attenuating effects of prior exposure. *Psychopharmacology*, **43**, 157–62.

Cappell, H. and LeBlanc, A.E. (1977). Parametric investigations of the effects of prior exposure to amphetamine and morphine on conditioned gustatory aversion. *Psychopharmacology*, **51**, 265–71.

Chaney, E.F., Roszell, D.K., and Cummings, C. (1982). Relapse in opiate addicts: a behavioural analysis. *Addictive Behaviours*, **7**, 291–7.

Childress, A.R., McLellan, A.T., Ehrman, R., and O'Brien, C.P. (1988). Classically conditioned responses in opioid and cocaine dependence: a role in relapse, *NIDA Research Monograph*, **84**, 25–43.

Choquette, K.A., Hesselbrock, M.N., and Babor, T.F. (1985). Discriminative control of alcoholics' drinking by the drinking situation. *Journal of Studies on Alcohol*. **46**, 412–7.

Coates, S. (1986). Cue exposure and cue avoidance in the modification of cigarette dependence. Unpublished BPS Diploma. British Psychological Society, Leicester.

Cooney, N.L., Gillespie, R.A., Baker, L.H., and Kaplan, R.F. (1987). Cognitive changes after alcohol cue exposure. *Journal of Consulting and Clinical Psychology*, **55**, 150–5.

Dafters, R. and Anderson, G. (1982). Conditioned tolerance to the tachycardia effect of ethanol in humans. *Psychopharmacology*, **78**, 365–7.

Dawe, S., Powell, J., Richards, D., Gossop, M., Strang, J., Marks, I., and Gray, J. (1993). Cue exposure in the treatment of opiate addiction: results from a clinical trial. *Addiction*, **88**, 1233–47.

Deardorff, C.M., Melges, F.T., Hout, C.N., and Savage, D.J. (1975). Situations related to drinking alcohol: a factor analysis of questionnaire responses. *Journal of Studies on Alcohol*, **36**, 1184–95.

Deutsch, J.A. and Koopmans, H.S. (1973). Preference enhancement for alcohol by passive exposure. *Science*, **179**, 1242–3.

de Wit, H. and Stewart, J. (1981). Reinstatement of cocaine reinforced responding in the rat. *Psychopharmacology*, **75**, 134–43.

de Wit, H. and Stewart, J. (1983). Drug reinstatement of heroin reinforced responding in the rat. *Psychopharmacology*, **79**, 29–31.

Drummond, D.C., Cooper, T., and Glautier, S.P. (1990). Conditioned learning in alcohol dependence: implications for cue exposure treatment. *British Journal of Addiction*, **856**, 725–43.

Drummond D.C. and Glautier S. The effects of cue exposure treatment on cue responsivity (in preparation).

Drummond, D.C. and Glautier, S. A controlled trial of cue exposure treatment in alcohol dependence. *Journal of Consulting and Clinical Psychology* (in press).

Edwards, G., Arif, A., and Hodgson, R. (1981). Nomenclature and classification of drug and alcohol-related problems: a shortened version of a WHO memorandum. *British Journal of Addiction*, **77**, 3–20.

Edwards, G.E. and Gross, M.M. (1976). Alcohol dependence: provisional description of a clinical syndrome. *British Medical Journal*, **1**, 1058–61.

Eikelboom, R. and Stewart, J. (1982). Conditioning of drug induced physiological responses. *Psychological Review*, **89**, 507–28.

Funderburk, F.R. and Allen, R.P. (1977). Alcoholic's disposition to drink. *Journal of Studies on Alcohol*, **38**, 410–25.

Glautier, S., Drummond, D.C., and Remington R. (1992). Different drink cues elicit different physiological responses in non-dependent drinkers. *Psychopharmacology*, **106**, 550–4.

Glautier, S. and Drummond, D.C. (1994). Alcohol dependence and cue reactivity. *Journal of Studies on Alcohol*, **55**, 224–9.

Goldberg, S.P., Woods, J.H., and Schuster, C.R. (1969). Morphine: conditioned increases in self-administration in rhesus monkeys. *Science*, **166**, 1306–7.

Goldberg, S.R., Hoffmeister, F., Schlichting, U., and Wuttke, W. (1971).

Aversive properties of nalorphine and naloxone in morphine dependent rhesus monkeys. *Journal of Pharmacology and Experimental Therapeutics*, **179**, 268–76.

Goudie, A.J. and Demellweek, C. (1986). Conditioning factors in drug tolerance. In *Behavioural analysis of drug dependence* (eds. S.R. Goldberg and I.P. Stolerman), Academic Press, London.

Harford, T.C. (1983). A contextual analysis of drinking events. *International Journal of the Addictions*, **18**, 825–34.

Hinson, J.M., Poulos, C.X., Thomas, W., and Cappell, H. (1986). Pavlovian conditioning and addictive behaviour: relapse to oral self-administration of morphine. *Behavioural Neuroscience*, **100**, 368–75.

Hodgson R., Rankin H., and Stockwell T. (1979). Alcohol dependence and the priming effect. *Behaviour Research and Therapy*, **17**, 387–97.

Hodgson, R.J. (1989). Resisting temptation: a psychological analysis. *British Journal of Addiction*, **84**, 251–7.

Hunt, T. and Amit, Z. (1987). Conditioned taste aversion induced by self-administered drugs: paradox revisited. *Neuroscience and Biobehavioral Reviews*, **11**, 107–30.

Hunt, W.A., Barnett, C.W., and Branch, L.G. (1971). Relapse rates in addiction progams. *Journal of Clinical Psychology*, **27**, 455–6.

Jaffe, J.H., Cascella, N.G., Kumor, K.M., and Sherer, M.A. (1989). Cocaine induced cocaine craving. *Psychopharmacology*, **97**, 59–64.

Jellinek, E.M. (1952). Current notes – phases of alcohol addiction. *Quarterly Journal of Studies on Alcohol*, **13**, 673–84.

Kaplan, R.F., Cooney, N.L., Baker, L.H., Gillespie, R.A., Meyer, R.E., and Pomerleau, O.F. (1985). Reactivity to alcohol related cues: physiological and subjective responses in alcoholics and non-problem drinkers. *Journal of Studies on Alcohol*, **464**, 267–72.

Kaplan, R.F., Meyer, R.E., and Stroebel, E.F. (1983). Alcohol dependence and responsivity to an ethanol stimulus as predictors of alcohol consumption. *British Journal of Addiction*, **78**, 259–67.

Kelsey, J.E., Aranow, J.S., and Matthews, R.T. (1990). Context-specific morphine withdrawal in rats: duration and effects of clonidine. *Behavioral Neuroscience*, **104**, 704–10.

Krank, M.D. (1987). Conditioned hyperalgesia depends on pain sensitivity measure. *Behavioral Neuroscience*, **101**, 854–7.

Krank, M.D. (1989). Environmental signals for ethanol enhance free choice ethanol consumption. *Behavioral Neuroscience*, **103**, 365–72.

Krank, M.D. and Wall, A.M. (1990). Cue exposure during a period of abstinence reduces the resumption of operant behaviour for oral ethanol reinforcement. *Behavioral Neuroscience*, **1045**, 725–33.

Laberg, J.C. and Ellertsen, B. (1987). Psychophysiological indicators of craving in alcoholics: effects of cue exposure. *British Journal of Addiction*, **82**, 1341–48.

Le, A.D., Poulos, C.X., and Cappell, H. (1979). Conditioned tolerance to the hyperthermic effects of ethyl alcohol. *Science*, **206**, 1109–10.

Litman, G.K., Stapleton, J., Oppenheim, A.N., Peleg, M., and Jackson, P. (1983). Situations related to alcoholism relapse. *British Journal of Addiction*, **78**, 381–89.

Ludwig, A.M., Wikler, A., and Stark, L.H. (1974). The first drink: psycho-biological aspects of craving. *Archives of General Psychiatry*, **30**, 539–47.

Mackintosh, N.J. (1987). Neurobiology, psychology and habituation. *Behaviour Research and Therapy*, **252**, 81–97.

Marlatt, G.A. and Gordon, J.R. (1980). Determinants of relapse: implications for the maintenance of behaviour change. In *Behavioural medicine: changing health lifestyles* (eds. P. Davidson and S. Davidson), Brunner Mazel, New York.

Marlatt, G.A. and Gordon, J.R. (1985). *Relapse prevention: maintenance strategies in the treatment of addictive behavior.* Guilford Press, New York.

Marlatt, G.A. and Rosenhow, D.J. (1980). Cognitive processes in alcohol use: expectancy and the balanced placebo design. In *Advances in substance abuse volume 1* (ed. N.K. Mello), JAI Press, Greenwich.

McCaul, M.E., Turkkan, J.S., and Stitzer, M.L. (1989). Conditioned opponent responses: placebo challenge in alcoholic subjects. *Alcoholism: Clinical and Experimental Research*, **134**, 631–5.

McLellen, A.T., Childress, A.R., Ehrman, R., and O'Brien, C.P. (1986). Extinguishing conditioned responses during opiate dependence treatment: turning laboratory findings into clinical procedures. *Journal of Substance Abuse Treatment*, **3**, 33–40.

Mello, N.K. and Mendelson, J.H. (1972). Drinking patterns during work contingent and non-contingent alcohol acquisition. *Psychosomatic Medicine*, **34**, 139–64.

Miller, P.M., Hersen, M., Eisler, R.M., Epstein, L.H., and Wooten, L.S. (1974). Relationship of alcohol cues to the drinking behavior of alcoholics and social drinkers: an analogue study. *Psychological Record*, **24**, 61–6.

Monti, P.M., Binkoff, J.A., Abrams, D.B., Zwick, W.R., Nirenberg, T.D., and Liepman, M.R. (1987). Reactivity of alcoholics and non-alcoholics to drinking cues. *Journal of Abnormal Psychology*, **962**, 122–6.

Niaura, R.S., Rosenhow, D.J., Binkoff, J.A., Monti, P.M., Pedraza, M., and Abrams, D.B. (1988). Relevance of cue reactivity to understanding alcohol and smoking relapse. *Journal of Abnormal Psychology*, **97**, 133–52.

Newlin, D.B. (1985). The antagonistic placebo response to alcohol cues. *Alcoholism: Clinical and Experimental Research*, **95**, 411–16.

Newlin, D.B., Hotchkiss, B., Cox, W.M., Rauscher, F., and Li, T.K. (1989). Autonomic and subjective responses to alcohol stimuli with appropriate control stimuli. *Addictive Behaviours*, **14**, 625–30.

O'Brien, C.P. (1976). Experimental analysis of conditioning factors in human narcotic addiction. *Pharmacological Reviews*, **274**, 533–43.

Pavlov, I.P. (1927). *Conditioned reflexes.* Dover Publications, (1960). New York.

Poulos, C.X., Hinson, R.E., and Siegel, S. (1981). The role of pavlovian processes in drug tolerance and dependence: implications for treatment. *Addictive Behaviours*, **6**, 205–11.

Powell, J., Bradley, B., and Gray, J. (in press). Subjective craving for opiates: evaluation of a cue exposure protocol for use with detoxified opiate addicts. *British Journal of Clinical Psychology*.

Powell, J., Gray, J.A., Bradley, B.P., Kasvikis, Y., Strang, J., Barrat, L., and Marks, I. (1990). The effects of exposure to drug-related cues in detoxified opiate addicts: a theoretical review and some new data. *Addictive Behaviours*, **15**, 339–45.

Rankin, H., Hodgson, R., and Stockwell, T. (1983). Cue exposure and response prevention with alcoholics: a controlled trial. *Behaviour Research and Therapy*, **214**, 435–46.

Raw, M. and Russell, M.A.H. (1980). Rapid smoking, cue exposure and support in the modification of smoking. *Behaviour Research and Therapy*, **18**, 363–72.

Remington, B., Roberts, P., and Glautier, S. Effects of drink familiarity on alcohol tolerance (in preparation).

Schwartz, K.S. and Cunningham, C.L. (1990). Conditioned stimulus control of morphine hyperthermia. *Psychopharmacology*, **101**, 77–84.

Sellers, E.M. and Kalant, H. (1982). Alcohol withdrawal and delirium tremens. In *Encyclopedic handbook of alcoholism* (eds. E.M. Pattisen and E. Kaufman), Gardner Press, New York.

Sherman, J.E., Zinser, M.C., Sideroff, S.I., and Baker, T. (1989). Subjective dimensions of heroin urges: influence of heroin-related and affectively negative stimuli. *Addictive Behaviours*, **14**, 611–23.

Shiffman, S. (1982). Relapse following smoking cessation: a situational analysis. *Journal of Consulting and Clinical Psychology*, **50**, 71–86.

Siegel, S. (1975). Evidence from rats that morphine tolerance is a learned response. *Journal of Comparative and Physiological Psychology*, **89**, 498–506.

Siegel, S. (1989). Pharmacological conditioning and drug effects. In *Psychoactive drugs: Tolerance and sensitisation* (eds. A.J. Goudie and M.W. Emmett-Oglesby), The Humana Press, Clifton, New Jersey.

Siegel, S., Hinson, R.E., and Krank, M.D. (1978). The role of predrug signals in morphine analgesic tolerance: support for a pavlovian conditioning model of tolerance. *Journal of Experimental Psychology: Animal Behavior Processes*, **4**, 188–96.

Solomon, R.L. and Corbit, J.D. (1973). An opponent-process theory of motivation: II. Cigarette addiction. *Journal of Abnormal Psychology*, **812**, 158–71.

Staiger, P.K. and White, J.M. (1988). Conditioned alcohol-like and alcohol-opposite Responses in humans. *Psychopharmacology*, **95**, 87–91.

Stewart, J. (1984). Reinstatement of heroin and cocaine self-administration behaviour in the rat by intracerebral application of morphine in the ventral tegmental area. *Pharmacology, Biochemistry and Behavior*, **20**, 917–23.

Stewart, J., de Wit, H., and Eikelboom, R. (1984). Role of unconditioned and conditioned drug effects in the self-administration of opiates and stimulants. *Psychological Review*, **91**, 251–68.

Stockwell, T.R., Hodgson, R.J., Rankin, H.J., and Taylor, C. (1982). Alcohol dependence, beliefs and the priming effect, *Behaviour Research and Therapy*, **20**, 513–22.

Strickler, D.P., Dobbs, S.D., and Maxwell, W.A. (1979). The influence of setting on drinking behaviours: the laboratory VS the barroom. *Addictive Behaviours*, **4**, 339–44.

Teasdale, J.D. (1973). Conditioned abstinence in narcotic addicts. *International Journal of the Addictions*, **8**, 273–92.

Wagner, A.R. (1976). Priming in STM: an information processing mechanism for self-generated or retrieval-generated depression in performance. In *Habituation: Perspectives from child development, animal behaviour and neurophysiology* (eds. T.J. Tighe and R.N. Leaton), Erlbaum Associates, Hillsdale, New Jersey.

Wagner, A.R. (1981). SOP: A model of automatic memory processing in animal behaviour. In *Information processing in animals: memory mechanisms* (eds N.E. Spear and R.R. Miller), Lawrence Erlbaum Associates, Hillsdale, New Jersey.

Ward, K.D., Garvey, A.J., and Bliss R.E. (1992). Evidence of transient heart rate change after smoking cessation. *Psychopharmacology*, **106**, 337–40.

West, R. and Schneider, N. (1988). Drop in heart rate following smoking cessation may be permanent. *Psychopharmacology*, **94**, 566–8.

Wikler, A. (1948). Recent progress in research on the neurophysiologic basis of morphine addiction. *American Journal of Psychiatry*, **105**, 329–38.

Wikler, A. and Pescor, F.T. (1967). Classical conditioning of a morphine abstinence phenomenon: reinforcement of opioid drinking behaviour and relapse in morphine addicted rats. *Psychopharmacologia*, **10**, 255–84.

World Health Organisation (1988). ICD 10, 1988 Draft of Chapter V, *Mental, behavioural and developmental disorders: clinical descriptions and diagnostic guidelines*, WHO, Geneva.

8

The learned nature of binge eating

Anita Jansen

BINGE EATING

Binge eating refers to the consumption of an amount of food in a discrete period of time, for example less than two hours, that is definitely larger than most people would eat in a similar period of time. During the binge a sense of lack of control, that is, the feeling that one cannot stop eating or control what or how much one is eating, is experienced (Walsh, 1992). Binge eating is one of the main diagnostic criteria of the eating disorder bulimia nervosa and nearly half of the patients with anorexia nervosa (Laessle *et al.*, 1989; Polivy and Herman, 1985; Wardle and Beinart, 1981) and obesity (Marcus, Wing, and Lamparsky, 1985) are characterized by recurrent episodes of binge eating. Binge eating has also been documented in non-clinical normal weight populations (Jansen, van den Hout and Griez, 1991; Marcus *et al.*, 1985; Wardle, 1980) and recently, Spitzer *et al.* (1991; 1992) proposed including a new eating disorder, the Binge Eating Disorder, in the fourth edition of the *Diagnostic and Statistical Manual of Mental Disorders* (DSM–IV; APA, in preparation). The Binge Eating Disorder will be characterized by recurrent binge eating with marked distress regarding binge eating but without the characteristic compensatory features of bulimia nervosa (that is, weight control methods such as self-induced vomiting, use of laxatives and extreme dieting).

A clinically relevant question is: how do we treat binge eating effectively? Treatment outcome studies on bulimia nervosa, in which efficacy is partly defined by the reduction in binge eating frequencies, show a mean of 70 per cent reduction of binge eating frequency and 34 per cent abstinence rates over 22 studies (Garner, 1987). Most of these therapies (behaviour-, cognitive-behaviour- and eclectic therapies) included a diversity of techniques, such as self-monitoring, diet management, self-control techniques, exposure and problem solving, which makes it impossible to identify the underlying processes which produce behaviour change. Moreover, for a more effective treatment of binge eating it might be wise to identify the causal mechanisms of the disorder. In the present chapter, two models of binge eating, the cognitive model and the model of learned anticipatory responses, will be discussed. After presentation of each model, empirical data pertaining to the model will be reviewed. Finally, treatment implications and outcome data will be discussed.

THE COGNITIVE MODEL

Description of the model

A crucial assumption of the cognitive model is that binge eating subjects are characterized by actual restrained eating or by the strong intention to restrain their food intake. Laboratory studies show that restrained eaters overeat when their restraint is broken (Herman and Mack, 1975; Hibscher and Herman, 1977; Herman and Polivy, 1980; Ruderman and Christensen, 1983) when they merely *believe* their restraint is broken (Spencer and Fremouw, 1979; Woody, Constanzo, Liefer, and Conger, 1981), and when they are in a strong emotional state (Baucom and Aiken, 1981; Frost *et al.*, 1982; Herman and Polivy, 1975; Ruderman, 1985; Schotte *et al.*, 1990).

The most typical finding is that restrained eaters eat more after diet violation (through forced consumption of a high-calorie pre-load such as a milk-shake) than without diet violation (eating no pre-load), whereas the food consumption of unrestrained eaters is smaller after a pre-load than without one. This so-called counterregulation of restrained eaters in the laboratory is considered to be a valid model of clinical binge eating: the antecedents for clinical binges seem remarkably similar to the stimuli for counterregulation or 'miniature binges' in the laboratory (Polivy and Herman, 1985).

According to cognitive theory, restrained eaters possess a cognitive 'diet boundary' and the start of a binge (or counterregulation) is held to be related to this boundary. The boundary model (Herman and Polivy, 1984) states that food consumption is regulated by biological needs as well as by psychological influences. When hunger or satiety passes a certain boundary, it is aversive and people start or stop eating. Between the boundaries of hunger and satiety there is an area of biological indifference. Normally an organism strives to be in the zone of biological indifference: the aversiveness of hunger keeps consumption above a minimum level while the aversiveness of satiety keeps consumption under a maximum level. In the zone of biological indifference, cognitive and social factors dominate the determination of human eating behaviour. According to the boundary model, restrained and unrestrained eaters differ in the place of their boundaries. In restrained eaters, the area of biological indifference is wider than in unrestrained eaters: restrained eaters have lower hunger boundaries and higher satiety boundaries, that is, they have to be more deprived to report hunger and they can eat more before reporting satiety. Furthermore, restrained eaters are supposed to have a 'diet boundary', somewhere between the hunger and satiety boundary in.

Normally (that is, when not dieting), a person eats until his satiety boundary is reached. That is, unrestrained eaters will eat less after a pre-load than without one. Restrained eaters usually eat until they reach their *diet* boundary, that is, without a pre-load they eat little. However, when passing their diet boundary, for example after forced eating of a high-calorie pre-load, restrained eaters eat until they reach their (high!) satiety boundary: they overeat.

The idea of passing the diet boundary leads to a complete loss of control: 'The slightest transgression from rigidly prescribed dieting leads the patient to conclude that she might as well give in to the urge to eat since perfect self-control has been blown.' (Garner, 1986, p.319). Even minor discretions are considered to be indicative of a complete absence of self-control: 'I try not to eat. But if I had pizza, it's over for the day' and 'If I ate that much, I might as well go ahead and eat more. Usually it ends up in a binge.' (Chiodo, 1987, p.42) Analogies to the notion that disinhibitive thoughts such as 'I've blown my diet, I might as well continue to eat' are held to be the antecedent of clinical binge eating behaviour, it is assumed that such thoughts trigger a counterregulatory response in the laboratory.

Empirical data

Until recently, the notion that disinhibitive thoughts such as 'I've blown my diet, I might as well continue to eat' trigger a clinical binge or lab counterregulation had never been tested *directly*. 'Despite the paucity of supporting evidence, the cognitive explanation for the putative association between dieting and overeating has a remarkable degree of acceptance. This is probably because it is credible to clinicians. Patients with bulimia nervosa describe abandoning their controls after breaking their rules.' (Fairburn, Cooper, and Cooper, 1986, p.401). However, credibility is no guarantee of validity.

From the cognitive theory, several predictions can be deduced. First, the most straightforward assumption is that dieters showing disinhibitive behaviour will be characterized by disinhibitive thoughts. By measuring self-talk of restrained and unrestrained eaters during a disinhibition challenge (eating a high-calorie pre-load), Jansen *et al.*

(1988) failed to find experimental confirmation for the widely held view that disinhibitive thoughts such as 'I've blown my diet, I might as well continue to eat' disinhibit restrained eaters.

Second, cognitive theory states that dieters overeat when they perceive their diet as broken. A logical implication of this assumption is that dieters who do not perceive their diet as broken will not overeat. Jansen and van den Hout (1991) showed that restrained eaters also 'counterregulate' after merely *smelling* a 'preload'. Restrained eaters who did not smell the pre-load and unrestrained eaters did not counterregulate in a subsequent taste test. Clearly, restrained eaters counterregulated *without* passing their diet boundary.

Third, the cognitive boundary model does *not* predict that dieters who are emotionally upset, overeat. Stronger than that, the model fails to explain the disinhibiting effect of emotions. It has repeatedly been found that strong negative and positive emotional states can trigger counterregulation and binge eating in restrained eaters (Baucom and Aiken, 1981; Frost *et al.*, 1982; Herman and Polivy, 1975; Ruderman, 1985; Schotte *et al.*, 1990). There is no reason to believe that someone passes his or her diet boundary when anxious, depressed, or merry. When it comes to explaining the overeating of restrained eaters in an emotional state, the model only holds by virtue of a weak auxiliary hypothesis: according to the model's proponents, emotions are more urgent than dietary concerns and, while coping with the stressor, restrained eaters forget to diet (Herman and Polivy, 1984).

Furthermore, the boundary model can be criticized for its lack of explanatory power. Due to its descriptive nature it fails to explain *why* restrained eaters regularly pass their diet boundary. When such descriptions of phenomena are used as explanations, circular reasoning may occur. For example, Westerterp *et al.* (1991) concluded that their restrained eaters, participating in a typical pre-load study, did not pass their diet boundary *because* they did not counterregulate. Restrained eaters who did not counterregulate did not pass their diet boundary and we know that they did not pass their diet boundary because they did not counterregulate. This is like saying that someone acts crazy because he is schizophrenic and we know he is schizophrenic because he acts crazy. To prevent circular reasoning one should determine independently the location of the diet boundary. In order to do so, operationalization and measurement of the hypothetical boundaries is required.

However, in spite of these conflicting data and criticisms, two studies convincingly showed that a breach of restraint did occur in restrained eaters who merely *believed* that the pre-load was high-calorie, whereas counterregulation did not take place in restrained eaters who believed the pre-load to be low-calorie (Spencer and Fremouw, 1979; Woody *et al.*, 1981). Spencer and Fremouw selected restrained and unrestrained subjects with Herman *et al.*'s Restraint Scale (1978). The subjects were given a liquid pre-load of 500 calories. Half of the subjects were told that the drink was 'very high calorie', the other half was told that the drink was 'very low calorie'. In fact, the calorie amounts of both pre-loads were identical. After drinking the liquid pre-load, the subjects were invited to taste three flavours of ice cream. High-restrained eaters ate significantly less ice cream when they believed they had eaten a low-calorie pre-load than when they believed they had eaten a high-calorie pre-load (96 vs 137 g of ice cream; $p<.01$). Low-restrained eaters, on the contrary, ate the same amount of ice cream in both conditions (118 g when they believed they had eaten a low-calorie pre-load vs 103 g when they believed they had eaten a high-calorie pre-load; $p=1.97$, NS). These data are usually put forward as strong evidence for the cognitive model. However, it is premature to conclude anything about mechanisms (that is, cognitions) from the disinhibiting effect of stimuli. As will become clear later in this chapter, these typical cognitions, or expectations, may elicit physiological anticipatory responses which trigger a binge.

Clinical implications

Cognitive theory predicts that binge eating will stop when people stop dieting. Although rather successful treatment packages such as cognitive behaviour therapy (Fairburn, 1985; Fairburn and Cooper, 1989) include strategies to discourage subjects from dieting, there is only one study on the pure effects of undieting. Polivy and Herman (1992) taught 18 overweight dieting female subjects to stop dieting in ten two-hour sessions. Bulimia scores on the Bulimia sub-scale of the Eating Disorder Inventory were indeed significantly decreased after treatment (unfortunately, the authors did not measure binge eating directly by, say, self-monitoring) and the subjects showed a marginal increase in weight ($F(2,14) = 2.52$, $p>.10$). However, no control groups were used and no manipulation check was performed. Concerning the latter, closer inspection of the data shows that, although restraint scores significantly declined during treatment, subjects were still highly restrained after treatment.

In summary, there is some evidence that cognitions might act as stimuli which trigger a counterregulation response. However, there are no convincing empirical data to support the cognitive boundary model of binge eating. Indeed, data from laboratory studies question the validity of the model. Studies are needed to prove that undieting is a *sine qua non* for the extinction of binge eating, as cognitive theory claims.

LEARNED ANTICIPATORY RESPONSES

Description of the model

Many physiological systems in our internal environment try to maintain a delicate homeostasis. Physiological variables usually vary around an optimal value and within a certain range. 'Caretakers' keep their eyes on the system and, when deviations from optimal values are signalled, they start correcting physiological responses to restore optimal values. For example, people shiver when it is cold whereas they sweat when it is hot.

From the experimental field of drug intake we already know that organisms, including humans, learn to anticipate the intake of a substance (e.g. Siegel, 1983). For example, experiments show that dogs injected with epinephrine show the usual tachycardia response to the epinephrine administration. After repeated administrations, the injection ritual becomes a cue or stimulus which is specifically associated with the supply of epinephrine and after a series of injection rituals and drug pairings, the injection ritual becomes a reliable *predictor* of the epinephrine. When the injection ritual predicts epinephrine intake reliably, the dogs will display a compensatory response in anticipation of the epinephrine. They learned that the injection ritual signals epinephrine and thus tachycardia. To compensate for the expected tachycardia, they show a bradycardia in advance (see Siegel, 1983). The counter-directional response is thus a learned response which prepares the organism for the intake of the substance. Another example shows that rats can learn to anticipate alcohol consumption. Normally, the intake of alcohol *lowers* core temperature: rats repeatedly injected with alcohol in room A show a strong *rise* in temperature when given a placebo in room A. Clearly, room A has become a reliable predictor of the intake of alcohol. When confronted with room A the rats expect to get alcohol and display a compensatory response in anticipation of the alcohol: they show an increase in temperature (see Siegel, 1983).

Compensatory responses prepare the organism for the intake of the drug and show the body's attempt to maintain homeostasis by counteracting the drug effect. Compensatory responses should, in this way, contribute much to tolerance: they increasingly cancel the effects of the substance taken, so that the response to a drug decreases in the course of successive administrations (Eikelboom and Stewart, 1982; Siegel, 1983). Moreover, the anticipatory compensatory responses are supposed to be subjectively experienced as craving (Pomerleau, Fertig, Baker, and Cooney, 1983).

The classical conditioning model of craving and tolerance thus states that, after repeated association of cues specifically related to a substance taken, these cues will elicit a learned physiological response which is opposite to the unlearned response of the substance, to prepare the organism for intake (Macrae *et al.*, 1987; Siegel, 1983). Note that the counterdirectional response will only be learned when the presence of a substance in the body can be reliably predicted. When cues reliably predict the intake of a substance, they are able to elicit responses which prepare for the actual intake of a substance, for example drugs or food (see also Glautier, this volume).

Preparatory responses for food intake

Woods (1991, p.488) states that, analogous to the intake of drugs, 'the act of eating, although necessary for the provision of energy, is a particularly disruptive event in a homeostatic sense'. The notion of preparatory responses associated with the intake of *food* has already been articulated many years ago by the physiologist Pavlov (1927). In the present section, an early theory on preparatory responses and overeating will be presented first. Secondly, attention will be paid to a crucial prediction which flows from the early theory and could not be corroborated. Finally, it will be argued that binge eating can be explained by preparatory responses on condition that the learned nature of the preparatory responses is taken into account.

The early theory

The idea that exaggerated cephalic[1] phase responses (CPRs) to food stimuli stimulated overeating, was presented many years ago. CPRs are the earliest physiological reactions of an organism which is exposed to food cues such as smell, taste, and appearance. They are fast pre-digestive hormonal reflexes which start in the first minute after stimulus presentation, peak within five minutes, and return to baseline within ten minutes (Powley, 1977; Powley and Berthoud, 1985). CPRs play an important metabolic anticipatory role. Functionally, they prepare the organism for the consumption of food by priming the mechanisms that will have to transport, break down, and store incoming nutrients (Berthoud *et al.*, 1981; Tordoff and Friedman, 1989). CPRs include the secretion of saliva, insulin, gastric juices, Free Fatty Acids mobilization, and greater gastric motility (Powley and Berthoud, 1985; Rodin, 1985).

With respect to binge eating, the original 'cephalic theory' stated that dieting or chronic hunger leads to an *over*responsiveness of CPRs which, in fact, reflect an irresistible biological imperative to

---

[1] The word *cephalic* means 'pertaining to the head' and here it refers to the activities of the afferent limb originating in the olfactory, visual, and gustatory receptors in the head (Berthoud *et al.*, 1981).

eat (Herman *et al.*, 1981; Johnson and Wildman, 1983; Klajner *et al.*, 1981). According to the theory, the exaggerated CPRs function as a corrective physiological defence against the energy shortage resulting from food deprivation: oversecretion (exaggerated CPRs) leads the organism to ingest enough calories to restore the metabolic balance.

A crucial prediction

The cephalic theory thus predicts that dieters will show stronger salivation responses than non-dieters. This hypothesis is not always supported. In several studies it was found that dieters did salivate more than non-dieters in response to palatable food items (Herman *et al.*, 1981; Klajner *et al.*, 1981; Leboff and Spigelman 1987). In other studies, however, subjects on low-calorie diets showed lower salivation responses than control subjects (Durrant, 1981 and Rosen, 1981 in Herman *et al.*, 1981; Wooley and Wooley, 1981). The inconsistent findings are probably due to the types of dieters participating in the different studies. In the 'low-salivation studies', dieters were institutionalized and put on a strict diet, whereas dieters in the 'high-salivation studies' were selected on the basis of their self-report scores on Herman *et al.*'s (1978) Restraint Scale. Dieters who are on a strict diet are really food deprived whereas dieters identified by the self-report questionnaire usually alternate periods of deprivation with spells of overeating. In line with this, LeGoff, Leichner, and Spigelman (1988) found that dieters who are on a highly unvaried diet (that is, anorexia nervosa restricters) salivated significantly less to food cues than dieters on a highly varied diet (bulimic patients). Note that this finding contradicts the cephalic theory, which states that dieting *per se* results in exaggerated CPRs. Data indicate that successful dieting produces low CPRs (salivation responses) whereas unsuccessful dieting, that is, alternation of dieting and overeating, produces exaggerated CPRs (salivation responses).

In summary, the findings of low salivation levels in 'real' dieters and high salivation flows in dieters who regularly overeat do not support the assumption of cephalic theory that it is deprivation *per se* which triggers exaggerated anticipatory responses. They suggest, rather, that it is the behaviour of occasional overeating which results in exaggerated CPRs. What is the cause of this?

The learned nature of CPRs

Classical conditioning refers to a procedure by which a previously neutral stimulus (the conditioned stimulus = CS) comes to elicit a response after systematically being paired with an unconditioned stimulus (UCS) (van den Hout and Merckelbach, 1991). If meat (UCS), for example, is reliably preceded by a bell (CS), salivation of a dog will begin to occur upon the dog hearing the bell (conditioned response = CR).

Food intake triggers metabolic responses. The intake may be considered a UCS, whereas the metabolic responses are unconditioned responses (UCRs). Sight, smell, taste, chewing, or swallowing of food naturally occur along with feeding. They may therefore start to act as conditioned stimuli (CSs) which can trigger a conditioned response (CR). The conditioned response in fact is a CPR which can be under the control of any arbitrary external stimulus that previously reliably preceded the actual ingestion of food (Berthoud *et al.*, 1981; Booth, 1981; Powley, 1977; Rodin, 1985; Wooley and Wooley 1973, 1981). The mere anticipation of food or sham feeding (that is, the sight, smell, taste, chewing, or swallowing of food without it entering the gastrointestinal tract) and cognitive processes (e.g. the thought of food or even hypnotic suggestion of food) have been found to elicit responses which may prepare the organism for the digestion of food (Goldfine *et al.*, 1970; Johnson and Wildman, 1983; Powley, 1977; Rodin, 1985; Sahakian *et al.*, 1981; Simon *et al.*, 1986).

When the learned nature of CPRs is taken into account, that is, CPRs being classically conditioned responses to cues that have come to predict food intake, it becomes understandable why anorexia nervosa restricters and systematically deprived subjects show decreased CPRs while unsuccessful dieters and bulimics show elevated CPRs. In the case of 'total' deprivation, that is, a low-calorie and unvaried diet, food cues (CS) are less predictive of extreme food intake (UCS) than in the case of a diet–splurge eating pattern, which is usually found in high scorers on the Restraint Scale. Clearly, it is not dietary restraint in itself, but it may be the nature of the CS (food cues)–UCS (extreme food intake) probability relationship which determines the salivation flow. Note that when someone restricts food intake successfully (e.g. anorectics), food cues (CSs), such as smell and sight, become less predictive of food intake (UCS). Classical conditioning theory then predicts an *extinction* of the conditioned response, that is, salivation. In the case of unsuccessful dieting (e.g. bulimics), CSs are regularly followed by particularly strong UCSs (large/extreme food intake). UCS strength is a powerful determinant of the strength of the CR. Classical conditioning theory therefore correctly predicts relatively high-salivation CRs in bulimics and unsuccessful dieters. Intermittent dieting (diet–splurge) will never fulfil the preconditions necessary for inhibitory conditioning or extinction, whereas real dieting does.

The idea of learned preparatory responses explains the differences in salivation responses between restricters and bulimics quite well.

But can the model also explain binge eating and counterregulation satisfactorily?

Insulin and blood sugar

One of the anticipatory CPRs is the release of insulin. Insulin, a small protein produced in the β cells of the pancreas, facilitates the entry of glucose to cells and, in that way, lowers the amount of glucose in the blood. Anticipatory insulin release can be elicited by any stimulus which has temporarily been associated with feeding (Deutsch, 1974). This is convenient: food intake heightens blood sugar level and anticipative insulin release allows a better tolerance of the glucose. The taste of sweetness, in particular, stimulates insulin release, which subsequently lowers blood sugar level and stimulates appetite (Berthoud *et al.*, 1981; Deutsch, 1974; Geiselman and Novin, 1982). Thus, CSs such as tasting or smelling food trigger anticipatory insulin release which, in its turn, elicits a decline in blood sugar level. Normally, food intake heightens blood sugar level: the hypoglycaemia in anticipation of food intake is therefore, in fact, a conditioned compensatory response (CCR). The hypoglycaemia may be subjectively experienced as hunger/craving and, in that way, may stimulate food intake in order to heighten blood sugar level.

Empirical data

Animal studies show that eating behaviour can be triggered by cues which have been associated with food consumption: rats which had already eaten till satiation were found to eat a large meal when exposed to a tone previously associated with food consumption (Weingarten, 1983). Also, physiological changes which prepare for food intake, such as the release of insulin and salivation, can be conditioned to cues: rats which were repeatedly exposed to a menthol odour at the start of their feeding showed an insulin response when exposed to the odour alone (see Wardle, 1990). Empirical data also support the notion that it is possible to condition blood sugar level. After repeated intravenous injections of insulin (which are usually followed by a decline in blood sugar level) rats learn to show a hyperglycaemic response to a placebo (Siegel, 1972). Rats thus learn to anticipate the insulin administration (and subsequent hypoglycaemia) with a compensatory, *hyper*glycaemic, response. Furthermore, conversely, after repeated intravenous injections with glucose, rats learn to show a hypoglycaemic response to a placebo (Deutsch, 1974). Rats thus learn to anticipate the glucose administration with a compensatory, *hypo*glycaemic, response. Deutsch (1974) also showed that, in rats, an initially neutral taste cue can elicit a glycometabolic effect if it has been paired with glucose administration in a classical conditioning paradigm.

Moreover, data from human studies are in line with the model: exposure to food cues (sight, smell, or slides of food) induces physiological responses such as the release of insulin and salivation (Rodin, 1985). In fact, *any* cue that predicts the actual ingestion of food may elicit preparatory responses (Rodin, 1985). Even cognitive processes such as thinking of food and hypnotic suggestion are found to be able to elicit a preparatory insulin release and restrained eaters lost control over food intake and overate after exposure to cues that typically predict food intake (that is, smelling a pre-load; Jansen and van den Hout, 1991). Also, human obesity has been attributed, by some authors, to hyperinsulinaemia and the hypoglycaemia resulting from it (Geiselman and Novin, 1982; Tordoff and Friedman, 1989).

In the literature on binge eating, however, the notion of a *learned* hypoglycaemia in anticipation of a binge has hardly been pointed out. Some authors have touched upon the idea of hypoglycaemia (e.g. Wooley and Wooley, 1985) but were unable to specify the exact, that is, learned, nature of the alleged hypoglycaemia. Others studied bingers' glucose and insulin levels *after* a meal or a glucose injection. The data are equivocal. Normal blood glucose and insulin levels in bulimics were reported by Hohlstein *et al.* (1986) and Weingarten *et al.* (1988), whereas Schweiger *et al.* (1987) reported abnormally high insulin and glucose levels in bulimics who had eaten a meal. It should be noted, however, that the present compensatory model for binge eating/counterregulation specifies *anticipatory* responses and not responses following a meal. Moreover, the studies mentioned were one-off, and did not use explicit CSs, which means that the learned nature of hypoglycaemic responses was not taken into account. As far as the present author knows, there is only one study on *anticipatory* glucose and insulin levels in bulimic subjects: in line with the hypothesis stated earlier, Thompson *et al.* (1988) found an elevated insulin/glucose ratio in counterregulating restrained subjects after they had eaten a pre-load.

Note that bulimics are usually restrained eaters who alternate dieting with bingeing: a very common eating pattern is that they resist eating during the day and binge eat late in the afternoon or in the evening. Such an eating pattern, eating large amounts with a limited range of cues, has the implication that classical conditioning will be strong.

The idea of learned anticipatory reponses is unique in the sense that it has, hitherto, been the only model which offers a unifying and satisfactory explanation for the motley collection of disinhibitors that have been identified. Binge eating occurs on several occasions. For the sake of parsimony one single mechanism that underlies all the counterregulatory challenges should be looked for. It is hypothesized that the different disinhibitors all act as conditioned stimuli with an identical consequence: CSs (*disinhibitors*) → CPR (*insulin oversecretion*) → CCR (*hypoglycaemia*) → *counterregulation/binge eating*. Eating a calorie-rich pre-load, smelling a tasty 'pre-load', the perceived breach of a diet, being in a low mood, or being anxious are all stimuli which could, hypothetically, be conditioned to the excessive intake of food (UCS) in dieters. These CSs may therefore elicit a hyperinsulinaemia response (CPR) which, in its turn, will be followed by a hypoglycaemia (CCR). The hypoglycaemia is subjectively experienced as craving or hunger and, therefore, leads to counterregulation or binge eating.

Clinical implications

Clinical implications follow from the assumption that binges result from exaggerated CCRs that are due to probabilistic CS (cue)–UCS (extreme food intake) contingencies. It is expected that the urge to binge is cue-dependent, that is, binges will occur in stereotyped stimulus configurations. There are clinical impressions that back up this inference and there is a therapeutic implication. If bingeing results from prior CS–UCS contingencies it follows that when the probabilistic connection between CS (cue) and UCS (extreme food intake) is broken, the exaggerated CCRs will be extinguished and so will actual bingeing behaviour. It thus is hypothesized that prolonged exposure to cues (the smell, sight, touch, and taste of food, mood states, time of day, binge room and so on) with response prevention (that is, not eating) will lead to the extinction of the preparatory responses and craving.

In a pilot study, we tested whether cue exposure is more effective in the reduction of the binge eating frequency than learning self-control techniques with relapse prevention (Jansen, Broekmate, and Heymans, 1992). Note that many self-control skills in fact mean learning avoidance behaviour; one mainly learns to avoid stimuli associated with binge eating. The conditioning model predicts that, by avoiding the cues, cue reactivity and craving will not extinguish. The model that has been presented states that it is only exposure to the cues associated with binge eating and response prevention (no binges) that will lead to the extinction of craving.

In our pilot study, the break of the relationship between cues and excessive intake was attempted in two ways. Subjects were treated individually. First, the subject was exposed to the contextual cues predicting a binge while she was prevented from eating (CS without UCS). During the one-hour exposure sessions, the subject was asked to prepare the food, to touch the food, to raise it to her mouth and nose, to smell it, to act if she was going to eat it, to lick the food, and to eat a very small piece of it. Second, before the sixth session, the subject was forced to eat a pre-load of binge food in a place not associated with a binge, for example eating ice-cream in the sports pavilion (UCS without CS). After having eaten binge food in a non-binge environment, the subject went home and confronted herself with the binge food and contextual binge cues without eating anything. Also outside of the sessions, the subject confronted herself with binge food during the day.

Cue exposure was indeed successful in the extinction of craving during therapy: habituation set in within and between sessions (see Fig. 8.1). Thus, during prolonged exposure to binge cues such as smelling and licking food, the urge to eat extinguished.

Both treatments were shown to be effective in reducing the binge frequency. In the self-control group the usual results were found: a 70 per cent reduction in binge frequency and an abstinence rate of 33 per cent. However, cue exposure was significantly more successful: *all* subjects treated with cue exposure were abstinent directly after treatment up to and including the one-year follow-up (see Fig. 8.2).

Although it should be noted that only 12 subjects were treated in the present pilot study, cue exposure seems to be promising in the treatment of binge eating. Of course, more controlled outcome data are needed before firm conclusions can be drawn.

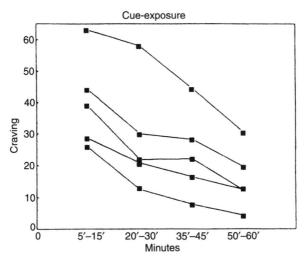

Fig. 8.1 The extinction of craving during cue exposure. Line A reflects mean craving scores (*n*=6) of exposure sessions 1 and 2, B reflects mean craving scores of sessions 3 and 4, C reflects mean craving scores of sessions 5 and 6, D reflects mean craving scores of sessions 7 and 8, and E reflects mean craving scores of sessions 9 and 10. (Reprinted from Jansen *et al.*, 1992.)

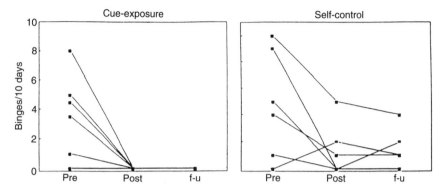

Fig. 8.2 The binge frequency between treatment, after treatment, and during the one-year follow-up. Each line is a subject. (Reprinted from Jansen *et al.*, 1992.)

CONCLUSIONS

The starting point of the present chapter was the observation that binge eating is a phenomenon of frequent occurrence in underweight as well as overweight and normal weight people. The question was: 'why?'.

Cognitive theory appeared to be untenable on theoretical and empirical grounds. By making use of experimental data on classically conditioned compensatory responses in addictive behaviours, an analogous model for binge eating was constructed. The idea is that binge eating is cue-dependent. Binge eating is supposed to result from learned compensatory responses (hypoglycaemia) which prepare the organism for the intake of food. The postulates of the learning model of binge eating are summarized in Table 8.1.

The model specifies the way in which dieters' binge eating after a variety of disinhibitors may take place. *Post hoc*, the model covers earlier findings quite well, and some predictions following from it could also be corroborated. It was, for example, predicted that if certain CSs are sometimes followed by strong UCSs, unsuccessful dieters will also counterregulate after any of these cues that typically predict food intake. Dieters did counterregulate after they had merely *smelled* a 'pre-load'. (Note again that this finding is in direct contradiction with cognitive theory, which states that dieters overeat because they perceive their diet as broken, whereas, here, this was not the case.)

Future research should further concentrate on the fundamental predictions that follow directly from the model. They are (i) that classical conditioning of food intake (UCS) to exteroceptive and

Table 8.1 Postulates of the conditioning model of binge eating

---

CPRs are conditioned responses to food cues
[*hyperinsulinaemia is a CPR*]

CPRs mediate compensatory responses (CCRs)
[*hyperinsulinaemia elicits hypoglycaemia*]

CPRs/CCRs are particularly strong if strong UCSs are presented
[*hypoglycaemia is particularly strong in the case of intermittent dieting/overeating*]

CPRs/CCRs are experienced as hunger or craving
[*hyperinsulinaemia/hypoglycaemia is experienced as hunger or craving*]

CPRs/CCRs promote overeating
[*hyperinsulinaemia/hypoglycaemia promote bingeing/counterregulation*]

---

interoceptive stimuli (CS) will, after repeated association, result in an anticipatory hyperinsulinaemia and a compensatory hypoglycaemic response (CCR); (ii) that after a variety of disinhibitors (cognitive manipulation, eating a pre-load, smelling a pre-load, and emotional agitation) individuals who overeat will show the anticipatory hyperinsulinaemia and compensatory decline in blood sugar level; (iii) that this hyperinsulinaemia/hypoglycaemia response will be subjectively experienced as craving,; and (iv) that inducing a hyperinsulinaemia/hypoglycaemia response in non-dieters will trigger craving and an overeating response.

ACKNOWLEDGEMENT

Thanks are expressed to Joost Overduin for his comments on an earlier draft of this chapter.

REFERENCES

American Psychiatric Association. *Diagnostic and statistical manual of mental disorders IV*. In preparation.

Baucom, D.H., and Aiken, P.A. (1981). Effect of depressed mood on eating among obese and nonobese dieting and nondieting persons. *Journal of Personality and Social Psychology*, **41**, 577–85.

Berthoud, H.R., Bereiter, D.A., Trimble, E.R., Siegel, E.G., and Jeanrenaud, B. (1981). Cephalic phase, reflex insulin secretion. Neuroanatomical and physiological characterization. *Diabetologica*, **20**, 393–401.

Booth, D.A. (1981). The physiology of appetite. *British Medical Bulletin*, **37**, 135–40.

208 *Anita Jansen*

Chiodo, J. (1987). Bulimia: An individual behavioral analysis. *Journal of Behavioral Therapy and Experimental Psychiatry*, **18**, 41–9.

Deutsch, R. (1974). Conditioned hypoglycaemia: A mechanism for saccharin-induced sensitivity to insulin in the rat. *Journal of Comparative and Physiological Psychology*, **86**, 350–8.

Eikelboom, R. and Stewart, J. (1982). Conditioning of drug-induced physiological responses. *Psychological Review*, **89**, 507–28.

Fairburn, C.G. (1985). The managemant of bulimia nervosa. *Journal of Psychiatric Research*, **3**, 465–72.

Fairburn, C.G. and Cooper, P.J. (1989). Eating disorders. In Hawton, K., Salkovskis, P., Kirk, J., and Clark, D.M. (eds.) *Cognitive behaviour therapy for psychiatric problems: A practical guide*, pp. 277–314. Oxford University Press.

Fairburn, C.G., Cooper, Z., and Cooper, P.J. (1986). The clinical features and maintenance of bulimia nervosa. K.D. Brownell, and J.P. Foreyt (eds.), *Handbook of eating disorders: physiology, psychology, and treatment of obesity, anorexia, and bulimia*, pp. 389–404. Basic Books, New York.

Frost, R.O., Goolkasian, G.A., Ely, R.J., and Blanchard, F.A. (1982). Depression, restraint and eating behavior. *Behaviour Research and Therapy*, **20**, 113–21.

Garner, D.M. (1986). Cognitive therapy for anorexia nervosa. In K.D. Brownell, and J.P. Foreyt (eds.), *Handbook of eating disorders: physiology, psychology, and treatment of obesity, anorexia, and bulimia*, pp. 301–327. Basic Books, New York.

Garner, D.M. (1987). Psychotherapy outcome research with bulimia nervosa. *Psychotherapy and Psychosomatics*, **48**, 129–140.

Geiselman, P.J. and Novin, D. (1982). The role of carbohydrates in appetite, hunger and obesity. *Appetite*, **3**, 203–23.

Goldfine, I.D., Abraira, C., Gruenewald, D., and Goldstein, M.S. (1970). Plasma insulin levels during imaginary food ingestion under hypnosis. *Proceedings of the Society for Experimental Biology and Medicine*, **133**, 274–6.

Herman, C.P. and Mack, D. (1975). Restrained and unrestrained eating. *Journal of Personality*, **43**, 647–60.

Herman, C.P. and Polivy, J. (1975). Anxiety, restraint, and eating behaviour. *Journal of Abnormal Psychology*, **84**, 666–72.

Herman, C.P. and Polivy, J. (1980). Restrained eating. In A.J. Stunkard (ed.), *Obesity*. pp. 208–25. W.B. Saunders, Philadephia.

Herman, C.P. and Polivy, J. (1984). A boundary model for the regulation of eating. In A.J. Stunkard, and E. Steller (eds.), *Eating and its disorders*. Raven Press, New York.

Herman, C.P., Polivy, J., Pliner, P., Threlkeld, J., and Munic, D. (1978). Distractability in dieters and nondieters: An alternative view of 'externality'. *Journal of Personality and Social Psychology*, **36**, 536–48.

Herman, C.P., Polivy, J., Klajner, F., and Esses, V.M. (1981). Salivation in dieters and nondieters. *Appetite*, **2**, 356–61.

Hibscher, J.A. and Herman, C.P. (1977). Obesity, dieting, and the expression of 'obese' characteristics. *Journal of Comparative and Physiological Psychology*, **91**, 374–80.

Hohlstein, L.A., Gwirtsman, H.E., Wahlen, F., and Enns, M.P. (1986). Oral glucose tolerance in Bulimia. *International Journal of Eating Disorders*, **5**, 157–60.

Jansen, A., Merckelbach, H., Oosterlaan, J., Tuiten, A. and Van den Hout,

M.A. (1988). Cognitions and self-talk during food intake of restrained and unrestrained eaters. *Behaviour Research and Therapy*, **26**(5), 393–8.

Jansen, A., Van den Hout, M.A., and Griez, E. (1990). Clinical and non-clinical binges. *Behaviour Research and Therapy*, **5**, 439–44.

Jansen, A. and van den Hout, M.A. (1991). On being led into temptation: 'Counterregulation' of dieters after smelling a 'preload'. *Addictive Behaviours*, **5**, 247–53.

Jansen, A., Broekmate, J., and Heymans, M. (1992). Cue-exposure vs self-control in the treatment of binge eating: a pilot study. *Behaviour Research and Therapy*, **3**, 235–41.

Johnson, W.G., and Wildman, H.E. (1983). Influence of external and covert food stimuli on insulin secretion in obese and normal persons. *Behavioral Neuroscience*, **97**, 1025–8.

Klajner, F., Herman, C.P., Polivy, J., and Chhabra, R. (1981). Human obesity, dieting, and anticipatory salivation to food. *Physiology and Behavior*, **27**, 195–8.

Laessle, R.G., Tuschl, R.L., Kotthaus, B.C., and Pirke, K.M. (1989). Behavioral and biological correlates of dietary restraint in normal life. *Appetite*, **12**, 83–94

Leboff, D.B. and Spigelman, M.N. (1987). Salivary response to olfactory food stimuli as a function of dietary restraint and body weight. *Appetite*, **8**, 29–35.

Leboff, D.B., Leichner, P., and Spigelman, M.N. (1988). Salivary response to olfactory stimuli in anorexics and bulimics. *Appetite*, **11**, 15–25.

Ludwig, A.M. and Wilker, A. (1974). The first drink: Psychobiological aspects of craving. *Archives of General Psychiatry*, **30**, 539–47.

Macrae, J, Scoles, M.T., and Siegel, S. (1987). The contribution of Pavlovian conditioning to drug tolerance and dependence. *British Journal of Addiction*, **82**, 371–80.

Marcus, M.D., Wing, R.R., and Lamparski, D.M. (1985). Binge eating and dietary restraint in obese patients. *Addictive Behaviors*, **10**, 163–8.

Pavlov, I.P. (1927). *Conditioned reflexes; An investigation of the physiological activity of the cerebral cortex*. Oxford University Press, London.

Polivy, J., and Herman, C.P. (1985). Dieting and bingeing: A causal analysis. *American Psychologist*, **40**, 193–201.

Polivy, J. and Herman, C.P. (1992). Undieting: a program to help people stop dieting. *International Journal of Eating Disorders*, **3**, 261–8.

Pomerleau, O., Fertig, J., Baker, L. and Cooney, N. (1983). Reactivity to alcohol cues in alcoholics and non-alcoholics: implications for a stimulus control analysis of drinking. *Addictive Behaviors*, **8**, 1–10.

Powley, T. (1977). The ventromedial hypothalamic syndrome, satiety and a cephalic phase hypothesis. *Psychological Review*, **84**, 89–126.

Powley, T.L. and Berthoud, H.R. (1985). Diet and cephalic phase insulin responses. *American Journal of Clinical Nutrition*, **42**, 991–1002.

Rodin, J. (1985). Insulin levels, hunger, and food intake: An example of feedback loops in body weight regulation. *Health Psychology*, **4**, 1–24.

Ruderman, A.J. (1985). Dysphoric mood and overeating: A test of restraint theory's disinhibition hypothesis. *Journal of Abnormal Psychology*, **94**, 78–85.

Ruderman, A.J., and Christensen, H. (1983). Restraint theory and its applicability to overweight individuals. *Journal of Abnormal Psychology*, **92**, 210–15.

Sahakian, B.J., Lean, M.E.J., Robbins, T.W., and James, W.P.T. (1981). Salivation and insulin in response to food in non-obese men and women. *Appetite*, **2**, 209–16.

Schotte, D.E., Cools, and J., McNally, R.J. (1990). Film-induced negative affect triggers overeating in restrained eaters. *Journal of Abnormal Psychology*, **99**(3), 317–20.

Schweiger, U., Poellinger, J., Laessle, R., Wolfram, G., Fichter, M.M., and Pirke, K.M. (1987). Altered insulin response to a balanced test meal in bulimic patients. *International Journal of Eating Disorders*, **6**, 551–6.

Siegel, S. (1972). Conditioning of insulin-induced glycaemia. *Journal of Comparative and Physiological Psychology*, **78**, 233–41.

Siegel, S. (1983). Classical conditioning, drug tolerance and drug dependance. In R. Smart, F. Glaser, Y. Israel, H. Kalant, R. Popham, and W. Schmidt (eds.), *Research advances in alcohol and drug problems*, pp. 207–46. Plenum Press, New York.

Simon, C., Schlienger, J.L., Sapin, R., and Imler, M. (1986). Cephalic phase insulin secretion in relation to food presentation in normal and overweight subjects. *Physiology and Behavior*, **36**, 465–69.

Spencer, J.A. and Fremouw, W.J. (1979). Binge eating as a function of restraint and weight classification. *Journal of Abnormal Psychology*, **88**, 262–7.

Spitzer, R., Devlin, M., Walsh, T., Hasin, D., Wing, R., Marcus, M., Stunkard, A., Wadden, T., Yanovski, S., Agras, S., Mitchell, J., and Nonas, C. (1991). Binge eating disorder: to be or not to be in DSM-IV. *International Journal of Eating Disorders*, **6**, 627–9.

Spitzer, R.L., Devlin, M., Walsh, B.T., Hasin, D., Wing, R., Marcus, M., Stunkard, A., Wadden, Th., Yanovski, S., Agras, S., Mitchell, J., and Nonas, C. (1992). Binge eating disorder: A multisite field trial of the diagnostic criteria. *International Journal of Eating Disorders*, **3**, 191–203.

Thompson, J.P., Palmer, R.L., and Petersen, S.A. (1988). Is there a metabolic component to counterregulation? *International Journal of Eating Disorders*, **7**, 307–19.

Tordoff, M.G., and Friedman, M.I. (1989). Drinking saccharin increases food intake and preference-IV. Cephalic phase and metabolic factors. *Appetite*, **12**, 37–56.

van den Hout, M. and Merckelbach, H. (1991). Classical conditioning: Still going strong. *Behavioural Psychotherapy*, **19**, 59–79.

Walsh, B.T. (1992). Diagnostic criteria for eating disorders in DSM-IV: Work in progress. *International Journal of Eating Disorders*, **4**, 301–4.

Wardle, J. (1980). Dietary restraint and binge eating. *Behaviour Analysis and Modification*, **4**, 201–9.

Wardle, J. (1990). Conditioning processes and cue exposure in the modification of excessive eating. *Addictive Behaviors*, **15**, 387–93.

Wardle, J., and Beinart, H. (1981). Binge eating: A theoretical review. *British Journal of Clinical Psychology*, **20**, 97–109.

Weingarten, H.P. (1983). Conditioned cues elicit feeding in sated rats: a role for learning in meal satiation. *Science*, **220**, 431–2.

Weingarten, H.P., Hendler, R., and Rodin, J. (1988). Metabolism and endocrine secretion in response to a test meal in normal-weight bulimic women. *Psychosomatic Medicine*, **50**, 273–85.

Westerterp-Plantenga, M.S., van den Heuvel, E., Wouters, L., and Ten Hoor,

F. (1991). Counter regulation as a function of cognitive restraint? In Ailhaud, G. *et al.* (eds.). *Obesity in Europe '91*, pp. 431–5. John Libbey.

Woody, E.Z., Costanzo, P.R., Liefer, H., and Conger, J. (1981). The effects of taste and caloric perceptions on the eating behaviour of restrained and unrestrained subjects. *Cognitive Therapy and Research*, **5**, 381–90.

Wooley, S.C. and Wooley, O.W. (1973). Salivation to sight and thought of food: A new measure of appetite. *Psychosomatic Medicine*, **35**, 136–42.

Wooley, O.W. and Wooley, S.C. (1981). Relationship of salivation in humans to deprivation, inhibition and the encephalization of hunger. *Appetite*, **2**, 331–50.

Wooley, S.C., and Wooley, O.W. (1985). Intensive outpatient and residential treatment for Bulimia. In: D.M. Garner, and P.E. Garfinkel (Eds.). *Handbook of psychotherapy for anorexia nervosa and bulimia*. Guilford Press, New York, pp. 391–401.

Woods, S.C. (1991). The eating paradox: How we tolerate food. *Psychological Review*, **4**, 488–505.

9

Neuropharmacology of appetite and taste preferences

Steven J. Cooper and Suzanne Higgs

INTRODUCTION

In this chapter we have not attempted to provide a comprehensive review of the neuropharmacology of appetite and feeding: good, general sources include Hoebel (1977*a,b*), Morley and Levine (1985), and Blundell (1987). Instead, our principal aim will be to compare the effects of some selected drugs on food intake with their effects on taste preferences, and, where available, with their effects on taste reactivity measures. Our purpose is to determine the extent to which it can be inferred that the effects of drugs on hedonic processes contribute to their effects on food ingestion. Placing an emphasis on the role of palatability represents a departure from the assumptions and experimental aims of the older literature, so, before discussing some of the most recent data, we will provide a brief, historical introduction.

A HISTORICAL INTRODUCTION

Thirty years ago, the study of the effects of drugs on ingestion had barely progressed beyond an early, rudimentary stage (Cooper, 1994). A motivation for the research was to try to develop new drugs that could be used therapeutically in the treatment of obesity, to help patients reduce their food intake. The normal starting point was to identify drugs, which, when given acutely or sub-chronically, could reduce food intake in hungry animals in the course of a relatively short test. Of course, there may be several reasons why drugs reduce feeding behaviour, not all of them having much to do with feeding as such. Control experiments have to be performed to exclude the possible contribution of non-specific effects to changes in feeding. Moreover, there are many steps between a demonstration of an acute anorectic effect, on the one hand, and meeting the clinical problems confronting obese individuals who aspire to lose substantial amounts of weight over an extended period, on the other. There may be only weak links between the initial starting point, an empirical demonstration of a reduction in food intake, and the ultimate therapeutic goal.

Nevertheless, originally it was a transfer in the opposite direction, from clinical observation to laboratory investigation, that encouraged the search for appetite-suppressant drugs. A sympathomimetic amine, *dl*-amphetamine (benzedrine), was identified as a central nervous system stimulant (Prinzmetal and Bloomberg, 1935), which could, in some individuals, bring about a loss of appetite (Nathanson, 1937). As clinical uses of amphetamine spread, it was widely adopted as an effective adjunct in therapeutic procedures designed to help obese people to stick to low-calorie diets, eliminate between-meal snacking, and exercise more (Colton *et al.*, 1943; Ersner, 1940). However, it was the careful investigational work of Harris, Ivy, and Searle (1947) which showed that the loss in weight produced by amphetamine could be accounted for in terms of a reduction in food intake. These authors also argued that amphetamine's effect must involve the central nervous system. Only much later did Silverstone and Stunkard (1968) conduct the first placebo-controlled, double-blind trial to assess the effects of *d*-amphetamine (dexedrine) on food intake and hunger ratings in normal-weight, male students. Their results confirmed that there was an anorectic effect of the drug, but there was considerable individual variability in the response.

Experience with amphetamine, nevertheless, gave rise to the idea that drug treatment with actions in the central nervous system could depress food consumption. During this time, Brobeck (1955) placed emphasis on the need to study feeding *behaviour* in any attempt to understand the neural regulation of food intake, and distinguished between two behavioural phenomena: *appetite* and *satiety*, respectively. Harris (1955) responded to Brobeck's proposal, and enquired if amphetamine reduces food intake because of inhibition of an 'appetite centre', or because of stimulation of an 'appetite inhibiting centre'. Brobeck's response, from work on the anaesthetized cat, was to favour an action of amphetamine to excite a medial hypothalamic 'feeding inhibitory centre' (Brobeck *et al.*, 1956), although later work disconfirmed this view (e.g. Epstein, 1959; Stowe and Miller, 1957). Instead, other experiments supported the alternative view that amphetamine acted in the lateral hypothalamus to reduce food intake (Booth, 1968; Carlisle, 1964; Leibowitz, 1975*a,b*), presumably by inhibiting the hypothetical 'appetite centre' thought to be located there (Stellar, 1954).

dl-Fenfluramine was reported to reduce food consumption in rats and mice (Le Douarec, 1963), in the absence of central stimulant effects

(Le Douarec *et al.*, 1966; van Rossum and Simons, 1969). Clinical studies confirmed its effectiveness in the treatment of obesity (Munro *et al.*, 1966; Silverstone *et al.*, 1970; Woodward, 1970). Significantly, Blundell and colleagues (1976) proposed that, while amphetamine might act to reduce hunger, fenfluramine produces its effect through a satiety system (that is an appetite inhibiting system).

Amphetamine and fenfluramine, therefore, were put forward as two contrasting drugs, the first of which directly reduces hunger whereas the second enhances the opposing process of satiety. This behavioural distinction between the effects of the two drugs would naturally support the idea of the two opposing processes governing food ingestion. The view that amphetamine and fenfluramine are distinctly different in their modes of action was further reinforced by evidence that their anorectic effects had different neurochemical bases. Amphetamine-induced anorexia is due, it was argued, to the activation of central catecholamine (noradrenaline, dopamine) pathways (Leibowitz, 1975*b*, 1976), whereas fenfluramine-induced anorexia is due, in contrast, to an increase in activity in central indoleamine (serotonin) pathways (Blundell *et al.*, 1976; Blundell and Latham, 1978).

By the middle of the 1970s, therefore, the study of drug effects on ingestion had moved from an early empirical phase to a more sophisticated theory-driven phase, in which emphasis was placed on multiple neurochemically defined systems, part of whose function is the control of the initiation and cessation of feeding. The behavioural distinction between 'appetite', on the one hand (leading to the initiation and maintenance of ingestion), and 'satiety' on the other (separate factors that come into play to terminate an episode of feeding), was further supported by detailed structural analyses of feeding behaviour (Blundell and Latham, 1978). Evolving from these ideas, a continuous sequence or stream of behavioural events was envisaged (appetitive behaviour as a prelude to feeding; bouts of feeding; a terminal satiety sequence), which was linked to the waxing and waning of neurochemical processes involving noradrenaline, serotonin, and dopamine pathways (Blundell, 1981).

Barbiturates and benzodiazepines

The prevailing preoccupation with anorectic drugs left other drugs, which increased food consumption, neglected. Among older sedative drugs, barbiturates were known to stimulate food intake (Jacobs and Farel, 1971; Watson and Cox, 1976). Historically of more importance, however, was the finding that the benzodiazepines (which include chlordiazepoxide, diazepam, oxazepam) also increase food consumption (Randall *et al.*, 1960). The benzodiazepine effect remained relatively obscure for 20 years, even though it was shown that benzodiazepines increased lever pressing for food (Wise and Dawson, 1974), reduced latencies to feed (Cooper and Francis, 1979a), overcame the effects of quinine adulteration of diet (Margules and Stein, 1967), and induced voracious eating in satiated animals (Fratta *et al.*, 1976). Cooper (1980) assembled sufficient evidence, however, to propose that benzodiazepines directly enhanced appetite for food, and suggested that their effects may mimic those of increased hunger. By this stage, it had become evident that benzodiazepines potentiate GABA (γ-amino butyric acid) inhibitory neurotransmission in the central nervous system (Costa and Guidotti, 1979), and this served to exclude them from neurochemical models for the control of feeding based exclusively on the monoamines. The discovery of specific receptors for benzodiazepines in the brain (Braestrup and Squires, 1977; Möhler and Okada, 1977) led to an explosion of pharmacological findings, which, in turn, stimulated much greater efforts to study the effects of benzodiazepines on ingestive behaviour. These further developments will be reviewed and discussed later in this chapter.

Neuropeptides: cholecystokinin and endorphins

A significant departure from the emphasis on central mechanisms arose with the suggestion that ingested food initiates the release of hormones from the gastrointestinal tract, which, in turn, generates satiety signals which are relayed to the brain (Smith and Gibbs, 1976). Cholecystokinin (CCK) was identified as a likely candidate for the role of an intestinal neuropeptide which signals satiety in response to food ingestion. It was shown to decrease food intake (Gibbs *et al.*, 1973a), inhibit sham feeding in gastric-fistulated rats (Gibbs *et al.*, 1973b), and elicit a behavioural sequence indicative of satiety (Antin *et al.*, 1975). Subsequent work on CCK helped to promote the idea of satiety factors involved in the termination of feeding (Smith and Gibbs, 1979), and encouraged an integrated view of the control of feeding responses, involving both central and peripheral mechanisms.

The discovery of specific opioid receptors in the brain (Pert and Snyder, 1973; Simon *et al.*, 1973; Terenius, 1973) led to the discovery of enkephalins in the brain (Hughes *et al.*, 1975), and these were the first of several kinds of endogenous opioid peptides to be found in the central nervous system (Akil *et al.*, 1988). Evidence that selective opioid antagonists, such as naloxone and naltrexone, could reduce food intake (Holtzman, 1974) and water intake (Maickel *et al.*, 1977) were interpreted in terms of the blockade of endogenous opioid peptide activity (Sanger, 1981, 1983). Morley (1980) proposed a scheme in which endogenous opioid activity in the hypothalamus contributed to an integrated neurochemical and neuroendocrine system in the control of food intake.

There was some attempt to attribute the effects of opioid antagonists to an increase in satiation (Kirkham and Blundell, 1984, 1986), but attention had begun to shift away from the prevailing 'appetite-satiety' dichotomy towards ideas of 'food reward' and palatability. Le Magnen and his colleagues (1980) first showed that naloxone abolished the preferred intake of saccharin or glucose solutions. This result suggested that brain opioids may have a part to play in the palatability of food-associated stimuli (Le Magnen, 1985). It was soon confirmed that naloxone suppressed the ingestion of highly palatable solutions, results that were interpreted in terms of the blockade of endogenous opioid peptide activity linked to the determination of food palatability (Sclafani *et al.*, 1982; Siviy *et al.*, 1982). This shift in interest led away from a simple feeding control model (starting and stopping feeding) towards the idea of hedonic evaluation of the sensory characteristics of the ingested food. It represented a step from measurement of simple, undifferentiated intake to behavioural indices of likes and dislikes, preferences and aversions.

Food reward and dopamine

Aside from an interest in palatability and opioid peptides, some authors attempted to link 'food reward' to the reward of electrical brain stimulation (Olds and Milner, 1954), and to the reward of drugs as revealed in drug self-administration procedures (Weeks, 1962; Thompson and Schuster, 1964). For example, Hoebel (1976) and colleagues (1982) took the two phenomena of brain-stimulation reward and aversion, respectively, and grafted them on to the older appetite–satiety dichotomy, to produce a lateral hypothalamic 'feeding-and-reward system' opposed by a more medial 'satiety-and-aversion' system. Wise (1981, 1982) has also consistently promoted the view that there is a common system which mediates the reward of brain stimulation, of drugs of abuse (e.g. psychomotor stimulants and opioids), and of food and water (see Wise, this volume). This system is the mesolimbic dopaminergic projection from the ventral tegmental area of the forebrain to the nucleus accumbens (ventral striatum) (Fallon, 1988). Much of the evidence supporting this general reward theory comes from experiments on the behavioural effects of dopamine receptor blockers (e.g. Wise *et al.*, 1978). Interactions between opioids and dopamine neurotransmission have been invoked to account for opioid participation in reward processes (Bozarth, 1988).

BENZODIAZEPINES AND INGESTIVE BEHAVIOUR

Food intake

As we have already noted, benzodiazepines have a powerful effect on stimulation of food consumption. Their hyperphagic effect has been documented not only in rats and dogs, as originally described (Randall *et al.*, 1960), but also in many other species: mice (Soubrié *et al.*, 1975; Stephens, 1973), hamsters (Birk and Noble, 1982), cats (Fratta *et al.*, 1976, Mereu *et al.*, 1976), rabbits (Mansbach *et al.*, 1984), horses (Brown *et al.*, 1976), cattle, sheep, and pigs (Baile and McLaughlin, 1979), grey wolves (Kreeger *et al.*, 1991), and several primates, squirrel monkeys (Locke *et al.*, 1982), rhesus monkeys (Foltin *et al.*, 1985), and baboons (Foltin *et al.*, 1985). Chlordiazepoxide also induces a hyperphagic response in pigeons (Cooper and Posadas-Andrews, 1979). Hence, there is no sense in which the benzodiazepine effect is species-specific, and it can have little to do with the type of diet or the mode of eating.

Margules and Stein (1967) hypothesized that benzodiazepines inhibit satiety, and thereby *disinhibit* feeding. One mechanism, for example, could be that benzodiazepines block the satiety-signalling effects of CCK. In fact, there is evidence that benzodiazepines counteract the satiety effect of exogenous CCK in mice (Kubota *et al.*, 1986), and in lean or obese rats (McLaughlin and Baile, 1979). Nevertheless, this evidence is ambiguous, since a 'hunger-promoting' effect of benzodiazepines might well oppose the effect of CCK. One way to investigate this further is to use sham-feeding animals which have a satiety–deficit (Young *et al.*, 1974). Our results indicated that the benzodiazepine, midazolam, enhanced sucrose consumption in sham-feeding rats, suggesting that inhibition of satiety is not a necessary requirement for benzodiazepine-induced hyperphagia (Cooper *et al.*, 1988).

Instrumental performance

Wise and Dawson (1974) found that diazepam induced lever pressing for food in rats that had previously been trained to respond under a food-deprivation schedule. They also found that a stomach load of food (but not of water) blocked the feeding induced by diazepam. These and other results led them to propose that 'diazepam makes the animals hungry'. Presumably, they thought that the benzodiazepine induces a state akin to hunger and this state was responsible for the enhancement of instrumental responding. However, recent data from Balleine and colleagues (1993) throw considerable doubt on this interpretation. While they confirmed that a benzodiazepine (in their case midazolam was used) increased instrumental performance for a food reward, additional careful experiments ruled out a non-specific effect of midazolam to increase arousal, or, indeed, to mimic the state of hunger. Instead, their data strongly suggested that midazolam enhanced the incentive value of instrumental outcomes, and only when animals experienced an increase in incentive value with the drug was the drug capable of enhancing instrumental performance. They considered that the most likely basis for the increase in incentive value of food pellets or sodium saccharin solution, which they employed as instrumental outcomes, was a modulation of palatability by the benzodiazepine. We shall now consider this fundamental hypothesis explicitly, looking at evidence that benzodiazepines enhance palatability, in the context of studies on palatable food consumption, taste preferences, and taste reactivity.

Palatable food consumption

Animals do not have to be food-deprived for benzodiazepines to promote overconsumption. Surprisingly, perhaps, even when non-deprived rats are given a highly palatable diet (sweetened wet mash) to consume, benzodiazepines prove to be very effective in elevating food consumption substantially above already high baseline values (Cooper and Gilbert, 1985; Cooper and Moores, 1985a; Cooper *et al.*, 1985). In this case, the hyperphagia was due to a lengthening of individual bouts of ingestion (Cooper and Yerbury, 1986a). β-Carbolines that act as agonists at benzodiazepine receptors also stimulate palatable food consumption (Cooper, 1986a), and drugs that act as antagonists or weak partial agonists at benzodiazepine receptors block the hyperphagic effect (Cooper, 1986a; Cooper and Moores, 1985b; Cooper and Yerbury, 1986b).

Interestingly, there is a category of drugs which show high affinity for benzodiazepine receptors but which produce effects that are opposite to those of the familiar benzodiazepines that we have been considering. Drugs belonging to this new category are usually referred to as 'inverse agonists' (Braestrup *et al.*, 1983). One important prediction to stem from their discovery is that these drugs should manifest anorectic properties. In confirmation, we have demonstrated that inverse agonists reduce palatable food consumption in rats (Cooper, 1985a, 1986a; Cooper *et al.*, 1985; Cooper and Yerbury, 1986a). It follows from this that there can be 'bi-directional' control of appetite through drug actions at benzodiazepine receptors: agonists, such as diazepam or chlordiazepoxide, induce hyperphagia, whereas inverse agonists cause anorexia (Cooper, 1985b). This is the first example of 'bi-directional' effects on ingestive behaviour achieved through the mediation of a single type of drug receptor. Whether it proves to be a unique example, or one of a larger class, remains to be seen.

Another pharmacological development has been the introduction of benzodiazepine receptor partial agonists, which retain significant main effects of classical full agonists such as diazepam, but exhibit fewer side-effects, for example sedation (Haefely *et al.*, 1990). Our work indicates that partial agonists are very effective in stimulating food intake, proving that the hyperphagic effect can be dissociated from the typical side-effects of benzodiazepine treatments (Yerbury and Cooper, 1987, 1989).

Taste preferences

Maickel and Maloney (1973) reported that chlordiazepoxide significantly increased the consumption of water by water-deprived rats. Their finding was confirmed and extended to other benzodiazepines in some of our work (Cooper, 1982*a,b*; Cooper and Francis, 1979*b*). This hyperdipsic effect of benzodiazepines is less significant, however, than the marked effect that these drugs have when animals are given access to a sweet-tasting solution. Maickel and Maloney (1974) subsequently observed that chlordiazepoxide had a dramatic effect to enhance consumption of a 'pleasant-tasting saccharin solution'. No explanation of this effect was offered. Later, in work on conditioned taste aversions, Roache and Zabik (1986) administered diazepam and chlordiazepoxide to water-deprived rats given a choice between water and a saccharin solution. Both benzodiazepines preferentially enhanced consumption of the saccharin solution, in a control group of animals for whom saccharin was preferred to water. In other words, the drugs appeared to potentiate a sweet taste preference. We (Cooper and Yerbury, 1988) explicitly tested this possibility using the potent benzodiazepine, clonazepam. Our results indicated that clonazepam enhanced saccharin consumption without significantly affecting water consumption in a two-choice test. This basic finding was fully confirmed in subsequent experiments using chlordiazepoxide (Parker, 1991), or abecarnil, a β-carboline which acts as an agonist at benzodiazepine receptors (Cooper and Greenwood, 1992), or two benzodiazepine partial agonists, bretazenil (Ro16–6028) and Ro17–1812 (Cooper and Green, 1993). Together, these data provide ample confirmation that benzodiazepine receptor agonists potentiate saccharin preferences in water-deprived rats. This class of drugs may, therefore, directly enhance the palatability of the sweet solution (Cooper, 1989).

The fact that inverse agonists act at benzodiazepine receptors to reduce food consumption, as we have already seen, suggests that these drugs may also act to block sweet taste preferences. This interesting possibility has been confirmed in three separate studies, using the β-carboline FG 7142 (Cooper, 1986*b*), the pyrazoloquinoline CGS 8216 (Kirkham and Cooper, 1986), and the imidazobenzodiazepine Ro15–4513 (Cooper *et al.*, 1989), all of which are benzodiazepine receptor inverse agonists. Hence, saccharin preference in the water-deprived rat can be bi-directionally modulated via drug actions at benzodiazepine receptors.

We also know, however, that benzodiazepines are effective in stimulating ingestion of a palatable 0.9 per cent sodium chloride solution in water-deprived rats (Turkish and Cooper, 1984; Estall and Cooper, 1987). Hence, it seemed probable that benzodiazepines might also potentiate salt taste preferences in water-deprived rats. When we tested this possibility, we found that the β-carboline, abecarnil, selectively enhanced the intake of a 0.9 per cent NaCl solution, without significantly affecting concurrent water consumption in a two-choice test (Cooper and Greenwood, 1992). Comparable results were obtained using the partial agonists, bretazenil or Ro17–1812 (Cooper and Barber, 1993*a*). Therefore, benzodiazepines not only potentiate saccharin preferences, they also potentiate the preference for isotonic saline. Somewhat surprisingly, we did not observe an abolition of salt taste preference following administration of the imidazobenzodiazepine Ro15–4513 (Cooper and Barber, 1993*a*. We noted, earlier, that this compound reduces saccharin preference (Cooper *et al.*, 1989). Before ruling out the possibility that inverse agonists acting at benzodiazepine receptors affect salt taste preferences, other examples must be tested. At the moment, although we can be confident that benzodiazepine agonists enhance both sweet and salt taste preferences, we have not established that inverse agonists are equally effective in blocking both sweet and salt taste preferences.

It is well-known that quinine adulteration lends an aversive taste to foods and fluids. Margules and Stein (1967) found that benzodiazepine, oxazepam, overcame the suppressant effect of quinine, while Niki (1965) reported that quinine adulteration blocked the hyperphagic effect produced by chlordiazepoxide. We (Cooper and Green, 1993) investigated whether or not benzodiazepines would affect aversion to a quinine solution in a two-choice test. The results were unequivocal. The two benzodiazepine partial agonists, Ro16–6028 and Ro17–1812, did not affect water consumption but enhanced the intake of the quinine solution, thereby abolishing the aversion. These data might be interpreted in terms of a disinhibitory or anti-aversive action of the benzodiazepines. However, this explanation fails to accommodate the findings that benzodiazepines also enhance taste preferences. A more parsimonious view is that benzodiazepines may act directly to enhance the palatability of ingested sapid fluids, whether they are sweet, salty, or bitter. This mechanism would account for the taste preference data we have reviewed so far.

Taste reactivity

This is a method which does not rely on an animal's ability to ingest fluids, but which can be used to determine its hedonic reactions to tastes (Grill *et al.*, 1987). Grill and Norgren (1978*a,b*) first observed that normal rats and neurologically impaired rats exhibit species-typical reactions to the intraoral infusions of sapid solutions. These reactions can be categorized as positively hedonic (ingestive) or aversive (rejection) (Norgren and Grill, 1982; Grill and Berridge, 1985). This taste reactivity paradigm has begun to prove to be very useful in determining the effects of pharmacological treatments on hedonic responses to taste stimuli.

Most interestingly, Berridge and Treit (1986) found that chlordiazepoxide selectively enhanced the positive ingestive reactions to infused solutions, but had no effect on aversive reactions. Their data suggest that benzodiazepines potentiate taste palatability in a direct sense, so that what is liked is liked better. This important result has been confirmed several times (Berridge, 1988; Cooper and Ewbank, in preparation; Treit *et al.*, 1987; Treit and Berridge, 1990). The taste-reactivity data are consistent with the results of the taste preference experiments described above, and strongly support the view that benzodiazepines enhance the hedonic value of ingested food and fluids.

Benzodiazepines and palatability

The hyperphagic effect of benzodiazepines, which is a very robust phenomenon that occurs in many species, is beginning to be better understood. It was interpreted originally in terms of a benzodiazepine-induced inhibition of satiety (Margules and Stein, 1967), and then in terms of making animals feel hungry (Wise and Dawson, 1974). An alternative view to both of these suggestions, and one which now receives a great deal of support, is that benzodiazepines specifically enhance the positive hedonic evaluation ('palatability') of ingested commodities. This effect would then be responsible for the effects of benzodiazepines to enhance palatable food consumption, to potentiate taste preferences, to increase positive reactions to taste stimuli, and to promote instrumental performance rewarded by food pellets or palatable solutions.

This evidence is sufficiently extensive and consistent that benzodiazepines now provide the paradigm case of pharmacological agents that act to enhance the palatability of ingested commodities and to increase the incentive value of instrumental outcomes. We consider that closely allied to the benzodiazepines in their effects are those drugs which act as opioid receptor agonists, and therefore we shall consider next the evidence available for these drugs and for their complementary receptor antagonists.

OPIOIDS AND INGESTION

Food intake

We took note, above, that selective opioid receptor antagonists reduce feeding and drinking responses (see Cooper, 1988, and Cooper *et al.*, 1988, for extensive reviews of the literature). The major inference to be drawn from these data is that endogenous opioid peptides are involved in mediating ingestive behaviour. Supporting this view are the findings that drugs which act as opioid receptor agonists enhance feeding responses. Thus, systemic administration of morphine (Kavaliers and Hirst, 1985; Sanger and McCarthy, 1980) or of kappa agonists (Cooper *et al.*, 1985) cause increased food consumption. Intracerebroventricular injection of opioid peptides stimulate food intake (Gosnell *et al.*, 1986; Jackson and Sewell, 1985*a*; McKay *et al.*, 1981; Morley and Levine, 1983).

While these data indicate a role for endogenous opioid peptides in the control of ingestive responses, they do not throw light on the behavioural mechanisms responsible for the drug-induced changes in consumption. Apfelbaum and Mandenoff (1981) discovered that the opioid antagonist, naltrexone, seemed to have a preferential effect to reduce the consumption of a high-palatability diet, while having little effect on normal feeding. This led them to suggest that endogenous opioid peptides may underlie the hyperphagia promoted by the availability of a high-palatability diet. Food preference studies also provide evidence for a relatively selective effect of opioid antagonists. Cooper and Turkish (1989), for example, found that naltrexone markedly decreased the time spent eating preferred chocolate-coated biscuits and reinstated a feeding response to less preferred food pellets. Their data implied that blocking opioid receptors greatly attenuated the preference for the more palatable food item. In contrast, a number of studies have shown that morphine is able to enhance the feeding response to preferred foodstuffs (Cooper and Kirkham, 1990; Evans and Vaccarino, 1990; Gosnell *et al.*, 1990). Mediating these drug-induced changes in preference may be corresponding changes in the incentive value of the food commodities.

In human volunteers, Yeomans *et al.* (1990) found that nalmefene, an opioid receptor antagonist, reduced food intake but had no effect on subjective ratings of hunger or satiety. However, nalmefene did appear to preferentially affect the ingestion of foods that were rated as highly palatable. Moreover, nalmefene reduced ratings of the pleasantness of the smell and taste, but not the appearance, of food items considered to be highly palatable (Yeomans and Wright, 1991).

Taken together, these studies point to the possibility that the palatability of a food item depends on endogenous opioid activity, and that preference is expressed for foods that are associated with greater opioid activity. Blocking opioid receptors with antagonists would then lead to a reduction in relatively high palatability values with a consequent loss of expressed preference.

Sham feeding

Weingarten and Watson (1982) suggested that sham feeding could provide an opportunity to investigate the effects of diet palatability on food consumption. It follows that opioid receptor antagonists, if they attenuate relatively high palatability values, should markedly affect sham feeding, particularly when a highly palatable solution is ingested. In fact, Rockwood and Reid (1982) confirmed that naloxone reduced sucrose sham feeding in gastric-fistulated rats, and postulated that naloxone affects the affective reactivity to palatable solutions. Subsequent experiments, in our laboratory, supported their results, and also showed that an increase in sucrose concentration could completely reverse the naloxone effect on sham feeding (Kirkham and Cooper, 1988*a,b*).

Hence, the high palatability value placed on the sucrose solution may depend critically upon endogenous opioid activity. The opioid-dependent palatability would, in turn, determine the high level of sucrose sham feeding.

Taste preferences

However, some of the most convincing evidence for opioid involvement in preferences derives from taste preference studies (Cooper and Kirkham, 1993). We considered above the highly consistent data for benzodiazepines, in respect of sweet and salt taste preferences, and, in this section, we shall see that the evidence for opioid involvement is also very strong.

Le Magnen and colleagues (1980) were the first to find evidence that opioid antagonists reduce the preference for saccharin solutions in rats.

Other investigators have amply confirmed their result (Cooper, 1983; Lynch, 1986; Lynch and Libby, 1983; Siviy and Reid, 1983). The opposite result has been obtained using opioid agonists. Thus Calcagnetti and Reid (1983) found that morphine increased the preference for saccharin solutions in water-deprived rats. Intracerebroventricular administration of a mu receptor agonist or a delta receptor agonist has also been found to potentiate saccharin preference (Gosnell and Majchrzak, 1989).

Salt preferences are also affected by drugs that are selective for opioid receptors. Naloxone was found to reduce saline consumption in a preference test (Cooper and Gilbert, 1984), while morphine was reported to increase the preference for isotonic saline in water-deprived rats (Bertino *et al.*, 1988). Intracerebroventricular administration of naloxone selectively reduced saline intake in a two-choice test, whereas either mu-selective or delta-selective agonists preferentially stimulated the ingestion of a preferred salt solution (Gosnell and Majchrzak, 1989; Gosnell *et al.*, 1990).

The evidence from taste preference experiments, therefore, strongly suggests that the hedonic value of preferred tastes depends upon the activity of endogenous opioid peptides.

Taste reactivity

If this hypothesis is correct, then we should seek supporting evidence from taste-reactivity data. Doyle and colleagues (1993) have recently conducted one relevant study, in which morphine was shown specifically to enhance hedonic taste reactions at a time when morphine exhibits a hyperphagic effect. These authors conclude that morphine increases the palatability of food, thus leading to increased food consumption. The data are clearly consistent with the general view, espoused above, that endogenous opioid peptides help to mediate the assigned hedonic value of ingested or tasted commodities.

Opioids and benzodiazepines

It is clear, from the evidence reviewed so far, that there are striking parallels between the ideas that have developed to account for the effects of benzodiazepines on ingestion and those which have evolved to explain opioid-dependent increases in ingestion. One can take the further step of suggesting that the benzodiazepine effects are closely interrelated with the opioid effects (Cooper, 1983; Reid, 1985). Assignment of hedonic value may be affected by benzodiazepines acting at benzodiazepine receptors, which in turn leads to the release of endogenous opioid peptides. Such a sequential model indicates that opioid antagonists should block not only benzodiazepine-induced hyperphagia (Britton *et al.*, 1981; Jackson and Sewell, 1985; Stapleton *et al.*, 1979), but also benzodiazepine-induced enhancement of taste preferences and hedonic reactions in taste reactivity tests. These last two predictions have still to be evaluated.

DOPAMINE AND INGESTION

Food intake

Much of the work that has dealt with dopaminergic mechanisms in relation to ingestion has been concerned with the effects of dopamine antagonists, such as haloperidol and pimozide. There is not the space here to deal with the literature on dopamine agonists, directly-and indirectly-acting, but a recent review covers much of the material (Cooper and Al-Naser, 1993).

It has been recognized for a considerable period that dopamine antagonists reduce food intake (Rolls *et al.*, 1974; Rowland and Engle, 1977; Wise and Colle, 1984, Wise and Raptis, 1986), and that they reduce instrumental responding for food (Wise *et al.*, 1978), for water (Gerber *et al.*, 1981), and for sucrose solutions (Bailey *et al.*, 1986). In an analysis of meal patterns, Blundell and Latham (1978) showed that pimozide reduced the average amount of food consumed in each bout of feeding, although there was also an increase in the duration of the feeding bouts. More recently, Clifton and colleagues (1991) reported that dopamine D_2 receptor antagonists (YM-09151–2, remoxipride and raclopride) decreased the rate of feeding within meals, while extending meal durations. In contrast, the selective D_1 receptor antagonist, SCH 23390, had little effect on meal size or duration. Rusk and Cooper (1994) have found that YM-09151–2 and SCH 23390 produce reductions in food intake and instrumental responding for food reward.

One of the influential hypotheses to account for the effect of dopamine antagonists on ingestive behaviour is that they block the reward quality or incentive value of food (Wise *et al.*, 1978). Sclafani and colleagues (1982) reported that pimozide depressed drinking of a palatable saccharin–glucose solution in non-deprived rats. Since pimozide suppressed consumption of the palatable solution to a greater degree than it affected deprivation-induced water-drinking, they concluded that the dopamine antagonist may block the incentive value of the sweet solution. With few exceptions, subsequent experiments with dopamine antagonists have taken the ideas of dopamine and food reward (Wise, 1981, 1982) as their principal frame of reference.

Sham feeding

Geary and Smith (1985) first observed that pimozide decreased sucrose sham feeding in rats with chronic gastric cannulas. They interpreted their data in terms of blockade of central dopaminergic activity, which, they suggested, mediates the reinforcing effect of sweet taste. Their work was extended with the observation that dopamine D_2 receptor antagonists were effective in reducing sucrose sham feeding (Schneider *et al.* 1986). The same group then showed that either the selective D_2 antagonist, raclopride, or the selective D_1 antagonist, SCH 23390, decreased sucrose sham-feeding (Schneider *et al.*, 1988). Effects of the dopamine antagonists were selective, although, at larger doses, sham drinking water was also affected by the dopamine receptor antagonists.

Their effects are not restricted to sucrose sham feeding, however, since both raclopride and SCH 23390 decreased corn oil sham feeding in rats with a gastric fistula (Weatherford *et al.*, 1988). Interestingly, Weatherford and colleagues (1990) found that the potency of both the D_2 and the D_1 antagonist was inversely related to the reward values of the sham-fed liquid. Adopting a microstructural approach to study patterns of licking, Schneider and colleagues (1990) showed that raclopride reduced sucrose sham feeding in a way that was equivalent to reducing sucrose concentration from 10 per cent to 5 per cent: the number of clusters of licks and the number of licks per cluster were reduced, while the intervals between clusters were increased. Raclopride did not affect licking rates, and, therefore, there was no evidence that the dopamine antagonist adversely affected the ability to lick. When raclopride and SCH 23390 were administered together, their effects on sucrose sham feeding were infra-additive (Schneider *et al.*, 1991), suggesting that the effects of the antagonists were not independent.

This line of work, from the laboratory of Smith and colleagues, provides strong support for the view that blockade of central dopamine receptors may attenuate the positive reward effect of sucrose during sham feeding.

Sucrose preference

A similar conclusion has been drawn by Willner and his colleagues, using dopamine antagonists in tests of sucrose ingestion and preference. Towell *et al.* (1987) found that pimozide decreased sucrose intake but increased water intake in a two-bottle choice test. In addition, pimozide decreased sucrose ingestion in a single-choice test, at low concentrations of sucrose but not at high. As we noted above, Weatherford and colleagues (1990) have also reported an inverse relation between effectiveness of dopamine antagonists in suppressing sham feeding and the reward value of the liquid consumed. Willner and colleagues also provided evidence that pimozide does not affect the threshold for perception of sucrose or the discrimination of a basely noticeable difference (Willner *et al.*, 1990). Hence, the effects of pimozide cannot be accounted for in terms of alterations in the perception of the sucrose solution. Muscat and Willner (1989) achieved similar findings to those of Towell *et al.* (1987) using the selective D_2 receptor antagonist, sulpiride and the D_1 receptor antagonist, SCH 23390. Later, their work was extended to include comparable data obtained with the selective D_2 receptor antagonist, raclopride (Muscat *et al.*, 1991; Phillips *et al.*, 1991).

This line of work indicates that dopamine antagonists, selective for either D_1 or D_2 receptors, may block the reward value of sucrose solutions. As such, the data are consistent with the results of the sham-feeding experiments described above.

Salt preference

In contrast with the wealth of work dealing with the effects of dopamine antagonists on sucrose ingestion and preference, very little has been reported for the ingestion of salt solutions by water-deprived rats. Gilbert and Cooper (1987) discovered that dopamine antagonists (pimozide, clozapine, sulpiride) did not attenuate preferences for salt drinking in two-choice tests. Any changes were in the direction of increases in preference. This result, if confirmed, suggests that dopamine may not be involved in the mediation of salt preference in the way that it appears to be involved in the reward effects of sweet solutions. The result is not consistent with the general hypothesis that dopamine is involved in all forms of reward.

Taste reactivity

Two reports, using taste-reactivity measures to assess changes in hedonic evaluation of taste stimuli, argue against the involvement of dopaminergic mechanisms in hedonic processes. Berridge and colleagues (1989) produced 6-hydroxydopamine lesions of ascending dopamine pathways to the forebrain, which rendered the animals aphagic. Not withstanding the effect of the lesioning technique on the ability of the animals to ingest, their taste-reactivity responses remained essentially unaltered. The authors conclude, therefore, that their results are not consistent with the notion that destruction of ascending dopamine pathways results in anhedonia (Wise, 1982). A pharmacological study by Treit and Berridge (1990) reached a similar conclusion. Neither apomorphine, a dopamine agonist, nor haloperidol, a dopamine antagonist, had significant effects on taste-reactivity measures. These authors concluded that dopaminergic mechanisms have little to do directly with hedonic processes.

These two studies represent a major challenge to a substantial body of data which supports the view that the palatability of ingested food and fluids is dopaminergically-mediated. However, a more recent taste-reactivity study by Leeb *et al.* (1991) has generated data which appears to be consistent with the anhedonia hypothesis (Wise, 1982). These authors found that pimozide shifted the pattern of taste-reactivity responses from highly ingestive to midly ingestive or neutral in rats receiving intraoral infusions of sucrose (17 per cent or 25 per cent solutions). They concluded that dopamine receptor blockade with pimozide produced a reduction in the palatability of the infused sucrose solutions. While there are differences in methodology between this study and the two preceding ones, it is clear that further investigation of possible dopaminergic involvement in determining taste-reactivity responses is warranted. Neuropharmacologically, a greater variety of drugs (dopamine agonists and antagonists) needs to be employed before any convincing conclusion about dopamine and taste reactivity can be reached. It is an important issue, and therefore some priority should be given to studies placing this critical issue under greater scrutiny.

5–HYDROXYTRYPTAMINE AND INGESTION

Food intake

One of the most influential hypotheses in the field of the neuro-pharmacology of feeding behaviour is that 5-hydroxytryptamine (serotonin) is fundamentally involved in satiety processes (Blundell 1977, 1984). In support of this hypothesis, it is well-established that drugs which enhance central serotonergic activity (5-HT receptor agonists, 5-HT re-uptake inhibitors, drugs that increase the release of 5-HT) act to suppress food intake, whereas 5-HT receptor antagonists increase food intake (Cooper, 1992). In contrast, comparatively little attention has been paid to the possibility that 5-HT mechanisms may play some part in determining the hedonic evaluation, or palatability, of ingested foods and fluids.

Borsini *et al.* (1985) showed that the indirectly-acting agonist, d-fenfluramine, reduced the intake of sucrose in freely-fed rats. Leander (1987) found that the 5-HT uptake inhibitor, fluoxetine, suppressed the ingestion of saccharin solutions, while Neill and Cooper (1989) reported that a number of 5-HT receptor agonists reduced the ingestion of a palatable mash by non-deprived rats. Furthermore, a range of serotonergic agonists are effective in reducing sucrose sham feeding (Neill and Cooper, 1988). Hence, there are some grounds for at least suspecting a role for serotonergic mechanisms in determining palatability. We would have to propose, however, that enhanced serotonergic activity would act to inhibit the hedonic evaluation of ingested items. As a further step in pursuing this idea, we have recently undertaken a series of taste preference experiments.

Salt and sweet taste preferences

Our results indicate that drugs which act as direct 5-HT receptor agonists (mCPP, TFMPP, MK212) reduce the preference for isotonic saline over water in thirsty rats (Cooper and Barber, 1993b; Cooper and Ciccocioppo, 1993). Moreover, the same drugs block the preference for a dilute saccharin solution over water (Cooper and Barber, 1994). These results strengthen the possibility that increased stimulation of 5-HT receptors may serve to inhibit the palatability of ingested sapid solutions.

CONCLUSIONS

We began this chapter noting that a few decades ago very little was known of the means by which drug treatments affected food ingestion. The first attempts to apply behavioural and neural interpretations to early pharmacological experiments focused on hypothalamic mechanisms, and opposing behavioural processes of hunger and satiety. In the last decade, in particular, we have witnessed a marked shift away from sole preoccupation with hunger and satiety as opposing processes to a position that also gives due regard to the hedonic evaluation of food- and fluid-related stimuli. Over the same period there has been a dramatic drop in investigations that centre upon hypothalamic functions. Several other brain regions have since come under close scrutiny for their involvement in the control of ingestional behaviour. Our present chapter is not primarily concerned with defining the neural bases of feeding behaviour, but it is concerned with specifying neurochemical and behavioural processes at work in determining responses to ingested items.

The early investigations using drugs were conducted at a time when great emphasis was placed on homeostatic or regulatory mechanisms in the control of feeding behaviour. In other words, food ingestion served a purpose in maintaining energy balance. Deprivation of food led to hunger, which initiated feeding when food was available, while satiety intervened to terminate feeding at an appropriate time to ensure repletion of energy availability. The shift towards an emphasis on food palatability reflects an acknowledgement of non-regulatory mechanisms at work in determining food intake. Several methods have evolved to help assess the effects that drugs may exert on hedonic evaluation of food-related stimuli.

We have demonstrated that, currently, the clearest example of drugs that affect palatability are those that act as agonists at benzodiazepine receptors linked to $GABA_A$ receptors. Approaching the question from several directions, recent results show a remarkable degree of consistency in supporting the view that benzodiazepines act to potentiate the hedonic evaluation of taste stimuli and thereby act to enhance food consumption. Data obtained with these drugs provide a strong basis for upholding the importance of hedonic processes in determining ingestive behaviour.

Probably linked to such benzodiazepine mechanisms in a closely inter-related functional sense, are opioid mechanisms. It now seems likely that opioid peptides also play a significant part in the hedonic evaluation of food-related stimuli. This, in turn, feeds into the expression of food and taste preferences, and helps to determine the quantities of food ingested.

Two monoaminergic systems may also be involved. There is a well-established hypothesis that dopamine helps to mediate the reward value of food. Although a great deal of evidence is consistent with this view, we still need more information on the critical point of whether or not dopamine is necessary for the hedonic evaluation of food-related stimuli. Less well considered, at the present time, is the possible involvement of central serotonergic pathways in the inhibition of food and taste preferences.

Clearly, the neuropharmacological scope of studies on ingestive behaviour has broadened considerably in recent years. There is no indication that this process is complete, and more complexities will be revealed as studies continue. At the same time, the growing evidence forces us to consider the important possibility that much of ingestive behaviour depends not simply on a purposeful refuelling, a homeostatic correction of energy imbalance, but on the competing attractions of food items available for consumption. Neuropharmacological studies may continue to provide valuable insights into neurochemical mechanisms involved in the evaluation of the appeal of ingested items. We are presently compiling a dossier of the most likely neurochemical candidates that figure in our decisions to like and accept, or to dislike and reject, items in our environment which can serve as food.

ACKNOWLEDGEMENTS

We would like to thank Mrs Dorothy Trinder and Miss Helen Jones for their help in the preparation of this chapter.

REFERENCES

Akil, H., Bronstein, D., and Mansour, A. (1988). Overview of the endogenous opioid systems: anatomical, biochemical and functional issues. In *Endorphins, opiates and behavioral processes* (eds. R.J. Rodgers and S.J. Cooper), pp. 1–23. Wiley, Chichester.

Antin, J., Gibbs, J., Holt, J., Young, R.C., and Smith, G.P. (1975). Cholecystokinin elicits the complete sequence of satiety in rats. *Journal of Comparative and Physiological Psychology*, **89**, 784–90.

Apfelbaum, M. and Mandenoff, A. (1981). Naltrexone suppresses hyperphagia induced in the rat by a highly palatable diet. *Pharmacology Biochemistry and Behavior*, **15**, 89–91.

Baile, C.A. and McLaughlin, C.L. (1979). A review of the behavioral and physiological responses to elfazepam, a chemical feed intake stimulant. *Journal of Animal Science*, **49**, 1371–95.

Bailey, C.S., Hsiao, S., and King, J.E. (1986). Hedonic reactivity to sucrose in rats: modification by pimozide. *Physiology and Behavior*, **38**, 447–52.

Balleine, B., Ball, J., and Dickinson, A. (1993). Benzodiazepine-induced incentive learning and the motivational control of instrumental action (in preparation).

Berridge, K.C. (1988). Brainstem systems mediate the enhancement of palatability by chlordiazepoxide. *Brain Research*, **447**, 262–8.

Berridge, K.C. and Treit, D. (1986). Chlordiazepoxide directly enhances positive ingestive reactions in the rat. *Pharmacology Biochemistry and Behavior*, **24**, 217–21.

Berridge, K.C., Venier, I.L., and Robinson, T.E. (1989). Taste reactivity analysis of 6-hydroxydopamine-induced aphagia: implications for arousal and anhedonia hypotheses of dopamine function. *Behavioral Neuroscience*, **103**, 36–45.

Bertino, M., Abelson, M.L., Marglin, S.H., Neuman, R., Burkhardt, C.A., and Reid, L.D. (1988). A small dose of morphine increases intake of and preference for isotonic saline among rats. *Pharmacology Biochemistry and Behavior*, **29**, 617–23.

Birk, J. and Noble, R.G. (1982). Bicuculline blocks diazepam-induced feeding in Syrian hamsters. *Life Science*, **30**, 321–5.

Blundell, J.E. (1977). Is there a role for serotonin (5-hydroxytryptamine) in feeding? *International Journal of Obesity*, **1**, 15–42.

Blundell, J.E. (1981). Bio-grammar of feeding: pharmacological manipulations and their interpretations. In *Theory in psychopharmacology*, Vol. 1 (ed. S.J. Cooper), pp. 233–276. Academic Press, London.

Blundell, J.E. (1984). Serotonin and appetite. *Neuropharmacology*, **23**, 1537–51.

Blundell, J.E. (1987). Structure, process and mechanism: case studies in the psychopharmacology of feeding. In *Handbook of psychopharmacology*, Vol. 19. (eds. L.L. Iversen, S.D. Iversen, and S.H. Snyder), pp. 123–82. Plenum, New York.

Blundell, J.E. and Latham, C.J. (1978). Pharmacological manipulation of feeding behavior: possible influences of serotonin and dopamine on food intake. In *Central mechanisms of anorectic drugs* (eds. S. Garattini and R. Samanin), pp. 83–109. Raven Press, New York.

Blundell, J.E., Latham, C.J., and Leshem, M.B. (1976). Differences between the anorexic actions of amphetamine and fenfluramine—possible effects on hunger and satiety. *Journal of Pharmacy and Pharmacology*, **28**, 471–7.

Booth, D.A. (1968). Amphetamine anorexia by direct action on the adrenergic feeding system of rat hypothalamus. *Nature*, **217**, 869–70.

Borsini, F., Bendotti, C., and Samanin, R. (1985). Salbutamol, *d*-amphetamine and *d*-fenfluramine reduce sucrose intake in freely fed rats by acting on different neurochemical mechanisms. *International Journal of Obesity*, **9**, 227–83.

Bozarth, M.A. (1988). Opioid reinforcement processes. In *Endorphins, opiates and behavioural processes* (eds. R.J. Rodgers and S.J. Cooper), pp. 53–75. Wiley, Chichester.

Braestrup, C., Nielsen, M., Honore, T., Jensen, L.H., and Petersen, E.N. (1983). Benzodiazepine receptor ligands with positive and negative efficacy. *Neuropharmacology*, **22**, 1451–1457.

Braestrup, C. and Squires, R.F. (1977). Specific benzodiazepine receptors in rat brain characterised by high-affinity ^{3}H-diazepam binding. *Proceedings of the National Academy of Science, USA*, **74**, 3805–9.

Britton, D.R., Britton, K.T., Dalton, D., and Vale, W. (1981). Effects of naloxone on anti-conflict and hyperphagic actions of diazepam. *Life Sciences*, **29**, 1297–1302.

Brobeck, J.R. (1955). Neural regulation of food intake. *Annals of the New York Academy of Sciences*, **63**, 44–55.

Brobeck, J.R., Larsson, S., and Reyer, E. (1956). A study of the electrical activity of the hypothalamic feeding mechanism. *Journal of Physiology*, **132**, 358–64.

Brown, R.F., Houpt, K.A., and Schryver, H.F. (1976). Stimulation of food intake in horses by diazepam and promazine. *Pharmacology Biochemistry and Behavior*, **5**, 495–7.

Calcagnetti, D.J. and Reid, L.D. (1983). Morphine and acceptability of putative reinforcers. *Pharmacology Biochemistry and Behavior*, **18**, 567–9.

Carlisle, H.J. (1964). Differential effects of amphetamine on food and water intake in rats with lateral hypothalamic lesions. *Journal of Comparative and Physiological Psychology*, **58**, 47–54.

Clifton, P.G., Rusk, I.N., and Cooper, S.J. (1991). Effects of dopamine D_1 and dopamine D_2 antagonists on the free feeding and drinking patterns of rats. *Behavioral Neuroscience*, **105**, 272–81.

Colton, N.H., Segal, H.I., Steinberg, A., Schechter, F.R., and Pastor, N. (1943). The management of obesity with emphasis on appetite control. *American Journal of Medical Science*, **206**, 75–86.

Cooper, S.J. (1980). Benzodiazepines as appetite-enhancing compounds. *Appetite*, **1**, 7–19.

Cooper, S.J. (1982a). Specific benzodiazepine antagonist Ro15–1788 and thirst-induced drinking in the rat. *Neuropharmacology*, **21**, 483–6.

Cooper, S.J. (1982*b*). Benzodiazepine mechanisms and drinking in the water-deprived rat. *Neuropharmacology*, **21**, 775–80.

Cooper, S.J. (1983*a*). Effects of opiate agonists and antagonists on fluid intake and saccharin choice in the rat. *Neuropharmacology*, **22**, 323–8.

Cooper, S.J. (1983*b*). Benzodiazepine-opiate antagonist interactions in relation to feeding and drinking behaviour. *Life Science*, **32**, 1043–51.

Cooper, S.J. (1985*a*). The anorectic effect of FG 7142, a partial inverse agonist at benzodiazepine recognition sites, is reversed by CGS 8216 and clonazepam but not by food deprivation. *Brain Research*, **346**, 190–4.

Cooper, S.J. (1985*b*). Bidirectional control of palatable food consumption through a common benzodiazepine receptor: Theory and evidence. *Brain Research Bulletin*, **15**, 391–6.

Cooper, S.J. (1986*a*). Hyperphagic and anorectic effects of β-carbolines in a palatable food consumption test: comparisons with triazolam and quazepam. *European Journal of Pharmacology*, **120**, 257–65.

Cooper, S.J. (1986*b*). Effects of β-carboline FG 7142 on saccharin preference and quinine rejection in the rat. *Neuropharmacology*, **25**, 213–6.

Cooper, S.J. (1988). Evidence for opioid involvement in controls of drinking and water balance. In *Endorphins, opiates and behavioural processes* (eds. R.J. Rodgers and S.J. Cooper), pp. 187–216. Wiley, Chichester.

Cooper, S.J. (1989). Benzodiazepine receptor-mediated enhancement and inhibition of taste reactivity, food choice and intake. *Annals of the New York Academy of Science*, **575**, 321–37.

Cooper, S.J. (1992). 5-HT and ingestive behavior. In *Central serotonin receptors and psychotropic drugs* (eds. C.A. Marsden and D.J. Heal), pp. 260–91. Blackwell Scientific, Oxford.

Cooper, S.J. (1994). Foundations in the study of the neuropharmacology of appetite. In *Neuropharmacology of appetite* (eds. S.J. Cooper and J.M. Liebman). Oxford University Press, New York, in press.

Cooper, S.J. and Barber, D.J. (1993*a*). The benzodiazepine receptor partial agonist bretazenil and the partial inverse agonist Ro15–4513: effects on salt preference and aversion in the rat. *Brain Research*, **612**, 313–18.

Cooper, S.J. and Barber, D.J. (1993*b*). Effects of *d*-fenfluramine, MK-212, and ondansetron on saline drinking in two-choice tests in the rehydrating rat. *Pharmacology Biochemistry and Behavior*, **45**, 593–6.

Cooper, S.J. and Barber, D.J. (1994). Evidence for serotonergic involvement in saccharin preference in a two-choice test in rehydrating rats. *Pharmacology Biochemistry and Behavior*, **47**, 541–6.

Cooper, S.J. and Al-Naser, H.A. (1993). D_1 : D_2 dopamine receptor interactions in relation to feeding responses and food intake. In D_1 : D_2 *dopamine receptor interactions* (ed. J.L. Waddington), pp. 203–33. Academic, London.

Cooper, S.J. and Ciccocioppo, R. (1993). Effects of selective 5–HT_1 receptor agonists in water-deprived rats on salt intake in two-choice tests. *Pharmacology Biochemistry and Behavior*, **45**, 513–18.

Cooper, S.J. and Francis, R.L. (1979*a*). Feeding parameters with two food textures after chlordiazepoxide administration, alone or in combination with *d*-amphetamine or fenfluramine. *Psychopharmacology*, **62**, 253–9.

Cooper, S.J. and Francis, R.L. (1979*b*). Water intake and time course of drinking after single or repeated chlordiazepoxide injections. *Psychopharmacology*, **65**, 191–5.

Cooper, S.J. and Gilbert, D.B. (1984). Naloxone suppresses fluid consumption in tests of choice between sodium chloride solutions and water in male and female rats. *Psychopharmacology*, **84**, 362–7.

Cooper, S.J. and Gilbert, D.B. (1985). Clonazepam-induced hyperphagia in non-deprived rats: tests of pharmacological specificity with Ro5–4864, Ro5– 3663, Ro15–1788 and CGS 9896. *Pharmacology Biochemistry and Behavior*, **22**, 753–60.

Cooper, S.J. and Green, A.E. (1993). The benzodiazepine receptor partial agonists, bretazenil (Ro16–6028) and Ro17– 1812, affect saccharin preference and quinine aversion in the rat. *Behavioural Pharmacology*, **4**, 81–5.

Cooper, S.J. and Greenwood, S.E. (1992). The β-carboline abecarnil, a novel agonist at central benzodiazepine receptors, influences saccharin and salt taste preferences in the rat. *Brain Research*, **59**, 144–7.

Cooper, S.J. and Kirkham, T.C. (1990). Basic mechanisms of opioids' effects on eating and drinking. In *Opioids, bulimia, and alcohol abuse and alcoholism* (ed. L.D. Reid), pp. 91–110. Springer, New York.

Cooper, S.J. and Kirkham, T.C. (1993). Opioid mechanisms in the control of food consumption and taste preferences. In *Handbook of experimental pharmacology*, Vol. 104/II (ed. A. Herz), pp. 239–62. Springer, Berlin.

Cooper, S.J. and Moores, W.R. (1985*a*). Benzodiazepine-induced hyperphagia in the non-deprived rat: comparisons with CL 218, 872, zopiclone, tracazolate and phenobarbital. *Pharmacology Biochemistry and Behavior*, **23**, 169–74.

Cooper, S.J. and Moores, W.R. (1985*b*). Chlordiazepoxide-induced hyperphagia in non-food-deprived rats: effects of Ro15–1788, CGS 8216 and ZK 93426. *European Journal of Pharmacology*, **112**, 39–45.

Cooper, S.J. and Posadas-Andrews, A. (1979). Food and water intake in the non-deprived pigeon after chlordiazepoxide administration. *Psychopharmacology*, **65**, 99– 101.

Cooper, S.J. and Turkish, S. (1989). Effects of naltrexone on food preference and concurrent behavioral responses in food-deprived rats. *Pharmacology Biochemistry and Behavior*, **33**, 17–20.

Cooper, S.J. and Yerbury, R.E. (1986*a*). Midazolam-induced hyperphagia and FG 7142-induced anorexia: behavioural characteristics in the rat. *Pharmacology Biochemistry and Behavior*, **25**, 99–106.

Cooper, S.J. and Yerbury, R.E. (1986*b*). Benzodiazepine-induced hyperphagia: antagonism by pyrazoloquinolines CGS 9895 and CGS 9896. *Psychopharmacology*, **89**, 462–6.

Cooper, S.J. and Yerbury, R.E. (1988). Clonazepam selectively increases saccharin ingestion in a two-choice test. *Brain Research*, **456**, 173–6.

Cooper, S.J., Barber, D.J., Gilbert, D.B., and Moores, W.R. (1985). Benzodiazepine receptor ligands and the consumption of a highly palatable diet in non-deprived male rats. *Psychopharmacology*, **86**, 348–55.

Cooper, S.J., Bowyer, D.M., and van der Hoek, G. (1989). Effects of the imidazobenzodiazepine Ro15–4513 on saccharin choice and acceptance, and on food intake, in the rat. *Brain Research*, **494**, 172–6.

Cooper, S.J., Jackson, A. and Kirkham, T.C., (1985). Endorphins and food intake: *kappa* opioid receptor agonists and hyperphagia. *Pharmacology Biochemistry and Behavior*, **23**, 889–901.

Cooper, S.J., Jackson, A., Kirkham, T.C., and Turkish, S. (1988). Endorphins, opiates and food intake. In *Endorphins, opiates and behavioural processes* (eds. R.J. Rodgers and S.J. Cooper), pp. 143–86. Wiley, Chichester.

Cooper, S.J., van der Hoek, G. and Kirkham, T.C. (1988). Bi-directional changes in sham feeding in the rat produced by benzodiazepine receptor ligands. *Physiology and Behavior*, **42**, 211–16.

Costa, E. and Guidotti, A. (1979). Molecular mechanisms in the receptor action of benzodiazepines. *Annual Review of Pharmacology and Toxicology*, **19**, 531–45.

Doyle, T.G., Berridge, K.C., and Gosnell, B.A. (1993). Morphine enhances hedonic taste palatability in rats. *Pharmacology Biochemistry and Behavior*, in press.

Epstein, A.N. (1959). Suppression of eating and drinking by amphetamine and other drugs in normal and hyperphagic rats. *Journal of Comparative and Physiological Psychology*, **52**, 37–45.

Ersner, J.S. (1940). The treatment of obesity due to dietary indiscretion (overeating) with benzedrine sulfate. *Endocrinology*, **27**, 776–80.

Estall, L.B. and Cooper, S.J. (1987). Differential effects of benzodiazepine receptor ligands on isotonic saline and water consumption in water-deprived rats. *Pharmacology Biochemistry and Behavior*, **26**, 247–52.

Evans, K.R. and Vaccarino, F.J. (1990). Amphetamine-and morphine-induced feeding: evidence for involvement of reward mechanisms. *Neuroscience and Biobehavioral Reviews*, **14**, 9–22.

Fallon, J.H. (1988). Topographic organization of ascending dopaminergic projections. *Annals of the New York Academy of Science*, **537**, 1–9.

Foltin, R.W., Ellis, S., and Schuster, C.R. (1985). Specific antagonism by Ro15–1788 of benzodiazepine-induced increases in food intake in rhesus monkeys. *Pharmacology Biochemistry and Behavior*, **23**, 249–52.

Fratta, W., Mereu, G., Chessa, P., Paglietti, E., and Gessa, G. (1976). Benzodiazepine-induced voraciousness in rats and inhibition of amphetamine-anorexia. *Life Science*, **18**, 1156–66.

Geary, N. and Smith, G.P. (1985). Pimozide decreases the positive reinforcing effect of sham fed sucrose in the rat. *Pharmacology Biochemistry and Behavior*, **22**, 787–90.

Gerber, G.J. Sing, J., and Wise, R. (1981). Pimozide attenuates lever pressing for water reinforcement in rats. *Pharmacology Biochemistry and Behavior*, **14**, 201–5.

Gibbs, J., Young, R.C. and Smith, G.P. (1973a). Cholecystokinin decreases food intake in rats. *Journal of Comparative and Physiological Psychology*, **84**, 488–95.

Gibbs, J., Young, R.C. and Smith, G.P. (1973b). Cholecystokinin elicits satiety in rats with open gastric fistulas. *Nature*, **245**, 323–5.

Gilbert, D.B. and Cooper, S.J. (1987). Effects of dopamine antagonists on fluid intake and salt preference in male and female rats. *Journal of Psychopharmacology*, **1**, 47–53.

Gosnell, B.A., Krahn, D.D., and Majchrzak, M.J. (1990a). The effects of morphine on diet selection are dependent upon baseline diet preferences. *Pharmacology Biochemistry and Behavior*, **37**, 207–12.

Gosnell, B.A., Levine, A.S., and Morley, J.E. (1986). The stimulation of food intake by selective agonists of mu, kappa and delta opioid receptors. *Life Science*, **38**, 1081–88.

Gosnell, B.A. and Majchrzak, M.J. (1989). Centrally administered opioid peptides stimulate saccharin intake in nondeprived rats. *Pharmacology Biochemistry and Behavior*, **33**, 805–10.

Gosnell, B.A. and Majchrzak, M.J. (1990). Effects of a selective mu opioid receptor agonist and naloxone on the intake of sodium chloride solutions. *Psychopharmacology*, **100**, 66–71.

Gosnell, B.A., Majchrzak, M.J. and Krahn, D.D. (1990*b*). Effects of preferential delta and kappa opioid receptor agonists on the intake of hypotonic saline. *Physiology and Behavior*, **47**, 601–3.

Grill, H.J. and Berridge, K.C. (1985). Taste reactivity as a measure of the neural control of palatability. In J.M. Sprague and A.N. Epstein (eds.), *Progress in psychobiology and physiological psychology*, Vol. 11, Academic Press, Orlando, FL, pp.1–61.

Grill, H.J., Spector, A.C., Schwartz, G.J., Kaplan, J.M., and Flynn, F.W. (1987). Evaluating taste effects on ingestive behavior. In *Feeding and drinking* (eds. F.M. Toates and N.E. Rowland), pp. 151–88. Elsevier Science, Amsterdam.

Grill, H.J. and Norgren, R. (1978*a*). The taste reactivity test, I: Mimetic responses to gustatory stimuli in neurologically normal rats. *Brain Research*, **143**, 263–79.

Grill, H.J. and Norgren, R. (1978*b*). The taste reactivity test, II: Mimetic responses to gustatory stimuli in chronic thalamic and chronic decerebrate rats. *Brain Research*, **143**, 281–97.

Haefely, W., Martin, J.R., and Schoch, P. (1990). Novel anxiolytics that act as partial agonists at benzodiazepine receptors. *Trends in Pharmacological Science*, **11**, 452–6.

Harris, S.C. (1955). Clinically useful appetite depressants. *Annals of the New York Academy of Science*, **63**, 121–31.

Harris, S.C., Ivy, A.C., and Searle, L.M. (1947). The mechanisms of amphetamine-induced loss of weight. *Journal of the American Medical Association*, **234**, 1468–75.

Hoebel, B.G. (1975). Brain-stimulation reward and aversion in relation to behavior. In *Brain-stimulation reward* (eds. A. Wauquier and E.T. Rolls), pp. 335–72. North-Holland, Amsterdam.

Hoebel, B.G. (1976). Satiety: hypothalamic stimulation, anorectic drugs, and neurochemical substrates. In *Hunger: basic mechanisms and clinical implications* (eds. D. Novin, W. Wyrwicka, and G. Bray), pp.33–50. Raven, New York.

Hoebel, B.G. (1977*a*). Pharmacologic control of feeding. *Annual Review of Pharmacology and Toxicology*, **17**, 605–21.

Hoebel, B.G. (1977*b*). The psychopharmacology of feeding. In *Handbook of psychopharmacology*, vol. 8. (eds. L.L. Iversen, S.D. Iversen, and S.H. Snyder), pp. 55–129. Plenum, New York.

Hoebel, B.G., Hernandez, L., McLean, S., Stanley, B.G., Aulissi, E.F., Glimcher, P., and Margolin, D. (1982). Catecholamines, enkephalin and neurotensin in feeding and reward. In *The neural basis of feeding and reward* (eds. B.G. Hoebel and D. Novin), pp. 465–78. Haer Institute, Brunswick, Maine.

Holtzman, S.G. (1974). Behavioral effects of separate and combined administration of naloxone and *d*-amphetamine. *Journal of Pharmacology and Experimental Therapeutics*, **189**, 51–60.

Hughes, J., Smith, T.W., Kosterlitz, H.W., Fothergill, L.A., Morgan, M.A., and Morris, H.R. (1975). Identification of two related pentapeptides from the brain with potent opiate agonist activity. *Nature*, **258**, 577–9.

Jackson, H.C. and Sewell, R.D.E. (1985*a*). Are β-opioid receptors involved in the regulation of food and water intake? *Neuropharmacology*, **24**, 885–8.

Jackson, H.C. and Sewell, R.D.E. (1985*b*). Involvement of endogenous enkephalins in the feeding response to diazepam. *European Journal of Pharmacology*, **107**, 389–91.

Jacobs, B.L. and Farel, P.B. (1971). Motivated behaviors produced by increased arousal in the presence of goal objects. *Physiology and Behavior*, **6**, 473–6.

Kavaliers, M. and Hirst, M. (1985). The influence of opiate agonists on day–night feedng rhythms in young and old mice. *Brain Research*, **326**, 160–7.

Kirkham, T.C. and Blundell, J.E. (1984). Dual action of naloxone on feeding revealed by behavioural analysis: separate effects on initiation and termination of eating. *Appetite*, **5**, 45–52.

Kirkham, T.C. and Blundell, J.E. (1986). Effect of naloxone and naltrexone on the development of satiation measured in the runway: comparisons with *d*-amphetamine and *d*-fenfluramine. *Pharmacology Biochemistry and Behavior*, **25**, 123–8.

Kirkham, T.C. and Cooper, S.J. (1986). CGS 8216, a novel anorectic agent, selectively reduces saccharin solution consumption in the rat. *Pharmacology Biochemistry and Behavior*, **26**, 145–51.

Kirkham, T.C. and Cooper, S.J. (1988*a*). Attenuation of sham feeding by naloxone is stereospecific: evidence for opioid mediation of orosensory reward. *Physiology and Behavior*, **43**, 845–7.

Kirkham, T.C. and Cooper, S.J. (1988*b*). Naloxone attenuation of sham feeding is modified by manipulation of sucrose concentration. *Physiology and Behavior*, **44**, 491–4.

Kreeger, T.J., Levine, A.S., Seale, U.S., Callahan, M., and Beckel, M. (1991). Diazepam-induced feeding in captive grey wolves (Canis lupus). *Pharmacology Biochemistry and Behavior*, **39**, 559–61.

Kubota, K., Matsuda, I., Sugaya, K., and Urunu, T. (1986). Cholecystokinin antagonism by benzodiazepines in the food intake in mice. *Physiology and Behavior*, **36**, 175–8.

Leander, J.D. (1987). Fluoxetine suppresses palatability-induced ingestion. *Psychopharmacology*, **91**, 285–7.

Le Douarec, J.-C. (1963). The taking of food. A physiologic study, pharmacologic action of drugs (English translation). Doctor of Pharmacy thesis, University of Paris.

Le Douarec, J.-C., Schmitt, H., and Laubie, M. (1966). Etude pharmacologique de la fenfluramine et de ses isomères optiques. *Archives Internationales Pharmacodynamie Thérapie*, **161**, 206–32.

Leeb, K., Parker, L., and Eikelboom, R. (1991). Effects of pimozide on the hedonic properties of sucrose: analysis by the taste reactivity test. *Pharmacology Biochemistry and Behavior*, **39**, 895–901.

Leibowitz, S.F. (1975*a*). Amphetamine: possible site and mode of action for producing anorexia in the rat. *Brain Research*, **84**, 160–7.

Leibowitz, S.F. (1975*b*). Catecholaminergic mechanisms of the lateral hypothalamus: their role in the mediation of amphetamine anorexia. *Brain Research*, **98**, 529–45.

Leibowitz, S.F. (1976). Brain catecholaminergic mechanisms for control of hunger. In *Hunger: basic mechanisms and clinical implications* (eds. D. Novin, W. Wyrwicka, and G. Bray, pp. 1–18. Raven Press, New York.

Le Magnen, J. (1985). *Hunger*. Cambridge University Press, Cambridge.

Le Magnen, J., Marfaing-Jallet, P., Miceli, D., and Devos, M. (1980). Pain modulating and reward systems: a single brain mechanism? *Pharmacology Biochemistry and Behavior*, 12, 729–33.

Locke, K.W., Brown, D.R., and Holtzman, S.G. (1982). Effects of opiate antagonists and putative *mu* and *kappa*-agonists on milk intake in rat and squirrel monkey. *Pharmacology Biochemistry and Behavior*, 17, 1275–9.

Lynch, W.C. (1986). Opiate blockade inhibits saccharin intake and blocks normal preference acquisition. *Pharmacology Biochemistry and Behavior*, 24, 833–6.

Lynch, W.C. and Libby, L. (1983). Naloxone suppresses intake of highly preferred saccharin in food deprived and sated rats. *Life Science*, 33, 1909–14.

Maickel, R.P., Braude, M.C., and Zabik, J.E. (1977). The effects of various narcotic agonists and antagonists on deprivation-induced fluid-consumption. *Neuropharmacology*, 16, 861–6.

Maickel, R.P. and Maloney, G.J. (1973). Effects of various depressant drugs on deprivation-induced water consumption *Neuropharmacology*, 12, 777–82.

Maickel, R.P. and Maloney, G.J. (1974). Taste phenomena influences on stimulation of deprivation-induced fluid consumption of rats. *Neuropharmacology*, 13, 763–67.

Mansbach, R.S., Stanley, J.A., and Barrett, J.E. (1984). Ro15-1788 and β-CCE selectively eliminate diazepam-induced feeding in the rabbit. *Pharmacology Biochemistry and Behavior*, 20, 763–66.

Margules, D.L. and Stein, L. (1967). Neuroleptics *v.* tranquilizers: evidence from animal studies of mode and site of action. In *Neuropsychopharmacology* (eds. H. Brill, J.O. Cole, P. Deniker, H. Hippius, and P.B. Bradley), pp. 108–20. Excerpta Medica Foundation, Amsterdam.

McKay, L.D., Kenney, N.J., Edens, N.K., Williams, R.H., and Woods, S.C. (1981). Intracerebroventricular beta-endorphin increases food intake in rats. *Life Sciences*, 29, 1429–34.

McLaughlin, C.L. and Baile, C.A. (1979). Cholecystokinin, amphetamine and diazepam and feeding in lean and obese Zucker rats. *Pharmacology Biochemistry and Behavior*, 10, 87–93.

Mereu, G.P., Fratta, W., Chessa, P., and Gessa, G.L. (1976). Voraciousness induced in cats by benzodiazepines. *Psychopharmacology*, 47, 101–3.

Möhler, H. and Okada, T. (1977). Properties of ^{3}H-diazepam binding to benzodiazepine receptors in the rat cerebral cortex. *Life Sciences*, 20, 2101–10.

Morley, J.E. (1980). The neuroendocrine control of appetite: the role of the endogenous opiates, cholecystokinin, TRH, gamma-amino-butyric acid and the diazepam receptor. *Life Sciences*, 27, 355–68.

Morley, J.E. and Levine, A.S. (1985). The pharmacology of eating behavior. *Annual Review of Pharmacology and Toxicology*, 25, 127–46.

Morley, J.E. and Levine, A.S. (1983). Involvement of dynorphin and the kappa opioid receptor infeeding. *Peptides*, 4, 797–800.

Munro, J.F., Seaton, D.A., and Duncan, L.J.P. (1966). Treatment of refractory obesity with fenfluramine. *British Medical Journal*, II, 624–5.

Muscat, R., Kyprionou, T., Osman, M., Phillips, G., and Willner, P. (1991). Sweetness-dependent facilitation of sucrose drinking by raclopride is unrelated to calorie content. *Pharmacology Biochemistry and Behavior*, 40, 209–13.

Muscat, R. and Willner, P. (1989). Effects of dopamine receptor antagonists on sucrose consumption and preference. *Psychopharmacology*, 99, 98–102.

Nathanson, M.H. (1937). The central action of beta-aminopropylbenzene (benzedrine). *Journal of the American Medical Association*, **108**, 528–31.

Neill, J.C. (1990). The effects of 5–hydroxytryptamine receptor agonists and antagonists on food and fluid intake in the rat. Unpublished PhD thesis, University of Birmingham.

Neill, J.C. and Cooper, S.J. (1988). Evidence for serotonergic modulation of sucrose sham-feeding in the gastric-fistulated rat. *Physiology and Behavior*, **44**, 453–9.

Neill, J.C. and Cooper, S.J. (1989). Evidence for 5-HT$_{1c}$ receptor mediation of anorexia in the rat. *British Journal of Pharmocology*, **97**, 433pp.

Niki, H. (1965). Chlordiazepoxide and food-intake in the rat. *Japanese Journal of Psychological Research*, **7**, 80–5.

Norgren, R. and Grill, H. (1982). Brain-stem control of ingestive behavior. In *The physiological mechanisms of motivation* (ed. D.W. Pfaff), pp.99–131. Springer-Verlag, New York.

Olds, J. and Milner, P. (1954). Positive reinforcement from electrical stimulation of septal area and other regions of the rat brain. *Journal of Comparative and Physiological Psychology*, **47**, 419–27.

Parker, L.A. (1991). Chlordiazepoxide nonspecifically enhances consumption of saccharin solution. *Pharmacology Biochemistry and Behavior*, **38**, 375–7.

Pert, C.B. and Snyder, S.H. (1973). Opiate receptor: demonstration in nervous tissue. *Science*, **179**, 1011–14.

Pfaffman, C. (1969). Taste preference and reinforcement. *In Reinforcement and behavior* (ed. J.T. Tapp), pp. 215–41. Academic, New York.

Phillips, G., Willner, P., and Muscat, R. (1991). Reward-dependent suppression or facilitation of consummatory behaviour by raclopride. *Psychopharmacology*, **105**, 355–60.

Prinzmetal, M. and Bloomberg, W. (1935). The use of benzedrine for the treatment of narcolepsy. *Journal of the American Medical Association*, **105**, 2051–4.

Randall, L.O., Schallek, W., Heise, G.A., Keith, E.F., and Bagdon, R.E. (1960). The psychosedative properties of methaminodiazepoxide. *Journal of Pharmacology and Experimental Therapeutics*, **129**, 163–71.

Reid, L.D. (1985). Endogneous opioid peptides and regulation of drinking and feeding. *American Journal of Clinical Nutrition*, **42**, 1099–132.

Roache, J.D. and Zabik, J.E. (1986). Effects of benzodiazepine on taste aversions in a two-bottle choice paradigm. *Pharmacology Biochemistry and Behavior*, **25**, 431–7.

Rockwood, G.A. and Reid, L.D. (1982). Naloxone modifies sugar-water intake in rats drinking with open gastric fistulas. *Physiology and Behavior*, **29**, 1175–8.

Rolls, E.T., Rolls, B.J., Kelly, P.H., Shaw, S.G., Wood, R.J., and Dale, R. (1974). The relative attenuation of self-stimulation, eating and drinking produced by dopamine receptor blockade. *Psychopharmacologia*, **38**, 219–30.

Rowland, N. and Engle, D.J. (1977). Feeding and drinking interactions after acute butyrophenone administration. *Pharmacology Biochemistry and Behavior*, **7**, 295–301.

Rusk, I.N. and Cooper, S.J. (1994). Parametric studies of selective D$_1$ and D$_2$ antagonists: effects on appetitive and feeding behaviour. *Behavioural Pharmacology*, in press.

Sanger, D.J. (1981). Endorphinergic mechanisms in the control of food and water intake. *Appetite*, **2**, 193–208.

Sanger, D.J. (1983). Opiates and ingestive behaviour. In *Theory in psychopharmacology*, vol. 2 (ed. S.J. Cooper), pp. 75–113. Academic Press, London.

Sanger, D.J. and McCarthy, P.S. (1980). Differential effects of morphine on food and water intake in food deprived and freely-feeding rats. *Psychopharmacology*, **72**, 103–6.

Schneider, L.H., Davis, J.D., Watson, C.A., and Smith, G.P. (1990). Similar effect of raclopride and reduced sucrose concentration on the microstructure of sucrose sham feeding. *European Journal of Pharmacology*, **186**, 61–70.

Schneider, L.H., Gibbs, J., and Smith, G.P. (1986). D-2 selective receptor antagonists suppress sucrose sham feeding in the rat. *Brain Research Bulletin*, **17**, 605–11.

Schneider, L.H., Greenberg, D., and Smith, G.P. (1988). Comparison of the effect of selective D_1 and D_2 receptor antagonists on sucrose sham feeding and water sham drinking. *Annals of the New York Academy of Science*, **537**, 534–537.

Schneider, L.H., Watson, C.A., Gibbs, J., and Smith, G.P. (1991). Infra-additivity of combined treatments with selective D_1 and D_2 receptor antagonists for inhibiting sucrose reinforcement. *Brain Research*, **550**, 122–4.

Sclafani, A., Aravich, P.E., and Xenakis, S. (1982). Dopaminergic and endorphinergic mediation of a sweet reward. In *The neural basis of feeding and reward* (eds. B.G. Hoebel and D. Novin), pp. 507–15. Haer Institute, Brunswick, Maine.

Silverstone, J.T. and Stunkard, A.J. (1968). The anorectic effect of dexamphetamine sulphate. *British Journal of Pharmacology and Chemotherapy*, **33**, 513–22.

Silverstone, J.T., Cooper, R.M., and Begg, R.R. (1970). A comparative trial of fenfluramine or diethylproprion in obesity. *British Journal of Clinical Practice*, **24**, 423–5.

Simon, E.J., Hiller, J.M., and Edelman, I. (1973). Stereospecific binding of the potent narcotic analgesic [^{1}H]etorphine to rat-brain homogenate. *Proceedings of the National Academy of Sciences USA*, **70**, 1947–9.

Siviy, S.M., Calcagnetti, D.J., and Reid, L.D. (1982). Opioids and palatability. In *The neural basis of feeding and reward* (eds. B.G. Hoebel and D. Novin), pp. 517–24. Haer Institute, Brunswick, Maine.

Siviy, S.M. and Reid, L.D. (1983). Endorphinergic modulation of acceptability of putative reinforcers. *Appetite*, **4**, 249–57.

Smith, G.P. and Gibbs, J. (1976). Cholecystokinin and satiety: theoretic and therapeutic implications. In *Hunger: basic mechanisms and clinical implications* (eds. D. Novin, W. Wyrwicka, and G. Bray), pp. 349–55. Raven Press, New York.

Smith, G.P. and Gibbs, J. (1979). Postprandial satiety. In *Progress in psychobiology and physiological psychology*, vol. 8 (eds. J.M. Sprague and A.N. Epstein), pp. 179– 242. Academic Press, New York.

Smith, G.P. and Schneider, L.H. (1988). Relationship between mesolimbic dopamine function and eating behavior. *Annals of the New York Academy of Sciences*, **537**, 254–61.

Soubrié, P., Kulkarni, S., Simon, P., and Boissier, J.R. (1975). Effets des anxiolytiques sur la prise de nourriture de rats et de souris placés en situation nouvelle ou familière. *Psychopharmacologia (Berl.)*, **45**, 203–10.

Stapleton, J.M., Lind, M.D., Merriman, V.J., and Reid, L.D. (1979). Naloxone inhibits diazepam-induced feeding in rats. *Life Sciences*, **24**, 2421–6.

Stellar, E. (1954). The physiology of motivation. *Psychological Review*, **61**, 5–22.

Stephens, R.J. (1973). The influence of mild stress on food consumption in untrained mice and the effect of drugs. *British Journal of Pharmacology*, **47**, 146pp.

Stowe, F.R. and Miller, A.T. (1957). The effect of amphetamine on food intake in rat with hypothalamic hyperphagia. *Experientia*, **13**, 114.

Terenius, L. (1973). Characteristics of the 'receptor' for narcotic analgesics in synaptic plasma membrane fraction from rat brain. *Acta Pharmacologica et Toxicologica*, **33**, 377–84.

Thompson, T. and Schuster, C.R. (1964). Morphine self-administration, food-reinforced, and avoidance behaviors in rhesus monkeys. *Psychopharmacologia*, **5**, 87–94.

Towell, A., Muscat, R., and Willner, P. (1987). Effects of pimozide on sucrose consumption and preference. *Psychopharmacology*, **92**, 262–4.

Treit, D. and Berridge, K.C. (1990). A comparison of benzodiazepine, serotonin and dopamine agents in the taste reactivity paradigm. *Pharmacology Biochemistry and Behavior*, **37**, 451–6.

Treit, D., Berridge, K.C. and Schulz, C.E. (1987). The direct enhancement of positive palatability by chlordiazepoxide is antagonized by Ro15–1788 and CGS 8216. *Pharmacology Biochemistry and Behavior*, **26**, 709–14.

Turkish, S. and Cooper, S.J. (1984). Enhancement of salt-intake by chlordiazepoxide in thirsty rats: antagonism by Ro15–1788. *Pharmacology Biochemistry and Behavior*, **20**, 869–73.

van Rossum, J.M. and Simons, F. (1969). Locomotor activity and anorexigenic action. *Psychopharmacologia*, **14**, 248–54.

Watson, P.J. and Cox, V.C. (1976). An analysis of barbiturate-induced eating and drinking in the rat. *Physiological Psychology*, **4**, 325–32.

Weatherford, S.C., Greenberg, D., Gibbs, J., and Smith, G.P. (1990). The potency of D-1 and D-2 receptor antagonists is inversely related to the reward value of sham-fed corn oil and sucrose in rats. *Pharmacology, Biochemistry and Behavior*, **37**, 317–23.

Weatherford, S.C., Smith, G.P., and Melville, L.D. (1988). D-1 and D-2 receptor antagonists decrease corn oil sham feeding in rats. *Physiology and Behavior*, **44**, 569–72.

Weeks, J.R. (1962). Experimental morphine addiction: method for automatic intravenous injections in unrestricted rats. *Science*, **138**, 143–4.

Weingarten, H.P. and Watson, S.D. (1982). Sham feeding as a procedure for assessing the influence of diet palatability on food intake. *Physiology and Behavior*, **28**, 401–7.

Willner, P. Papp, M., Phillips, G., Maleeh, M., and Muscat, R. (1990). Pimozide does not impair sweetness discrimination *Psychopharmacology*, **102**, 278–82.

Wise, R.A. (1981). Brain dopamine and reward. In *Theory in psychopharmacology*, Vol. 1 (ed. S.J. Cooper), pp. 233–76. Academic Press, London.

Wise, R.A. (1982). Common neural basis for brain stimulation reward, drug reward, and food reward. In *The neural basis of feeding and reward* (eds. B.G. Hoebel and D. Novin), pp. 445–54. Haer Institute, Brunswick, Maine.

Wise, R.A. and Colle, L.M. (1984). Pimozide attenuates free feeding: best scores analysis reveals a motivational deficit. *Psychopharmacology*, **84**, 446–51.

Wise, R.A. and Dawson, V. (1974). Diazepam-induced eating and lever pressing for food in sated rats. *Journal of Comparative and Physiological Psychology*, **86**, 930–41.

Wise, R.A. and Raptis, L. (1986). Effects of naloxone and pimozide on initiation and maintenance measures of free feeding. *Brain Research*, **368**, 62–8.

Wise, R.A., Spindler, J., de Wit, H. and Gerber, G.J. (1978). Neuroleptic-induced 'anhedonia' in rats: pimozide blocks the reward quality of food. *Science*, **201**, 262–4.

Woodward, E. (1970). Clinical experience with fenfluramine in the United States. In *Amphetamines and related compounds* (eds. E. Costa and S. Garattini), pp. 685–91. Raven, New York.

Yeomans, M.R., Wright, P., Macleod, H.A., and Critchley, J.A.J.H. (1990). Effects of nalmefene on feeding in humans: dissociation of hunger and palatability. *Psychopharmacology*, **100**, 426–34.

Yeomans, M.R. and Wright, P. (1991). Lower pleasantness of palatable foods in nalmefene-treated human volunteers. *Appetite*, **16**, 249–59.

Yerbury, R.E., and Cooper, S.J. (1987). The benzodiazepine partial agonists, Ro16–6028 and Ro17–1812, increase palatable food consumption in nondeprived rats. *Pharmacology Biochemistry and Behavior*, **28**, 427–31.

Yerbury, R.E. and Cooper, S.J. (1989). Novel benzodiazepine receptor ligands: palatable food consumption following administration of zolpidem, CGS 17867A or Ro23–0364, in the rat. *Pharmacology Biochemistry and Behavior*, **33**, 303–7.

Young, R.C., Gibbs, J., Antin, J., Holt, J. and Smith, G.P. (1974). Absence of satiety during sham feeding in the rat. *Journal of Comparative and Physiological Psychology*, **87**, 795–800.

10

A brief history of the anhedonia hypothesis

Roy A. Wise

INTRODUCTION

The anhedonia hypothesis holds that dopamine receptor antagonists (neuroleptic drugs) block the positive reinforcement and positive affect that is associated with rewarding events. The hypothesis began to take shape in the mid 1970s, when my students and I were studying the effects of dopamine receptor blockers on the rewarding effects of the 'psychomotor' stimulants amphetamine and cocaine and of hypothalamic electrical stimulation. We first used the term 'anhedonia' in 1978, when, in an attempt to present the 'news' succinctly, we asserted that 'pimozide blocks the reward quality of food' (Wise *et al.*, 1978a). Soon it became apparent that the dopamine system played a role in opiate reward as well, and I reviewed the literature which suggested a role for dopamine in brain stimulation, psychomotor stimulant, food, water, and opiate reinforcement and formally named the hypothesis (Wise, 1982). The paper was widely cited (Wise, 1990), often, in the early years, by workers who took issue with it (Wise, 1985).

The hypothesis was questioned at two levels. First, the more traditional assumption (Barbeau, 1974; Hornykeiwicz, 1975) was that dopamine blockers interfered with the ability to initiate the voluntary movements from which reward and pleasure are, in the end (Hebb, 1981), inferred. It was evidence of deficits that could not be explained by such a simple motor hypothesis that gave rise to the anhedonia hypothesis in the first place, and more such evidence has been uncovered since the hypothesis was published. However, the hypothesis suggested not only that neuroleptics block the rewarding effects of food, hypothalamic brain stimulation, and a variety of drugs of abuse, but also that they block the pleasure or euphoria that is often associated with these rewards. The evidence discussed in my early papers was evidence that neuroleptics blocked objectively measured reward function, not evidence that neuroleptics blocked subjective pleasure. By 'reward'

I intend to imply somewhat more than what is usually meant by the phrase 'operant reinforcement' (Wise, 1989). We most frequently study the maintenance of established habits rather than the increase in response probability that accompanies habit development and that is the defining characteristic of operant reinforcement (but see Wise and Schwartz, 1981). Moreover, the brain stimulation reward specialist typically indicates the sum of reinforcement and 'priming', an incentive motivational consequence of a rewarding stimulus that is often not appreciated by operant psychologists. I believe that neuroleptics attenuate priming as well as reinforcing effects of drugs and food, although Wasserman *et al.* (1982) have argued against such a notion in the case of brain stimulation reward. Finally, neuroleptics block development of conditioned place preferences, which is most properly viewed as an autoshaping phenomenon involving Pavlovian rather than operant reinforcement. Each of these phenomena is related to my notion of reward and each has been operationally specified and examined. The anhedonia component of the hypothesis, unlike the reward component, has always been a speculation to be tested rather than an hypothesis on which any substantial direct evidence already existed. My assumption of 1982 was that subjective pleasure usually accompanied reward and would be blunted by treatments that blunt reward; I no longer make this assumption, but it was at the root of the original hypothesis.

PSYCHOMOTOR STIMULANT REINFORCEMENT

When given to trained animals that have the opportunity for intravenous psychomotor stimulant self-administration, neuroleptics cause a condition in which there is first a compensatory increase in drug taking and then, if the neuroleptic dose is high enough, there is extinction of the lever-pressing (or other) habit. These effects are inconsistent with the suggestion that neuroleptic treatment might simply be causing motoric difficulties, since the animals respond more, not less, than usual following treatment (deWit and Wise, 1977; Yokel and Wise, 1975, 1976). It was this observation that first suggested a motivational rather than a motor interpretation of neuroleptic effects on stimulant self-administration (Wilson and Schuster, 1972), but the neuroleptic first tested was chlorpromazine, which blocks noradrenergic as well as dopaminergic receptors. Our subsequent (Yokel and Wise, 1975) demonstration was that a selective dopamine antagonist had the same effect. This and the fact that selective dopamine agonists, such as apomorphine, piribedil, and bromocriptine, are self-administered in much the same way as are the psychomotor stimulants amphetamine and cocaine (Baxter *et al.*, 1974; Wise *et al.*, 1976, 1990; Woolverton *et al.*, 1984; Yokel and Wise, 1978), confirmed that it is their ability to activate the dopamine system that makes the psychomotor stimulants habit-forming (Wise, 1978; Wise and Rompré, 1989).

BRAIN STIMULATION REWARD

The earliest suggestions that brain dopamine might play an important role in reward function came from studies of brain stimulation reward. Crow (1971) called attention to the close relation of the dopamine cell groups to reward sites in the ventral tegmental area. Lippa *et al.* (1973) reported that selective damage to dopamine systems disrupted self-stimulation; Liebman and Butcher (1973, 1974) reported that selective pharmacological blockade of dopamine systems did also. My colleagues and I, like others (e.g. Fibiger *et al.*, 1976) were initially concerned with the obvious possibility that dopaminergic impairment might merely be causing the motoric deficits associated with Parkinson's disease. However, when we examined the temporal pattern of responding caused by pre-treatment with selective dopamine antagonists, we found that our animals were capable of responding at normal or near-normal rates and did so in the early minutes of a test session (after ample time had been allowed for drug absorption); the animals responded in a typical extinction pattern, with initially normal response rates, gradual slowing, and eventual response cessation. There were periods of 'spontaneous recovery' when an animal went to the lever and re-initated responding at normal rates for a moment or two, only to lose interest and move off to groom or rear. It was not that neuroleptics made the animals incapable of responding but, rather, that they rendered the stimulation ineffective in maintaining such responding (Fouriezos *et al.*, 1978; Fouriezos and Wise, 1976). This conclusion was soon confirmed by others using the same general strategy (Franklin and McCoy, 1979; Gallistel *et al.*, 1982), which came to be known as the 'extinction paradigm'.

That neuroleptics attenuated the rewarding effects of brain stimula-tion was subsequently confirmed by an even more powerful approach involving the 'curve-shift' paradigm of Edmonds and Gallistel (1974). This paradigm essentially offers a dose–response analysis of brain stimulation reward (Liebman, 1983), with the 'dose' of stimulation manipulated through variations in the frequency, intensity, or duration of the trains of rewarding stimulation pulses that the animal earns with each response. In this paradigm the reward-attenuating and the performance-impairing effects of neuroleptics can be demonstrated and dissociated (Gallistel, 1987; Miliaressis *et al.*, 1986; Fig. 10.1). Low doses of dopamine antagonists cause parallel rightward shifts in the

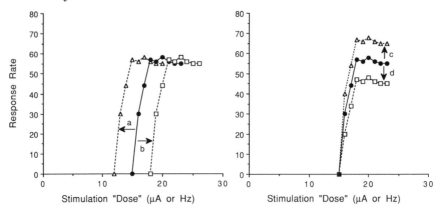

Fig. 10.1 Brain stimulation reward rate-frequency or 'dose-response' functions. On the left are illustrated the leftward and rightward shifts of the normal rate-frequency function (solid circles) that would be associated with (a) reward-synergism or (b) reward-antagonism as caused by reward-enhancing or reward-suppressing treatments. Reward-enhancing treatments (a) reduce the 'dose' of stimulation required to sustain performance at a selected response level (without affecting the *maximum* level of performance). Reward-suppressing treatments (b) increase the dose of stimulation needed to sustain a given response level (without altering the maximum level of performance). On the right are illustrated the upward and downward shifts that would be associated with (c) enhanced performance capacity (or an easier task) or (d) decreased performance capacity (or a more difficult task).

dose–response curve, increasing the amount of stimulation required for a given level of responding but not changing the maximum level of responding demonstrated when the animal is given maximal stimulation (Stellar *et al.*, 1983). The dopamine releaser amphetamine has the opposite effect causing parallel leftward shifts of the curve and reversing the rightward shifts caused by dopamine antagonists (Gallistel and Freyd, 1987). High doses of dopamine antagonists not only shift the curve to the right; they also shift it down, reducing the maximal response rate of the animal as well as increasing the stimulation required to produce responding at maximal rates (Gallistel and Davis, 1983; Rompré and Wise, 1989; Stellar *et al.*, 1983). Morphine injections that shift the curve to the left reverse the rightward shift but fail to reverse the downward shift caused when high doses of neuroleptics are given (Rompré and Wise, 1989); this finding confirms the assumption (Gallistel, 1987; Miliaressis *et al.*, 1986) that the rightward and downward shifts caused by neuroleptics reflect independent mechanisms.

The fact that neuroleptic treatment can reduce the effectiveness of stimulation at doses that do not reduce the maximum response rate of the animals confirms that neuroleptics have a low-dose action above and beyond any performance-impairing effects of these drugs; this conclusion is now apparently accepted (Fibiger *et al.*, 1987), even by those who initially questioned it (Fibiger *et al.*, 1976).

FOOD REWARD

The anhedonia hypothesis was advanced in the context of food reward, and it is in this context that it was most energetically challenged. The hypothesis (Wise, 1982) was based on a number of specific findings, each of which involved periods of normal responding that appeared to rule out explanation by any simple form of motoric impairment. Dopamine-selective neuroleptics block or retard acquisition of food-rewarded operant habits (acquisition effect; Wise and Schwartz, 1981) and cause extinction of already learned operant habits despite continued food reward (extinction effect; Wise *et al.*, 1978a,b). When an operant habit undergoes extinction, initial responding is normal, but normal response rates are not maintained as they would be if the reward were given. In the neuroleptic-treated rat, responding follows the same pattern (initially normal, then slowing, then essentially nil) despite the fact that the reward is still being given. The inability of the reward to maintain normal responding suggests that the reward is simply not rewarding to the neuroleptic-treated rat. The problem is not simply that the neuroleptic-treated rat fatigues more quickly, since operants such as alley running or lever pressing that have been extinguished under neuroleptics can still be elicited (spontaneous recovery effect) by environmental manipulations (such as presentation of a reward-associated conditioned stimulus: Fouriezos and Wise, 1976; Franklin and McCoy, 1979), even during the period of peak neuroleptic effectiveness. Neuroleptic-induced extinction is progressively more rapid with repeated trials, despite the use of a constant neuroleptic dose (resistance-to-extinction effect; Wise *et al.*, 1978a); thus animals that show their ability to lever-press the first time they are tested under a given dose of a given neuroleptic do so less and less on subsequent (though distributed) days of neuroleptic testing. Further, animals having previous experience with the frustration of non-reward extinguish more quickly under subsequent neuroleptic treatment than do extinction-naïve animals (transfer effect: Wise *et al.*, 1978a but see Mason *et al.*, 1980, and rebuttal, Wise, 1982); it is the *frustration* of non-reward that is assumed to transfer between the non-reward and the neuroleptic conditions. The fact that animals without prior experience with non-reward maintain almost normal responding for the first day of testing in this paradigm rules out the possibility that this dose of neuroleptic renders the previously non-rewarded animals (animals with the identical pharmacological histories with the neuroleptic) incapable of normal responding. Thus, the anhedonia hypothesis was essentially an alternative offered in the context of what was viewed as a falsified motor hypothesis. Since neuroleptic-treated rats had been shown capable of responding under several circumstances that could not be related to the drug treatment or drug history itself, a motivational hypothesis was needed to explain why capable animals fail to respond under just the circumstances where a non-rewarded animal would fail to respond.

The anhedonia hypothesis was challenged on several grounds. It was already clear that neuroleptic treatment usually did less than completely block the reward system, since, in animals trained under continuous reinforcement, neuroleptic-induced extinction was always slower than extinction induced by withholding the food (Wise, 1982, 1985). This finding might have suggested a term implying a less-than-total reduction in reward effectiveness, such as 'dysphoria' (Wise, 1985) or Liebman's (1982) 'neuroleptothesia'. Our own experiments made it clear that neuroleptics also do more than *merely* attenuate the rewarding impact of food, however, since neuroleptic-treated animals previously trained (drug-free) under partial reinforcement conditions extinguish faster under pimozide treatment than do non-rewarded animals; indeed, they begin to slow their responding under neuroleptic treatment well before they would normally receive their first earned food pellet (Gray and Wise, 1980). This fact suggested an incentive-motivational deficit (Gray and Wise, 1980) that has, along with other important considerations (Wise, 1989), encouraged me to continue to use the term 'reward', which implies more than simply the 'stamping in' (Thorndike, 1898) of stimulus–response associations (Thorndike, 1933) or response–consequence associations (Skinner, 1938) that are usually associated with the term 'reinforcement' and, recently, to broaden my view of the role of dopamine in behaviour (Wise, 1989).

Of those who published early challenges to the anhedonia hypothesis, several have subsequently come to support it. Beninger and Phillips, who were involved in early studies that favoured a motor interpretation (Mason *et al.*, 1980), have subsequently done a good deal of work (Beninger and Freedman, 1982; Beninger and Phillips, 1980; Beninger *et al.* 1987; Hoffman and Beninger, 1985) that supports a reward interpretation (Beninger, 1983, 1989; Miller *et al.*, 1990). Ettenberg, who once went so far as to suggest that the effects of neuroleptics on brain stimulation reward reflected a 'response artifact' rather than a reward deficit (Ettenberg *et al.*, 1981), has developed the most subtle—and perhaps the most convincing—evidence that neuroleptics attenuate the reward function. Here animals are trained for 30 days to traverse a runway for food (Ettenberg and Camp, 1986a) or water (Ettenberg and Camp, 1986b). A single training trial is given each day, and one group of animals receives reinforcement each of these days while one group receives it on only two days out of every three. The latter group, the 'partial reinforcement' group, subsequently runs longer under conditions of non-reward ('extinction'). Similarly, animals given food or water every day but trained every third day under haloperidol run longer under subsequent conditions of non-reward. Here is a task where the animals are not given drug during testing, so the problem of performance impairment does not arise; moreover, partial training under drug produces *increased* responding during subsequent testing, just as does partial training under non-reward. Since responding is supra-normal on the test day, it cannot be explained by any presumed motoric effects of the previous drug treatment.

Another line of evidence in support of the view that neuroleptics reduce the rewarding effects of food comes from our demonstration that, contrary to an unconfirmed assertion of Tombaugh *et al.* (1979), neuroleptics interfere with the maintenance of feeding in response to the taste of food rather than with the initiation of feeding in response to the sight of food (Koechling *et al.*, 1988; Wise and Colle, 1984; Wise and Raptis, 1986); when we carefully examined the latency to initiate eating of small sequential meal segments as well as the speed of eating once the first bite was taken, we found that it was the latter, not the former, that deteriorated under neuroleptic treatment. Rats continued to take up the freshly presented food with short latency long after they slowed their eating and began to leave portions of each meal segment uneaten. Moreover, neuroleptics impair free-feeding by increasing its variability rather than by impairing peak performance; the best scores under neuroleptic treatment remain as good as the best scores under control conditions, but the frequency of good scores decreases and the frequency of irrelevant responses increases (Koechling *et al.*, 1988; Wise and Colle, 1984; Wise and Raptis, 1986).

Much more compelling evidence on this point has been reported by Schneider *et al.* (1990), who have compared lick rates in neuroleptic-treated and normal rats engaged in sham-feeding of sucrose solutions. Neuroleptic-treated sham-feeding rats (rats with an opened gastric fistula, such that there is no significant post-ingestive absorption of the sucrose) decrease their intake of sucrose as do animals given a sucrose solution of reduced concentration (and, thus, of less sweetness). However, the motor capability of the animals as reflected in their inter-lick interval is perfectly normal in both the neuroleptic-treated and the reduced concentration conditions (see Schneider *et al.*, 1990, Fig. 3); the animals lick at a rate of 5–7 licks per second within a cluster of consecutive licks and they do so whether treated with neuroleptics or saline and whether given 5% or 10% sucrose. However, neuroleptic-treated rats and rats given 5% sucrose lick fewer times per cluster than do saline-treated rats given 10% sucrose. In addition, neuroleptic-treated rats and rats given 5% sucrose pause longer between clusters of licks than do saline-treated rats given 10% sucrose. Because there is no slowing of the inter-lick interval, it is clear that the neuroleptic-treated animals in this experiment were, at the dose tested, capable of making the rapid motoric responses of a normal animal. Because neuroleptic-treated rats receiving 10% sucrose behaved in a manner identical to that of drug-free rats given 5% sucrose, it would seem that the reward value of sucrose was, for the neuroleptic-treated animals, reduced by roughly half.

Despite the fact that neuroleptic-induced motor deficits are not sufficient to explain the observed patterns of deteriorating commerce with rewarding stimuli, neuroleptics are clearly capable of causing significant motor deficits if given in sufficient doses (the threshold doses for reward deficits seem to be well below those for motor deficits), as is revealed nicely in the curve-shift paradigm that was first developed for use with brain stimulation reward (Rompré and Wise, 1989; Stellar et al., 1983; see above). The curve-shift paradigm has been adapted to the assessment of sucrose reward, where, again, reward deficits can be distinguished from decreased performance capacity and where, again, neuroleptics can be demonstrated to cause the former without the latter when low neuroleptic doses are given (Bailey et al., 1986). Essentially, the neuroleptic pimozide (at 0.2 mg/kg) does not alter the maximum bar-press rate of rats rewarded with sucrose, but does change the concentration of sucrose necessary to produce maximum rates of bar pressing; under this dose of pimozide rats require 1.7 M sucrose to motivate bar pressing as avid as that motivated by 0.1 M sucrose in untreated animals. Indeed, the pimozide-treated rats responded for sucrose in the same way as undrugged rats responded for sucrose adulterated with quinine. Similar effects of neuroleptics have been reported in free-feeding tests in normal animals (Xenakis and Sclafani, 1981, 1982) and in animals with open gastric fistulas (Geary and Smith, 1985).

Motor deficits may account for the decrease in lick rate in a frequently cited sucrose licking experiment by Gramling et al. (1984). Examination of their Fig. 1 indicates that the neuroleptic-treated animals licked only marginally slower than untreated animals but that their tongues frequently failed to reach the fluid cup on successive licks in the high-dose condition; indeed, the animals appeared to make contact with the sucrose only on approximately every-other lick. Decreased tongue protrusion is arguably a motoric deficit, though this question might bear closer scrutiny. In any case, Schneider et al. (1990) and

Weatherford *et al.* (1990) failed to find any difference in lick rate between neuroleptic-treated and normal rats; in their studies neuroleptics decreased the number of licks, rather than the rate of licking, in a cluster. The most obvious possibility is that the tongue extension required in the Fowler apparatus taxed the neuroleptic-treated rat to near the limits of its capacity. It is perhaps not surprising that such a test would be sensitive to the motoric debilitation that can be caused by neuroleptic treatment (Rompré and Wise, 1989; Stellar *et al.*, 1983). Several tests of free feeding suggest that neuroleptics have effects on the drinking of sweet solutions that parallel the effects of reward-dilution (Bailey *et al.*, 1986; Geary and Smith, 1985; Schneider *et al.*, 1986*a,b*; Weatherford *et al.*, 1990; Xenakis and Sclafani, 1981, 1982).

Two recent lines of study suggest directions for further consideration. The suggestion that neuroleptics reduce the subjective enjoyment of food reward would appear on the surface to be amenable to test with the taste-reactivity paradigm of Grill and Norgren (1978). While originally viewed as a measure of taste-elicited fixed action patterns of ingestion (Grill and Berridge, 1985), this paradigm has increasingly come to be viewed as a measure of subjective hedonic responses to food (Berridge and Grill, 1984; Berridge *et al.*, 1981, 1989; Berridge and Valenstein, 1991; Zellner *et al.*, 1985). Berridge *et al.* (1989) found no evidence that sweet solutions became less palatable or that bitter solutions became more aversive in animals with extensive damage to their dopamine systems. On the other hand, Leeb *et al.* (1991) found decreased sensitivity to sucrose in the same taste reactivity test in neuroleptic-treated rats. These animals showed progressively less appetitive tongue movements and progressively more neutral mouth movements both within (an extinction-like effect) and across (an apparent decrease in resistance-to-extinction) daily test sessions. To the degree that the taste-reactivity test measures more than simply the fixed action patterns of ingestion, Leeb *et al.* found evidence consistent with the hypothesis that neuroleptics do reduce the hedonic impact of sucrose. My own inclination, however, is to view the taste-reactivity test as it was originally characterized by Grill and Berridge (1985), as simply a measure of consummatory responses of food presented to the mouth. Consummatory responses might be expected to be refractory to extinction phenomena. Acts such as alley running lever pressing are termed 'preparatory' (Sherrington, 1906), 'appetitive' (Craig, 1918), 'operant' (Skinner, 1937), or 'instru-mental' (origins unknown) responses and have been distinguished from 'consummatory' (Craig, 1918; Sherrington, 1906) responses on the presumption that their control is very different. In my own experience neuroleptics have been far more effective in reducing the effectiveness of food-associated cues of an operant situation than in reducing effectiveness of the proximal cues of food once it is in the mouth. My personal opinion is that the taste-reactivity paradigm simply measures the consummatory responses of ingestion or rejection, and adds little to what we can infer from other consummatory measures as to the hedonic impact of food. This is a view that has changed considerably since I first raised the question of whether neuroleptics alter the hedonic impact of rewarding stimuli; I now see the issue of hedonics as largely irrelevant to the issue of reward. In any case, it is my view that in order to assess the effects of neuroleptics on the subjective hedonic impact of food objectively, we must rely either on studies of the facial expression of emotion in humans (e.g. Ekman *et al.*, 1969; Izzard, 1971)—which, unlike the facial responses of the rat, reflect more than simply the components of ingestion or rejection—or on subjective human reports from paradigms such as that of Cabanac (1971), which, unfortunately, can give only momentary estimates of relative hedonic impact (Helson, 1948).

The second line of recent relevant study involves extracellular recordings of the activity of dopamine-containing neurons of the ventral tegmental area and substantia nigra (the presumed substrate of this particular behavioural function). Schultz and his colleagues (Ljungberg *et al.*, 1992; Romo and Schultz, 1990*a,b*) have recorded dopaminergic neuronal activity during food-rewarded behavior in freely moving monkeys, and find that while dopaminergic neurons initially respond to food stimuli with a burst of firing, the same neurons soon come to fire in response to stimuli that *predict* the presentation of food and lose their responsiveness to the food itself. This is true in both free-feeding and instrumental (lever-pressing) feeding situations; thus the dopamine system seems more responsive to the *anticipation* of food reward than to the *receipt* of food reward. *In vivo* voltammetry studies also suggest that the dopamine system may be more involved in anticipatory than consummatory aspects of naturally rewarded behaviours (Phillips *et al.*, 1991). As more data are gathered using these direct physiological probes of dopaminergic activation, it seems likely that major revisions of the anhedonia hypothesis will be necessary.

OPIATE REINFORCEMENT

The anhedonia hypothesis was based largely on studies of psychomotor stimulant, brain stimulation, and food and water reinforcement. It implied, however, that the effectiveness of many or even all reinforcers might depend critically on dopamine function. The most extensive test of this prediction has involved opiate reinforcement, and the findings both support and challenge the hypothesis that opiate reward depends on dopaminergic function.

First, it is increasingly clear that opiates cause activation of the dopamine system, and that this activation is reinforcing. Opiates act in the ventral tegmental area to inhibit the activity of GABA-containing interneurons (Lacey *et al.*, 1989) that, in turn, normally inhibit dopaminergic activity (Johnson and North, 1992; Lacey *et al.*, 1988); thus opiate actions in the region of the dopamine cell bodies cause disinhibition of dopamine cell firing (Lacey *et al.*, 1989). When injected into the ventral tegmental area, opiates cause dopamine-mediated locomotion (Holmes *et al.*, 1983; Joyce and Iversen, 1979; Kalivas *et al.*, 1983), produce dopamine-mediated conditioned place preferences (Bozarth and Wise, 1981*b*; Phillips and LePiane, 1980; Spyraki *et al.*, 1983), facilitate the rewarding effects (Rompré and Wise, 1989) of hypothalamic brain stimulation (Broekkamp *et al.*, 1976), serve as operant reinforcers in their own right (Bozarth and Wise, 1981*a*; van Ree and de Weid, 1980; Welzl *et al.*, 1989), and reinstate operant habits that were learned under opiate reinforcement and then extinguished (Stewart, 1984).

However, it also seems clear that opiates have rewarding actions that are independent of dopaminergic activation *per se*. Opiates also appear to have rewarding actions in the nucleus accumbens, as shown by both place preference (van der Kooy *et al.*, 1982) and self-administration tests (Goeders *et al.*, 1984; Olds, 1982). It is thought that opiate rewarding actions in nucleus accumbens are independent of the dopamine system (Goeders *et al.*, 1984), but it is presumed that rewarding action is mediated by cells intrinsic to the nucleus, which is an anatomical target of the dopamine projection from the ventral tegmental area. Thus, if this system is activated by the levels of drug that are normally taken intravenously, it represents a dopamine-independent (though intimately dopamine-related) mechanism of opiate reward. Vaccarino *et al.* (1985) have reported evidence suggesting that this system is activated by self-administered intravenous heroin, but we have been unable to replicate their findings and have findings of our own that suggest the contrary (Britt and Wise, 1983); these seemingly contradictory results may one day be resolved by adjustment of injection coordinates. However, it remains reasonably well established that ten times higher doses of opiates are required to activate nucleus accumbens mechanisms than are required to activate ventral tegmental mechanisms (Kalivas *et al.*, 1983; West and Wise, 1988); thus it would appear likely that the effects of intravenous opiates in the ventral tegmental area will prove to be stronger than those in the nucleus accumbens. In either case, where it was once argued that opiate reward was completely independent of the dopaminergic mechanism that undeniably mediates the rewarding effects of psychomotor stimulants (Ettenberg *et al.*, 1982) it is now assumed by the same authors that opiates do activate the same ventral tegmental–nucleus accumbens–ventral pallidal circuit as is activated by the psychomotor stimulants, perhaps one synapse downstream (Hubner and Koob, 1990; Koob and Bloom, 1988) from the dopamine link that is disinhibited by opiate actions in the ventral tegmental area.

OTHER DRUGS OF ABUSE

Several other drugs of abuse activate the dopamine system. In addition to amphetamine (Zetterstrom *et al.*, 1983), cocaine (Church *et al.*, 1987), and opiates (Di Chiara and Imperato, 1988), nicotine (Imperato *et al.*, 1986), ethanol (Di Chiara and Imperato, 1985), cannabis (Ng Cheong Ton *et al.*, 1988), and phencyclidine (Gerhardt *et al.*, 1987) are known by direct measurement to elevate extracellular dopamine levels in the nucleus accumbens. This fact, taken with the fact that dopamine itself (and also amphetamine: Hoebel *et al.*, 1983) is rewarding when injected into the nucleus accumbens (Guerin *et al.*, 1984), strongly suggests that at least some portion of the habit-forming effects of these drugs is dopamine-dependent. Barbiturates and benzodiazepines, on the other hand, appear to inhibit dopamine release (Wood, 1982). These drugs may act in the same circuitry—efferent to the dopaminergic link—or they may act in independent reward circuitry, circuitry that has no dopaminergic link.

CURRENT ISSUES

The work of Schultz and his colleagues makes it obvious that brain dopamine plays a more general role than simply serving in brain circuitry specialized for reinforcement function. With the early success of operant psychology it was once attractive to speculate as to the specialized reward centres (Olds, 1956) and the identity of the mysterious substance 'X' (Olds and Olds, 1965) that 'stamped in' the S–R connections of Thorndike or the response probabilities of Skinner. It is becoming increasingly clear, however, that there is more to reward than operant reinforcement (Wise, 1989). Like a salted peanut, brain stimulation (Deutsch *et al.*, 1964; Gallistel, 1966) and drug (Gerber and Stretch, 1975; Stewart and de Wit, 1987) rewards have proactive as well as retroactive effects that can be reliably demonstrated and do not fit well within the simple conception of response-contingent operant reinforcement. The proactive effects of rewards do not require that the reward be given in a response-contingent manner; indeed, they are studied more in the paradigm of Pavlov than that of Skinner

(Wise, 1989). So, too, is the conditioned place-preference paradigm—in which the conditioned attachments of the addict to the drug-taking environment are modelled—a Pavlovian rather than a Skinnerian paradigm. Since Skinner originally (1933) took the term 'reinforcement' from Pavlov (personal communication, 2 December 1986), it is fitting that the notion of the role of dopamine in reinforcement be broadened to include more than simply the response-contingent reinforcement on which Skinner (1938) and Thorndike (1933) and their followers have focussed their attention.

The current views of the role of dopamine in motivational function include a good deal more than the narrow concept of 'stamping in' of stimulus–response associations or operant probabilities. They must at the very least include a role in incentive motivation, the motivational arousal induced by the 'priming' effects of the incentive stimulus itself (Gallistel, 1966; Stewart and de Wit, 1987). They must also include roles in conditioned reinforcement (Davis and Smith, 1975; Taylor and Robbins, 1984) and conditioned incentives—the sights and sounds that usually predict reward (Ljungberg *et al.*, 1992; Phillips *et al.*, 1991; Romo and Schultz, 1990*a,b*). They must also include roles in the conditioned approach of stimuli that have been paired with reward (Beach, 1957; Spragg, 1940) and in the response-independent potentiation by rewarding drugs of the response-contingent reward of brain stimulation (Kornetsky *et al.*, 1979; Levitt *et al.*, 1977; Wise, 1980). Our own attempts at such a formulation (Wise, 1989; Wise and Bozarth, 1987) appeal to a loose concept of 'psychomotor arousal' or 'psychomotor activation'. While this concept is a throwback to the arousal theory of the 1950s (e.g. Hebb, 1955), I expect it to fit better than a strict reinforcement hypothesis with the data of the 1990s.

With hindsight, I believe that the anhedonia hypothesis wrongly linked subjective pleasure with objective reward. When human subjects self-administer intravenous cocaine and nicotine, they report that the levels of euphoria accompanying successive injections become progressively weaker (Fischman *et al.*, 1985; Henningfield, 1984). Similarly, the pleasure of subsequent cigarettes is reported never to match that of the first cigarette of the day. This decrease in hedonic impact is referred to as 'within-session' or 'acute' tolerance (LeBlanc *et al.*, 1975). Yet the response-maintaining effects of these drugs seem quite constant; human subjects respond at very regular intervals for intravenous cocaine and nicotine, as do lower animals (Henningfield 1984; Pickens and Thompson, 1971). Thus the rewarding effects of cocaine and nicotine do not undergo acute tolerance, while the subjective euphoria caused by these drugs does. This dissociation between the rewarding and hedonic effects of cocaine and nicotine makes it seem clear that we cannot seek the explanation of the one in the other. It seems quite possible to me that, as Skinner cautioned many years ago—and current trends in psychology notwithstanding—our persistent appeal to mental causes may well hinder, rather than help, the human quest for self-understanding.

REFERENCES

Bailey, C. S., Hsiao, S., and King, J. E. (1986). Hedonic reactivity to sucrose in rats: Modification by pimozide. *Physiology and Behavior*, **38**, 447–52.

Barbeau, A. (1974). Drugs affecting movement disorders. *Annual Review of Pharmacology*, **14**, 91–113.

Baxter, B. L., Gluckman, M. I., Stein, L., and Scerni, R. A. (1974). Self-injection of apomorphine in the rat: Positive reinforcement by a dopamine receptor stimulant. *Pharmacology Biochemistry and Behavior*, **2**, 387–391.

Beach, H. D. (1957). Morphine addiction in rats. *Canadian Journal of Psychology*, **11**, 104–12.

Beninger, R. J. (1983). The role of dopamine in locomotor activity and learning. *Brain Research Reviews*, **6**, 173–96.

Beninger, R. J. (1989). Dissociating the effects of altered dopaminergic function on performance and learning. *Brain Research Bulletin*, **23**, 365–71.

Beninger, R. J., Cheng, M., Hahn, B. L., Hoffman, D. C., Mazurski, E. J., Morency, M. A., Ramm, P., and Stewart, R. J. (1987). Effects of extinction, pimozide, SCH 23390, and metoclopramide on food-rewarded operant responding of rats. *Psychopharmacology*, **92**, 343–49.

Beninger, R. J. and Freedman, N. L. (1982). The use of two operants to examine the nature of pimozide-induced decreases in responding for brain stimulation. *Physiological Psychology*, **10**, 409–12.

Beninger, R. J. and Phillips, A. G. (1980). The effect of pimozide on the establishment of conditioned reinforcement. *Psychopharmacology*, **68**, 147–53.

Berridge, K. C. and Grill, H. J. (1984). Isohedonic tastes support a two-dimensional hypothesis of palatability. *Appetite*, **5**, 221–31.

Berridge, K. C. and Valenstein, E. S. (1991). What psychological process mediates feeding evoked by electrical stimulation of the lateral hypothalamus? *Behavioral Neuroscience*, **105**, 3–14.

Berridge, K. C., Grill, H. J., and Norgren, R. (1981). Relation of consummatory responses and preabsorptive insulin release to palatability and learned taste aversions. *Journal of Comparative and Physiological Psychology*, **95**, 363–82.

Berridge, K. D., Venier, I. L., and Robinson, T. E. (1989). Taste reactivity analysis of 6–hydroxydopamine-induced aphagia: Implications for arousal and anhedonia hypotheses of dopamine function. *Behavioral Neuroscience*, **103**, 36–45.

Bozarth, M. A. and Wise, R. A. (1981a). Intracranial self-administration of morphine into the ventral tegmental area in rats. *Life Sciences*, **28**, 551–5.

Bozarth, M. A. and Wise, R. A. (1981b). Heroin reward is dependent on a dopaminergic substrate. *Life Sciences*, **29**, 1881–6.

Britt, M. D. and Wise, R. A. (1983). Ventral tegmental site of opiate reward: antagonism by a hydrophilic opiate receptor blocker. *Brain Research*, **258**, 105–8.

Broekkamp, C. L. E., Van den Bogaard, J. H., Heijnen, H. J., Rops, R. H., Cools, A. R., and Van Rossum, J. M. (1976). Separation of inhibiting and stimulating effects of morphine on self-stimulation behavior by intracerebral microinjections. *European Journal of Pharmacology*, **36**, 443–6.

Cabanac, M. (1971). Physiological role of pleasure. *Science*, **173**, 1103–7.

Church, W. H., Justice, J. B., Jr., and Byrd, L. D. (1987). Extracellular dopamine in rat striatum following uptake inhibition by cocaine, nomifensine and benztropine. *European Journal of Pharmacology*, **139**, 345–8.

Craig, W. (1918). Appetites and aversions as constituents of instincts. *Biological Bulletin*, **34**, 91–107.

Crow, T. J. (1971). The relation between electrical self-stimulation sites and catecholamine-containing neurones in the rat mesencephalon. *Experientia*, **27**, 662.

Davis, W. M. and Smith, S. G. (1975). Effect of haloperidol on (+)-amphetamine self-administration. *Journal of Pharmacy and Pharmacology*, **27**, 540–2.

Deutsch, J. A., Adams, D. W., and Metzner, R. J. (1964). Choice of intracranial stimulation as a function of delay between stimulations and strength of competing drive. *Journal of Comparative and Physiological Psychology*, **1964**, 241–3.

deWit, H. and Wise, R. A. (1977). Blockade of cocaine reinforcement in rats with the dopamine receptor blocker pimozide but not with the noradrenergic blockers phentolamine or phenoxybenzamine. *Canadian Journal of Psychology*, **31**, 195–203.

Di Chiara, G. and Imperato, A. (1985). Ethanol preferentially stimulates dopamine release in the nucleus accumbens of freely moving rats. *European Journal of Pharmacology*, **115**, 131–2.

Di Chiara, G. and Imperato, A. (1988). Drugs of abuse preferentially stimulate dopamine release in the mesolimbic system of freely moving rats. *Proceedings of the National Academy of Sciences (U.S.A.)*, **85**, 5274–8.

Edmonds, D. E. and Gallistel, C. R. (1974). Parametric analysis of brain stimulation reward in the rat: III. Effect of performance variables on the reward summation function. *Journal of Comparative and Physiological Psychology*, **87**, 876–83.

Ekman, P., Sorenson, E., and Friesen, W. (1969). Pan-cultural elements in facial displays of emotions. *Science*, **164**, 86–8.

Ettenberg, A. and Camp, C. H. (1986a). Haloperidol induces a partial reinforcement extinction effect in rats: Implications for a dopamine involvement in food reward. *Pharmacology Biochemistry and Behavior*, **25**, 813–21.

Ettenberg, A. and Camp, C. H. (1986b). A partial reinforcement extinction effect in water-reinforced rats intermittently treated with haloperidol. *Pharmacology Biochemistry and Behavior*, **25**, 1231–5.

Ettenberg, A., Koob, G. F., and Bloom, F. E. (1981). Response artifact in the measurement of neuroleptic-induced anhedonia. *Science*, **213**, 357–9.

Ettenberg, A., Pettit, H. O., Bloom, F. E., and Koob, G. F. (1982). Heroin and cocaine intravenous self-administration in rats: Mediation by separate neural systems. *Psychopharmacology*, **78**, 204–09.

Fibiger, H. C., Carter, D. A., and Phillips, A. G. (1976). Decreased intracranial self-stimulation after neuroleptics or 6-hydroxydopamine: Evidence for mediation by motor deficits rather than by reduced reward. *Psychopharmacology*, **47**, 21–7.

Fibiger, H. C., LePiane, F. G., Jakubovic, A., and Phillips, A. G. (1987). The role of dopamine in intracranial self-stimulation of the ventral tegmental area. *Journal of Neuroscience*, **7**, 3888–96.

Fischman, M. W., Schuster, C. R., Javaid, J., Hatano, Y., and Davis, J. (1985). Acute tolerance development to the cardiovascular and subjective effects of cocaine. *Journal of Pharmacology and Experimental Therapeutics*, **235**, 677–82.

Fouriezos, G. and Wise, R. A. (1976). Pimozide-induced extinction of intracranial self-stimulation: response patterns rule out motor or performance deficits. *Brain Research*, **103**, 377–80.

Fouriezos, G., Hansson, P., and Wise, R. A. (1978). Neuroleptic-induced attenuation of brain stimulation reward in rats. *Journal of Comparative and Physiological Psychology*, **92**, 661–71.

Franklin, K. B. J. and McCoy, S. N. (1979). Pimozide-induced extinction in rats: Stimulus control of responding rules out motor deficit. *Pharmacology Biochemistry and Behavior*, **11**, 71–5.

Gallistel, C. R. (1966). Motivating effects in self-stimulation. *Journal of Comparative and Physiological Psychology*, **62**, 95–101.

Gallistel, C. R. (1987). Determining the quantitative characteristics of a reward pathway. In *Biological determinants of reinforcement* (eds. R. M. Church, M. L. Commons, J. R. Stellar and A. R. Wagner), pp. 1–30. Lawrence Erlbaum Associates, Hillsdale, NJ.

Gallistel, C. R. and Davis, A. J. (1983). Affinity for the dopamine D2 receptor predicts neuroleptic potency in blocking the reinforcing effect of MFB stimulation. *Pharmacology Biochemistry and Behavior*, **19**, 867–72.

Gallistel, C. R. and Freyd, G. (1987). Quantitative determination of the effects of catecholaminergic agonists and antagonists on the rewarding efficacy of brain stimulation. *Pharmacology Biochemistry and Behavior*, **26**, 731–41.

Gallistel, C. R., Boytim, M., Gomita, Y., and Klebanoff, L. (1982). Does pimozide block the reinforcing effect of brain stimulation? *Pharmacology Biochemistry and Behavior*, **17**, 769–81.

Geary, N. and Smith, G. (1985). Pimozide decreases the positive reinforcing effect of sham fed sucrose in the rat. *Pharmacology Biochemistry and Behavior*, **22**, 787–90.

Gerber, G. J. and Stretch, R. (1975). Drug-induced reinstatement of extinguished self-administration behavior in monkeys. *Pharmacology Biochemistry and Behavior*, **3**, 1055–61.

Gerhardt, G. A., Pang, K., and Rose, G. M. (1987). In vivo electrochemical demonstration of the presynaptic actions of phencyclidine in rat caudate nucleus. *Journal of Pharmacology and Experimental Therapeutics*, **241**, 714–21.

Goeders, N. E., Lane, J. D., and Smith, J. E. (1984). Self-administration of methionine enkephalin into the nucleus accumbens. *Pharmacology Biochemistry and Behavior*, **20**, 451–55.

Gramling, S. E., Fowler, S. C., and Collins, K. R. (1984). Some effects of pimozide on nondeprived rats licking sucrose solutions in an anhedonia paradigm. *Pharmacology Biochemistry and Behavior*, **21**, 617–24.

Gray, T. and Wise, R. A. (1980). Effects of pimozide on lever-pressing behavior maintained on an intermittent reinforcement schedule. *Pharmacology Biochemistry and Behavior*, **12**, 931–35.

Grill, H. J. and Berridge, K. C. (1985). Taste reactivity as a measure of the neural control of palatability. In *Progress in psychobiology and physiological psychology* (eds. J. M. Sprague and A. N. Epstein), pp. 1–61. Academic Press, Orlando, FL.

Grill, H. J. and Norgren, R. (1978). The taste reactivity test. I. Mimetic responses to gustatory stimuli in neurologically normal rats. *Brain Research*, **143**, 263–79.

Guerin, G. F., Goeders, N. E., Dworkin, S. I., and Smith, J. E. (1984). Intracranial self-administration of dopamine into the nucleus accumbens. *Society for Neuroscience Abstracts*, **10**, 1072.

Hebb, D. O. (1955). Drives and the C.N.S. (conceptual nervous system). *Psychological Review*, **62**, 243–54.

Hebb, D. O. (1981). *Essay on mind*. Erlbaum, New York.

Helson, H. (1948). Adaptation level as a basis for a quantitative theory of frames of reference. *Psychological Review*, **55**, 297–313.

Henningfield, J. E. (1984). Behavioral pharmacology of cigarette smoking. *Advances in Behavioral Pharmacology*, **4**, 131–210.

Hoebel, B. G., Monaco, A. P., Hernandez, L., Aulisi, E. F., Stanley, B. G., and Lenard, L. (1983). Self-injection of amphetamine directly into the brain. *Psychopharmacology*, **81**, 158–63.

Hoffman, D. C. and Beninger, R. J. (1985). The effects of pimozide on the establishment of conditioned reinforcement as a function of the amount of conditioning. *Psychopharmacology*, **87**, 454–60.

Holmes, L. J., Bozarth, M. A., and Wise, R. A. (1983). Circling from intracranial morphine applied to the ventral tegmental area in rats. *Brain Research Bulletin*, **11**, 295–98.

Hornykiewicz, O. (1975). Parkinsonism induced by dopaminergic antagonists. In *Advances in neurology* (eds. D. B. Kalne, T. N. Chase and A. Barbeau), pp. 155–164. Raven Press, New York.

Hubner, C. B. and Koob, G. F. (1990). The ventral striatum plays a role in mediating cocaine and heroin self-administration in the rat. *Brain Research*, **508**, 20–9.

Imperato, A., Mulas, A., and Di Chiara, G. (1986). Nicotine preferentially stimulates dopamine release in the limbic system of freely moving rats. *European Journal of Pharmacology*, **132**, 337–8.

Izzard, C. E. (1971). *The face of emotion*. Academic Press, New York.

Johnson, S. W. and North, R. A. (1992). Opioids excite dopamine neurons by hyperpolarization of local interneurons. *Journal of Neuroscience*, **12**, 483–8.

Joyce, E. M. and Iversen, S. D. (1979). The effect of morphine applied locally to mesencephalic dopamine cell bodies on spontaneous motor activity in the rat. *Neuroscience Letters*, **14**, 207–12.

Kalivas, P. W., Widerlov, E., Stanley, D., Breese, G., and Prange, A. J. (1983). Enkephalin action on the mesolimbic system: A dopamine-dependent and a dopamine-independent increase in locomotor activity. *Journal of Pharmacology and Experimental Therapeutics*, **227**, 229–37.

Koechling, U., Colle, L. M., and Wise, R. A. (1988). Effects of SCH 23390 on latency and speed measures of deprivation-induced feeding. *Psychobiology*, **16**, 207–12.

Koob, G. F. and Bloom, F. E. (1988). Cellular and molecular mechanisms of drug dependence. *Science*, **242**, 715–23.

Kornetsky, C., Esposito, R. U., McLean, S., and Jacobson, J. O. (1979). Intracranial self-stimulation thresholds: A model for the hedonic effects of drugs of abuse. *Archives of General Psychiatry*, **36**, 289–92.

Lacey, M. G., Mercuri, N. B., and North, R. A. (1988). On the potassium conductance increase activated by GABA-B and dopamine D-2 receptors in rat substantia nigra neurones. *Journal of Physiology*, **401**, 437–53.

Lacey, M. G., Mercuri, N. B., and North, R. A. (1989). Two cell types in rat substantia nigra zona compacta distinguished by membrane properties and the actions of dopamine and opioids. *Journal of Neuroscience*, **9**, 1233–41.

LeBlanc, A. E., Kalant, H., and Gibbins, R. J. (1975). Acute tolerance to ethanol in the rat. *Psychopharmacologia*, **41**, 43–6.

Leeb, K., Parker, L., and Eikelboom, R. (1991). Effects of pimozide on the hedonic properties of sucrose: Analysis by the taste reactivity test. *Pharmacology Biochemistry and Behavior*, **39**, 895–901.

Levitt, A., Baltzer, J. H., Evers, T. M., Stilwell, D. J., and Furby, J. E. (1977). Morphine and shuttle-box self-stimulation in the rat: a model for euphoria. *Psychopharmacologia*, **54**, 307–11.

Liebman, J. (1982). Understanding neuroleptics: From 'anhedonia' to 'neuro-leptothesia'. *Behavioral and Brain Sciences*, **5**, 64–5.

Liebman, J. M. (1983). Discriminating between reward and performance: A critical review of intracranial self-stimulation methodology. *Neuroscience and Biobehavioral Reviews*, **7**, 45–72.

Liebman, J. M. and Butcher, L. L. (1973). Effects on self-stimulation behavior of drugs influencing dopaminergic neurotransmission. *Naunyn-Schmiedeberg's Archives of Pharmacology*, **277**, 305–18.

Liebman, J. M. and Butcher, L. L. (1974). Comparative involvement of dopamine and noradrenaline in rate-free self-stimulation in substantia nigra, lateral hypothalamus, and mesencephalic central gray. *Naunyn-Schmiedeberg's Archives of Pharmacology*, **284**, 167–94.

Lippa, A. S., Antelman, S. M., Fisher, A. E., and Canfield, D. R. (1973). Neurochemical mediation of reward: A significant role for dopamine. *Pharmacology Biochemistry and Behavior*, **1**, 23–8.

Ljungberg, T., Apicella, P., and Schultz, W. (1992). Responses of monkey dopamine neurons during learning of behavioral reactions. *Journal of Neurophysiology*, **67**, 145–63.

Mason, S. T., Beninger, R. J., Fibiger, H. C., and Phillips, A. G. (1980). Pimozide-induced suppression of responding: Evidence against a block of food reward. *Pharmacology Biochemistry and Behavior*, **12**, 917–23.

Miliaressis, E., Rompré, P.-P., Laviolette, L. P., Philippe, L., and Coulombe, D. (1986). The curve-shift paradigm in self-stimulation. *Physiology and Behavior*, **37**, 85–91.

Miller, R., Wickens, J. R., and Beninger, R. J. (1990). Dopamine D-1 and D-2 receptors in relation to reward and performance: A case for the D-1 receptor as a primary site of therapeutic action of neuroleptic drugs. *Progress in Neurobiology*, **34**, 143–83.

Ng Cheong Ton, J. M., Gerhardt, G. A., Friedemann, M., Etgen, A., Rose, G. M., Sharpless, N. S., and Gardner, E. L. (1988). The effects of Δ^9-tetrahydrocannabinol on potassium-evoked release of dopamine in the rat caudate nucleus: An in vivo electrochemical and in vivo dialysis study. *Brain Research*, **451**, 59–68.

Olds, J. (1956). Pleasure centers in the brain. *Scientific American*, **195**, 105–16.

Olds, M. E. (1982). Reinforcing effects of morphine in the nucleus accumbens. *Brain Research*, **237**, 429–40.

Olds, J. and Olds, M. E. (1965). Drives, rewards, and the brain. In *New directions in psychology* (ed. T. M. Newcombe), pp. 327–410. Holt, Rinehart and Winston, New York.

Phillips, A. G. and LePiane, F. G. (1980). Reinforcing effects of morphine microinjection into the ventral tegmental area. *Pharmacology Biochemistry and Behavior*, **12**, 965–8.

Phillips, A. G., Pfaus, J. G., and Blaha, C. D. (1991). Dopamine and motivated behavior: Insights provided by *in vivo* analyses. In *The mesolimbic dopamine system: From motivation to action* (eds. P. Willner and J. Scheel-Krüger), pp. 199–224. Wiley and Sons, New York.

Pickens, R. and Thompson, T. (1971). Characteristics of stimulant reinforcement. In *Stimulus properties of drugs* (eds. T. Thompson and R. Pickens), pp. 177–192. Appleton-Century-Crofts, New York.

Romo, R. and Schultz, W. (1990a). Dopamine neurons of the monkey midbrain: Contingencies of responses to active touch during self-initiated arm movements. *Journal of Neurophysiology*, **63**, 592–606.

Romo, R. and Schultz, W. (1990b). Dopamine neurons of the monkey midbrain: Contingencies of responses to stimuli eliciting immediate behavioral reactions. *Journal of Neurophysiology*, **63**, 607–24.

Rompré, P.-P. and Wise, R. A. (1989). Opioid-neuroleptic interaction in brain stem self-stimulation. *Brain Research*, **477**, 144–51.

Schneider, L. H., Davis, J. D., Watson, C. A., and Smith, G. P. (1990). Similar effect of raclopride and reduced sucrose concentration on the microstructure of sucrose sham feeding. *European Journal of Pharmacology*, **186**, 61–70.

Schneider, L. H., Gibbs, J., and Smith, G. P. (1986a). D-2 selective receptor antagonists suppress sucrose sham feeding in the rat. *Brain Research Bulletin*, **17**, 605–11.

Schneider, L. H., Gibbs, J., and Smith, G. P. (1986b). Selective D-1 or D-2 receptor antagonists inhibit sucrose sham feeding in rats. *Appetite*, **7**, 294–5.

Sherrington, C. S. (1906). *The integrative action of the nervous system*. Yale University Press, New Haven, CT.

Skinner, B. F. (1933). The rate of establishment of a discrimination. *Journal of General Psychology*, **9**, 302–50.

Skinner, B. F. (1937). Two types of conditioned reflex: A reply to Konorski and Miller. *Journal of General Psychology*, **16**, 272–9.

Skinner, B. F. (1938). *The behavior of organisms*. Appleton-Century-Crofts, New York.

Spragg, S. D. S. (1940). Morphine addiction in chimpanzees. *Comparative Psychology Monographs*, **15**, 1–132.

Spyraki, C., Fibiger, H. C., and Phillips, A. G. (1983). Attenuation of heroin reward in rats by disruption of the mesolimbic dopamine system. *Psychopharmacology*, **79**, 278–83.

Stellar, J. R., Kelley, A. E., and Corbett, D. (1983). Effects of peripheral and central dopamine blockade on lateral hypothalamic self-stimulation: Evidence for both reward and motor deficits. *Pharmacology Biochemistry and Behavior*, **18**, 433–42.

Stewart, J. (1984). Reinstatement of heroin and cocaine self-administration behavior in the rat by intracerebral application of morphine in the ventral tegmental area. *Pharmacology Biochemistry and Behavior*, **20**, 917–23.

Stewart, J. and de Wit, H. (1987). Reinstatement of drug-taking behavior as a method of assessing incentive motivational properties of drugs. In *Methods of assessing the reinforcing properties of abused drugs* (ed. M. A. Bozarth), pp. 211–27. Springer Verlag, New York.

Taylor, J. R. and Robbins, T. W. (1984). Enhanced behavioural control by conditioned reinforcers produced by intracerebral injections of *d*-amphetamine in the rat. *Psychopharmacology*, **84**, 405–12.

Thorndike, E. L. (1898). Animal intelligence: An experimental study of the associative processes in animals. *Psychological Monographs*, **8**, 1–109.

Thorndike, E. L. (1933). A theory of the action of the after-effects of a connection upon it. *Psychological Review*, **40**, 434–9.

Tombaugh, T. N., Tombaugh, J., and Anisman, H. (1979). Effects of dopamine receptor blockade on alimentary behaviors: Home cage food consumption, magazine training, operant acquisition, and performance. *Psychopharmacology*, **66**, 219–25.

Vaccarino, F. J., Bloom, F. E., and Koob, G. F. (1985). Blockade of nucleus accumbens opiate receptors attenuates intravenous heroin reward in the rat. *Psychopharmacology*, **86**, 37–42.

van der Kooy, D., Mucha, R. F., O'Shaughnessy, M., and Bucenieks, P. (1982). Reinforcing effects of brain microinjections of morphine revealed by conditioned place preference. *Brain Research*, **243**, 107–17.

van Ree, J. M. and de Wied, D. (1980). Involvement of neurohypophyseal peptides in drug-mediated adaptive responses. *Pharmacology Biochemistry and Behavior*, **13**(Suppl.1), 257–63.

Wasserman, E. M., Gomita, Y., and Gallistel, C. R. (1982). Pimozide blocks reinforcement but not priming from MFB stimulation in the rat. *Pharmacology Biochemistry and Behavior*, **17**, 783–7.

Weatherford, S. C., Greenberg, D., Gibbs, J., and Smith, G. P. (1990). The potency of D-1 and D-2 receptor antagonists is inversely related to the reward value of sham-fed corn oil and sucrose in rats. *Pharmacology Biochemistry and Behavior*, **37**, 317–23.

Welzl, H., Kuhn, G., and Huston, J. P. (1989). Self-administration of small amounts of morphine through glass micropipettes into the ventral tegmental area of the rat. *Neuropharmacology*, **28**, 1017–23.

West, T. E. G. and Wise, R. A. (1988). Nucleus accumbens opioids facilitate brain stimulation reward. *Society for Neuroscience Abstracts*, **14**, 1102.

Wilson, M. C. and Schuster, C. R. (1972). The effects of chlorpromazine on psychomotor stimulant self-administration in the rhesus monkey. *Psychopharmacologia*, **26**, 115–26.

Wise, R. A. (1978). Neuroleptic attenuation of intracranial self-stimulation: Reward or performance deficits? *Life Sciences*, **22**, 535–42.

Wise, R. A. (1980). Action of drugs of abuse on brain reward systems. *Pharmacology Biochemistry and Behavior*, **13**(1), 213–23.

Wise, R. A. (1982). Neuroleptics and operant behavior: The anhedonia hypothesis. *The Behavioral and Brain Sciences*, **5**, 39–87.

Wise, R. A. (1985). The anhedonia hypothesis: Mark III. *The Behavioral and Brain Sciences*, **8**, 178–86.

Wise, R. A. (1989). The brain and reward. In *The neuropharmacological basis of reward* (eds. J. M. Liebman and S. J. Cooper), pp. 377–424. Oxford University Press.

Wise, R. A. (1990). Drugs against pleasure. *Current Contents*, **22**, 20.

Wise, R. A. and Bozarth, M. A. (1987). A psychomotor stimulant theory of addiction. *Psychological Review*, **94**, 469–92.

Wise, R. A. and Colle, L. (1984). Pimozide attenuates free-feeding: Best scores analysis reveals a motivational deficit. *Psychopharmacology*, **84**, 446–51.

Wise, R. A. and Raptis, L. (1986). Effects of naloxone and pimozide on initiation and maintenance measures of free feeding. *Brain Research*, **368**, 62–8.

Wise, R. A. and Rompré, P.-P. (1989). Brain dopamine and reward. *Annual Review of Psychology*, **40**, 191–225.

Wise, R. A. and Schwartz, H. V. (1981). Pimozide attenuates acquisition of lever pressing for food in rats. *Pharmacology Biochemistry and Behavior*, **15**, 655–6.

Wise, R. A., Murray, A., and Bozarth, M. A. (1990). Bromocriptine self-administration and bromocriptine-reinstatement of cocaine-trained and heroin-trained lever-pressing in rats. *Psychopharmacology*, **100**, 355–60.

Wise, R. A., Spindler, J., deWit, H., and Gerber, G. J. (1978a). Neuroleptic-induced 'anhedonia' in rats: Pimozide blocks the reward quality of food. *Science*, **201**, 262–4.

Wise, R. A., Spindler, J., and Legault, L. (1978b). Major attenuation of food reward with performance sparing doses of pimozide in the rat. *Canadian Journal of Psychology*, **32**, 77–85.

Wise, R. A., Yokel, R. A., and deWit, H. (1976). Both positive reinforcement and conditioned taste aversion from amphetamine and from apomorphine in rats. *Science*, **191**, 1273–5.

Wood, P. L. (1982). Actions of GABAergic agents on dopamine metabolism in the nigrostriatal pathway of the rat. *Journal of Pharmacology and Experimental Therapeutics*, **222**, 674–9.

Woolverton, W. L., Goldberg, L., I., and Ginos, J. (1984). Intravenous self-administration of dopamine receptor agonists by rhesus monkeys. *Journal of Pharmacology and Experimental Therapeutics*, **230**, 678–83.

Xenakis, S. and Sclafani, A. (1981). The effects of pimozide on the consumption of a palatable saccharin-glucose solution in the rat. *Pharmacology Biochemistry and Behavior*, **15**, 435–42.

Xenakis, S. and Sclafani, A. (1982). The dopaminergic mediation of a sweet reward in normal and VMH hyperphagic rats. *Pharmacology Biochemistry and Behavior*, **16**, 293–302.

Yokel, R. A. and Wise, R. A. (1975). Increased lever-pressing for amphetamine after pimozide in rats: Implications for a dopamine theory of reward. *Science*, **187**, 547–9.

Yokel, R. A. and Wise, R. A. (1976). Attenuation of intravenous amphetamine reinforcement by central dopamine blockade in rats. *Psychopharmacology*, **48**, 311–8.

Yokel, R. A. and Wise, R. A. (1978). Amphetamine-type reinforcement by dopaminergic agonists in the rat. *Psychopharmacology*, **58**, 289–96.

Zellner, D. A., Berridge, K. C., and Ternes, J. W. (1985). Rats learn to like the taste of morphine. *Behavioral Neuroscience*, **99**, 290–300.

Zetterstrom, T., Sharp, T., Marsden, C. A., and Ungerstedt, U. (1983). *In vivo* measurement of dopamine and its metabolites by intracerebral dialysis: Changes after d-amphetamine. *Journal of Neurochemistry*, **41**, 1769–73.

11

The appetite for nicotine

David M. Warburton

INTRODUCTION

Smoking is one of the most peculiar habits adopted by man. People are the only animals who take smoke into their lungs for pleasure. Certainly, inhalation of smoke into the lungs is contrary to the normal use of those organs. One of the most widespread smoke inhalation practices is the use of tobacco leaves.

Tobacco-producing plants (*Nicotiana*) occur naturally in South and North America, Australia, on several islands of the South Pacific and in Africa. Not all of the 64 Nicotiana species synthesize nicotine; some species of the genus produce nicotine in relatively large quantities, some only in small amounts, and others not at all. So it is only a dozen or so of the 64 species which have been cultivated and only the two highest nicotine yielders (*Nicotiana rustica* and *Nicotiana tabacum*), that have achieved wide dissemination throughout Indian America (Wilbert, 1987) and the rest of the World.

From the arrival of Christopher Columbus in the Americas, in 1492, it was only 50 years to the cultivation of tobacco in Europe and only 100 years until it was introduced to Japan by the Portuguese. We know that Zen monks were using tobacco as a gift at this time. The diary of the Zen Abbott of the Rokuonji Monastery in Kyoto, in 1593, records that he 'went to Shuyo's cloister in the evening; brought tobacco with me' (Collcutt, Jansen, and Kamakura, 1988).

How did this appetite for nicotine develop and why was this strange habit of puffing on dried leaves and inhaling the smoke adopted in the Americas, Europe, Asia, and indeed in all parts of the world?

Some answers to that question will be given in this chapter.

APPETITE AND SATIETY FOR NICOTINE

Appetites are the dispositions to take in a substance in whatever materials contain it, for example hunger is the specific disposition to take nourishment (Booth, 1981). Satiation is the reduction of such a behavioural tendency of intake behaviour. The innate appetites and satieties are few, elicited by extreme conditions, such as gross salt deficiency, or by stimuli poorly related to nutrient supply, such as sweetness (Booth, 1981). Most other appetites and satieties are acquired. This chapter considers the acquired appetite for nicotine and the satiation of that appetite. The major focus will be on cigarette smoking, the most common method for taking in nicotine.

Appetites derive from external cues and a context from internal bodily cues, some of which signal a deficit or excess. Attribution of causation into internal and external categories is doomed because the sets of cues interact. External and internal cues normally act in combination to elicit preferences or aversions. Thus, appetite or satiety signals are those that give appetizing or satiating patterns of internal and external cues their control over behaviour (Booth, 1981).

Four processes can be identified as underlying the satiety and appetite signals that form the desire and satisfaction of that desire (see Blundell, Hill, and Rodgers, 1989). For food, these factors are cognitive, sensory, post-intake, and post-absorptive (see Fig. 11.1). This classification will be used to demonstrate how all of these factors influence the desire to smoke, before smoking and during the early and late phases of satiety.

Cognitive factors represent the beliefs held by the smoker about the properties of cigarettes. Sensory effects are generated through the smell of the tobacco and the smell, taste, and temperature of the cigarette smoke. It is likely that these factors could prevent smoking or stop the smoking process and inhibit smoking in the short term. Post-smoking processes include a number of possible consequences. The post-intake phase includes those effects arising from the action of nicotine and smoke constituents on the lungs. In this chapter, these effects will be included in the sensory effects. The post-absorptive processes include the effects of nicotine and its metabolites after absorption into the blood system. It would include nicotine's actions on the brain as well as the release of hormones and the chemicals (e.g. glucose) which are released by hormones.

Smoking a cigarette has the capacity to take away the desire for a cigarette and further desire to smoke is inhibited for a period. It is likely that the mechanisms which are involved in terminating smoking and in maintaining inhibition range from those which occur when a cigarette is initially experienced, the repeated sensory stimulation, the absorbed nicotine, and its effects on the body.

Satiety is not an instantaneous event, but occurs over a period of time. Therefore, it is useful to distinguish the phases of the satiety process and associate these with different mechanisms. The approximate timing of these phases is shown in Fig. 11.1.

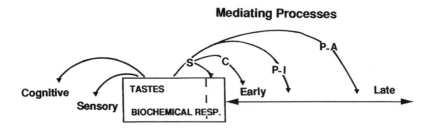

Mediating Processes

Fig. 11.1 Illustration of the major components of satisfaction: S, sensory; C, cognitive; p-I, post-ingestive; P-A, post-absorptive; and postulated changes in motivation (perceived) accompanying smoking.

Of course, the processes will overlap and their effects will be integrated to produce a conjoint effect. For example, cognitive and sensory aspects may act proactively, so that the sight and smell of a cigar, which have become associated with the effects of nicotine (see Chapter 7 on conditioning processes in drug use by Glautier, this volume), would augment the desire to smoke.

Therefore, in assessing the overall effect of individual cigarettes on smoking, it is necessary to take into account *both* the facilitatory and inhibitory actions. As the overall satiating capacity of cigarettes will depend upon facilitatory and inhibitory effects, measures of a number of variables before, during, and after smoking, for example temporal profiles of motivation (e.g. wanting a cigarette) and behaviour (e.g. smoking) must be considered in order to provide a complete description of appetite.

COGNITIVE FACTORS

Cognitive factors represent the beliefs held by the smoker about the properties of cigarettes (as represented by pack and brand image) and about their effect upon the smoker. They also constitute the context which may inhibit or facilitate use.

I have not been able to find any published studies on the effects of beliefs about products influencing nicotine use. Anecdotally, it is clear from conversations that smokers have views about products which influence their choice, 'such-and-such a brand is rough', etc. In addition, it is said that pack colour can influence beliefs about nicotine yields. In the drug literature, capsule colour has a significant effect on the expected effect of a drug (Jacobs and Nordan, 1979) and so this claim is plausible.

More interesting are the effects of social context on nicotine use. Smoking motive surveys have identified the importance of the social situation on smoking behaviour (McKennell, 1970).

In a study of smoking in social groups, Foss (1972) found that the majority of smokers report smoking most often in small groups or at parties and other social gatherings. In a follow-up study, Glad and Adesso (1976) recorded the number of cigarettes smoked, the number of minutes spent smoking, the number of puffs taken and the number of flicks of the cigarette.

Both light and heavy smokers increased the number of cigarettes, puffs, flicks, and time spent smoking in social groups. However, only light smokers were induced to smoke under conditions of behavioural contagion, which is most easily explained in terms of a ceiling effect for heavy smokers. Thus, this study represents clear-cut evidence for the view that some people smoke mainly because those around them are smoking.

The effect of social influence is even found when subjects watch a film (Surawy, Stepney, and Cox, 1985). While watching a video containing shots of people smoking and in the ten-minute period immediately afterwards, smokers smoked significantly more than while watching a non-smoking video; the number of cigarettes smoked while watching the smoking video was over 40 per cent higher, and their rate of puffing 20 per cent greater, than while watching the non-smoking video. This experiment demonstrates that social cues have a clear effect on the behaviour of smokers.

The dependence of smoking on social cues contradicts one of the criteria of the Surgeon General's Report for nicotine being addictive (USDHHS, 1988), that nicotine use is stereotypic. Substance use is stereotyped when the behavioural repertoire is narrowed and use has come under the control of withdrawal symptoms. It implies less flexible use, more an activity done for its own sake and less an activity with a social meaning (Orford, 1985). However, it is very clear that smoking has definite social meanings.

THE SENSORY AND OTHER POST-INTAKE EFFECTS OF SMOKING

As previously stated, sensory effects are generated through the smell of the tobacco and the smell, taste, and temperature of the cigarette smoke. It is likely that the smell of tobacco could prime smoking, while the remaining factors could prevent nicotine intake or bring intake to a halt and inhibit further nicotine intake in the short term. In this respect, nicotine use also shares a close affinity with other ingesting behaviours, such as eating, with pleasurable sensory effects.

The sensory pleasure of smoking occurs because it stimulates taste and smell. However, the sense of smell plays only a small role in smoking and the term 'taste' is used imprecisely when applied to cigarettes. The traditional taste qualities, such as bitter, salty, sour and sweet, play little role in the sensory impact of tobacco smoke. The one sensory attribute which predominates is stimulation of the common chemical sense. The term common chemical sense refers to the irritancy that can be felt in the nose, mouth, and throat, via the sensory nerves. Cain (1976) has discussed nicotine's ability to stimulate the common chemical sense—a property which it has in common with foods, such as spicy dishes. In this way, stimulation of the chemical senses makes tobacco use more like chili pepper use than drug use.

Consequently, it has been argued that nicotine use may not only be for obtaining plasma levels of nicotine, but also for sensory stimulation of the airways (Chamberlain and Higenbottam, 1985). Evidence from the work of West and Kranzler (1990) indicates that pure nicotine, injected into a person, does not satisfy the desire for cigarettes and it is a conclusion from his work and others that the sensory aspects are a significant part of the smoking habit. These sensory characteristics are important discriminators of nicotine use from the use of drugs such as heroin or cocaine. The latter do not have sensory pleasure properties, but produce dramatic pharmacological effects. The role of sensory effects with these drugs is limited to the conditioning processes, which act proactively to initiate use.

In summary, an important aspect of nicotine use is its sensory effects. While they are pleasurable in their own right, it is also worth anticipating the later section on nicotine control, in which it will be argued that the taste, smell, and irritation of nicotine control the puffing on the cigarette. In addition, they probably also serve as signals of the impending psychological effects from the absorbed nicotine and so to predict the absorptive consequences of nicotine.

POST-ABSORPTIVE FACTORS

The factors include the effects of nicotine and its metabolites after absorption across the alveolar wall into the blood system. It would include actions on the brain as well as the release of hormones and chemicals, such as glucose, which are released by hormones.

Nicotine does not have the pharmacological salience of drugs such as heroin and cocaine, in comparison with the strong sensory effects. Thus, many smokers are surprised to discover that even some of the larger pharmacological effects that occur, like increased heart rate, are effects of nicotine. It has taken relatively subtle testing to demonstrate its effects on mood and cognition.

Smoking and mood

The calming effects of smoking are the day-by-day experience of many smokers (McKennell, 1970; McKennell, 1973; Tomkins, 1966; Tomkins, 1968). Surveys have found that 80 per cent of smokers say that they smoke more when they are worried, 75 per cent say that they light up a cigarette when they are angry, and 60 per cent feel that smoking cheers them up (Russell *et al.*, 1974; Warburton and Wesnes, 1978).

However, anyone who has experienced both alcohol and nicotine would agree that the calming effects of nicotine are mild in comparison with alcohol. For example, Kozlowski *et al.* (1989) did a retrospective comparison of pleasure from cigarettes with other substances. He asked some problem users to compare smoking with their own problem substance. Of the problem users of alcohol, 57.5 per cent said that their pleasure from cigarettes was less than that from alcohol, 28.7 per cent said that it was similar, and only 13.8 per cent rated smoking as giving more pleasure than alcohol. Of the cocaine users, only 2.7 per cent said that their pleasure from cigarettes was greater, 1.4 per cent said that their pleasure was similar, 96 per cent said that their pleasure was less strong. These data show clearly that smokers do not experience cigarettes as strongly pleasurable, like cocaine and alcohol, but only as mildly pleasurable.

In our own work (Warburton, 1988a), we compared the pleasurable stimulation and pleasurable relaxation from different substances and activities. Alcohol, amphetamines, cocaine, heroin, marijuana, and sex were significantly more stimulating than tobacco. Sleeping tablets and tranquillizers were significantly less stimulating than tobacco, while there were no statistically reliable differences between tobacco, coffee, or chocolate, in terms of pleasurable stimulation. On the pleasurable relaxation dimension, alcohol, heroin, sex, sleeping tablets, and tranquillizers were significantly more relaxing than tobacco. Amphetamine, cocaine, and coffee were significantly less relaxing than tobacco, while there were no statistically reliable differences between tobacco and chocolate in terms of pleasurable relaxation.

In laboratory studies, we assessed the mood effects of nicotine with visual analogue scales (Warburton, Revell, and Walters, 1988). Puff-by-puff, subjects reported that they became calmer, more tranquil, more sociable, more friendly, more contented, more relaxed, and happier.

Non-nicotine cigarettes produced no improvements, suggesting that the effects were due to nicotine.

The mood changes were correlated with plasma nicotine so that, as plasma nicotine increased throughout the cigarette, the mood changes increased (Warburton, 1988b). When a second cigarette was given 30 minutes later, (that is, no nicotine deprivation), the pre-smoking mood level was below that achieved at the end of the first cigarette changes, but during smoking, it increased until it was above the level that was achieved at the end of the first cigarette.

This pattern is precisely what one would expect if nicotine was responsible for the mood improvement. With the first cigarette, the mood improved as the nicotine levels increased. During the 30-minute interval, the plasma levels of nicotine would have decreased as the drug was rapidly metabolized. After 30 minutes, the serum nicotine values would not have returned to zero and, at the end of the second cigarette, the levels would have exceeded those achieved after the first cigarette.

Other studies with no nicotine deprivation have shown that nicotine abstinence was not required for the effects. In an earlier paper, Pomerleau, Turk, and Fertig (1984) found that anxiety, as measured by the Profile of Mood States Questionnaire, could be generated using anagrams. The anxiety was markedly decreased in all subjects after smoking their own nicotine-containing cigarettes in comparison with smoking non-nicotine cigarettes, showing the beneficial effects of nicotine on mood.

An important part of the study was that subjects were only deprived of cigarettes for half an hour prior to the study and in our own studies *ad lib* smoking was allowed prior to the test sessions and improvement was again found. Thus, the results could not have been due to a reversal of nicotine withdrawal.

Similar findings of nicotine calming people down have been found in real-life situations. It dampened down the body's stress response and calmed people down when they were watching a video showing horrible mutilation scenes (Gilbert and Hagen, 1980). It reduced the annoyance (Woodson et al., 1986) and the physiological stress response to high-intensity noises (Marlatt, 1979; Woodson et al., 1986). Nicotine enabled smokers to tolerate higher levels of electric shock than when they had not been allowed to smoke beforehand (Schachter, 1978). Smoking even helped smokers to be less angry when they knew that they were being cheated by another player in a gambling game (Cherek, 1981).

If the beliefs of smokers and the laboratory findings are true, then nicotine is an important resource for smokers for reducing their feelings of anxiety and anger (Warburton, Revell and Walters, 1988). Certainly, people increase their nicotine intake when experiencing stressors (Ashton and Stepney, 1982; Frith, 1971; Schachter, 1978; Warburton, 1987).

It is not surprising that smokers miss nicotine when they stop smoking. More anxiety and anger are two of the common complaints of people who cut down or give up (Shiffman and Jarvik, 1976). Some become so nasty that their partners complain that they cannot live with them any more (Schachter, 1978).

Nicotine and performance

Surveys have indicated that the majority of smokers believe that nicotine helps them process information more efficiently, by aiding thought and concentration (Russell, Peto, and Patel, 1974; Warburton and Wesnes, 1978). Clearly, the normal person is continuously engaged in processing information throughout their waking day. The belief of smokers, that smoking improves their information processing throughout the day, argues against the idea that there is tolerance to this effect of nicotine.

One type of performance test is the rapid visual information processing test in which a series of digits are presented at a rapid rate by computer, and subjects are required to detect certain specified three-digit sequences. Measures of both the speed and the accuracy of detection are made, in order to assess the ability of the subjects to sustain their attention.

We have found that smoking after ten hours' deprivation produced improved performance in terms of both speed and accuracy (Wesnes and Warburton, 1984a). Of course, these results could merely be a reversal of a withdrawal effect. Accordingly, we tested the same smokers after deprivation for only one hour and after ten hours' deprivation. There was no difference in the improved performance when the subjects were smoking after one or ten hours' deprivation, that is, there was no evidence of short-term tolerance.

In another test of tolerance, we tested oral doses of nicotine which were given to non-smokers. The taste of the nicotine was masked by capsaicin which was placed on both the active and placebo tablets. Then the subjects performed the rapid visual information processing task (Wesnes and Warburton, 1984b). Doses of nicotine produced a performance improvement of both speed and accuracy in non-smokers which closely resembled that produced by smoking in smokers. This finding provides strong evidence that nicotine plays the major role in the improvements in focussed attention tasks that are produced by smoking. The use of capsaicin as an irritancy control argues against the performance improvements being due to sensory arousal.

The improvement in the performance of non-smokers contradicts the idea that the improvement was only a reversal of nicotine withdrawal. This laboratory finding matches the beliefs of smokers that smoking during the working day helps them think and concentrate better (Russell *et al.*, 1974; Warburton and Wesnes, 1978). Studies in the workplace have supported the idea of smoking being important for work. A survey of 2000 union representatives and managers in business, industry, and government revealed that smoking in the workplace can lift employee productivity and certainly does not retard it (Response Analysis Corporation, 1984). A similar survey among bank credit managers found smokers were 2.5 per cent more effective at their work (Dahl *et al.*, 1984). A study of academic performance among university students revealed better examination marks and essay marks for smokers compared with non-smokers (Warburton *et al.*, 1984).

Nicotine not only helps young, healthy people, but can also benefit the elderly who are suffering from dementia. Doses of nicotine produced a dose-related improvement in performance in the detection of signals and reaction time in the rapid visual information processing task so that they approached the performance of the normal elderly. A comparison of smokers with non-smokers found no differences in the effect of nicotine, which was in accord with the results using healthy volunteers (Jones *et al.*, 1992; Sahakian *et al.*, 1989).

The evidence from this section is consistent in both the healthy young and impaired Alzheimer patients. Nicotine improves processing capacity and the results do not depend on deprivation from nicotine and so the effects cannot be attributed to the reversal of withdrawal. More recently, studies have shown that nicotine-containing cigarettes improve memory directly and via attention (Colrain *et al.*, 1992; Rusted and Warburton, 1992; Warburton *et al.*, 1992).

Functional model

Nicotine use can be seen as a purposive activity, with many functions in everyday life, which has important psychological benefits. Consequently, nicotine use is not an irrational behaviour but the behaviour is adopted because it enables users to effectively enhance their lives, at a personal and inter-personal level. It can be seen as a psychological resource that the individual uses for control of his or her psychological state (Warburton, 1987; 1988*b*).

Controllable, predictable effects are more pleasurable than effects which are produced without control (Warburton, 1990*b*). In fact, uncontrollable events can very often be aversive, while identical effects which are produced under the control of the person, can be pleasurable. All aspects of smoking contribute to this feeling that smokers have that they are in control of their own lives—a feeling that is very important to the smoker (see Warburton, Revell, and Thompson, 1991).

NICOTINE CONTROL

In order to compare the variety of cigarette products on the market they are smoked in machines to standard values. However, smokers do not smoke in the same unvarying way as machines. The intake of nicotine from any brand of cigarette by individuals may span a considerable range of deliveries and, with the reduction in yields, smoking patterns of the smoker may change in order to compensate for any alteration in nicotine delivery shown under machine-smoked conditions.

This compensation could take the form of increased cigarette consumption, increased smoke generation (including puffing) and smoke manipulation (including inhaling). Thus, smoking lower nicotine yield brands will not necessarily be safer, because compensation will result in levels of exposure to smoke which the smoker had not anticipated.

Consumption

Increasing the number smoked is the most obvious way for smokers to compensate for lower yield. Evidence from the brand switching studies in a major epidemiological study conducted by Garfinkel (1979) suggests that reported cigarette consumption shows only a very small increase, if any, when subjects switch to lower yielding products. Similarly, Stepney (1980), for instance, showed that, based on laboratory studies, a reduction in machine-estimated yield of about 20 to 30 per cent only led to a small increase in consumption of up to 5 per cent.

The problem for the smoker is the increase in use. In one study, smokers were switched from their usual brand (1.34 mg of nicotine and 18 mg tar average) to cigarettes of less than 0.3 mg nicotine and 4 mg of tar (Russell, Wilson, Patel, Cole, and Feyerabend, 1973). The consumption of the group increased by 17 per cent after the switch, but, in terms of cigarette yield, subjects would have needed to increase their use from 11 cigarettes to over 53 if they did not change their smoking behaviour in any way.

Smoke generation

Changes in smoke generation occur by modifying the flow of smoke into the mouth. In a series of studies, Creighton (Creighton and Lewis,

1978; Creighton, Noble, and Whewell, 1978) recorded the pattern of smoking in terms of number of puffs, puff interval, puff volume, and puff shape. Smoking pattern data were recorded on a smoking analyser, which measures and records the pressures and flows in a cigarette holder connected to a pair of transducers. Both the pressure and flow signals are recorded on computer disk, together with the volume and duration of each puff, the pressure used to draw each puff, and the interval between puffs (see Fig. 11.2).

In order to provide a more detailed, comprehensive, and accurate analysis of smoke delivery during human smoking, machines have been developed which will exactly duplicate human smoking profiles from the pressure and flow signals (Creighton *et al.*, 1978). The particulate matter in the smoke drawn from the cigarettes, smoked by the puff duplicator, is passed through a filter pad and the nicotine delivery can be estimated.

Creighton and Lewis (1978) found that there were marked inter-individual differences and the patterns did not conform to the standard variables of the smoking machine. The consequence of these variations in smoking pattern was a divergence of the actual nicotine deliveries from the smoking machine yields. For example, a group of male smokers derived an average of 2.25 mg of nicotine and a group of female smokers obtained an average of 1.4 mg of nicotine from a product with a machine-estimated yield of 1.0 mg nicotine.

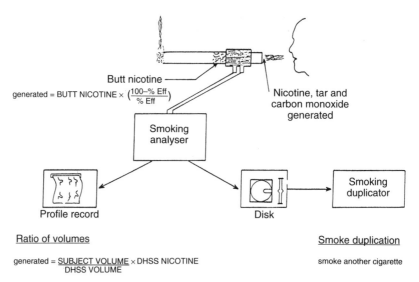

Fig. 11.2 Methods of estimating subject nicotine levels.

Smoke manipulation

A crucial part of cigarette smoking is further manipulation of the smoke, which usually includes inhalation. In fact, smoking might now be more appropriately described as a three-stage process, because the puff and the inhalation are usually separated by a variable time period during which a significant amount of the puff may be lost from the mouth—waste smoke.

About 90 per cent of cigarette smokers say that they inhale to some extent and 77 per cent say that they usually inhale 'a lot' or 'a fair amount' (US Department of Health, Education, and Welfare, 1979). Since nicotine from tobacco smoke is easily absorbed by the lungs, it follows that a high percentage of the mouth nicotine is made available for absorption by inhalation. Smoke inhalation results in very efficient absorption of nicotine and the large percentage of smokers who do inhale provides evidence that an aim of smoking is to obtain nicotine.

In order to measure the actual nicotine intake by the smoker, one has either to measure nicotine or its metabolites in a body fluid (blood, urine, saliva, or expired air), or one has to calculate the figure as the difference between delivery and wasted plus exhaled nicotine. The latter measures indicate that over 95 per cent of nicotine is retained in the body.

A good example of compensation by changes in inhalation is an eleven-week cross-over study in which smokers switch from their own 1.4 mg nicotine brand with 18 mg of tar to 0.6 mg cigarettes with 6.5 mg of tar, that is, a decrease of 64 per cent in machine-estimated tar yield (Ashton, Stepney, and Thompson, 1979). They found that the plasma carboxyhaemoglobin levels, an index of inhalation, were only 19 per cent lower after the switch, indicating increased inhalation. In addition, consumption was increased significantly and 24-hour values for urinary nicotine and cotinine excretion showed that the subjects were obtaining just as much nicotine from the reduced-yield cigarette as from their own.

In summary, smokers can control their nicotine intake by smoke manipulation. Clearly, the smokers are sensitive in some way to nicotine yield and control inhalation accordingly.

Control mechanisms

Clearly, the machine-estimated yield can give a totally misleading picture of the nicotine entering a smoker's plasma. Therefore, it is important that we understand the control mechanisms for this smoke generation and smoke manipulation.

In an attempt to understand the mechanism or mechanisms that are involved in nicotine control, we presented a series of cigarettes for which there was co-varying yield of total particulate matter ('tar') and nicotine. Then, we examined the changes in the amount of nicotine presented to the smoker's mouth, from the analysis of the nicotine that was deposited in the cigarette filter (Warburton and Wesnes, 1984). Nicotine changed systematically when smokers were presented with cigarettes of co-varying yield. As yield increased, nicotine presented also increased, but the best-fitting curve was exponential with an exponent of 0.50 and the constant of -0.024 (virtually zero) indicates that it is a reasonable assumption that the curve passed through the origin. An exponent less than one means that puffing increased much more for increments in yield at low levels than at high.

Exponents in the range 0.5–0.8 are found for the relation between subjective experience and the physical intensity of taste and odour stimuli. It seemed a reasonable hypothesis that puffing intensity could be controlled by the flavour impact of the cigarette smoke. In order to obtain support for this idea, we presented a series of cigarettes of differing yields to smokers and obtained their subjective estimates of the flavour of the cigarette smoke after four puffs by the technique of magnitude estimation (Warburton, Wesnes, and Revell, 1984). The subjective estimates of flavour were plotted against machine-smoked nicotine yield. The best-fitting curve for the subjective sensory experience of the cigarette flavour was exponential with an exponent of 0.51. There was no consistent relation between estimates of flavour and tar levels. This argues for a relation between nicotine and flavour.

We have investigated this relationship, using products matched for nicotine yields (1.4–1.7 mg), but varying in tar (17 mg and 10 mg), and a third product with 0.8 mg nicotine and 9 mg tar (Kochhar and Warburton, 1990). A puff-by-puff analysis showed that there was linear increase over successive puffs for mouth and throat impact, intensity of flavour, and roughness for all three cigarettes. However, the magnitude of these intensity-related characteristics was related to the nicotine yields of the products rather than to the tar yields. This finding argued for nicotine being crucial for estimates of flavour.

In summary, there was an analogous exponential relation between flavour and nicotine yield and between puffing intensity and nicotine yield. The similarity of the function suggests that cigarette puffing is under the control of the taste receptors in the buccal cavity which are sensitive to nicotine.

Smoke manipulation

Given that nicotine impact is an important cue for smoke generation, it would not be surprising if oral cues were also part of the mechanism that controlled smoke manipulation, especially inhalation. In order to investigate the involvement of mouth cues in judgments of cigarette strength, three cigarettes with varying nicotine (1.3 mg, 1.1 mg, and 0.9 mg), but constant tar (0.8 mg), were made with and without menthol (Warburton, Wesnes, and Revell, 1984). Strong mentholation desensitizes the taste receptors in the mouth and so minimizes oral cues.

These six cigarettes were ranked for strength, 'its physiological effect', by subjects, with and without inhalation. There was clear evidence that subjects could distinguish the three cigarettes when they were given both oral cues and cues from the inhaled nicotine. There was clearly no differentiation of the products in two non-inhale conditions, showing that oral cues are not sufficient for differentiating the strength of the cigarettes. These two pieces of evidence point strongly to physiological effects of absorbed nicotine being the cues for strength discrimination.

There was some discrimination in the menthol-inhale condition, which supports the idea of differentiation by the effects of nicotine after inhalation from the mouth. However, the discrimination was not as good as with non-mentholated products, which suggests that nicotine was producing some sensory cues between the mouth and the lungs, perhaps due to stimulation of the trigeminal nerve receptors in the respiratory tract. Menthol would block these receptors in the menthol-inhale condition and would allow only internal physiological cues to be used for judging strength. The nature of this internal mechanism, which we will call the 'nicotinostat', will be considered next.

It is obvious that a necessary condition for controlled, self-administration of a drug is the ability to discriminate the level of drug in the body. In a study which was designed in order to gather direct evidence for this 'nicotinostat', we gave subjects nicotine tablets to pre-load them with nicotine and stimulate the 'nicotinostat', prior to smoking a 0.6 mg nicotine cigarette. The oral absorption from tablets containing 1.5 mg nicotine gave venous levels of 10.5 ng/ml at pH 9. Puffing behaviour, butt nicotine, and exhaled carbon monoxide were measured. No differences were seen in puffing variables or butt nicotine levels for nicotine tablet and placebo conditions. However, there was a significant reduction of end-tidal carbon monoxide after the subjects had received a nicotine tablet, indicating reduced inhalation. Clearly, the smokers were reducing their nicotine intake according to a nicotinostat sensitive to plasma nicotine levels.

The interesting question is how this mechanism operates and where it is located. There is evidence, from drug discrimination studies in animals, that one cue is based on cholinergic action (Rosecrans and Meltzer, 1977). Animals show strong discrimination of nicotine from saline which could be blocked by intraventricular injections of nicotinic, cholinergic antagonists and mimicked by intraventricular injections of nicotine agonists (Romano, Goldstein, and Jewell, 1981). Thus, there are some cholinergic systems in the brain which are sensitive to the absorbed nicotine, but their location is a matter for speculation. One possible mechanism is the ascending cholinergic pathways to the cortex, and there is abundant evidence in the biofeedback literature showing that people can learn to discriminate their states of cortical arousal.

Summary

From the evidence which has been discussed in this section and previous sections, it is clear that the appetite for nicotine depends on the integration of a variety of cues. It is apparent that nicotine intake is not merely restoration of a biochemical deficit. It does not explain why people smoke as they do, varying their intake according to the situation. Smoking cannot always be classified as regulatory or non-regulatory. The evidence from titration studies indicates that down-regulation is very precise so that people can avoid the adverse effects of too much nicotine, but up-regulation is often only partial.

NICOTINE USE—AN ACQUIRED APPETITE

In this Section, I will consider the acquisition of the appetite for nicotine. Studies of the history of smoking among young people show that there is linear increase in the early teens of the number of adolescents who smoke (e.g. Balding, 1987; Dobbs and Marsh, 1985; Stanton, Silva, and Oei, 1989). The intriguing question is: Why should it occur at this point in early adolescence and why should it now be 1.64 times more likely in girls than boys?

It is clear that experimental smoking and nicotine exposure at an early age do not increase the probability of becoming a daily smoker by age 15 years (Stanton, Silva, and Oei, 1989). Daily users at age 15 years were equally as likely to come from the 'infrequent' group and the 'never smoked' group at age nine years. These data clearly contradict the simple 'one puff of nicotine and you are hooked' model of nicotine use (Russell, 1990).

In the past, it has been proposed that initiation into smoking is linked to personality type (Eysenck, 1980), which interacts with the pharmacological effect of nicotine (Warburton, 1990). In addition, family influence has been said to be an important factor in the young person's decision to smoke, but the greatest environmental influence on initiation is the young person's family and peers (Bewley and Bland, 1977; Bewley, Bland, and Harris, 1974; Goddard, 1990).

In a school-based survey of over 10 000 adolescents, Eiser, Morgan, and Gammage (1987) found that young smokers predominantly attributed their smoking to the intrinsic rewards of smoking itself, rather than to external pressure or the desire to conform to group norms. They regarded smoking as enjoyable, calming, and helpful for coping with problems. Thus, the rewards from smoking seem to be no different for the adolescent from those for more regular and older smokers.

Given these findings, it is interesting to look at the predictors for smoking at 15 years. In a New Zealand study, daily smokers at 15 years tended to experience more life stress events (Stanton *et al.*, 1989). Parents of daily smokers had sought professional help for their children's emotional or behavioural problems, and more of the daily, adolescent smokers had sought help for themselves. In agreement with the self-reports, more parents of 15-year-old daily smokers reported that their children had been in trouble with the police in the previous two years (23 per cent), compared with the remainder of the sample (6 per cent). As well as being a stressor, delinquency is associated with specific, rebellious social groups and smoking has been related to adolescent rebellion and insensitivity to social pressures (Matarazzo and Saslow, 1960; Wills, 1985).

Girls were significantly more likely to smoke if they had young parents or their mother had her first baby before 20 years of age, and boys were significantly more likely to smoke if they came from broken homes or they had poor relations with their families. A broken home was also found to be a predictor of smoking in a study of Swiss adolescents (Sieber and Angst, 1990).

Thus, the predictors of smoking were not so much experimentation, as factors which result in problems for the individual. This suggests that it may not be simple exposure to nicotine that results in adolescent smoking, but that smoking results from the situations in which the young people find themselves at this most stressful time of life (see also Wills, 1985). Smoking continues because it provides nicotine which ameliorates the effects of stressors.

CONCLUSIONS

In this chapter, I have tried to show that the appetite for nicotine is purposive and represents an attempt by the smoker to adapt to the environment. In this respect, it has features in common with other appetites, such as eating, drinking, and sex. This approach gives a functional analysis of nicotine appetite. It considers questions about how smoking occurs and examines the conditions that initiate and sustain nicotine use. The answers have avoided explanations of nicotine use in terms of 'need' and the 'reward or reinforcement' derived from 'satisfying' this need.

Instead, nicotine appetite has been seen as an integration of sets of factors such as situation, psychological state, and sensory factors, as well as plasma nicotine level. None of these factors is considered more important than the others. The primary factor in nicotine appetite is the functional interrelationship between the factors.

This approach differs from the addiction view of nicotine use (USDHHS, 1988). In this view, a 'need for nicotine' has developed through exposure which manifests itself as a withdrawal syndrome during abstinence. Nicotine use is 'reinforcing', because it 'satisfies the nicotine need'. In this model, the reasons for nicotine use are exclusively endogenous.

In contrast, the causes in the functional model can be both exogenous and endogenous, the situation and the individual. A smoker may have more than one motive for nicotine use and use may have different functions in different situations. In addition, nicotine appetite can be the outcome of not only the characteristics of the situation, but the personality of the individual. Personality characteristics will determine the way in which the person interacts with situations. Consequently, differences in nicotine appetite will be the result of the interaction of the individual with the situation.

REFERENCES

Ashton, H. and Stepney, R. (1982). *Smoking: psychology and pharmacology.* Cambridge University Press.

Ashton, H., Stepney, R., and Thompson, J.W. (1979). Self-titration in cigarette smokers. *British Medical Journal*, **2**, 357–60.

Balding, J. (1987). *Young people in 1986.* Health Education Authority Schools Education Unit, University of Exeter.

Bewley, B. R. and Bland, J. M. (1977). Academic performance and social factors related to cigarette smoking by schoolchildren. *British Journal of Preventive and Social Medicine*, **31**, 18–24.

Bewley, B. R., Bland, J. M., and Harris, R. (1974). Factors associated with the starting of cigarette smoking by primary school children. *British Journal of Preventive and Social Medicine*, **28**, 37–44.

Blundell, J. E., Hill, A. J., and Rogers, P. J. (1989). Hunger and satiety cascade—their importance for food acceptance in the late 20th century. In *Food acceptability*, (ed. D. M. H. Thompson), pp. 233–50. Elsevier, London.

Booth, D. A. (1981). Physiology of appetite. *British Medical Bulletin*, **37**, 135–40.

Cain, W.S. (1976). Olfaction and the common chemical sense: some psychophysical contrasts. *Sensory Processes*, **1**, 57.

Cain, W. S. (1980). Sensory attributes of cigarette smoking. In *Banbury Report 3: a safe cigarette?*, (eds. G. B. Gori and F. G. Bock), pp. 239–49. Cold Spring Harbor Laboratory, New York.

Chamberlain, A. T., and Higenbottam, T. W. (1985). Nicotine and cigarette smoking: an alternative hypothesis. *Medical Hypotheses*, **17**, 285–97.

Cherek, D. R. (1981). Effects of smoking different doses of nicotine on human aggressive behavior. *Psychopharmacology*, **75**, 339–45.

Cherry, N. and Kiernan, K. (1976). Personality scores and smoking behaviour. *British Journal of Preventive and Social Medicine*, **30**, 123–31.

Colcutt, M., Jansen, M., and Kamakura, I. (1988). *Cultural atlas of Japan*. Phaidon, Oxford.

Colrain, G. L., Mangan, O. L., Pellett, O.L., and Bates, T. C. (1992). Effects of post-learning smoking on memory consolidation. *Psychopharmacology*, **108**, 448–51.

Creighton, D. E. and Lewis, P. H. (1978). The effect of smoking pattern on smoke deliveries. In *Smoking behaviour* (ed. R. E. Thornton), pp. 301–14. Churchill Livingstone, Edinburgh.

Creighton, D. E., Noble, M. J., and Whewell, R. T. (1978). Instruments to measure, record and duplicate human smoking patterns. In *Smoking behaviour: physiological and psychological influence* (ed. R. E. Thornton), pp. 277–88. Churchill Livingstone, Edinburgh.

Dahl, T., Gunderson, B., and Kuehnast, K. (1984). *The influence of health improvement programs on white collar productivity.*University of Minnesota, Minneapolis.

Dobbs, J. and Marsh, A. (1985). *Smoking among secondary school children in 1984*. Her Majesty's Stationery Office, London.

Eiser J. R., Morgan, M., and Gammage, P. (1987). Belief correlates of perceived addiction in young smokers. *European Journal of Psychology of Education*, **2**, 307–10.

Eysenck, H. J. (1963). Smoking, personality and psychosomatic disorders. *Journal of Psychosomatic Research*, **7**, 107–30.

Eysenck, H.J. (1980). (With contributions from Eaves, L.J.) *The causes and effects of smoking*. Temple Smith, London.

Foss, R. (1972). Personality, social influence and cigarette smoking. *Journal of Health and Social Behavior*, **14**, 279–86.

Frith, C. D. (1971). Smoking behaviour and its relationship to the smoker's immediate experience. *British Journal of Social and Clinical Psychology*, **10**, 73–8.

Garfinkel, L. (1979). Changes in the cigarette consumption of smokers in relation to changes in tar/nicotine content of cigarettes smoked. *American Journal of Public Health*, **69**, 1274–6.

Gilbert, D. G., and Hagen, R. L. (1980). The effects of nicotine and extraversion on self-report, skin conductance, electromyographic, and heart responses to emotional stimuli. *Addictive Behaviors*, **5**, 247–57.

Glad, W., and Adesso, V.J. (1976). The relative importance of socially induced tension and behavioral contagion for smoking behavior. *Journal of Abnormal Psychology*, **85**, 119–21.

Goddard, E. (1990). *Smoking among secondary school children in England in 1988*. Her Majesty's Stationery Office, London.

Jacobs, K. W. and Nordan, F. M. (1979). Classification of placebo drugs: effect of colour. *Perceptual and Motor Skills*, **49**, 367–72.

Jones, G.M.M., Sahakian, B.J., Levy, R., Warburton, D.M., and Gray, J.A. (1992). Effects of acute sub-cutaneous nicotine on attention, information processing and short-term memory in Alzheimer's Disease. *Psychopharmacology*, **108**, 485–94.

Kochhar, N. and Warburton, D.M. (1990). Puff-by-puff sensory evaluation of a low to middle tar medium nicotine cigarette designed to maintain nicotine delivery to the smoker. *Psychopharmacology*, **102**, 343–9.

Kozlowski, L. T., Wilkinson, D. A., Skinner, W., Kent., C., Franklin, T., and Pope, M. (1989). Comparing tobacco cigarette dependence with other drug dependencies: Greater or equal 'difficulty quitting' and 'urges to use'. but less pleasure from cigarettes. *Journal of the American Medical Association*, **261**, 898–901.

Marlatt, A. (1979). A cognitive-behavioral model of the relapse process. In *Behavioural analysis and treatment of substance abuse* (ed. J. Krasnegor), pp. 191–99. National Institute for Drug Abuse, Washington, DC.

Matarazzo, J.D. and Saslow, G. (1960). Psychological and related characteristics of smokers and non-smokers. *Psychological Bulletin*, **57**, 493–513.

McKennell, A. C. (1970). Smoking motivation factors. *British Journal of Social and Clinical Psychology*, **9**, 8–22.

McKennell, A. C. (1973). *A comparison of two smoking typologies. Research Paper No. 12*. Tobacco Research Council, London.

Orford, J. (1985). *Excessive appetites: a psychological view of addictions*. Wiley, Chichester.

Pomerleau, O.F., Turk, D.C., and Fertig, J.B. (1984). The effects of cigarette smoking on pain and anxiety. *Addictive Behaviors*, **9**, 265–71.

Response Analysis Corporation. (1984). *Smoking and productivity in the workplace: overall report. A nationwide survey among: first level supervisors in business and industry: first level supervisors in government, and local union officials*. Response Analysis Corporation, Princeton, NJ.

Romano, C., Goldstein, A., and Jewell, N. P. (1981). Characterization of the receptor mediating the nicotine discriminative stimulus. *Psychopharmacology*, **74**, 310–15.

Rosecrans, J. A. and Meltzer, L. T. (1982). Central sites and mechanisms of action of nicotine. *Neuroscience and Biobehavioral Reviews*, **5**, 489–97.

Royal College of Physicians (1962). *Smoking and health*. Royal College of Physicians, London.

Russell, M. A. H. (1990). The nicotine addiction trap: a 40– year sentence for four cigarettes. *British Journal of Addiction*, **85**, 293–300.

Russell, M. A. H., Peto, J., and Patel, U.A. (1974). The classification of smoking by factorial structure of motives. *Journal of the Royal Statistical Society. Series A (General)*, **137**, 313–46.

Russell, M. A. H., Wilson, C., Patel, U. A., Cole, P. V., and Feyerabend, C. (1973). Comparison of the effect on tobacco consumption and carbon monoxide absorption of changing to high and low nicotine cigarettes. *British Medical Journal*, **4**, 512–16.

Rusted, J. M. and Warburton, D. M. (1992). Facilitation of memory by post-trial administration of nicotine: evidence of an attentional explanation. *Psychopharmacology*, **108**, 452–5.

Sahakian, B., Jones, G., Levy, R., Gray, J., and Warburton, D.M. (1989). The effects of nicotine on attention, information processing, and short-term memory in patients with dementia of the Alzheimer type. *British Journal of Psychiatry*, **154**, 797–800.

Schachter, S. (1978). Pharmacological and psychological determinants of smoking. In *Smoking behaviour* (ed. R. E. Thornton), pp. 208–28. Churchill Livingstone, Edinburgh.

Shiffman, S. M. and Jarvik, M. E. (1976). Smoking withdrawal symptoms in two weeks of abstinence. *Psychopharmacology*, **50**, 35–9.

Sieber, M. F. and Angst, J. (1990). Alcohol, tobacco and cannabis: 12–year longitudinal associations with antecedent social context and personality. *Drug and Alcohol Dependence*, **25**, 281–92.

Stanton, W. R., Silva, P. A., and Oei, T. P. S. (1989). *The origins and development of an addictive behaviour: a longitudinal study of smoking*. The Dunedin Multidisciplinary Health and Development Research Unit, Dunedin, New Zealand.

Stephen, A., Frost, C., Thompson, S., and Wald, N.J. (1988). Estimating the extent of compensatory smoking. In *Smoking and the low tar programme* (eds. N. J. Wald and P. Froggatt), pp. 100–15. Oxford University Press.

Stepney, R. (1980). Cigarette consumption and nicotine delivery. *British Journal of Addiction*, **75**(1), 81–8.

Suraway, C., Stepney, R., and Cox, T. (1985). Does watching others smoke increase smoking? *British Journal of Addiction*, **80**, 207–10.

Tomkins, S. S. (1966). Psychological model of smoking behaviour. *American Journal of Public Health*, **56**, 17–20.

Tomkins, S. S. (1968). A modified model of smoking behaviour. In *Smoking, health and behaviour* (eds. E. Borgatta and R. Evans), pp. 165–6. Aldine, Chicago.

U.S. Department of Health, Education, and Welfare (1979). *Smoking and health. A report of the Surgeon General*. U.S. Department of Health, Education, and Welfare. Public Health Service, Office of the Assistant Secretary for Health, Office on Smoking and Health. DHEW Publication No. (PHS)79–50066.

U.S. Department of Health and Human Services (1988). *The health consequences of smoking: nicotine addiction. A report of the Surgeon-General*. DHHS Publication Number (CDC) 88–8406, U. S. Department of Health and Human Services, Office of the Assistant Secretary for Health, Office on Smoking and Health, Rockville, MD.

Warburton, D. M. (1987). The functions of smoking. In *Tobacco smoking and nicotine: a neurobiological approach* (eds. W. R. Martin, G. R. Van Loon, E. T. Iwamoto, and D. L. Davis), pp. 51–61. Plenum Press, New York.

Warburton, D. M. (1988a). The puzzle of nicotine use. In *The psychopharmacology of the addiction* (ed. M. Lader), pp. 27–49. Oxford University Press.

Warburton, D. M. (1988b). The functional use of nicotine. In *Nicotine, smoking and the low tar programme* (ed. N. Wald and P. Froggatt), pp. 182–99. Oxford University Press.

Warburton, D. M. (1990). Psychopharmacological aspects of nicotine. In *Nicotine psychopharmacology* (eds. S. Wonnacott, M. A. H. Russell, and I. P. Stolerman), pp 76–111. Oxford University Press.

Warburton, D. M. and Wesnes, K. (1978). Individual differences in smoking and attentional performance. In *Smoking behaviour* (ed. R. E. Thornton), pp. 19–43. Churchill-Livingstone, Edinburgh.

Warburton, D. M., Revell, A., and Walters, A. C. (1988). Nicotine as a resource. In *The pharmacology of nicotine* (eds. M. J. Rand and K. Thurau), pp. 359–73. IRL Press, Oxford.

Warburton, D.M., Wesnes, K., and Revell, A.D. (1984). Nicotine and the control of smoking behaviour. In *Smoking and the lung* (eds. G. Cumming and G. Bonsignore), pp. 217–232. Plenum, New York.

Warburton, D.M., Wesnes, K., and Revell, A.D. (1984) Smoking and academic performance. *Current Psychological Research and Reviews*, **3**, 25–31.

Warburton, D. M., Revell, A. D., and Thompson, D. H. (1991). Smokers of the future. *British Journal of Addiction*, **86**, 621–5.

Warburton, D.M., Rusted, J.M., and Fowler, J. (1992). A comparison of the attentional and consolidation hypotheses for the facilitation of memory by nicotine. *Psychopharmacology*, **108**, 443–447.

Wesnes, K. and Warburton, D. M. (1983). Smoking, nicotine and human information processing performance. *Neuropsychobiology*, **9**, 223–9.

Wesnes, K. and Warburton, D. M. (1984*a*). The effects of cigarettes of varying yield on rapid information processing performance. *Psychopharmacology*, **82**, 338–42.

Wesnes, K. and Warburton, D. M. (1984*b*). Effects of scopolamine and nicotine on human rapid information processing performance. *Psychopharmacology*, **82**, 147–50.

Wesnes, K., Warburton, D. M., and Matz, B. (1983). The effects of nicotine on stimulus sensitivity and response bias in a visual vigilance task. *Neuropsychobiology* **9**, 41–4.

West, R. W. and Kranzler, H. R. (1990). Craving for cigarettes and psychoactive drugs. In *Addiction controversies* (ed. D. M. Warburton), pp. 250–60. Harwood Academic Publishers, London.

Wilbert, J. (1987). *Tobacco and Shamanism in South America*. Yale University Press, New Haven, Conn.

Wills, T.A. (1985). Stress, coping, and tobacco and alchol use in early adolescence. In *Coping and substamce use* (eds. S. Shiffman and T.A. Wills), pp. 67–94. Academic Press, Orlando, Fl.

Woodson, P. P., Buzzi, R., Nil, R., and Bättig, K. (1986). Effects of smoking on vegetative reactivity to noise in women. *Psychophysiology*, **23(3)**, 272–82.

12

Young people and fruit machine gambling

Douglas Carroll and Justine A.A. Huxley

INTRODUCTION

Gambling is a strikingly ubiquitous human activity. For most people, though, it constitutes a fairly casual pastime: one recreational distraction amid a varied matrix of social and leisure pursuits. For many, though, gambling is anything but a casual activity. For the dependent or pathological gambler, gambling is preoccupying, consuming substantial time and money.

The *Diagnostic and Statistical Manual* (DSMIII) of the American Psychiatric Association characterizes dependent or pathological gambling as an addictive disorder akin to substance addiction. Indeed, the criteria for substance addiction and pathological gambling are virtually identical if one substitutes gambling for the substance abused. In contrast to the recreational gambler, the pathological gambler has lost control over his/her gambling behaviour. Gambling has, for such an individual, reached the point of disrupting not only his/her life but also the lives of close family members and friends. Like the substance addict, the pathological gambler has been observed to display withdrawal symptoms of disturbed mood and behaviour (Wray and Dickerson, 1981) as well as tolerance (Dickerson, 1984). Indeed, some authors have noted occasions of cross-addictions in pathological gamblers (see, e.g. Jacobs, Pettis, and Linda, 1981; McCormick, Russo, Ramirez, and Taber, 1984).

It is curious, then, that the study of gambling has, for the most part, proceeded quite separately from the study of other dependencies. In addition, gambling has received far less academic attention than substance abuse. It would seem that the time and money devoted to the study of social and personal problems depends very much on perceived public concern. Until recently, problem gambling has been decidedly less in the public eye than substance abuse. The last few years, though, have seen a marked increase, certainly within the United Kingdom, of concern over one particular manifestation of problem gambling: young people and fruit machines.

FRUIT MACHINE GAMBLING

Legislation covering access to fruit machines in the United Kingdom is exceptionally liberal. The 1968 Gaming Act, which legalized gaming for profit, allowed licences to be granted for fruit machine installations in amusement arcades, cafes, leisure centres, etc. Thus, in contrast to other forms of commercial gambling, fruit machines, at the very outset, were deemed appropriate for young people. At present, the only restrictions on fruit machine use by young people are those arising from the British Amusement and Catering Trade Association's (BACTA) voluntary code of conduct. This prohibits those under 16 years of age from entering amusement arcades. However, the code does not apply to seaside arcades, does not bind owners who are not members of the Association, and does not apply to non-arcade sites. In addition, it is a commonplace observation that the code is sometimes applied in a lax manner by those arcade owners who are BACTA members.

This is in sharp contrast to the much stricter regulation of fruit machine access elsewhere in the world. In the USA, for example, fruit machines are permitted in eight states only (Colorado, Louisiana, Maryland, Montana, Nevada, New Jersey, South Carolina, and South Dakota) and the legal age limit is either 18 or 21. In Australia fruit machines are again largely restricted to certain states (New South Wales and the Australian Capital Territory) and to special venues, such as rugby league football clubs and retired servicemen's clubs, for which membership is limited to those over the age of 18. Similar age restrictions characterize access in virtually all European countries which permit fruit machines. While other countries are not without problems related to fruit machine gambling (see Griffiths, Lea, and Webley, 1989), it would appear that the heavy involvement of young people is a particularly British phenomenon.

In recent years, newspapers have printed numerous examples of the apparent 'fallout' from excessive fruit machine gambling among the young. Instances of stealing and prostitution in order to support gambling have been recounted, along with reports of attempted suicide. The following reports are fairly typical:

Paul began playing the fruit machine in a cafe near his family home in Slough at the age of 10. It was not long before he began stealing from his parents in order to play more. By the time he was 15, he was playing truant from school and committing one burglary after another in order to finance his compulsive gambling. (*Observer*, 11 September, 1988, p.6)

Davina Patterson returned from a two-week holiday to find her smart West London maisonette had been ransacked. Everything of value had gone . . .

The culprit was Davina's eldest son, Bill. He sold the haul, worth nearly £6000, for £400 to pay for his addiction to gambling machines. While Davina was coming to terms with her son's behaviour, Bill tried to kill himself with a drugs overdose. (*Sunday Mirror*, 7 August, 1988, p.21)

It is possible to discern in some newspaper reports a selectivity and excessiveness all too often typical of press treatment of deviant behaviour: ever eager to alert the public to yet another contemporary folk devil. However, in the case of adolescent fruit machine gambling, more sober organizations offer parallel testimony.

Organizations such as Gamblers Anonymous (GA) report an increasingly large number of young people seeking help for problems relating to excessive or uncontrolled fruit machine use. In 1964, the typical GA member was a 40–50-year-old horse race gambler; by 1986, approximately 50 per cent of new members were fruit machine users, half of these being adolescents (Moody, 1987). Excessive fruit machine use among the young is also reflected in the formation of Parents of Young Gamblers, a parental support group, and pressure groups such as the Amusement Arcade Action Group, which campaigns for an increase in the powers possessed by local authorites to control the location of amusement arcades and their accessibility to young people.

RESEARCH INTO ADOLESCENT FRUIT MACHINE GAMBLING

Given its liberal legislative stance on fruit machine gambling, it is not surprising that the bulk of the research on young people and fruit machines has been conducted in the United Kingdom. However, it constitutes anything but a substantial literature, and much of it comprises questionnaire surveys, concerned mainly with the prevalence of fruit machine gambling among the young, its association with broad demographic variables, such as age and gender, on the one hand, and its possible consequences for deliquent behaviours, such as truanting and stealing, on the other. Hardly any studies have attempted to elucidate potential mechanisms of dependency in this context.

SURVEYS OF YOUNG PEOPLE AND FRUIT MACHINES

The major surveys that have been published to date are summarized in Table 12.1, which lists the sample size, age range, and percentage considered to be regular users of fruit machines. Given variations in sample size and composition, the context and nature of the questions posed, the different operationalizations of 'regular', discrepancies in the apparent incidence of regular playing are hardly unexpected. Nevertheless, a brief discussion is warranted; the incidence of frequent play, and of possible dependency, are not trivial matters, since they are likely, along with data on possible consequent delinquency, to inform any consideration of appropriated regulatory provision.

Table 12.1 records regular use values varying from less than 2 to 14 per cent. At the high end we find the Huff and Collinson (1987) study. However, special factors pertain. Subjects in this survey were 100 consecutive admissions to a young people's custody centre in Feltham. The primary aim of the study was to explore the possible link between crime and amusement machine use. Sixty per cent of the sample reported that they used fruit machines and 23 per cent of these (14 per cent of the total sample) claimed to have committed an offence in order to obtain money specifically for gambling on machines. Thus, as we shall see, relative to other surveys, the sample was somewhat atypical and the derived definition of regularly, in terms of the prevalence of purportedly related offences, was also atypical. Most studies have opted for reported frequency of play.

Next in terms of magnitude of regular use is the Spectrum Children's Trust (1988) study of schoolchildren in the Taunton and Minehead area. However, the value of 8.7 per cent is derived from the very liberal criterion of regular use of at least twice per week. Even with such a liberal criterion of regularity, Waterman and Atkin (1985) reported only 6.3 per cent of their sample of Birmingham schoolchildren to be regular users. Caution may be warranted, though. Waterman and Atkin's survey was the earliest conducted, since which time the number

Table 12.1 *Surveys on young people and amusement machines*

Authors	Sample size	Age range	% regular users
Waterman & Atkin (1985)	451	14–18	6.3
Huff & Collinson (1987)	100	15–21	14.0
Barham & Cornell (1987)	329	11–16	5.0
Spectrum Children's Trust (1988)	2423	11–16	8.7
National Housing and Town Planning Council (1988)	9752	13–16	3.0
Graham (1988)	1946	10–16	<0.5
Huxley & Carroll (1992)	1332	11–15	6.0
Fisher (1993)	460	11–16	5.7

of arcades and fruit machines has increased markedly (Griffiths, 1989). Between 1987 and 1988 alone, the number of licensed fruit machines rose by 6000.

In general, it has been more usual for studies to adopt the stricter criterion of regularity of four times a week or more. Two studies deploying this criterion found similar results. Barham and Cornell (1987) reported that 5 per cent of their sample of Bognor Regis schoolchildren visited amusement arcades to play fruit machines four times per week or more. In Huxley and Carroll's (1992) study, 6 per cent of the Birmingham schoolchildren questioned admitted to gambling in arcades with such regularity. The demographic similarity between this latter study and the earlier Waterman and Atkin research reinforces the contention that an increase in the availability of fruit machines has contributed to an increase in the proportion of young people making regular use of them. For example, in the Huxley and Carroll study, 16 per cent reported using fruit machines in arcades at least twice a week, and whereas Waterman and Atkin reported that only 9 per cent of their sample admitted playing machines at least once a week, the analogous figure in the Huxley and Carroll survey was 28 per cent. The most recent published survey (Fisher, 1993) used an even stricter criterion: the provisional DSM-IV classification scheme for diagnosing pathological gambling. Even so, some 5.7 per cent of her sample of South-west of England schoolchildren met the criterion.

At the other end of the scale we have the National Housing and Town Planning Council (1988) Survey and the Home Office Survey (Graham, 1988). The data from the former are just about reconcilable with those reported by other surveys using the four times a week or more definition of regularity, and, as we shall see, the data dealing with apparently consequential delinquent behaviours broadly match those revealed by other surveys. On the other hand, the Home Office Survey registered less than 0.5 per cent of its total sample of respondents as regular users. While this may, to an extent, be accounted for by a stringent criterion of regularity (every day or nearly every day), it is unlikely that this affords anything but a partial explanation for the untypically low incidence. After all, less than 2 per cent of their respondents admitted to playing fruit machines once a week or more. The analogous figure from the National Housing and Town Planning Council study was 14 per cent. Clearly, other factors are at work here. It has been proposed that the overall strikingly low incidences recorded in the Home Office study might owe much to the absence of clear assurances about confidentiality (Griffiths, 1989; Carroll and Huxley, 1992). Given that interviewees were asked for their name, address, and telephone number, it is reasonable to presume a certain amount of reticence in disclosing frequent fruit machine gambling.

Taken together, surveys of young people's gambling habits suggest that somewhere around half of them admit to playing fruit machines at some time or another: the figures reported by the National Housing and Town Planning Council (1988), Huxley and Carroll (1992), and Fisher (1993) are 58 per cent, 40 per cent, and 62 per cent respectively. For the vast majority of these, fruit machine gambling is a rare or occasional activity. For a minority, it would appear to be a much more consuming pursuit. The best estimate from the survey literature is that somewhere between 3 and 6 per cent of young people engage in fruit machine gambling with a regularity that could, for some, intimate dependency. In 1986, official population statistics reveal that there were almost three million schoolchildren aged 13–16 years of age in England and Wales. Simple extrapolation indicates the scale of regular fruit machine gambling among these young people; that is, it engages somewhere around 90 000 and 180 000 of them.

Frequency of usage is not the only issue. If regular fruit machine gambling involved little financial outlay, it would almost certainly be far less of a concern. However, the recent surveys, with one apparent exception, suggest that for some young people expenditure on fruit machines is considerable. As might be anticipated, the apparent exception is the Home Office survey. Graham (1988) reported that 71 per cent of fruit machine players spent less than £1 per week on fruit machines, 17 per cent spent between £1 and £2 per week. However, Graham also found that 15 per cent of fruit machine players spent all or most of the money they had available for spending each week on playing fruit machines. In contrast to Graham's absolute expenditure statistics, the National Housing and Town Planning Council (1988) study found that 9 per cent of the fruit machine players in their sample were spending more than £3 per session; 4 per cent were spending more than £5 per session. In addition, expenditure per gambling session was related to the frequency of gambling. Nearly one-fifth of the young people who gambled on fruit machines at least four times a week revealed that they usually spent more than £10 during each session, that is, at least £40 per week. A further 34 per cent of this group admitted to spending at least £3 per session or £12 per week. In contrast, only 7 per cent of young people who played infrequently, that is, once a month or less, indicated this level of expenditure per session.

The percentages reporting high spending were even larger in the Huxley and Carroll (1992) study. Nearly 12 per cent of the fruit machine users in their survey admitted that they usually spent between £3 and £5 per session, and a further 14 per cent declared spending over £5 per session. Further, when questioned about maximum as opposed to usual expenditure, 19 per cent of young gamblers revealed that they had spent more than £10 at one session. In line with the results of the National

Housing and Town Planning Council study, Huxley and Carroll found that both the usual and maximum expenditure per session were related to frequency of play. Huxley and Carroll also examined expenditure as a proportion of income in the sub-sample of 201 fruit machine users who played once a week or more. Approximately 17 per cent of this sub-sample (2.5 per cent of the total sample of schoolchildren) spent more money on fruit machines than they usually received from pocket money and/or a part-time job. While Fisher (1993) presents fewer data on expenditure, they are broadly in accord with those presented by Huxley and Carroll; more than 25 per cent of her fruit machine players had spent more than £5 in one session.

A number of these surveys have attended to the question of the relationship between fruit machine gambling in young people and other undesirable behaviours. Articles in the popular press would seem to leave no doubt that a causal relationship exists. However, Graham (1988) was decidedly unconvinced, although he did not address the issues of stealing, borrowing, and truanting directly, highlighted to an extent in the earlier study by Barham and Cornell (1987). Instead a small sub-sample of respondents (24 regular users and 12 occasional users) in the Home Office study were asked in the context of group discussions where they usually obtained the money for gambling. No dishonest means of acquiring funds were reported. In addition, sub-sample members completed a general delinquency questionnaire. The questions, however, were concerned with more widespread manifestations of delinquent behaviour. As Fisher (1989) pointed out, it is difficult to see the relevance of activities such as 'written or sprayed paint on buildings' or 'broken windows in an empty house'. Save for a relatively high proportion of the sub-sample owning up to smashing bottles in the street, travelling on public transport without a ticket, and deliberately damaging school property, there was little in the responses to disturb the Queen's peace or, for that matter, the Home Office's. Again, it is also worth reminding the reader of the lack of subject anonymity in the Home Office study.

Other surveys paint a different picture. In the Spectrum Children's Trust (1988) study, 7 per cent of those who gambled admitted stealing to finance machine playing, 7 per cent to truancy, and 25 per cent to borrowing money to play machines. In the National Housing and Town Planning Council (1988) Survey, 35 per cent of fruit machine gamblers owned up to borrowing money to gamble, 7 per cent had stolen, 17 per cent had used their school dinner money to play fruit machines, and 6 per cent had truanted. The prevalence of these activities was directly related to the amount of money spent gambling and the frequency of fruit machine play. For example, 38 per cent of those who gambled four times a week or more admitted that they had stolen to finance their gambling. Of the fruit machine users in the Huxley and Carroll (1992) survey the following frequencies of undesirable behaviours were found: 40 per cent had borrowed money to play machines; 24 per cent had used their school dinner money; 12 per cent had stolen from their parents; 5 per cent had stolen from outside their immediate family; 8 per cent had sold their possessions in order to obtain money for playing machines. Highly significant relationships were found between all these behaviours, on the one hand, and frequency of play and the amount of money spent, on the other.

A consensus seems to be emerging. In addition, two other, as yet unpublished surveys, appear to provide further confirmation. Lee (1989) reported that 4 per cent of fruit machine users admitted stealing to play, 7 per cent had truanted or missed work, and 27 per cent had borrowed money. Rands and Hooper (1990) found that 6 per cent of fruit machine users had stolen to play machines, 17 per cent had used school dinner money, 6 per cent had truanted, and 28 per cent had borrowed.

In summary, a small but, in population terms, hardly negligible proportion of young people gamble regularly on fruit machines. Expenditure appears to be related to frequency of play, but not merely as a simple arithmetic function; more frequent play is associated with greater expenditure per session of play. However, as Graham (1988) pointed out, it could be income which is determining; those who spend the most may simply have more money at their disposal. Nevertheless, what is apparent from both Graham's data and those reported by Huxley and Carroll is that not insignificant numbers of young people are spending all of their income on fruit machines, and in some cases amounts that exceed their incomes. It is perhaps hardly surprising, then, that some fruit machine users borrow, or even steal, to support their gambling. While the surveys which have inquired about truanting, using school dinner money, borrowing, and stealing, report slightly varying prevalences of these behaviours, a broad consistency is evident. In addition, those studies which have examined the association between such behaviours and the extent of gambling, whether in terms of regularity or expenditure, report substantial positive relationships.

ADDITIONAL CORRELATES OF FRUIT MACHINE GAMBLING

The survey literature also highlights a number of other variables associated with the frequency of fruit machine playing in young people. Some of these might provide clues as to the factors which encourage and sustain fruit machine play.

Graham (1988) was the first to present evidence on social class background in this context. While the class background of those who had gambled in the previous month was fairly evenly spread, there was some over-representation of young people from social classes C2, D, and E (skilled manual to unskilled). Fisher (1993) reported slightly stronger social class effects with regard to pathological gambling in her sample; her data suggested an increasing gradient of prevalence of pathological gambling from the highest to the lowest social class. Although social class background was not determined in other surveys, Huxley and Carroll (1992) did analyse gambling in terms of the broad areas of Birmingham that their respondents were drawn from. Young people from the outer suburban areas were less likely to play fruit machines four times a week or more than were their inner suburban or city centre counterparts. They argued that this effect could simply reflect the concentration of amusement arcades in these areas. Indeed, it remains possible that any social class effect could be determined similarly.

Gender has also been implicated, with fruit machine gambling very much regarded as a male preserve. Certainly the early survey research revealed that boys were more likely than girls to have played fruit machines and more likely than girls to play frequently. They were also found to spend more and to engage in other socially undesirable behaviours in order to find the time and money to play (see, e.g., Ide-Smith and Lea, 1988; National Housing and Town Planning Council, 1988). More recent studies, however, have reported less marked gender differences. Huxley and Carroll (1992) found that girls were just as likely as boys to have played fruit machines, although high-frequency play still characterized boys more than girls. However, Fisher (1993) failed to find gender differences in play frequency; boys were not reliably over-represented among the pathological gamblers in her sample. These trends lend support to the notion that gender differences in this context may have been decreasing over time. They also suggest that efforts be made to correct the current male bias in gambling research, a point made by others (e.g. Mark and Lesieur, 1992).

There emerges from the survey literature a broad consensus that many of the young people studied began playing fruit machines . exceptionally early in life; mean age of first exposure to fruit machines seems, on average, to be somewhere between nine and ten years old. In addition, age at first exposure appears to be reliably related to subsequent frequency of play and the extent of subsequent financial commitment. For example, the National Housing and Town Planning Council (1988) found that young people who started gambling when they were under nine years of age were twice as likely as later starters to gamble four times a week or more. Further, there was a clear relationship between the amount spent on gambling and age at first exposure. If one takes £3 per session or more as the cut off, young people who started playing before they were nine were three times more likely to be spending this amount per session than late starters. Huxley and Carroll (1992) reported almost identical effects. In Fisher's (1993) study the prevalence of pathological gambling among her sample of young people was again related to age of first exposure. Most 'at risk' were children who started playing at the age of eight or younger; 20 per cent of such subjects registered as pathological on Fisher's DSM-IV criterion.

Retrospective studies of adult pathological gamblers reveal that the vast majority started gambling in their teens (e.g. Custer, 1982; Livingston, 1974). With problem teenage fruit machine gambling in the UK, it would appear that the age of introduction to fruit machines is even younger, implying that the earlier the initiation, the earlier the manifestation of problem gambling.

Related to this is the finding from surveys of young fruit machine players that the youngest cohorts often tended to play machines with their parents, suggesting that, in many instances, parents may be the key to children's initial acquaintance with fruit machines. There is certainly evidence from studies of general gambling behaviour, that parental gambling is a good predictor of their offspring's participation (see, e.g., Lesieur and Rothschild, 1989). Recent evidence suggests that this relationship holds for fruit machine gambling among the young. Fisher (1993) reported that pathological fruit machine gambling among her sample of young people was predicted by the frequency of gambling by their parents on fruit machines, as well as by the extent of parental involvement in other gambling activities, such as betting on horses and dog racing.

AETIOLOGY OF PATHOLOGICAL FRUIT MACHINE GAMBLING

Although the survey literature presents reasonably consistent evidence as to the scale of the problem in the UK, it offers few clues to the processes which produce pathological fruit machine gambling among the young. Nevertheless, clearly implied is that ease of access renders young people more vulnerable, and, as with adult gamblers, the earlier the initiation into gambling the more likely it is that gambling will become a pathological pursuit. Other clues emerge from the few available in-depth studies of smaller samples of young pathological and non-pathological fruit machine gamblers.

Griffiths (1990a,b,c, and d) reported data from two field studies of adolescent fruit machine gamblers in Exeter. Both pathological (identified by DSM-III or an equivalent) and non-pathological young gamblers were questioned about the acquisition and maintenance of their gambling behaviours. A number of recurring themes emerged. First of all, pathological fruit machine gamblers were prone to regard the activity, at least partially, as skilled-based; non-pathological gamblers were much more likely to attribute outcomes to chance. Secondly, Griffiths identified excitement as a key maintaining variable. Many of his young pathological gamblers claimed that fruit machine gambling produced a 'high'. When questioned as to the nature of the high, the majority of answers were vague or non-existent. However, a few described it as immediate, while others insisted that it was the next best thing to sex. Some said they could feel their heart beat getting faster. Crucially, pathological gamblers reported reliably higher levels of excitement during gambling than non-pathological gamblers, and were significantly more likely to affirm that they needed to gamble more to get more excited.

Slightly different factors emerged as discriminating between young pathological and non-pathological fruit machine gamblers in an interview study conducted in Birmingham by Carroll and Huxley (1991a). Pathological gamblers were defined in terms of their responses to DSM-III and by the amount of money spent per week. Pathological gamblers spent on average £66 per week, compared with an average of £5 spent by the non-pathological gamblers. Excitement during play was rarely mentioned as a rationale by pathological gamblers, although they did cite reasons centred around risk, suspense, and uncertainty. More compelling by far was the constant reference by pathological gamblers to a broader affective context of boredom. The following exchange between the interviewer (JH) and a young pathological gambler is fairly typical:

JH: So you would like to stop playing?

R: If I could yeah, if there's a cure for it I would.

JH: Have you tried?

R: I have, I have, it's just when you're bored, when you've got money in your pocket, or when you see a machine in the chip shop or you're walking past shops like in town looking for clothes and seeing amusements like in Oasis that you'll see the machine, you'll think I'll have one go on it and you end up putting the money in that was for a £20 pair of jeans.

In contrast the non-pathological gamblers in the Carroll and Huxley study claimed to play fruit machines for 'fun', 'entertainment', and because their friends did. Many of the pathological gamblers in this study recounted having gambled originally for similar reasons. However, few claimed to gamble for those reasons now. For the pathological gamblers fun and entertainment appeared to have given way to compulsion.

Very much in line with Griffiths' finding, though, were the indications from the Carroll and Huxley interviews concerning control versus chance. Pathological gamblers were much more likely than non-pathological gamblers to claim that fruit machines involved skill and to attribute wins to their own abilities. The following two exchanges, the first with a pathological and the second with a non-pathological respondent are indicative of the difference in beliefs.

JH: How important do you think skill is in winning?

R: Quite important.

JH: Where does the skill come in?

R: The gamble button, I think that's skill.

In contrast the non-pathological gambler dismissed the idea that the gamble button was responsive to skill:

JH: What about the gamble button?

R: Oh that's luck. It'll gamble [between] 20 and 80 perhaps and it's alternating very, very fast. That's pure luck.

In order to determine whether the different narrative accounts of pathological and non-pathological reflected relatively stable dispositional variations, Carroll and Huxley administered a questionnaire to measure Locus of Control (Rotter, 1966) and the Eysenck Personality Questionnaire (Eysenck and Eysenck, 1975) to their interviewees. The pathological gamblers registered as reliably more 'internal' in terms of locus of control than their non-pathological counterparts, a result which suggests that their beliefs about fruit machines and skill are part of a more general orientation. With regard to the Eysenck Personality Questionnaire, the two groups of young gamblers did not differ in terms of extraversion or neuroticism. However, differences appeared for the psychoticism sub-scale. Pathological fruit machine gamblers recorded scores that were higher than both non-pathological gamblers and age-appropriate norms.

It is perhaps worth reminding the reader what this scale purports to capture. Eysenck and Eysenck (1975) provided the following pen picture of the high Psychoticism scorer.

. . . solitary, not caring for people; he is often troublesome, not fitting in anywhere. He may be cruel and inhumane, lacking in feeling and empathy, and altogether insensitive. He is hostile to others, even his own kith and kin, and aggressive even to loved ones. He has a liking for odd and unusual things, and a disregard for danger; he likes to make fools of other people and to upset them. (Eysenck and Eysenck, 1975, p.11).

In the case of young people, Eysenck and Eysenck state:

we obtain a fairly congruent picture of an odd, isolated, troublesome child; glacial and lacking in human feelings for his fellow beings and for animals, aggressive and hostile, even to near and dear ones. Such children try to make up for lack of feeling by indulging in sensation-seeking 'arousal jags' without thinking of the dangers involved. Socialization is a concept which is relatively alien to both adults and children; empathy, feelings of guilt and sensitivity to other people are notions which are strange and unfamiliar to them. (Eysenck and Eysenck, 1975, p.11).

In a subsequent study Carroll and Huxley (1991*b*, 1992) explored the matter of control further, as well as issues arising from the Eysenck Personality Questionnaire results. A sample of adolescent pathological and non-pathological gamblers were observed while playing fruit machines. All were given £5 for this purpose, and the time it took them to use up the money was noted, as was the extent of their winnings. Subjects were also asked how much they expected to win, first on their favourite machine and secondly on an unfamiliar machine. Finally, heart rate and blood pressure were monitored before, during, and after fruit machine play. In this study, pathological gamblers were defined in terms of the amount of money spent, since, in the previous Carroll and Huxley (1991*a*) interview study, this simple index was found to correlate highly with answers to diagnostic questions.

A number of findings emerged from comparing the two groups. First of all, as would be predicted from earlier results, pathological gamblers anticipated more substantial winnings than their non-pathological counterparts; the respective average estimates were £5.80 and £4.40 for their favourite machine, and £4.50 and £2.80 for an unfamiliar machine. However, in reality, both groups managed almost identical average winnings of £3. In addition, for both groups the original £5 lasted the same time: a paltry five minutes. The difference between anticipated and actual winnings met the criterion for statistical significance in only one instance: pathological gamblers' anticipated winnings on a favourite machine, although it approached the criterion in this group for unfamilar machines ($0.05 < p < 0.10$). Taken together, these data lend support to the interview revelations. Pathological gamblers would seem to harbour the belief that skill matters in this context and that they can exercise considerable control over the fruit machines they play. Non-pathological gamblers, on the other hand, are far more likely to presume success rates in line with chance. In addition, the data confirm that the former's belief in control is illusory, since, in reality, they fared no better than non-pathological gamblers.

With regard to the psychophysiological data, there was a significant increase in cardiovascular activity during fruit machine play, although pathological and non-pathological gamblers did not differ reliably with respect to the magnitude of that increase. However, what did emerge was that the pathological gamblers showed lower basal levels of physiological activity than non-pathological gamblers. Group differences in this regard, though, were statistically reliable only in the case of diastolic blood pressure. Nevertheless, this result is interesting in the light of the high psychoticism scores that seem to characterize adolescent pathological fruit machine gamblers. It could be argued that, to an extent, pathological fruit machine gambling may be driven by sensation-seeking for arousal 'jags', which in turn may reflect conventionally low arousal levels. Coupled to this, one would have to include in any model of pathological fruit machine gambling a compelling susceptibility to an illusion of control. Finally, such dispositional tendencies have to be regarded in a particular developmental context, characterized by parental modelling and an early introduction to gambling, as well as the social context of continuing ease of access to fruit machines.

EXPLANATIONS OF PATHOLOGICAL GAMBLING

Early attempts to account for pathological gambling relied either on psychodynamic metaphor or on a strict application of reinforcement theory. In the former, gambling was regarded as an attempt to resolve conflicts with parental figures through symbolic contests with a surrogate, 'Lady Luck'. Bergler (1957) proposed that pathological gambling reflected an unconscious desire to lose such contests, thus appeasing the parental figures. In the latter, Skinner (1953) regarded gambling as a learned response to irregular schedules of financial reinforcement. Pathological gambling, from this perspective, was the result of repeated exposure to these powerful schedules. Neither provide a satisfactory answer. While psychodynamic explanations are couched in a manner that renders empirical examination extremely difficult, strict reinforcement theory, with its emphasis on purely financial contingencies, gives improper regard to other motivating agencies and to intra-individual factors.

More recent theoretical models of pathological gambling (e.g. Brown, 1986; Dickerson and Adcock, 1987) are much more multifactorial in character, and, although retaining variable financial reinforcement schedules as part of the explanatory matrix, have incorporated a range of other factors. Most prominent among these are cognitive bias, personal disposition, and arousal.

Cognitive bias

One of the most influential contributions to a cognitive psychology of gambling has been the work of Ellen Langer on the illusion of control (e.g. Langer, 1975, 1983). Langer defines the illusion of control as an expectancy of personal success inappropriately higher than the objective probability would warrant. In an elegant series of laboratory studies Langer demonstrated that subjects' appropriate orientations towards chance events could be altered by a range of manipulations. For example, subjects who cut cards against a nervous competitor bet more than when playing against a confident competitor. Subjects would pitch the sale price of a lottery ticket that they had chosen themselves at a higher price than they would a ticket chosen for them. Subjects given the opportunity to practise a novel game of chance would bet more than those denied such an opportunity. Finally, subjects led to believe that they were particularly successful during the early trials of a coin-tossing task rated themselves as significantly better predictors of outcome than subjects led to believe they performed poorly in the early stages of the task.

In summary, if devices conventionally characteristic of skill situations are introduced into chance situations, individuals will inappropriately shift their expectations of success to levels better than chance. Studies of gamblers in naturalistic settings yield confirmatory data. Gadboury and Ladouceur (1989) had gamblers verbalize their thoughts while playing roulette and other gaming machines. Subjects attributed success to personal factors such as skill, while external factors such as bad luck were invoked to account for losses. Fruit machine manufacturers have made very profitable use of such devices; contemporary fruit machine design would seem optimally facilitative of an illusion of control.

It is also clear that individuals vary in the degree to which they generally attribute outcomes to internal factors, such as skill, or external factors, such as luck (Rotter, 1966). Thus, some individuals may be more likely to adopt a skill or control perspective in essentially chance situations. There is certainly evidence from studies by Carroll and Huxley (1991*a*) and Griffiths (1989) that an internal locus of control may be particularly characteristic of young pathological fruit machine gamblers.

Personal disposition

Aside from orientations regarding the locus of control, other dispositional variables have been implicated as predisposing in this context. Given the variety of personality questionnaires that have been deployed and variations in the populations studied, it is perhaps hardly surprising that not all studies point in the same direction. Nevertheless, some consistent themes can be discerned. Sensation-seeking, impulsivity, and lack of concern for others emerge as characteristic of pathological gamblers in a number of studies. As reported previously, Carroll and Huxley (1991*a*) found that young pathological fruit machine gamblers registered very high scores on the psychoticism scale of the Eysenck Personality Questionnaire. Eysenck and Eysenck's pen picture of high scorers certainly resonates with the characteristics listed above. Blaszczynski, Buhrich, and McConaghy (1985) also reported higher psychoticism scores among pathological gamblers. In addition, they found high scores in a group of heroin addicts, suggesting that high psychoticism scores may be typical of those who succumb to a range of addictive behaviours. In support, Gossop and Eysenck (1980) reported high psychoticism scores in a sample of poly-drug addicts. Interestingly, in this context, Dell, Ruzicka, and Palisi (1981) found that pathological gamblers scored high on the Drug Abuse Scale of the Million Multiaxial Clinical Inventory, even though none of the gamblers were drug abusers.

Results from studies that have administered Zuckerman's (1979) sensation-seeking scale have yielded, at best, equivocal results (see, e.g. Anderson and Brown, 1984; Dickerson, Hinchy, and Fabre, 1987). However, as Brown (1986) pointed out, sensation-seeking should be regarded in the context of prevailing levels of stimulation. Evidence seems to indicate that pathological gamblers, apart from their gambling, endure a lifestyle noticeably low in stimulation. Carroll and Huxley's (1991a) young pathological fruit machine gamblers certainly reported relief from boredom as a major motivating force. Accordingly, to the extent that sensation-seeking is implicated in gambling, it is perhaps less as a personality trait, but more as a response to conventional low levels of stimulation and arousal.

Impulsivity and a lack of concern for others also emerges from studies that have administered the Minnesota Multiphasic Personality Inventory to pathological gamblers. Bolen, Caldwell, and Boyd (1975) and Lowenfeld (1979) presented evidence that pathological gamblers score particularly highly on the psychopathic deviate sub-scale. High scores on this scale are deemed to reflect an inability to form and sustain interpersonal relationships, and impulsivity.

Further evidence on the latter emerges from the electroencephalographic studies of Carlton and his associates (Carlton, Manowitz, McBride, Nora, Swartzburg, and Goldstein, 1987; Goldstein, Manowitz, Nora, Swartzburg, and Carlton, 1985). Drawing on the theory that hemispheric dysregulation is related to poor impulse control, hemispheric activation was examined in response to simple verbal versus non-verbal tasks. Pathological gamblers showed a pattern of activation dissimilar to normal control subjects, but similar in many ways to children with attention deficit disorder. Probably the major behavioural characteristic of such children is impulsivity. Carlton and Manowitz (1987) speculated that at the neurochemical level poor control of impulses may be a manifestation of a serotonin deficit. Recently, Moreno, Saiz-Ruiz, and

Lopez-Ibor (1991) presented evidence in line with this speculation. A serotonergic probe was used to measure the degree of activity of the serotonin system in pathological gamblers and matched control subjects. The pathological gamblers showed hypoactivity relative to the controls, a result that led the authors to conclude that pathological gambling shared common neurochemical features with other behavioural disturbances characterized by poor impulse control.

Arousal

A number of recent theorists have proposed an important role for arousal. Dickerson (1984), for example, added arousal, as a reinforcer on a fixed interval schedule, to the more commonly hypothesized variable financial schedule, to explain what sustained a pathological gambler. Indeed, Dickerson argued that arousal as a reinforcer may be a more important determinant of loss of control. This view has been echoed by Blaszczynski, Wilson, and McConaghy (1986). Anderson and Brown (1984) proposed a not dissimilar model. Individual differences on autonomic arousal, as expounded by Nebylitsyn and Gray (1972), combined with irregular financial schedules, were regarded as the driving force behind pathological gambling.

Early laboratory investigations of heart rate as an index of arousal suggested that gambling was not particularly provocative (Rule and Fischer, 1970; Rule, Nutler, and Fischer, 1971). However, the ecological validity of these studies has been questioned. Tellingly, Anderson and Brown (1984) found only modest increases in heart rate among students and regular gamblers in the context of a laboratory casino. For the regular gamblers in a real casino, though, substantial increases in heart rate accompanied gambling. In subsequent studies, reliable increases in cardiovascular activity have been observed during fruit machine play (Carroll and Huxley, 1991*b*; Leary and Dickerson, 1985).

Nevertheless, we are still without strong evidence that individual variation in arousal underlies pathological gambling. In the Anderson and Brown (1984) study only regular gamblers were monitored in the real casino setting. Further, Carroll and Huxley's study comparing pathological and non-pathological fruit machine gamblers suggested that it might be conventional levels of arousal that are discriminating, and not the magnitude of the increase provoked by gambling.

CONCLUDING REMARKS

The study of gambling in general, and fruit machine playing in particular, has still to yield a satisfactory account of the mechanisms which lead some individuals to dependency and gambling of pathological proportions. A variety of factors is undoubtedly involved. It is also likely that these various factors assume a different importance during progression from induction to addiction (see Brown, 1986). For example, at the induction stage, positive cultural attitudes towards gambling, legislative *laissez-faire*, parental participation, and early age of initiation all undoubtedly increase risk. Subsequently, the consistently arousing nature of gambling in the context of an otherwise unfulfilling and unstimulating lifestyle, coupled with a susceptibility to presume control when it is chance which operates, and a personality high on impulsivity and low on social concern, are all likely to be significant factors. However, this is very much the bare bones of a model, and, aside from the proposed role of hemispheric dysregulation and serotonergic deficits in impulsivity, we are without any account of the mechanisms operating at a neurobiological level. Given that pathological gambling may not be phenomenally distinct from other addictive behaviours, it is perhaps to the neurobiology of other, more fully studied, addictions that research into gambling should look for clues.

In the meantime, though, substantial numbers of young people in Britain will continue to fall foul of fruit machines. While a deeper understanding of the processes that have led to their dependency is certainly important, simple legislative reform would undoubtedly yield more immediate dividends.

REFERENCES

Anderson, G. and Brown, R.I.F. (1984). Real and laboratory gambling, sensation-seeking and arousal. *British Journal of Psychology*, **75**, 401–10.

Barham, B. and Cornell, M. (1987). *Teenage use of amusement arcades in Bognor Regis*. West Sussex Institute of Higher Education, Bognor Regis.

Bergler, E. (1957). *The psychology of gambling*. Hill and Wang, New York.

Blaszczynski, A.P., Buhrich, N., and McConaghy, N. (1985). Pathological gamblers, heroin addicts and controls compared on the EPQ 'addiction' scale. *British Journal of Addiction*, **80**, 315–19.

Bolen, D.W., Caldwell, A.B., and Boyd, W.H. (1975). Personality traits of pathological gamblers. Paper presented at the Second Annual Conference on Gambling, Lake Tahoe, Nevada.

Brown, R.I.F. (1986). Arousal and sensation-seeking components in the general explanation of gambling and gambling addictions. *International Journal of the Addictions*, **21**, 1001–16.

Carlton, P.L. and Manowitz, P. (1987). Physiological factors in determinants of pathological gambling. *Journal of Gambling Behavior*, **3**, 274–85.

Carlton, P.L., Manowitz, P., McBride, H., Nora, R., Swartzburg, M., and Goldstein, L. (1987). Attention deficit disorder and pathological gambling. *Journal of Clinical Psychiatry*, **48**, 487–8.

Carroll, D. and Huxley, J.A.A. (1991*a*). *Young people and fruit machine gambling.* Unpublished report to the Children's Society.

Carroll, D. and Huxley, J.A.A. (1991*b*). Personality and psychophysiological activity in dependent and non-dependent young slot machine players. *Psychophysiology,* **28,** S-16.

Carroll, D. and Huxley, J.A.A. (1992). Cardiovascular responses of high and low frequency adolescent gamblers. *Journal of Psychophysiology,* **6,** 350.

Custer, R.L. (1982). An overview of compulsive gambling. In P.A. Carone, S.F. Yoles, S.N. Kieffer, and L. Krinsky (eds.), *Addictive disorders update: Alcoholism, drug abuse, gambling.* Human Sciences Press, New York.

Dell, L.J., Ruzicka, M.F., and Palisi, A.T. (1981). Personality and other factors associated with the gambling addiction. *International Journal of the Addictions,* **16,** 149–56.

Dickerson, M.G. (1984). *Compulsive gamblers.* Longman, London

Dickerson, M.G. and Adcock, S.G. (1987). Mood, arousal and cognitions in persistent gambling: Preliminary investigation of a theoretical model. *Journal of Gambling Behavior,* **3,** 3–15.

Dickerson, M., Hinchy, J., and Fabre, J. (1987). Chasing, arousal and sensation seeking in off-course gamblers. *British Journal of Addiction,* **82,** 673–80.

Eysenck, H.J. and Eysenck, S.B.G. (1975). *Manual of the Eysenck personality questionnaire.* Hodder and Stoughton, Sevenoaks.

Fisher, S.E. (1989). The use of friut machines by children in the UK. *Society for the Study of Gambling Newsletter,* **16,** 13–33.

Fisher, S.E. (1993). Gambling and pathological gambling in adolescents. *Journal of Gambling Studies,* in press

Gadboury, A. and Ladouceur, R. (1989). Erroneous perceptions and gambling. *Journal of Social Behavior and Personality,* **4,** 411–20.

Goldstein, L., Manowitz, P., Nora, R., Swartzburg, M., and Carlton, P.L. (1985). Differential EEG activation and pathological gambling. *Biological Psychiatry,* **20,** 1232–4.

Gossop, M.R. and Eysenck, S.B.G. (1980). A further investigation into the personality of drug addicts in treatment. *British Journal of Addiction,* **75,** 305–11.

Graham, J. (1988). *Amusement machines: Dependency and delinquency.* HMSO, London.

Griffiths, M. (1989). Gambling in children and adolescents. *Journal of Gambling Behavior,* **5,** 66–83.

Griffiths, M. (1990*a*). Addiction to fruit machines: A preliminary study among young males. *Journal of Gambling,* **6,** 113–26.

Griffiths, M. (1990*b*). The acquisition, development and maintenance of fruit machine gambling in adolescents. *Journal of Gambling Behavior,* **6,** 193–204.

Griffiths, M. (1990*c*). The role of cognitive bias and skill in fruit machine gambling. In S.E..G. Lea, P. Webley, and B. Young (eds.), *Applied economic psychology in the 1990s.* Washington Singer Press, Exeter.

Griffiths, M. (1990*d*). Psychobiology of the near-miss in fruit machine gambling. *Journal of Psychology,* **125,** 347–57.

Griffiths, M., Lea, S.E.G., and Webley, P. (1989). *Slot machine playing in the western world.* Internal Report, University of Exeter.

Huff, G. and Collinson, F. (1987). Young offenders, gambling and video game playing. *British Journal of Criminology,* **27,** 401–10.

Huxley, J.A.A. and Carroll, D. (1992). A survey of fruit machine gambling in adolescents. *Journal of Gambling Studies,* **8,** 167–79.

Ide-Smith, S.G. and Lea, S.E.G. (1988). Gambling in young adolescents. *Journal of Gambling Behavior*, **4**, 110–18.

Jacobs, D.F., Pettis, J.L., and Linda, L. (1981). The 'addictive personality syndrome': A new theoretical for understanding and treating addictions. In W. Eadington (ed.) *The Gambling Papers: Proceedings of the Fifth International Conference on Gambling and Risk Taking*. Bureau of Business and Economic Research, University of Nevada, Reno.

Langer, E.J. (1975). The illusion of control. *Journal of Personality and Social Psychology*, **32**, 311–28.

Langer, E.J. (1983). *The psychology of control*. Sage, Beverly Hills.

Leary, K. and Dickerson, M. (1985). Levels of arousal in high and low frequency gamblers. *Behavior Research and Therapy*, **23**, 635–40.

Lee, J. (1989). It's good fun pressing buttons: Young people and video and fruit machine use. Unpublished manuscript.

Lesieur, H.R. and Rothschild, J. (1989). Children of Gamblers Anonymous members. *Journal of Gambling Behavior*, **5**, 269–82.

Livingston, J. (1974). *Compulsive gamblers: Observations on action and abstinence*. Harper and Row, New York.

Lowenfeld, B.H. (1979). Personality dimensions of the pathological gambler. *Dissertation Abstracts International*, **40**, 456.

Mark, E.M., and Lesieur, H.R. (1992). A feminist critique of problem gambling. *British Journal of Addiction*, **87**, 549–65.

McCormick, R.A., Russo, A.M., Ramirez, L.F., and Taber, J.I. (1984). Affective disorders among pathological gamblers seeking treatment. *American Journal of Psychiatry*, **141**, 215–18.

Moody, G. (1987). Parents of young gamblers. Paper presented at the 7th *International Conference on Gambling and Risk Taking*. Reno, Nevada.

Moreno, I., Saiz-Ruiz., J., and Lopez-Ibor, J.J. (1991). Serotonin and gambling dependency. *Human Psychopharmacology*, **6**, S9–12.

National Housing and Town Planning Council (1988). *Gambling machines and young people*. National Housing and Town Planning Council, London.

Nebylitsin, V.D. and Gray, J.A. (ed.) (1972). *Biological basis of individual behavior*. Academic Press, New York.

Rands, J. and Hooper, M. (1990). Survey of young people's use of slot machines within the Sedgemoor district. Unpublished manuscript.

Rotter, J.B. (1966). Generalized expectancies for internal versus external control of reinforcement. *Psychological Monographs*, **80**, 1–28.

Rule, B.G. and Fischer, D.G. (1970). Impulsivity, subjective probability, cardiac response and risk taking: Correlates and factors. *Personality*, **1**, 251–260.

Rule, B.G., Nutler, R.W., and Fischer, D.G. (1971). The effect of arousal on risk-taking. *Personality*, **2**, 239–47.

Skinner, B.F. (1953). *Science and human behavior*. Macmillan, New York.

Spectrum Children's Trust (1988). *Slot machine playing by children*. Spectrum Children's Trust, London.

Waterman, J. and Atkin, K. (1985). Young people and fruit machines. *Society for the Study of Gambling Newsletter*, **7**, 23–7.

Wray, I. and Dickerson, M.G. (1981). Cessation of high frequency gambling and 'withdrawal' symptoms. *British Journal of Addiction*, **76**, 401–5.

Zuckerman, M. (1979). Sensation seeking and risk taking. In C.E. Izard (ed.), *Emotions in personality and psychopathology*. Plenum, New York.

13

Comparing motivational systems— an incentive motivation perspective

Frederick Toates

INTRODUCTION

The framework for this review is an incentive motivation model (Bindra, 1978; Toates, 1981, 1986), based on the assumption that motivation can be understood in terms of behaviour being directed *towards incentives*. The term 'incentive' covers such things as food, water, and a mate, as well as conditional incentives such as a location associated with food. For drug studies on animals, strictly speaking, all incentives are conditional since the animal never negotiates towards the chemical itself but the similarities between behaviour motivated by drugs and by direct commerce with food or water are profound. Incentives both help to arouse motivation and form the target of the animal's goal-directed behaviour. In such terms, dichotomies of the kind 'feeding is internally controlled and sex externally controlled' are seen to be meaningless, since both motivations are determined by incentive objects and internal states.

Some assumptions of the model provide organizing themes for the present chapter:

(1) Motivational states arise from an interaction between (a) internal states and (b) both unconditional (e.g. the taste of sucrose) and conditional incentive stimuli. For example, in feeding, internal state is made up of such things as glucose level and gut contents, while the incentive contribution comprises such things as the sensory properties of food. It was argued (Toates, 1986) that internal factors can be represented by a parameter which, in effect, multiplies the incoming signal to determine motivation (see also Wise, 1987, for a similar model). The parameter can be positive (e.g. low energy reserves), which will promote commerce with a food-related incentive or negative (e.g. energy surfeit or a taste associated with aversion) which, together with the food, will produce an avoidance motivational state.

(2) Neutral stimuli paired with incentive presentation can acquire incentive value; they can acquire some of the motivation-arousing properties of the unconditional incentive. Such conditional incentives can give strength and direction to behaviour (apparent in the animal's pursuit of incentives).

(3) The power of an unconditional incentive stimulus to arouse motivation depends in part upon associations formed between the stimulus and its consequences (e.g. a substance might be favoured if it yields calories).

(4) Given that motivation is aroused by a complex of factors, external and internal, it can only be understood in terms of *interactions* between components. For example, the role of the internal metabolic stimulus for feeding is revealed in the context of a matrix of external stimuli and associations between external and metabolic signals. Similarly, satiety of feeding involves events at several levels (oral, gastric, intestinal, post-absorptive) with a particular time-course of relationship between them.

(5) Given its multiple determinants, motivation is not a fixed attribute of a given animal at a given time. An animal might show motivation in the presence of one food but not another. For example, it might show motivation as indexed by appetitive behaviour (lever pressing for food) but not consummatory behaviour (eating).

Examination of behaviour in the light of these five assumptions shows there to be important similarities between different motivational systems. The present review focusses upon results obtained since 1985 and their interpretation in terms of the model. Emphasis will be upon general principles applicable to more than one motivational system.

THE CAPACITY OF INCENTIVES TO AROUSE MOTIVATION

Incentives (e.g. taste of food, presence of a partner) have the capacity to arouse motivation directed towards the incentive and associated cues.

In feeding, the power of external stimuli to arouse ingestion even in satiated human subjects was shown by Cornell, Rodin, and Weingarten (1989). Priming with a brief exposure to the taste of either pizza or ice-cream selectively increased the intake of the primed food relative to the unprimed. The differential effectiveness according to the food primed suggests a cognitive effect of holding food-related items in memory.

If an incentive such as food can increase motivation directed towards itself, this defines a positive feedback system. In time, behaviour would be dominated by the delayed effects of negative feedback. One possible basis of positive feedback is the opioid system. There is evidence that opioids both potentiate, and are released by, feeding, particularly of sweet solutions (Fantino, Hosotte, and Apfelbaum, 1986; Lieblich, Yirmiya, and Liebeskind, 1991), which could constitute positive feedback.

In the context of drug taking, incentive motivation models and the possibility of positive feedback (the action of the drug would be to sensitize the motivational pathways underlying drug craving) have attracted much attention. Thus Bozarth (1991) considers the situation where a rat that has learned to lever-press for either intravenous drug or electrical brain stimulation, is placed in the apparatus but sits grooming. A priming reward is given by the experimenter. On a reinforcement interpretation, this should merely increase the frequency of grooming. What in practice occurs is that the animal initiates lever pressing. Thus the priming could be described as rewarding but not reinforcing. In terms that echo an incentive motivation interpretation, Bozarth identifies:

'. . . an important attribute of reward mechanisms—they increase behaviours associated with their activation. Brain reward function thus describes processes that elicit approach behaviour and processes that the subject 'seeks' to activate. Reward functions to direct the animal's behaviour toward whatever stimulus or response is most strongly associated with reward expectancy . . .'

In this context, the evidence from human drug addicts and alcoholics suggests that craving can be induced by the *presence* of the drug or alcohol in the body (Kassel and Shiffman, 1992; Robinson and Berridge, 1993; Stewart, de Wit, and Eikelboom, 1984). Thus craving can be highest immediately after taking the drug or alcohol.

Incentives themselves can arouse motivation but incentives normally occur embedded within a matrix of other stimuli and events. Events precede their arrival and follow the animal's commerce with them. The nervous system forms associations between the incentive object and these events. This topic forms the subject of the next three sections.

ADAPTIVE CONTROL—FEEDBACK EFFECTS

The model incorporates the feature that the capacity of incentive objects to control behaviour depends upon the consequences of the animal's commerce with them. This section looks at some recent evidence and theories that concern this.

In sexual behaviour, lesions to the preoptic area of rats disrupt *performance* of copulation but do not immediately disrupt appetitive behaviour. However, over a number of sessions, with repeated failure to achieve intromission, loss of appetitive motivation is seen (Everitt and Stacey, 1987). Preference for a place associated with a female falls to zero (Everitt, 1990), indicating a feedback effect from the consequences of consummatory behaviour to appetitive arousal.

Much of the evidence on the modification of behaviour with experience comes from feeding; the consequences of ingestion, whether positive (gain of nutrients) or negative (illness) modify preferences and future intake. The conditions under which a shift in preference can be shown to occur following post-ingestive consequences can give insight into the unconditional signal. Tordoff and Friedman (1986) found both (i) a satiating effect of hepatic portal vein infusions of glucose (but not jugular infusions); and (ii) a preference for flavours tasted during the infusion. The post-ingestive consequence that supports a shift of preference is fuel oxidation (Tordoff, Tepper, and Friedman, 1987; Tordoff, Ulrich, and Sandler, 1990). Whereas ingested glucose modulates a previously neutral taste in a positive direction for normal rats, for diabetic rats it produces an aversion for the previously neutral flavour (Tordoff, Tepper, and Friedman, 1987).

Some researchers employ sham feeding to study these processes. In sham feeding, ingested nutrients either fail to get beyond the stomach or are transported in much smaller amounts. Bédard and Weingarten (1989) examined lowered responsivity to taste (negative alliesthesia) as a factor terminating a meal. They looked at the ability of intraperitoneal (ip) glucose to attenuate sham feeding, varying the time of loading from before, to during, feeding. A *combination* of sham feeding followed by ip glucose suppressed subsequent sham feeding. The ip load in the absence of the prior five-minute sham feeding suppressed little. They noted the synergistic suppression between, on the one hand, taste stimulation and, on the other, either CCK, gastric loads or duodenal loads. Injection needed to be made at the same time as, or following, feeding to be suppressive. As palatability of the solution decreased (by lowering its sucrose concentration), so the size of load that was sufficient to suppress sham feeding decreased.

It is possible to imagine at least two ways in which consequences could alter motivation. Taste-aversion learning can be used to illustrate this. First, what Grill and Berridge (1985) term the 'hedonic evaluation' of the unconditional incentive (e.g. food) might be altered by experience. They described a set of functionally related reactions to substances placed on the tongue, ranging from hedonically positive (maximizing ingestion) to aversive (eliminating contact). For example, sodium depletion converts a negative evaluation of a hypertonic saline solution to a positive one (Berridge and Schulkin, 1989), showing the role of internal state as a modulator of the power of the taste stimulus. Pairing a taste with gustatory illness converts the palatability evaluation from positive to negative (Grill and Berridge, 1985). Bolles (1991) proposes, as a general theory, that changes in intake as a result of consequences are mediated by changes in hedonic evaluation but we have reason to doubt the universality of this process. Thus, as a second possibility for how experience might affect intake, under some conditions the animal might form a predictive association between taste and outcome but the hedonic rating of the incentive would remain unaltered.

In accounting for taste-aversion learning, Garcia (1989) argues that nausea provides feedback to modulate the hedonics of taste. This is in preference to the terminology that taste is a CS and ionizing radiation a UCS and accounts better for the fact that, for example, a steadily growing tumour can produce a steadily increasing aversion to the diet. In this situation, there is no clear time of onset of the UCS. Modulation of hedonic value would also fit with the disgust reaction that animals show to the previously acceptable solution. According to Garcia, non-taste cues paired with nausea can acquire a negative incentive value to the extent that they are able to predict a taste that has been devalued.

However, there are procedures that modify the approach behaviour towards foods but the hedonic rating of the food, if applied to the tongue, remains unchanged. Thus, following ingestion by immediate electric shock reduces future ingestion but does not do so by modulating hedonic evaluation (Pelchat, Grill, Rozin, and Jacobs, 1983). Conversely, experimenter-controlled electrical stimulation of the lateral hypothalamus (ESLH), the area also implicated in electrical self-stimulation, evokes feeding in satiated rats. However, its capacity to do so cannot be explained by hedonic enhancement of food. Berridge and Valenstein (1991) found using the taste-reactivity test that the affective reactions were shifted in an overall negative, rather than positive, direction by simultaneous ESLH.

The phenomenon of sham feeding is relevant to theorizing about hedonic re-evaluation. For animals sham feeding, intake increases over successive daily presentations. How is this to be explained? One imagines any hedonic re-evaluation would be in the direction of devaluing the food, since ingestion fails to deliver normal consequences. Of course, any such devaluation would not explain increased intake, since it would contribute to decreased intake over days. Davis and Smith (1990) discuss the increase in intake and the assumption that the rat is relearning the relationship between ingestion and its post-absorptive consequences. Normally intake is thought to be restrained by (i) unconditional satiety (from nutrients in and beyond the gut); and (ii) conditional factors (expectation of nutrients). The surgery either eliminates, or drastically reduces (i), but (ii) would take time to extinguish. Davis and Smith interspersed days of normal feeding between days of sham feeding and found that this prevented the rise in amount sham fed. This is what would be expected on the basis of learning.

The usual interpretation of increasing intake in sham feeding is that rats have a prior (taste/ingestion) → (caloric consequence) expectation, which, during sham feeding, is not realized. Weingarten and Kulikovsky (1989) argued that one would expect to see such an increase for diets that the rat had earlier eaten normally (revision of expectation based upon failure to realize consequences) but not for diets that it had not consumed normally (intake would be expected to be elevated from the start). The data supported this.

Can the sham-feeding results be reconciled with any hedonic re-evaluation taking place? As noted, the contribution of such re-evaluation would presumably be a tendency to subsequent *decreasing* intake over days. Such devaluation might indeed occur but it is difficult to tell from ingestion alone; it could occur but be masked. Only the taste-reactivity test would enable us to know. Since both a change in hedonic value and some additional process of learning about consequences would determine ingestion, increased intake could arise from the latter (learning about the decreased nutrient consequences of ingestion), in spite of a decrease in the former. Whatever the processes postulated, it is necessary to explain why (i) intake increases over days, including the first five minutes of sham feeding; and (ii) following experience of sham feeding, the first non-sham ingested meal is larger than normal.

Exteroceptive cues such as visual stimuli from the environment paired with ingestion can also play a role in modulating intake as a function of the consequences of ingestion. For example, tolerance to the anorexic effect of amphetamine is determined by environmental cues and the consequences of ingestion (Poulos and Cappell, 1991). It seems unlikely that the effect of exteroceptive cues is mediated via changes in taste hedonics given that amphetamine itself does not alter taste hedonics (Treit and Berridge, 1990). (However it is mediated, it raises the interesting question of whether human subjects taking dieting agents should be encouraged to change regularly the environmental context associated with the act of eating).

In rats, Lucas and Timberlake (1992) presented a 0.15 per cent saccharin solution followed by either a preferred 32 per cent sucrose solution or a non-preferred saccharine solution. For the group receiving 32 per cent sucrose, preference conditioning associated with the taste of 0.15 per cent saccharin occurred; its intake increased over days. Presumably the (taste of A) → (nutrient gain of B) association enhanced the preference for A. However, acting in the opposite direction, environmental (that is, non taste-related) cues present at the time of ingesting the 0.15 per cent saccharin conditioned a decrease in intake of A, termed a negative anticipatory contrast effect; presumably an (environmental cue) → (presentation of B) association was responsible. The net effect was determined by the difference between these two conditioning processes. It is interesting to speculate that taste hedonics might be modulated in the first association but not in the second.

The notion that, in the control of intake, changes in physiological state can modulate taste reactivity might fit the observations that those rats that manage to learn to lever press for intravenous or intragastric reward sometimes lick the lever or wall at the time of pressing (reviewed by Toates, 1981). As a thought experiment, would a taste-reactivity test reveal the rat's reaction to the taste of the lever to be modified by the gain of nutrients following such interaction? The relationship between (i) incentives, for example the exteroceptive cue of the lever and its click combined with the response of pressing itself, and (ii) nutrient gain could be mediated via the stimulus of taste of the metal. By this means, rats would be able to generate exteroceptive and proprioceptive information that would normally accompany ingestion.

It is suggested that, normally, the motivation to maintain feeding derives from taste, the accompanying motor patterns of ingestion (Toates and Jensen, 1991) and tactile stimulation associated with ingestion. In support of such an interpretation, Jacquin and Zeigler (1983) found that rats with trigeminal section, thereby denied orosensation, lost body weight and reduced the frequency of meals. Berridge and Fentress (1985) found that, in rats, transection of the sensory branches of the trigeminal nerve shifted palatability. Fewer ingestive reactions were shown to a normally palatable solution placed on the tongue. A possible interpretation deriving from both studies is that (i) loss of palatability by trigeminal section, as reflected in consummatory behaviour, is followed by (ii) a lowering of the incentive value of food at a distance as a stimulus to initiate a meal, which thereby reduces meal frequency. The phenomenon of air-licking by thirsty rats (Oatley and Dickinson, 1970) might also make better sense in such terms. It seems that a combination of the sensory detection of cold air combined with motor action has sufficient in common with normal drinking to maintain this action.

CONDITIONAL INCENTIVE STIMULI AND THE CONTROL OF BEHAVIOUR

A number of results show that stimuli paired with incentive presentation and/or consummatory behaviour acquire a capacity to exert control over behaviour. Thus, cues paired with the presentation of food (Weingarten, 1984) and opiate drugs (Stewart, de Wit, and Eikelboom, 1984) acquire appetitive value. The observation of conditional incentive motivational effects across motivational systems encourages the development of general models of motivation. The present section looks at the behavioural effects of presenting such conditional incentives and asks what are the processes underlying this effect.

Sexual behaviour

In quail, the incentive value of a conspecific, as indexed by approach behaviour, can be increased by mating experience (Domjan, Akins, and Vandergriff, 1992). In rats, the strength of sexual motivation would appear to be increased by conditional incentives, as indexed by, for example, lever pressing in an operant task. Bar pressing for a light CS+ that had been paired with presentation of a receptive female was looked at by Everitt, Fray, Kostarczyk, Taylor and Stacey (1987). Omission of the CS+ resulted in a lowering of appetitive responding. The post-ejaculatory interval, a period of non-arousability, was characterized by a sharp drop in appetitive responding.

Ingestive behaviour

In an operant situation, the contextual cue of the Skinner box is paired with reward. This association was investigated by Dickinson (1989), which allowed him to reinterpret the 'irrelevant incentive effect' experiment. In this, animals learn an instrumental task for a reward that has two properties, one relevant to their motivational state and one irrelevant. For example, a hungry rat might learn a task for a sucrose solution. The reward's energy content is relevant, but its fluid content is irrelevant, to hunger. Subsequently, rats are tested in extinction when made thirsty. As normally carried out, the rats have never experienced a sucrose solution in a state of thirst. Typically, such rats press more in extinction under thirst than those trained with an incentive irrelevant to thirst (e.g. dry pellets). As Dickinson notes, one's intuitive explanation of the process underlying this effect is that (i) when hungry, animals encode a relationship between a response and its outcome; (ii) the sucrose solution is desirable under thirst; and (iii) this is reflected in greater responding in extinction.

Superficially, the result is compatible with this interpretation but further experimentation forces a different interpretation (Dickinson and Dawson, 1988). Rats were food deprived and learned that, in a given Skinner box, pressing a lever delivered one reinforcer (e.g.

sucrose solution) and pulling a chain delivered another (e.g. food pellets). Motivation was then shifted to thirst and rats were tested in extinction with access to just the lever. If the irrelevant incentive effect is based upon learning an instrumental relationship between response and reinforcer, it could be predicted that rats would respond in extinction by pressing the lever more in those cases where the lever had delivered sucrose than where it had delivered food pellets. Surprisingly this was not the case.

So what does mediate the irrelevant incentive effect, if not an instrumental contingency between response and reinforcer? Dickinson suggested a Pavlovian association between the contextual cues within the Skinner box and the reinforcer. Later experimentation confirmed this. Thus, although the irrelevant incentive effect is not to be explained in terms of an instrumental expectancy, it shows that information on the reinforcer is encoded in the Pavlovian association. Dickinson concludes that: 'Presenting a conditioned stimulus activates a *representation* of the reinforcer whose sensitivity to the activation is directly enhanced by the presence of a relevant drive state. The excited representation then appears to have a potentiating effect on any prepotent actions.' But does this mean that animals do not learn response → reinforcer relationships? No. It shows that (i) Pavlovian associations can mediate incentive motivation; and (ii) under the conditions *traditionally tested* the effect is mediated by such an association rather than an R→S one (however, see also the following section).

In the case of ingestive behaviour, the taste-reactivity test enables one of the effects of conditional incentives to be elucidated. Delamater, LoLordo and Berridge (1986) gave a neutral cue (a tone) at the time of presenting either sucrose or quinine. When the tone and water were given later, the tone endowed the water with some of the hedonic attribute of the solution with which it had earlier been paired, suggesting that part of the power of conditional incentive stimuli is exerted through modulation of taste hedonics. This fits with Garcia's argument (see above) that the effect of exteroceptive cues on ingestive behaviour is mediated via taste. Berridge and Schulkin (1989) paired a neutral taste with application of NaCl solution to the tongues of rats that were not sodium depleted (when NaCl is not hedonically positive). They were then tested both in sodium balance and when depleted (when NaCl is hedonically positive). For rats tested sodium depleted, palatability was shifted in the direction of positive hedonics by the prior experience. This was not so for rats tested in sodium balance. The result is evidence that, as a result of learning, neutral cues acquire hedonic properties.

Results such as these lead to the conclusion that one function served by conditional incentive stimuli is to increase the strength of consummatory behaviour, revealed by increased hedonic evaluation of a taste if accompanied by conditional incentive cues. Stimuli not localized in space (e.g. sounds or smells) could easily serve this role. According to incentive motivation theory, spatially localized incentive stimuli (e.g. food at a particular site) also have the function of giving *direction* to behaviour. In this context, Berridge and associates argue that a role of incentives is to act as attractors to the animal: goal-directed behaviour is directed towards them. For example, Berridge and Valenstein (1991) propose that electrical stimulation of the lateral hypothalamus potentiates the salience of food-related external stimuli. Incentive *salience attribution* is '. . . the active assignment of salience and attractiveness to visual, auditory, tactile, or olfactory stimuli that are themselves intrinsically neutral'. Incentive salience will be discussed further in the next section.

Drug taking

In the case of an animal working for intravenous reward of drugs in a Skinner box, there are not, of course, natural sensory associations (sight, taste) in the way that there are in the process of earning food or water. However, reward can be associated with sensory events in a contingency arranged by the experimenter. There is some evidence that such arbitrary response-associated exteroceptive stimuli acquire a strong incentive value. Although it is possible to obtain responding on an operant task rewarded with intravenous nicotine (Goldberg, Spealman, and Goldberg, 1981) or cocaine (Spealman and Goldberg, 1978), omission of a light that had been paired with delivery caused responding to fall sharply. A possible role of classical conditioning might be found in reports of opioid-like conditioned effects in humans following injection of saline when opioid was expected or hoped for (O'Brien, Ehrman, and Ternes, 1986).

Theories of drug taking and relapse emphasize different underlying processes but all are agreed that a major factor is classical conditioning (Glautier, this volume; Robinson and Berridge, 1993; Siegel, Krank and Hinson, 1987; Stewart, de Wit, and Eikelboom, 1984). Craving for cigarettes, alcohol, cocaine and heroin can be increased by presenting cues that in the past were paired with the substance, for example injecting equipment, a placebo beverage (see review by Kassel and Shiffman, 1992).

Recently, based upon incentive motivation theory, Robinson and Berridge (1993) argue that a major factor in drug addiction is the allocation of *incentive salience* to drug-related stimuli. This postulation involves a quite distinct process from any associations also formed between drug-related stimuli and either euphoria or withdrawal symptoms. The process underlying such allocation increases in strength with each drug experience. Thus although the pleasure derived from drugs might *decrease* with each experience the salience attributed to drug-related stimuli can increase. Elevated dopamine turnover (discussed later) induced by the drug appears to be responsible for the pathological levels of incentive salience attribution, a positive feedback system.

There is every reason to suppose that multiple factors underlie drug craving and taking, and conditional stimuli might control behaviour by different means at different times. Thus, Baker, Morse and Sherman (1986) present evidence for two distinct and mutually inhibitory states, termed positive- and negative-affect urge networks, each able to trigger craving. The power of a conditional stimulus might depend to some extent upon mood or physiological state congruence between the current time of drug taking and the time of initial exposure to the cue. Further evidence that could be advanced in support of this interpretation is as follows:

(1) The motivational basis of drug abuse appears to vary both between individuals and within a given individual as a function of time (O'Brien, Ehrman, and Ternes, 1986).

(2) The development of abuse following medication with opiates as analgesics is rare (reviewed by Henningfield, Lukas, and Bigelow, 1986; Melzack, 1990). This might be explained in terms of motivation arising exclusively within a negative-affect urge network at times of pain and opiate-linked associations being formed neither within a positive-affect urge network nor with conditional incentive stimuli outside the medical context.

(3) Relapse rate among Vietnam veterans was relatively low on their return home (reviewed by O'Brien, Ehrman, and Ternes, 1986), which could be seen as removal of the support stimuli for abuse.

(4) The same CSs (e.g. pre-injection ritual) can elicit either opioid-like or withdrawal-like CRs, depending upon internal state at the time. Extinction to drug-related stimuli can be mood-specific (O'Brien, Ehrman, and Ternes, 1986). A patient showing extinction of responses in a normal mood state can sometimes show a reaction (e.g. craving) the following day when depressed.

The possibility of various conditioned associations, (i) cues to hedonism; (ii) cues to withdrawal; and (iii) salience attribution means that it might be difficult to predict when relapse will occur. By processes (i) and (ii), opportunistic encounters with drug-related cues might trigger intake/relapse at times when craving is not particularly high (Kassel and Shiffman, 1992).

THE INSTRUMENTAL CONTINGENCY AND INCENTIVE MOTIVATION

The last section emphasized the role of classical conditioning between neutral cues and incentives in the control of behaviour. It was noted that the irrelevant incentive effect, which is often interpreted in terms of learning a relationship between an action and an outcome, can, at least under the condition described, be explained in terms of classical conditioning between the cage and reward.

However, the assumption is commonly made that behaviour in the Skinner box is mediated, at least in part, via a (response) → (outcome) association. In this context, Dickinson cites Tolman, who suggested that behaviour is determined by the expectancy for a particular reinforcer and the value attributed to that reinforcer in a given drive state. This value derives from past experience with the reinforcer in the particular drive state. Thus, based upon such principles, one would not expect the irrelevant incentive effect to be mediated via an R→S association, since typically the irrelevant incentive has been one never before experienced in the drive state under which the effect is sought. For example, rats trained under hunger and tested under thirst had no prior experience of sucrose solution in the state of thirst.

Suppose rats are given prior experience of sucrose solution under the condition of thirst, trained under hunger in a concurrent task (one response leading to sucrose and another to food pellets), and then tested for an irrelevant incentive shift. Under these conditions, in extinction under thirst there is increased responding on the manipulandum previously delivering sucrose.

To summarize in the terms of Bindra (1978), the Pavlovian expectancy would be seen as follows. The context acts as a CS which creates an expectancy of a UCS. This expectancy acts in combination with a physiological state to arouse a central motivational state that plays a role in instrumental behaviour. Dickinson showed that this process survives a shift from one physiological state (e.g. water imbalance) appropriate to an incentive (e.g. mild saline) to another appropriate physiological state (e.g. sodium deficiency) whether or not the animal has had prior experience of the incentive under the new physiological state.

Behaviour can also be controlled in part by an instrumental expectancy (R→S) between response and reinforcer. However, for this expectancy to be revealed by particular goal-directed behaviour (e.g. pressing a lever rather than pulling a chain), the animal must have had prior experience of the incentive (even in a context outside the Skinner box) in the physiological state tested in extinction. As Dickinson notes, the results suggest that: '. . . a desire for a particular reinforcer under a given drive state depends on prior experience with that incentive in the appropriate motivational state. This, in turn, suggests that desires must be based on beliefs about the value of reinforcers which have their origins in experience.'

Balleine (1992) looked at the effect of changing motivation level on lever pressing in extinction. Suppose rats are trained under conditions of strong hunger and then tested in extinction under either a high or low hunger. It might be expected that activity in extinction would reflect the level of hunger existing at the time of observation. However, Balleine found that animals trained under one magnitude of food deprivation and then tested in extinction under another only sometimes show a shift in responding commensurate with the shift in deprivation. Balleine showed that whether they do so depends upon whether they had prior experience of the reinforcer under the deprivation condition tested in extinction. For example, suppose a rat is trained to earn a particular sort of pellet under low hunger and then tested in extinction under a high hunger. The elevated hunger level will be reflected in a higher rate of lever pressing in extinction provided the rat had experienced the pellets in question earlier (either in, or outside, the operant context) when under a high hunger. This discounts a model of the kind that drive level multiplies with habit strength to determine behaviour. Incentive value in the operant context retains the value allocated on experiencing the incentive unless modified by experience in the current state of motivation. Thus, there is a dissociation between consummatory and appetitive measures of motivation; changing drive levels are reflected more in consummatory than appetitive measures until the animal has experience with the substance in the new drive state. This is comparable to the results of taste-aversion learning (discussed earlier), where a rat might show operant behaviour towards a food which it will decline to ingest. (A somewhat analogous effect for sexual behaviour was noted by Everitt (1990). Male rats with mPOA lesions show normal appetitive behaviour, which is only revised following (abortive) contact with a female.)

INCENTIVE MOTIVATION, AND THE ROLE OF DOPAMINE

Dopamine is assumed to play a central role in motivational processes, and the incentive motivation model (Toates, 1986) has been shown to have explanatory value in elucidating this role (Berridge, Venier, and Robinson, 1989).

Presentation of a conditional stimulus signalling food results in increased dopamine utilization in the nucleus accumbens (Blackburn,

Phillips, Jakubovic, and Fibiger, 1989). By contrast, feeding was not associated with an increase, leading Blackburn *et al.* to conclude that: 'dopamine systems are more importantly involved in *preparatory* than in *consummatory* feeding behaviours'. On presenting a cue predictive of food, normal rats orient towards the cue and explore the feeding tray. Pimozide decreased the vigour of such behaviour but had little effect upon consummatory behaviour (Phillips, Pfaus, and Blaha, 1991), a result compatible with that of Salamone, Steinpreis, McCullough, Smith, Grebel, and Mahan (1991), though other researchers have failed to find a similar effect (Wise and Raptis, 1986). In the terms of incentive motivation theory and those of Berridge, Venier, and Robinson (1989), an interpretation of the result of Phillips *et al.* would be that pimozide lowers the incentive value (salience) of food at a distance from the animal.

Antagonists which affect ventral striatal dopamine receptors delay *initiation* of copulation but not performance (Everitt, 1990). *d*-Amphetamine injection into the nucleus accumbens of male rats reduces mount latency without changing copulatory pattern. Activation of DA neurons in the nucleus accumbens of a male rat occurs as a result of being in the presence of a female, even where the male is denied access. Ejaculation is associated with a decrease in level of nucleus accumbens dopamine (Everitt, 1990; Phillips *et al.*, 1991). Phillips *et al.* suggest that the increase in DA levels in the male elicited by the presence of a receptive female represents a neural substrate for sexual arousal. Further, they suggest that the drop in DA activity in the nucleus accumbens following ejaculation fits an incentive model in which ejaculation desensitizes arousal processes (Toates, 1986). For rats having experienced a classical contingency between a light CS+ and presentation of a female, pressing for the CS+ was increased by amphetamine infused into the ventral striatum (Everitt, Cador, and Robbins, 1989).

Dopamine depletion by 6-OHDA lesions of the substantia nigra causes severe aphagia but does not alter ingestive behaviour in response to oral infusion (Berridge, Venier, and Robinson, 1989). Berridge *et al.* propose that '. . . mesostriatal dopamine neurons belong to a system that assigns salience or motivational significance to the perception of intrinsically neutral events'. The result is what would be predicted from Crow's (1973) hypothesis. He discussed a fundamental distinction between the roles of olfaction and taste in feeding. Whereas olfaction serves to orient the animal towards food, the role of taste can only be served once food is in the mouth. Olfaction would seem to serve an incentive motivational role, whereas taste might more clearly fit a reinforcing role. In its evolutionary roots, Crow suggests that dopaminergic neurons mediate the effects of olfactory inputs on incentive motivation.

For rats under the influence of a DA blocker, even before the first pellet is obtained there is evidence of some reduction in motivation (Wise, 1982). This led Wise to propose, in a similar vein to the incentive motivation interpretation, that 'environmental cues lost their normal effectiveness because of neuroleptic treatment'. One of Wise's (1982) arguments in favour of a motivational rather than a motor fatigue explanation can, as a motivational explanation, be used to favour incentive devaluation. Wise rightly notes that fatigue should be context-independent, whereas the decline in performance seen in DA-blocked rats is context-specific (discussed by Berridge and Valenstein, 1991). Context specificity is what would be expected on the basis of loss of incentive salience. Berridge and Valenstein explain the loss of motivation arising from DA-blockers by claiming that 'such drugs prevent the continual reboosting of salience attribution to an incentive that normally occurs during a meal or reward' and: 'Task specificity can be explained by supposing that neuroleptics have prevented the reboosting of salience attribution to the specific incentive stimuli that are associated with the "extinguished" task.' In such terms dopamine would be implicated in the process of tagging incentives. (There is also a report of a dopamine-induced increase in food intake that is specific to the testing situation (Friedman and Coons, 1983).)

Superficially, at least, the process of reboosting incentive salience would seem to resemble priming (increased responding as a result of the prior application of non-contingent reward). However, in a study of rewarding brain stimulation, Wasserman, Gomita, and Gallistel (1982) found that, whereas reward impact is reduced by pimozide (a dopamine blocker), the effect of priming stimulation is not blocked. This result is not easy to explain in terms of an incentive motivation model; an interpretation of priming is that it motivates the rat by reminding it of the reward. One might argue that, since priming took place in a different environment to that used for testing, its effect was one of a general increase in motivation. By contrast, dopamine might be implicated in the more specific tagging of a goal with a reward label. Reboosting would occur at the time of incentive contact. However, Wasserman *et al.* also found the more specific effect that priming increased the choice of brain stimulation over water and this is not blocked by pimozide.

Dopamine appears to be involved in the processes whereby neutral stimuli become incentive stimuli as a result of their pairing with reward (Beninger, 1989; Taylor and Robbins,1984). Franklin and McCoy (1979) investigated the loss of responding for brain stimulation reward induced by pimozide. They found that presenting a light previously paired with brain-stimulation reward (not during DA blockage) can temporarily restore responding. This suggests that DA blocking produces a deficit in incentive motivational processes which can be temporarily overcome by presenting a conditioned incentive stimulus that has not been devalued by DA blocking (Beninger, 1989).

Beninger observes that rats are still able to learn a spatial discrimination in a T-maze (e.g. turn left) even under the effect of a DA blocker, and suggests that this result remains the strongest challenge to an incentive motivation model of DA function. A possible explanation might need to appeal to a rather different process from that of incentive motivation. Animals are able to learn by various processes (Dickinson, 1989) and they might be forming an S–R association under these conditions. A possible reason for the difference between results in the Skinner box and the T-maze is that, in the maze, if the rat is motivated to run, it would presumably have a relatively high probability of performing the correct response by chance, whereas this might be low in the Skinner box. If it repeatedly gets rewarded for turning left, it might acquire an S–R association, whereas the Skinner box might, initially at least, require cognitions and incentive attribution for its solution. It would be interesting to compare the effects of DA blocking on response learning and place learning strategies in a given maze. The prediction would be that place learners would be more disrupted than response learners.

The incentive motivational perspective adopted in this chapter allows similarities to be seen not only between appetitive motivational systems but also those based on aversion, where dopamine is also implicated in the control of behaviour. Rats subjected to tone–shock pairings while under the influence of a dopamine receptor blocker learn the association as indexed by a conditioned emotional response (CER) (Beninger, 1989). However, they fail to learn one-way shock avoidance (Fibiger, Zis, and Phillips, 1975). Beninger (1989) is specific about what DA-depleted rats cannot learn in an avoidance task. Their failure is in 'the acquisition by the safety-related environmental stimuli of the ability to elicit reactions that involve instrumental responses that serve to bring the animal closer to them'.

Why do DA-depleted rats fail to learn avoidance? Where physical movement is concerned, avoidance involves not simply getting away from somewhere but getting *to a safe situation* (Masterson and Crawford, 1982). Under the influence of a DA-block, they seem to fail to attribute positive salience to the safe platform or side of the shuttle box as cued by the CS (Crow and Deakin, 1985). Recently, the importance of the length of time spent in the safe location in achieving one-way avoidance has been established (Candido, Maldonado, Megias, and Catena, 1992; Candido, Maldonado, and Vila, 1989) and interpreted in incentive motivation terms.

Recently evidence has emerged to implicate nucleus accumbens dopamine in aversively motivated behaviour, in this case lever-pressing to avoid shock, as well as that appetitively motivated (McCullough, Sokolowski, and Salamone, 1993). Dopamine depletion disrupts this behaviour and McCullough *et al.* suggest interpreting this result in a broad incentive motivation framework, that is, that dopamine plays a role attributing motivational significance to temporal cues predictive of shock. In such a situation, by responding the rat is of course not actually moving anywhere and so, to account for this result, an adaptation of Beninger's claim (see above) is needed. The rat is achieving a shock-free period by its active behaviour, so if in Beninger's statement 'closer to them' is replaced by 'a situation of safety' the result might be encompassed. That neither the CER (Beninger, 1989) nor freezing (McCullough *et al.*, 1993) is disrupted by DA-blockage suggests that the animal is still sensitive to aversive stimulation and is able to effect appropriate passive behaviour but active goal-directed behaviour is disrupted.

CONCLUSIONS

Results from feeding, sexual behaviour, and drug taking confirm the emphases of the earlier model in pointing to the crucial role of incentives and their context as determinants of motivation. The similarity of incentive motivational processes across motivations encourages the development of general models. Results with DA-depletion encourage looking for features common to appetitive and aversively motivated behaviour. In a similar vein, within an incentive motivational framework, Kassel and Shiffman (1992) argue for the usefulness of the notion of craving in drug taking. They note its similarity to that of hunger in the context of feeding control, both being under multi-factor control and powerfully triggered by incentives. To these authors, the fact that hunger, the paradigm of physiological regulation, could not simply be tied down to tissue needs encouraged speculation on the similarity of hunger and drug seeking.

The chapter has emphasized the power of incentive motivation theory to explain behaviour. Positive feedback was described. However, implied in the discussion of feeding, drinking, and sex is also the existence of negative feedback effects that exert an influence through modulation of incentive value. There is also evidence for negative feedback effects in drug taking and so far the model does not address these. They require further insights. For example, in the case of rats that are lever pressing for self-administration of drugs, changing the size of reward or changing its impact by giving antagonists is typically followed by compensatory changes in frequency of lever-pressing (Bozarth, 1987; Koob, Vaccarino, Amalric, and Bloom, 1987; Yokel and Pickens, 1974; Yokel and Wise, 1975). It might be interpreted that there is some kind of expectation regarding the outcome of pressing. R.A.Wise (personal communication) might well be right that the kind of model proposed here can handle these effects and 'that the case of drug reward is little different from the case of food reward with respect to the fact that the animal is not interested in the incentive stimuli when post-ingestional consequences of the last meal or injection are still present'. However, both conceptually and experimentally, we need more insight into the satiety pathway for drugs.

There is evidence for a substitution process between exogenous opioids and natural behaviours that appear to involve endogenous opioids, which also suggests a negative feedback process. Thus availability of sucrose reduces the amount of morphine solution drunk by rats (Kanarek and Marks-Kaufman, 1988). The time infant guinea pigs spend in the proximity of their mother is decreased by morphine (Herman and Panksepp, 1978). Keverne, Martensz, and Tuite (1989) found that cerebrospinal beta-endorphin levels increased during grooming in Talpoin monkeys. Morphine administration reduced the number of invitations and time spent grooming whereas the opiate blocker naltrexone increased them. There is a tendency for isolation to increase both alcohol (Wolffgramm, 1991) and opiate (Alexander and Hadaway, 1982; Bozarth, Murray, and Wise, 1989) intake.

Finally, in application to humans, it hardly needs to be stated that caution is needed. The extent to which such principles as classical conditioning, derived from laboratory-based rat studies, can be applied to ecologically viable human situations is still open to some discussion (Hammersley, 1992).

ACKNOWLEDGEMENT

I am most grateful to Kent Berridge and Roy Wise for their insightful comments on the chapter.

REFERENCES

Alexander, B.K. and Hadaway, P.F. (1982). Opiate addiction: The case for an adaptive orientation. *Psychological Bulletin*, **92**, 367–81.

Baker, T.B., Morse, E., and Sherman, J.E. (1986). The motivation to use drugs: A psychobiological analysis of urges. In *Alcohol and Addictive Behaviour, Nebraska Symposium on Motivation*, Vol. 34, (ed. P.C.Rivers), University of Nebraska Press, Lincoln, pp.257–323.

Balleine, B. (1992). Instrumental performance following a shift in primary motivation depends upon incentive learning. *Journal of Experimental Psychology: Animal Behavior Processes*, **18**, 236–50.

Bédard, M. and Weingarten, H.P. (1989). Postabsorptive glucose decreases excitatory effects of tastes on ingestion. *American Journal of Physiology*, **256**, R1142–7.

Beninger, R.J. (1989). Methods for determining the effects of drugs on learning. In *Neuromethods*, Vol. 13, *Psychopharmacology* (eds. A.A. Boulton, G.B. Baker, and A.J. Greenshaw), The Humana Press, Clifton, pp.623–85.

Berridge, K.C. (1991). Modulation of taste affect by hunger, caloric satiety and sensory-specific satiety in the rat. *Appetite*, **16**, 103–20.

Berridge, K.C. and Fentress, J.C. (1985). Trigeminal-taste interaction in palatability processing. *Science*, **228**, 747–50.

Berridge, K.C. and Schulkin, J. (1989). Palatability shift of a salt-associated incentive during sodium depletion. *Quarterly Journal of Experimental Psychology*, **41B**, 121–38.

Berridge, K.C. and Valenstein, E.S. (1991). What psychological process mediates feeding evoked by electrical stimulation of the lateral hypothalamus. *Behavioural Neuroscience*, **105**, 3–14.

Berridge, K.C., Venier, I.L., and Robinson, T.E. (1989). Taste reactivity analysis of 6–hydroxydopamine-induced aphagia: Implications for arousal and anhedonia hypotheses of dopamine function. *Behavioral Neuroscience*, **103**, 36–45.

Bindra, D. (1978). How adaptive behaviour is produced: a perceptual–motivational alternative to response-reinforcement. *The Behavioral and Brain Sciences*, **1**, 41–91.

Blackburn, J.R., Phillips, A.G., Jakubovic, A., and Fibiger, H.C. (1989). Dopamine and preparatory behaviour: II. A neurochemical analysis. *Behavioral Neuroscience*, **103**, 15–23.

Bolles, R.C. (1991). *The hedonics of taste*. Lawrence Erlbaum Associates, Hillsdale, NJ

Bozarth, M.A. (1987). Ventral tegmental reward system. In *Brain reward systems and abuse* (eds. J. Engel, L. Oreland, D.H. Ingvar, B. Pernow, S. Rossner and L.A. Pellborn), Raven Press, New York, pp. 1–17.

Bozarth, M.A. (1991). The mesolimbic dopamine system as a model reward system. In *The mesolimbic dopamine system: From motivation to action* (eds. P.Willner and J.Scheel-Krüger), Wiley, Chichester, pp.301–30.

Bozarth, M.A., Murray, A., and Wise, R.A. (1989). Influence of housing conditions on the acquisition of intravenous heroin and cocaine self-administration in rats. *Pharmacology Biochemistry and Behavior*, **33**, 903–7.

Candido, A., Maldonado, A., Megias, J.L., and Catena, A. (1992). Successive negative contrast in one-way avoidance learning in rats. *Quarterly Journal of Experimental Psychology*, **45B**, 15–32.

Candido, A., Maldonado, A. and Vila, J., (1989) Relative time in dangerous and safe places influences one-way avoidance learning in the rat. *Quarterly Journal of Experimental Psychology*, **41B**, 181–99

Cornell, C.E., Rodin, J. and Weingarten, H. (1989), Stimulus-induced eating when satiated. *Physiology and Behavior*, **45**, 695–704.

Crow, T.J. (1973). Catecholamine-containing neurones and electrical self-stimulation: 2. A theoretical interpretation and some psychiatric implications. *Psychological Medicine*, **3**, 66–73.

Crow, T.J. and Deakin, J.F.W. (1985). Neurohumoral transmission, behaviour and mental disorder. In *Handbook of psychiatry*, Volume 5—*The scientific foundations of psychiatry*, (ed. M. Shepherd), Cambridge University Press, pp.137–82.

Davis, J.D. and Smith, G.P. (1990). Learning to sham feed: behavioural adjustments to loss of physiological postingestional stimuli. *American Journal of Physiology*, **259**, R1228–35.

Delamater, A.R., LoLordo, V.M., and Berridge,K.C. (1986). Control of fluid palatability by exteroceptive Pavlovian signals. *Journal of Experimental Psychology: Animal Behaviour Processes*, **12**, 143–52.

Dickinson, A. (1989). Expectancy theory in animal conditioning. In *Contemporary learning theories: Pavlovian conditioning and the status of traditional learning theory*, (eds. S.B. Klein and R.R. Mowrer), Lawrence Erlbaum Associates, Hillsdale N.J., pp.279–308.

Dickinson, A. and Dawson, G.R. (1988). Motivational control of instrumental performance: The role of prior experience of the reinforcer. *The Quarterly Journal of Experimental Psychology*, **40B**, 113–34.

Domjan, M., Akins, C., and Vandergriff, D.H. (1992) Increased responding to female stimuli as a result of sexual experience: Tests of mechanisms of learning. *The Quarterly Journal of Experimental Psychology*, **45B**, 139–57.

Everitt, B.J. (1990). Sexual motivation—A neural and behavioural analysis of the mechanisms underlying appetitive and copulatory responses of male rats. *Neuroscience and Biobehavioural Reviews*, **14**, 217–32.

Everitt, B.J. and Stacey, P. (1987). Studies of instrumental behaviour with sexual reinforcement in male rats *(Rattus norvegicus)*: II. Effects of preoptic area lesions, castration and testosterone. *Journal of Comparative Psychology*, **101**, 407–19.

Everitt,B.J., Cador, M., and Robbins, T.W. (1989). Interactions between the amygdala and ventral striatum in stimulus-reward associations: Studies using a second-order schedule of sexual reinforcement. *Neuroscience*, **30**, 63–75.

Everitt, B.J., Fray, P., Kostarczyk, E., Taylor, S., and Stacey, P. (1987). Studies of instrumental behaviour with sexual reinforcement in male rats *Rattus norvegicus*: I. Control by brief visual stimuli paired with a receptive female. *Journal of Comparative Psychology*, **101**, 395–406.

Fantino, M., Hosotte, J. and Apfelbaum, M. (1986). An opioid antagonist, naltrexone, reduces preference for sucrose in humans. *American Journal of Physiology*, **251**, R91–6.

Fibiger, H.C., Zis, A.P., and Phillips, A.G. (1975). Haloperidol-induced disruption of conditioned avoidance responding: Attenuation by prior training or by anticholinergic drugs. *European Journal of Pharmacology*, **30**, 309–14.

Franklin, K.B.J. and McCoy, S.N. (1979). Pimozide-induced extinction in rats: Stimulus control of responding rules out motor deficit. *Pharmacology Biochemistry and Behaviour*, **11**, 71–5.

Friedman, H.R. and Coons, E.E. (1983). Dopaminergic modulation of consummatory behaviour in hungry and sated rats. *Society for Neuroscience Abstracts*, **9**, 468.

Garcia, J. (1989). Food for Tolman: Cognition and cathexis in concert. In: *Aversion, avoidance and anxiety*. (eds. T. Archer and L-G. Nilsson), Lawrence Erlbaum Associates, Hillsdale, N.J., pp.45–85.

Goldberg, S.R., Spealman, R.D., and Goldberg, D.M. (1981). Persistent behaviour at high rates maintained by intravenous self-administration of nicotine. *Science*, **214**, 573–5.

Grill, H.J. and Berridge, K.C. (1985). Taste reactivity as a measure of the neural control of palatability. In *Progress in psychobiology and physiological psychology* (Vol.11) (eds. J.M. Sprague and A.N. Epstein), Academic Press, Orlando, pp.1–61.

Hammersley, R. (1992). Cue exposure and learning theory. *Addictive Behaviour*, **17**, 297–300.

Henningfield, J.E., Lukas, S.E. and Bigelow, G.E. (1986). Human studies of drugs as reinforcers. In *Behavioral analysis of drug dependence* (eds. S.R. Goldberg and I.P. Stolerman), Academic Press, Orlando, Fl, pp.69–122.

Herman, B.H. and Panksepp, J. (1978). Effects of morphine and naloxone on separation distress and approach attachment: Evidence for opiate mediation of social affect. *Pharmacology Biochemistry and Behavior*, **9**, 213–20.

Jacquin, M.F. and Zeigler, H.P. (1983). Trigeminal orosensation and ingestive behaviour in the rat. *Behavioral Neuroscience*, **97**, 62–97.

Kanarek, R.B. and Marks-Kaufman, R. (1988). Animal models of appetitive behaviour: Interaction of nutritional factors and drug seeking behaviour. In *Control of appetite* (ed. M. Winick), John Wiley, New York, pp.1–25.

Kassel, J.D. and Shiffman, S. (1992). What can hunger teach us about drug craving? A comparative analysis of the two construct. *Advances in Behaviour Research and Therapy*, **14**, 141–67.

Keverne, E.B., Martensz, N.D., and Tuite,B. (1984). Beta-endorphin concentrations in cerebrospinal fluid of monkeys are influenced by grooming relationships. *Psychoneuroendocrinology*, **14**, 155–61.

Koob, G.F., Vaccarino, F., Amalric, M. and Bloom, F.E. (1987). Positive reinforcement properties of drugs: Search for neural substrates. In *Brain reward systems and abuse* (eds. J. Engel, L. Oreland, D.H. Ingvar, B. Pernow, S. Rossner, and L.A. Pellborn), Raven Press, New York, pp.35–50.

Lieblich, I., Yirmiya, R., and Liebeskind, J.C. (1991). Intake of and preference for sweet solutions are attenuated in morphine-withdrawn rats. *Behavioral Neuroscience*, **105**, 965–70.

Lucas, G.A. and Timberlake, W. (1992). Negative anticipatory contrast and preference conditioning: Flavour cues support preference conditioning and environmental cues support contrast. *Journal of Experimental Psychology: Animal Behavior Processes*, **18**, 34–40.

McCullough, L.D., Sokolowski, J.D., and Salamone, J.D. (1993). A neurochemical and behavioural investigation of the involvement of nucleus accumbens dopamine in instrumental avoidance. *Neuroscience*, **52**, 919–25.

Masterson, F.A. and Crawford,M. (1982). The defense motivaton system: A theory of avoidance behaviour. *The Behavioral and Brain Sciences*, **5**, 661–96.

Melzack, R. (1990). The tragedy of needless pain. *Scientific American*, **262**(2), 19–25.

Oatley, K. and Dickinson,A. (1970). Air drinking and the measurement of thirst. *Animal Behaviour*, **18**, 259–65.

O'Brien, C.P., Ehrman, R.N., and Ternes, J.W. (1986). Classical conditioning in human dependence. In *Behavioural analysis of drug dependence* (eds. S.R. Goldberg and I.P. Stolerman), Academic Press, Orlando, Fl, pp.329–56

Pelchat, M.L., Grill, H.J., Rozin, P., and Jacobs, J. (1983). Quality of acquired responses to tastes by *Rattus norvegicus* depends on type of associated discomfort. *Journal of Comparative Psychology*, **97**, 140–53.

Phillips, A.G., Pfaus, J.G., and Blaha, C.D. (1991). Dopamine and motivated behaviour: Insights provided by *in vivo* analyses. In *The mesolimbic dopamine system: From motivation to action*, (ed. P. Willner and J. Scheel-Krüger), Wiley, Chichester, pp.199–224.

Pfaus, J.G. and Phillips, A.G. (1991). Role of dopamine in anticipatory and consummatory aspects of sexual behaviour in the male rat. *Behavioural Neuroscience*, **105**, 727–43.

Poulos, C.X. and Cappell, H. (1991). Homeostatic theory of drug tolerance: A general model of physiological adaptation. *Psychological Review*, **98**, 390–408.

Robinson, T.E. and Berridge, K.C. (1993). The neural basis of drug craving: An incentive-sensitization theory of addiction. *Brain Research Reviews*, **18**, 247–91.

Salamone, J.D., Steinpreis, R.E., McCullough, L.D., Smith, P., Grebel, D. and Mahan, K. (1991). Haloperidol and nucleus accumbens dopamine depletion suppress lever pressing for food but increase free food consumption in a novel food-choice procedure. *Psychopharmacologia*, **104**, 515–21.

Siegel, S, Krank, M.D., and Hinson, R.E. (1987). Anticipation of pharmacological and nonpharmacological events: Classical conditioning and addictive behaviour. *Journal of Drug Issues*, **17**, 83–110.

Spealman, R.D. and Goldberg, S.R. (1978). Drug self-administration by laboratory animals: Control by schedules of reinforcement. *Annual Review of Pharmacology and Toxicology*, **18**, 313–39.

Stewart, J., de Wit, H., and Eikelboom, R. (1984). Role of unconditioned and conditioned drug effects in the self-administration of opiates and stimulants. *Psychological Review*, **91**, 251–68.

Taylor, J.R. and Robbins, T.W. (1984). Enhanced behavioural control by conditioned reinforcers following microinjections of *d*-amphetamine into the nucleus accumbens. *Psychopharmacology*, **84**, 405–12.

Toates, F. (1981). The control of ingestive behaviour by internal and external factors—A theoretical review. *Appetite*, **2**, 35–50.

Toates, F. (1986). *Motivational systems*. Cambridge University Press.

Toates, F. and Jensen, P. (1991). Ethological and psychological models of motivation—towards a synthesis. In *From animals to animals*, (eds. J-A. Meyer and S.W. Wilson), The MIT Press, Cambridge, pp.194–205.

Tordoff, M.G. and Friedman, M.I. (1986). Hepatic portal glucose infusions decrease food intake and increase food preference. *American Journal of Physiology*, **251**, R192–6.

Tordoff, M.G., Tepper, B.J., and Friedman, M.I. (1987). Food flavour preferences produced by drinking glucose and oil in normal and diabetic rats: Evidence for conditioning based on fuel oxidation. *Physiology and Behavior*, **41**, 481–7.

Tordoff, M.G., Ulrich, P.M., and Sandler, F. (1990). Flavour preferences and fructose: Evidence that the liver detects the unconditioned stimulus for calorie-based learning. *Appetite*, **14**, 29–44.

Treit, D. and Berridge, K.C. (1990). A comparison of benzodiazepine, serotonin and dopamine agents in the taste-reactivity paradigm. *Pharmacology, Biochemistry and Behavior*, **37**, 451–6.

Wasserman, E.M., Gomita, Y., and Gallistel, C.R. (1982). Pimozide blocks reinforcement but not priming from MFB stimulation in the rat. *Pharmacology Biochemistry and Behavior*, **17**, 783–7.

Weingarten, H.P. (1984). Meal initiation controlled by learned cues: Basic behavioral properties. *Appetite*, **5**, 147–58.

Weingarten, H.P. and Kulikovsky, O.T. (1989). Taste-to-postingestive consequence conditioning: Is the rise in sham feeding with repeated experience a learning phenomenon? *Physiology and Behavior*, **45**, 471–6.

Wise, R.A. (1982). Neuroleptics and operant behaviour: The anhedonia hypothesis. *The Behavioral and Brain Sciences*, **5**, 39–87.

Wise, R.A. (1987). Sensorimotor modulation and the variable action pattern (VAP): Toward a noncircular definition of drive and motivation. *Psychobiology*, **15**, 7–20.

Wise, R.A. and Raptis, L. (1986). Effects of naloxone and pimozide on initiation and maintenance measures of free feeding. *Brain Research*, **368**, 62–8.

Wolffgramm, J. (1991). An ethopharmacological approach to the development of drug addiction. *Neuroscience and Biobehavioral Reviews*, **15**, 515–19.

Yokel, R.A. and Pickens, R. (1974). Drug level of *d*- and *l*-amphetamine during intravenous self-administration. *Psychopharmacologia*, **34**, 255–64.

Yokel, R.A. and Wise, R.A. (1975). Increased lever pressing for amphetamine after pimozide in rats: Implications for a dopamine theory of reward. *Science*, **187**, 547–9.

Index